D0990705

EYEWITNESS ◉ HANDBOOKS

MUSHROOMS

EYEWITNESS ✺ HANDBOOKS

MUSHROOMS

THOMAS LÆSSØE

Editorial Consultant
GARY LINCOFF

Photography by
NEIL FLETCHER

DK PUBLISHING, INC.

A DK Publishing Book

Important Notice
The author and publishers strongly advise anyone
gathering fungi for eating to seek the help of an
experienced mycologist. Never eat any fungus
unless you are 100% certain of its identity.
We accept no responsiblity for readers who
do not follow this advice.

US Editor Mary Sutherland
Project Editor Jo Weeks
Project Art Editor Colin Walton
Picture Research Mollie Gillard and Sean Hunter
Production Controller Michelle Thomas
Managing Editor Jonathan Metcalf
Managing Art Editor Peter Cross

First American Edition, 1998

2 4 6 8 10 9 7 5 3 1

First published in the United States by
DK Publishing, Inc. 95 Madison Avenue
New York, New York 10016
Visit us on the World Wide Web at
http://www.dk.com

Copyright © 1998
Dorling Kindersley Limited, London
Text copyright © 1998 Thomas Læssøe

All rights reserved under International and Pan-American
Copyright Conventions. No part of this publication may
be reproduced, stored in a retrieval system, or transmitted
in any form or by any means, electronic, mechanical,
photocopying, recording, or otherwise, without the prior
written permission of the copyright owner. Published in
Great Britain by Dorling Kindersley Limited.

Læssøe, Thomas.
    Mushrooms / by Thomas Læssøe and
Gary Lincoff. -- 1st American ed.
        p. cm. -- (Eyewitness handbooks)
    Includes index.
    ISBN 0-7894-3286-2 hardcover
    ISBN 0-7894-3335-4 flexibinding
1. Mushrooms--Identification.
2. Mushrooms--Pictorial works.
I. Lincoff, Gary. II. Title. III. Series.
QK617.L248 1998
579.6--dc21   97-44418
                                           GIP

Reproduction by Colourscan, Singapore
Film output by The Right Type, England
Printed and bound in Singapore
by Kyodo Printing Co.

CONTENTS

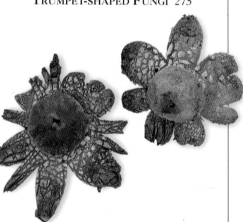

INTRODUCTION

The fungal kingdom is enormous, with fungi occurring in all habitat types all over the world. Ranging in size from microscopic yeasts to large, fleshy mushrooms, fungi also have highly diverse lifestyles, some forming beneficial relationships with living plants, others degrading or even killing their hosts. All play a vital role in the processes that govern life on our planet.

THE STUDY of the fungal kingdom is referred to as mycology. Until comparatively recently, fungi were simply considered to be a lower form of plant life and were studied as part of botany. They were also often regarded with suspicion due to their habit of appearing seemingly out of nowhere after rain. These factors perhaps help explain why there are so many fungi as yet undescribed, although the sheer volume of species is also an important reason. Current estimates put the number of species in the fungal kingdom at approximately 1.5 million, compared to, for example, flowering plants at 250,000 species.

Mycologists believe that only about 80,000 of these species have been properly documented – fewer than five percent of the estimated total number in existence. Of the undescribed species up to this point, many are thought to inhabit tropical rain forest areas, but even in much more accessible regions such as northern Europe, which have been quite closely studied, new species are still being discovered, including some that are large and fleshy.

△ FLY AMANITA
The colorful but poisonous Amanita muscaria *is perhaps the best known of all fungus species.*

SECRET LIFE

Most of us are familiar with mushrooms and toadstools, found mostly in wooded areas in the fall, but fewer people are aware that each of these is simply the "fruitbody" of a much larger organism

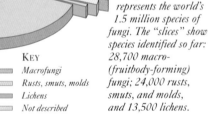

◁ FUNGUS COUNT
This pie chart represents the world's 1.5 million species of fungi. The "slices" show species identified so far: 28,700 macro- (fruitbody-forming) fungi; 24,000 rusts, smuts, and molds, and 13,500 lichens.

KEY
- Macrofungi
- Rusts, smuts, molds
- Lichens
- Not described

LICHENS ▷
*A lichen is a compound organism, the result of an association between a fungus and algae. Lichens survive on nutrients filtered from the air, aided by the photosynthesis of the algal partner. They also take up air pollutants, so are useful indicators of air quality. The picture shows the very common lichen Yellow Scales (*Xanthoria parietina*).*

Useful Fungi ▷

Fungi are an essential part of life, playing vital roles in many areas. They are used as food, as flavoring, and to produce alcohol. Antibiotics are made from them, and they contain enzymes that are used in detergents.

Detergent
The cleaning agents in detergents contain enzymes that have been extracted from fungi.

Penicillin
Penicillium *molds produce a chemical that kills bacteria and is used in antibiotics.*

Blue Cheese
The flavoring in blue cheese is produced by the mold Penicillium roqueforti.

Salami Sausages
Salami is flavored and protected by the mold Penicillium nalgiovense.

that is concealed in the soil, wood, or other material (substrate) on which the fruitbody is growing. Fruitbodies are produced to enable the dispersal of spores, by which fungi reproduce. However, there are many other species that never produce fruitbodies. Most of these are molds, such as those that occur on old foods like stale bread.

Bread
Bread dough rises through the action of the yeast fungus Saccharomyces.

Beer
Beer is brewed using a yeast fungus like Saccharomyces carlsbergensis.

Macrofungi

Only those fungi that produce more or less conspicuous fruitbodies are featured in this book. Mycologists refer to them as "macrofungi," but most are popularly known as mushrooms or toadstools. They are diverse in form, varying from the well-known cap and stem type to those species with shelflike fruitbodies and those that grow flat (see pp.12–13). Despite this diversity, the fruitbodies of some closely related fungi can look very similar and thus require careful examination for accurate identification. This book will assist in identification and increase your understanding and enjoyment of the fungal kingdom.

Edible Fungi

Although not common in all cultures, the gathering of fungi for eating is an ancient practice. The Shiitake (*Lentinula edodes*) has been cultivated in China and Japan for hundreds of years, and the cultivated mushroom (*Agaricus bisporus* p.161) has long been grown commercially. Today, oyster mushrooms (*Pleurotus* species pp.178–79) and several other species are widely cultivated, while huge quantities of morels, chanterelles, and boletes are wild-collected and sold worldwide.

Before eating any mushroom that has been collected from the wild, be sure it is correctly identified as edible (see also p.23). If poisoning is suspected, seek medical advice immediately and take along a sample of the mushroom.

Shiitake Mushrooms

Agaricus bisporus

Oyster Mushroom

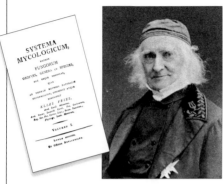

△ ELIAS FRIES *(1794–1878)*
*Elias Fries was an outstanding early mycologist.
His* Systema Mycologicum *(1821–1832) laid the
foundations for the modern classification system.*

EATING WILD MUSHROOMS

As well as making identification easier,
the species section of this book also
details edibility. However, it is strongly
recommended that beginners take
along an experieced forager if they are
gathering mushrooms for eating; many
fungi are, or can be, poisonous. There
are also some edible species that look
very similar to poisonous ones (see
p.23). The species entries warn of any
specific dangers relating to each fungus.
The effects of eating a poisonous
mushroom vary from a
stomach upset to severe or
even fatal liver damage,
so it is not advisable
to experiment.

◁ DEADLY SPECIES
Amanita virosa *(far
left) and* Amanita
phalloides *(left) cause
severe liver damage or
death if they are eaten.*

AMERICAN MUSHROOMS

This edition is based on the premise
that mushrooms whose photographs
and original descriptions come
primarily from Europe can be used to
identify North American collections.
To make a usable field guide for both
beginners and more experienced
collectors, many of the common names
used incorporate part of the scientific
generic name and are based on field-
observed characteristics.

CLASSIFICATION OF FUNGI

Within the fungal kingdom there are
three major phyla (see p.11). These are
divided into classes, then orders.
Within orders, fungi with similar traits
are grouped into families and then
genera, which link closely related
species. Each subdivision has its own
scientific (Latin) name; the name for
individual species consists of the genus
name and a specific epithet.
As an example, the full classification
for Common Chanterelle (*Cantharellus
cibarius* p.28) is shown below.

KINGDOM
Fungi

PHYLUM
Basidiomycota

CLASS
Hymenomycetes

ORDER
Cantharellales

FAMILY
Cantharellaceae

GENUS (PLURAL GENERA)
Cantharellus

SPECIES
Cantharellus cibarius

*Cantharellus
cibarius* ▷

HOW THIS BOOK WORKS

THE FUNGI FEATURED in this book are placed in one of 16 main sections, based on their most obvious visual characteristics (see pp.24–27). To make identification even simpler, the larger sections are divided into subsections according to more detailed traits. Most of the fungi are shown at slightly smaller than life size; a few are enlarged to show more detail.

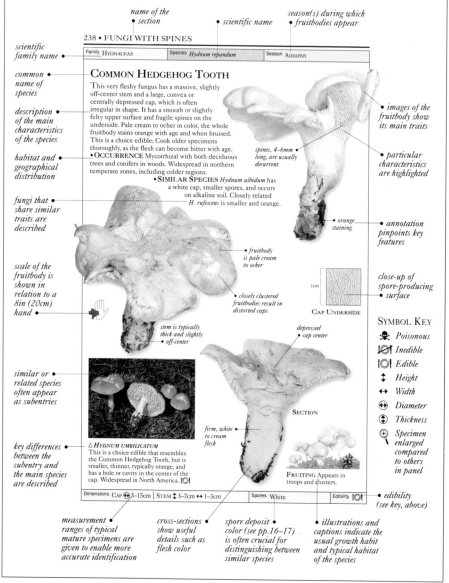

name of the section

scientific name

season(s) during which fruitbodies appear

238 • FUNGI WITH SPINES

scientific family name •

Family HYDNACEAE | Species Hydnum repandum | Season Autumn

common name of species •

COMMON HEDGEHOG TOOTH

description of the main characteristics of the species •

This very fleshy fungus has a massive, slightly off-center stem and a large, convex or centrally depressed cap, which is often irregular in shape. It has a smooth or slightly felty upper surface and fragile spines on the underside. Pale cream to ocher in color, the whole fruitbody stains orange with age and when bruised. This is a choice edible; Cook older specimens thoroughly, as the flesh can become bitter with age.

habitat and geographical distribution •

• OCCURRENCE Mycorrhizal with both deciduous trees and conifers in woods. Widespread in northern temperate zones, including colder regions.

fungi that share similar traits are described •

• SIMILAR SPECIES *Hydnum albidum* has a white cap, smaller spores, and occurs on alkaline soil. Closely related *H. rufescens* is smaller and orange.

images of the fruitbody show its main traits

particular characteristics are highlighted

spines, 4–6mm long, are usually decurrent

orange staining

annotation pinpoints key features

fruitbody is pale cream to ocher

scale of the fruitbody is shown in relation to a 8in (20cm) hand •

closely clustered fruitbodies result in distorted caps

1cm

close-up of spore-producing surface

CAP UNDERSIDE

stem is typically thick and slightly off-center

depressed cap center

SYMBOL KEY

☠ Poisonous

🚫 Inedible

🍴 Edible

↕ Height

↔ Width

⊕ Diameter

⊕ Thickness

⊕ Specimen enlarged compared to others in panel

similar or related species often appear as subentries •

SECTION

key differences between the subentry and the main species are described •

△ HYDNUM UMBILICATUM
This is a choice edible that resembles the Common Hedgehog Tooth, but is smaller, thinner, typically orange, and has a hole or cavity in the center of the cap. Widespread in North America. 🍴

firm, white to cream flesh

FRUITING Appears in troops and clusters.

Dimensions CAP ⊕ 5–15cm | STEM ↕ 3–7cm ↔ 1–3cm | Spores White | Edibility 🍴

edibility (see key, above)

measurement ranges of typical mature specimens are given to enable more accurate identification

cross-sections show useful details such as flesh color

spore deposit color (see pp.16–17) is often crucial for distinguishing between similar species

illustrations and captions indicate the usual growth habit and typical habitat of the species

WHAT IS A MUSHROOM?

IN POPULAR USAGE, mushrooms are fungi that produce conspicuous fruitbodies. Often the only visible part of a fungus, fruitbodies vary from the well-known cap and stem type shown below to the variety illustrated on pp.12–13. Their function is to produce sexual spores, and mycologists divide most fungi into three groups, or phyla, according to the way in which they do this (see p.11). The majority of species in this book belong to Basidiomycota; all but two of the others to Ascomycota. Zygomycota is represented by two mushroom parasites.

ANATOMY OF A FRUITBODY

Every fungus, including its fruitbodies, consists of masses of minute threads called *hyphae*. Hidden in the substrate, the hyphae form into *mycelia*, which produce fruitbodies on the surface when conditions are favorable. All fruitbodies have an area of fertile, spore-producing tissue, known as the *hymenium*, which is often supported by a fleshy structure, such as a cap on a stem.

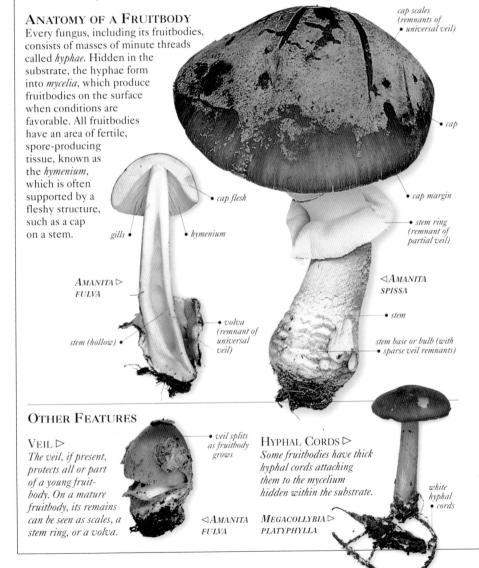

cap scales (remnants of universal veil)

cap

cap flesh

cap margin

stem ring (remnant of partial veil)

gills •

hymenium

△ *AMANITA SPISSA*

AMANITA ▷
FULVA

stem

stem (hollow) •

volva (remnant of universal veil)

stem base or bulb (with *sparse veil remnants*)

OTHER FEATURES

VEIL ▷
The veil, if present, protects all or part of a young fruit-body. On a mature fruitbody, its remains can be seen as scales, a stem ring, or a volva.

veil splits as fruitbody grows

△ *AMANITA FULVA*

HYPHAL CORDS ▷
Some fruitbodies have thick hyphal cords attaching them to the mycelium hidden within the substrate.

MEGACOLLYBIA ▷
PLATYPHYLLA

white hyphal cords

ASCOMYCOTA

Ascomycetes form spores inside tiny saclike structures called asci, each typically producing eight spores. Asci are sited within the hymenium. The hymenium may be on the outside of the fruitbody, such as in morels, or the asci may be loosely distributed inside the fruitbody, as they are in truffles. Many ascomycetes do not produce fruitbodies, but reproduce by asexual spores (*conidia*).

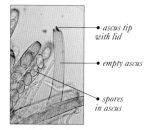

COMMON MOREL ▷
Morchella esculenta *forms spores within asci lining the honeycomb-like structure of the cap.*

CUP-FUNGUS ASCI ▷
Here, some of the asci have discharged their spores, while others still contain spores that are not yet mature.

• ascus tip with lid

• empty ascus

• spores in ascus

FALSE FLASK-FUNGUS ASCI ▷
Once the spores in these asci have reached maturity, they are released through an opening in the top.

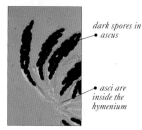

dark spores in • ascus

• asci are inside the hymenium

BASIDIOMYCOTA

Nearly all basidiomycetes produce fruitbodies. The hymenium consists of club-shaped cells (*basidia*) with outgrowths (*sterigmata*) at one end, on which the spores are formed. On each basidium there are typically four sterigmata, each producing one spore. Many basidiomycetes are further distinguished from other fungi by clamp connections between their hyphae.

COMMON PUFFBALL ▷
Lycoperdon perlatum *forms spores on basidia in the hymenium, which is in the top of the fruitbody.*

GILL SURFACE ▷
Basidia with spores at different stages of maturity can be seen on this gill surface.

basidium with four mature • spores

hymenium

HYPHAL CLAMP ▷
Clamp connections between hyphae are a typical feature of many basidiomycetes.

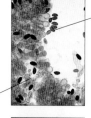

• hypha

• clamp connection

hypha •

ZYGOMYCOTA

Zygomycetes do not have fruitbodies. Their sexual spores (zygospores) are long lived and are able to wait for perfect conditions before germination. Zygomycetes also form asexual spores in structures called sporangia at the end of threadlike sporangiophores. The gray molds found on foods or dung are mainly zygomycetes.

SPINELLUS FUSIGER ▷
This species consists of masses of threadlike sporangiophores.

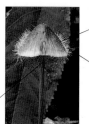

sporangio- • phores

• sporangia containing asexual spores

Spinellus *growing on* Mycena

FRUITBODY SHAPES

FUNGAL FRUITBODIES occur in a wide range of forms, with several different ways of arranging the spore-producing hymenium. This may be found on gills, in tubes, or on smooth surfaces on the fruitbody; in some fungi it is concealed inside. When the fruitbody is mature the spores are dispersed either actively or passively (see also pp.16–17). The shape of the fruitbody can reveal the method of spore dispersal. For example, tuber-like, rounded fruitbodies, found below ground (pp.258–59), have internal spores that are passively dispersed.

CAP AND STEM ▷
The hymenium lines the sides of the gills under the cap. The spores are actively discharged.

STEM OFF-CENTER OR ABSENT ▷
The hymenium lines the gills under the cap. The spores are actively discharged.

SADDLE-LIKE CAP ▷
The hymenium lines the folds of the cap. The spores are actively discharged.

HONEYCOMB-LIKE CAP ▷
The hymenium lines the cavities in the cap. The spores are actively discharged.

BRACKETLIKE ▷
The underside is smooth or has tubes lined with the hymenium. The spores are actively discharged.

SKINLIKE, GROWING FLAT OR CRUSTLIKE ▽
The hymenium covers most of the fruitbody surface. The spores are actively discharged.

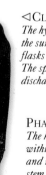

◁**CLUB-SHAPED**
The hymenium either covers the surface or is situated in flasks embedded in the flesh. The spores are actively discharged.

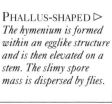

PHALLUS-SHAPED ▷
The hymenium is formed within an egglike structure and is then elevated on a stem. The slimy spore mass is dispersed by flies.

◁**ANTLERLIKE**
The hymenium covers most of the surface. The spores are actively discharged.

CORAL-LIKE ▷
The hymenium covers most of the surface. The spores are actively discharged.

ROUNDED ▷
The hymenium is formed internally or in flasks. The spores are passively or actively discharged.

◁**PEAR- TO PESTLE-SHAPED**
The hymenium is formed internally. The spores are passively dispersed, often by raindrops.

△ **CUP- OR DISK-SHAPED**
The hymenium lines the inner or upper side. The spores are actively discharged.

CUP-SHAPED CONTAINING "EGGS" △
The "eggs" have an internal hymenium. The whole "egg" is propelled by rain splashes.

◁**TRUMPET-SHAPED**
The hymenium is on the smooth to wrinkled outer surface. The spores are actively discharged.

STAR-SHAPED ▷
The hymenium is formed in a closed structure that splits. The spores are dispersed by rain splashes or flies.

CAGELIKE ▷
The hymenium is within a structure that splits into a mesh. The spores are dispersed by insects.

EARLIKE ▷
The hymenium is on the surface of the lobes. The spores are actively discharged.

LOBED AND GELATINOUS ▷
The hymenium is on the surface of the lobes. The spores are actively discharged.

CAP FEATURES

THE CAP can provide lots of clues to the identity of a species. Its overall shape and features on the surface, such as scales or marginal threads (indicating remains of the veil) are important. Key characteristics include any structures on the underside of the cap, such as gills or pores, and their attachment to the stem.

CAP SHAPES AND SURFACES

Cap shape and surface texture can change as the fruitbody matures, so try to examine several specimens. A usually sticky surface may become nonsticky in dry weather. Test it by touching it with a moistened lower lip (the "kiss" test). If it sticks to the lip, it will have been sticky in more humid conditions.

CONVEX
Cap is more or less the shape of a bun

CONICAL
Cap is cone- or almost cone-shaped

FUNNEL-SHAPED
Cap has a depressed center

UMBONATE
Raised boss in center of cap

LOOSE SCALES
Removable veil scales

PLEATED
Surface of cap is folded radially into pleats

SCALY
Cap skin is covered with fixed scales

STRIATE
Striations are gills seen through cap skin

GROOVED MARGIN
Distinct radial ridges at edges of cap

CONCENTRIC ZONES
Different color zones

SHAGGY
Dense layer of long, fibrous scales on cap

STICKY
Cap skin is sticky-slimy (may dry up)

INROLLED MARGIN
Cap edge rolls inward, especially when young

FOLDED
Whole cap consists of many folds of flesh

SADDLE-SHAPED
More or less folded cap, shaped like a saddle

HONEYCOMBED
Cap with indented cells similar to a honeycomb

GILLS IN SECTION

If the cap has gills it is vital to note how, and if, they are attached to the stem (if present). This is seen by cutting out a section with a sharp knife. Free gills are not connected to the stem, which can often be loosened from the cap by twisting. If only a very narrow part of the gill runs down the stem, this is often called decurrent with a tooth.

DECURRENT
Gills run down stem, slightly or markedly

ADNATE
Broadly attached gills

ADNEXED
Narrowly attached gills appear almost free

FREE
Gills not joined to stem, which can be removed

NOTCHED
Gills indented just before joining stem

SINUATE NOTCHED
Curved and indented before joining stem

GILLS FROM BENEATH

Taking note of the cap underside can be useful in identification. For example, the proportion of full-length gills to shorter gills is an important feature, as is the number of gills and the distance between them.

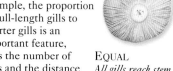

EQUAL
All gills reach stem and are the same length

UNEQUAL
Full-length gills mixed with shorter ones

FORKED
Gills divide one or several times

CROWDED
Gills are arranged very close together

WIDELY SPACED
Gills are far apart from each other

JOINED TO COLLAR
Gills joined at a collar instead of reaching stem

RADIATING
Gills radiate from the margin of the cap

OTHER SPORE-PRODUCING SURFACES

Instead of having gills, some cap and stem fungi and bracketlike species have the hymenium on surfaces that are smooth to wrinkled, toothed, or in tubes. Rounded to angular pores on the fruitbody underside indicate that the hymenium is in tubes.

GILL-LIKE VEINS
Hymenium covers folds and wrinkles on the undersurface

TUBES WITH PORES
Hymenium lines tubes, which are vertical with porelike openings

SPINES
Hymenium positioned vertically on spine-shaped structures

SPORES AND SPORE DISPERSAL

FUNGI PRODUCE SPORES to colonize suitable substrates, and just one fruitbody can produce billions of them. Spores can be asexual or sexual. Asexual spores (conidia) may produce individual mycelia that can then grow on their own. Sexual spores can sometimes establish independent mycelia, but often a fusion with another mycelium has to take place before they can continue to grow.

HOW SPORES ARE DISPERSED

Spores can be dispersed either passively or actively. Passive dispersal relies on animals, wind, or water; active discharge occurs when the fruitbody itself has a special mechanism that ejects or propels the spores when they reach maturity.

EJECTION
In flask fungi, including this Xylaria, *the mature asci eject the spores some distance through the mouths of the tiny fruitbodies.*

BY ANIMAL
Sticky spore masses, such as on this Phallus *species, are eaten by insects. Some spores stick to the insects and are borne away.*

BY WATER AND WIND
As rain falls on the fruitbodies of puffballs like this Lycoperdon, *they compress and the spores are released, to be dispersed by wind.*

SPORE DEPOSITS

A useful way of confirming the genus to which a fungus belongs is to find out the color of its spore deposit. Taking a spore deposit from a gilled mushroom (agaric) is an easy process and can produce fascinating results: it reveals both the pattern of the gill spaces and the color of the spores. Cut the cap from a fresh specimen and place it gill-side down on paper. Use black paper to take pale spore deposits; for unknown colors, place the cap half over white paper and half over black paper.

1 COVERING THE CAP
Remove the stem and place the cap, gills down, on the paper. A drop of water on the cap keeps it moist. Cover with glass – a bowl or tumbler – and leave for several hours or overnight.

2 REMOVING THE CAP
Gently lift the glass, then the cap to reveal the spore deposit. The thicker the deposit, the easier it is to get an accurate idea of the spore color. The deposit should be observed in natural light.

SPORE COLOR

Species within a genus typically have spore deposits of more or less the same color, so the genus of a specimen can be revealed by its spore color. For example, all *Agaricus* species have spores in dark brown shades. In some genera, such as *Russula* (pp.120–31), the spore color can also be used to differentiate between similar species. Spore deposits are usually black, white to cream, or red, purple, or brown shades. Exceptions include *Chlorophyllum molybdites* (p.166), which has a green deposit.

PINKISH TO RED

OCHER TO CLAY

BLACK

WHITE TO CREAM

PURPLE-BROWN

RUST-BROWN

SPORE SHAPE AND SIZE

Spore shape and size can be very important in the final correct identification of a species. Most spores are less than 20 microns (µm) long or wide (0.02mm), and many are smaller than 5µm, although some can be up to about 2mm in diameter. Their shape varies according to the method of their dispersal: actively discharged spores are typically asymmetrical, whereas those dispersed by passive means tend to be symmetrical. The spore chart on pp.284–88 gives spore shapes and average sizes, as well as other details, for species in this book.

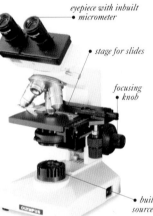

eyepiece with inbuilt • micrometer

• stage for slides

focusing • knob

• built-in light source

◁ **MICROSCOPE**
To identify spore shapes and sizes, you will need a good quality, but not necessarily very expensive, microscope. Ideally, enlargement should be × 1000, but good results can be obtained at only × 400. A built-in light source is very useful.

all of these close-ups are × 2000 • life size

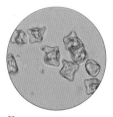

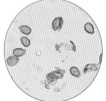

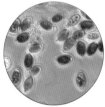

ENTOLOMA CONFERENDUM
Entoloma *species have angular spores. Those of* E. conferendum *are starlike in shape and many faceted.*

GANODERMA APPLANATUM
G. applanatum *has rough-textured spores that are truncated at one end and have a double skin.*

COPRINUS ATRAMENTARIUS
Like many Coprinus *species, the black spores of this species each have a tiny pore from which the hyphae germinate.*

CONIOPHORA PUTEANA
The ellipsoid spores of C. puteana *have a smooth surface and appear yellow-brown in color.*

MUSHROOM LIFESTYLES

ONCE A MUSHROOM has established itself by forming a mycelium, it has to find a way to continue to grow and live. Different types of fungi have different methods of survival. Many have to form a mutually beneficial, or mycorrhizal, relationship with a living partner, such as a tree, which enables both to survive; others, known as saprotrophs, degrade (break down) dead material. There are also some fungi that kill plants or animals. These are called necrotrophs. Through their ability to break down dead matter or provide suitable growing conditions for other living things, fungi play a vital role in the ecological balance of the environment.

◁ THE HOST TREE
A single tree species can provide different fungi with what they need to survive. The spruce, shown here, can support mycorrhizal fungi, saprotrophs can live off its litter, and necrotrophs may kill it and live off its remains.

MYCORRHIZAL

Mycorrhizae are the basis for a close beneficial relationship between the tree and the fungus, in which the tree gives the fungus sugars, while the fungus provides water and nutrients. A mycorrhizal relationship is formed when the hyphae of fungi species, including some agarics and most boletes, penetrate roots of a suitable living host tree.

SPECIAL RELATIONSHIP ▷
These fruitbodies of Amanita muscaria *(p.146) are near a spruce tree with which they may have formed mycorrhizae. Other trees, such as birch and oak, also form mycorrhizae with fungi.*

BELOW GROUND ▷
Where there is a mycorrhizal partnership, the fungus grows a mantle around the tiniest tree roots and a net of hyphae in between the outer root cells. Nutrients are exchanged between the partners via complex chemical pathways.

plant host is a
• spruce tree

• *fungal partner is a Fly Amanita*

• *forked tips*

pine roots •

a pale, forked •
mantle typifies
pine mycorrhizae

SAPROTROPHIC

With the aid of enzymes, which they release externally, saprotrophic fungi degrade many types of dead organic matter, including fungi and animals. Some saprotrophs, such as *Strobilurus esculentus* (right), occur only on one substrate, in this case a spruce cone. Others are wider in their range. Some fungal species are even present in a passive form in living plants, waiting to start their activity once the plant dies.

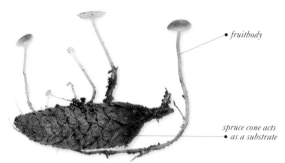

fruitbody

spruce cone acts as a substrate

△ *STROBILURUS ESCULENTUS* (p.133)
This specialized saprotroph degrades only fallen spruce cones. It produces fruitbodies after obtaining the materials it needs from the substrate.

NECROTROPHIC

Necrotrophs, or parasites, live off of, and eventually kill living plants. Some kill their host by blocking or destroying the plant's water and nutrient systems with hyphae or specially produced, yeastlike cells; others use toxins. After killing the plant, the necrotroph acts like a saprotroph (see above), degrading the plant as a substrate. Parasitic fungi include *Fomes fomentarius* (p.219), and *Armillaria* species (pp.42 and 80).

stump of spruce tree

fruitbody

△ *HETEROBASIDION ANNOSUM* (p.222)
This species causes extensive damage in large spruce stands, spreading from tree to tree via the roots. Following the death of the tree, the wood is degraded by the fungus and brackets are produced.

BIOTROPHIC

Like mycorrhizal fungi, biotrophic fungi, such as rusts and mildews, depend on a living host. However, in this case the plant does not benefit. Special hyphae are often produced by the fungus, which penetrate the host cells and transport the nutrients back to the fungus. Although the plant is not killed, its life processes may be affected. For example, spores may infect seeds and germinate in seedlings.

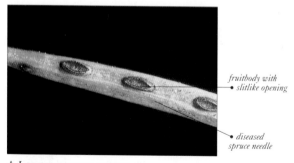

fruitbody with slitlike opening

diseased spruce needle

△ *LOPHODERMIUM PICEAE*
This tar-spot fungus produces black marks on spruce needles. Other Lophodermium *species may cause severe leaf fall on pines and other trees.*

MUSHROOM HABITATS

FUNGI OCCUR throughout the world, but most of the species in this book can be found in the northern temperate zones. Some are widespread, occurring in North America, Europe, and Asia; others are restricted to a single continent or a very localized region within it. Most fungi are confined to a very specific environment, so it is important to be able to recognize the main habitats, including their indigenous plants, and which mushrooms occur in them.

WOODLAND

The many varieties of woodland support different types of fungal life. Alkaline loam dominated by ash trees tends to contain non-mycorrhizal species, such as *Lepiota*. Acidic, peaty soil, with beech or birch trees, has a high proportion of mycorrhizal fungi, such as boletes, trichs, and russulas. Mineral-laden soil, along paths or beside ditches, can support species of *Lepiota*, *Psathyrella*, and *Peziza*, which thrive on comparatively small amounts of organic matter.

△ PINE WOODLAND
Sandy pine woods are home to many boletes, such as Suillus bovinus *(p.200), as well as russulas (pp.120–29). Wetter, mossy pine forests are also rich in fungi.*

△ SUILLUS
BOVINUS

◁ OAK WOODLAND
Mycorrhizal fungi and sapro-trophs, such as Fistulina *species, occur with oak trees. Some of the same species are also found growing with chestnuts.*

◁ FISTULINA
HEPATICA

CONIFEROUS TREES

Most coniferous trees, or conifers, form important mycorrhizal relationships with fungi. Many fungus species are found only under one particular type of conifer, so knowing the tree's name makes an accurate identification of the fungus more likely. The trees shown are among the most important.

LARCH (*LARIX*)   SPRUCE (*PICEA*)   PINE (*PINUS*)

GRASSLAND

There are many types of grassland, from the basic monocultures of wheat and barley to heavily fertilized pastures or near-natural, unfertilized but grazed or mown grassland. The mushrooms in such habitats may be directly associated with the grass or other plants in the turf, or they may be dung-fungi, living on the droppings of the animals that graze there. Soil composition is also important, with different fungi species occuring in very acidic grassland compared to more neutral or very alkaline soils.

△ FERTILIZED PASTURE
Typically grazed by farm animals, and with limited flora other than grass, fertilized pasture is a suitable habitat for many species of Agaricus, Coprinus, *and* Panaeolus, *which like dung-rich environments.*

△ AGARICUS
CAMPESTRIS

◁ UNFERTILIZED MEADOW
This type of grassland is rich in plant and mushroom species. Dominant fungi include species of Clavaria, Entoloma, *and* Hygrocybe, *which do not thrive in fertilized pasture, possibly because they cannot compete with other fungi that flourish where nutrient levels are high.*

◁ HYGROCYBE
PUNICEA

DECIDUOUS TREES

Mycorrhizal relationships often exist between fungi and deciduous trees shown here. There are several other important deciduous trees, including ash, elm, and maple, which have less direct relationships with fungi.

BIRCH (*BETULA*)   BEECH (*FAGUS*)   OAK (*QUERCUS*)

FORAGING FOR MUSHROOMS

W HEN LOOKING FOR FUNGI, remember to leave some fruitbodies in place so that they can mature, and, after your studies, throw leftovers on a compost heap or put them back in the woods. Check for maggots before gathering edibles.

EQUIPMENT
A sharp knife and a basket or a compartmentalized collection box are essential equipment for foragers. Tweezers are helpful for handling tiny specimens, and a hand lens reveals small details. A camera and note pad are useful for documenting finds.

FLAT BASKET

KNIFE   TWEEZERS

HAND LENS

COLLECTION BOX WITH COMPARTMENTS

CAMERA WITH MACRO LENS

NOTEPAD AND PENCILS

HOW TO PICK
Although most species can be gathered using a knife, shears, or a small pruning saw can be useful for collecting specimens on twigs or pieces of wood. Once picked, keep the fungi in closed containers so that important features are not lost and they do not dry out. Take a sniff when opening the container to detect diagnostic smells. Avoid picking poisonous or endangered species by making a preliminary attempt at identification before lifting specimens.

CUTTING WITH A KNIFE
When picking a mushroom, use a knife to lift out the stem base. Do not handle specimens more than absolutely necessary; this could damage or destroy useful identification characteristics.

THINGS TO NOTE

• **STAINING** Scratch with a finger nail to test for color changes.
• **TEXTURE** Rub the flesh between your fingers to check its texture.
• **SMELL** Check for any distinctive fragrance.
• **TASTE** Test only with a tiny piece and always spit the sample out.
• **CHEMICAL TESTS** Join a local mycology group to get help with chemical tests, which can be very useful in identification.

TAKING MEASUREMENTS

Standard measurements for different types of fungi are shown here. Although mushrooms vary in size, and can grow quite a bit before they are fully mature, it is useful to take measurements as an aid to identification. The dimensions given in the species descriptions are of average mature specimens.

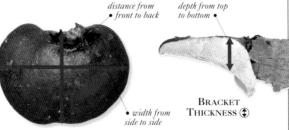

distance from front to back

depth from top to bottom

width from side to side

BRACKET THICKNESS ⊕

BRACKET WIDTH BY DEPTH ⊕

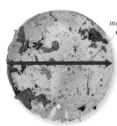

measure largest diameter

height from top to bottom of cap

measure to just under cap

STEM WIDTH ↔

STEM HEIGHT ↕

width of base

CAP DIAMETER ⊕

CAP HEIGHT ↕

POISONOUS OR EDIBLE?

Some poisonous mushrooms look similar to edible ones, so foragers are strongly advised to familiarize themselves with dangerous species. Never eat anything you cannot identify accurately. If you suspect poisoning, seek medical advice and take along a sample of the fungus. Of the fungi here, *Amanita pantherina* can be lethal; *Agaricus xanthoderma* and *Russula mairei* produce minor poisonings. **Note also:** *Amanita phalloides* p.151, *A. virosa* p.150, *Cortinarius rubellus* p.72, and *C. orellanus* p.73.

☠

AMANITA PANTHERINA p.149

🍽

AMANITA RUBESCENS p.147

☠

RUSSULA MAIREI p.129

🍽

RUSSULA XERAMPELINA p.127

☠

AGARICUS XANTHODERMA p.159

🍽

AGARICUS ARVENSIS p.158

IDENTIFICATION

To identify a mushroom, use the keys on the following pages to find out what type it is and where it is most likely to be described in the species section. Answer the question (right), then follow the instructions and illustrations to the end. If at any point you become "stuck," start over again and double-check each characteristic. **Note:** Remember, never eat a mushroom unless you are absolutely certain of its identity.

DOES IT HAVE A CAP AND STEM?

YES
SEE BELOW ▽

NO
SEE PAGE 26 ▷▷

CAP AND STEM FUNGI: MAIN TYPES

Examine the cap, especially the underside, and choose the most similar illustration below to proceed to the next step. If the underside has gills, decide whether they are decurrent, adnexed to adnate, or free. A section will reveal this more clearly. If there are pores or spines instead (see p.15), choose a different illustration. Also check the stem is central. **Note:** the illustrations are for example only; your specimen could differ in color or shape.

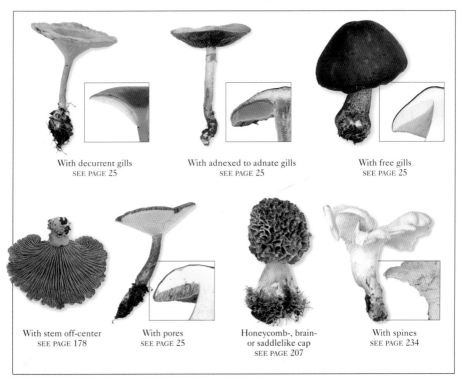

With decurrent gills
SEE PAGE 25

With adnexed to adnate gills
SEE PAGE 25

With free gills
SEE PAGE 25

With stem off-center
SEE PAGE 178

With pores
SEE PAGE 25

Honeycomb-, brain-
or saddlelike cap
SEE PAGE 207

With spines
SEE PAGE 234

CAP AND STEM FUNGI: OTHER CHARACTERISTICS

In this book, cap and stem fungi with gills or pores are divided into the subsections shown below. Choose the illustration and description that is closest to the fruitbodies you wish to identify, then turn to the page given. Be prepared to try again with any fruitbodies that fit more than one subsection. Spore color and size is often required to confirm identity.

DECURRENT GILLS

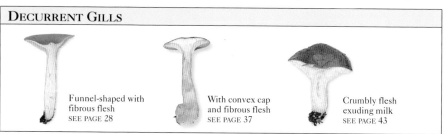

Funnel-shaped with fibrous flesh
SEE PAGE 28

With convex cap and fibrous flesh
SEE PAGE 37

Crumbly flesh exuding milk
SEE PAGE 43

ADNEXED TO ADNATE GILLS

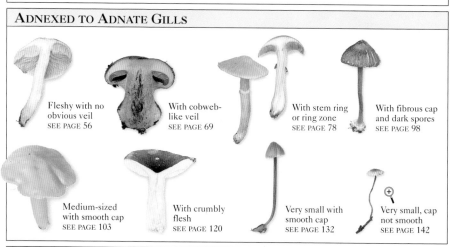

Fleshy with no obvious veil
SEE PAGE 56

With cobweb-like veil
SEE PAGE 69

With stem ring or ring zone
SEE PAGE 78

With fibrous cap and dark spores
SEE PAGE 98

Medium-sized with smooth cap
SEE PAGE 103

With crumbly flesh
SEE PAGE 120

Very small with smooth cap
SEE PAGE 132

Very small, cap not smooth
SEE PAGE 142

FREE GILLS

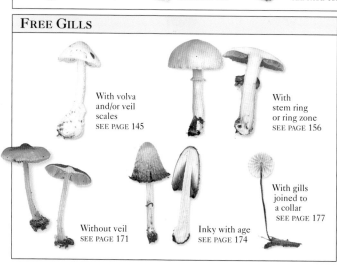

With volva and/or veil scales
SEE PAGE 145

With stem ring or ring zone
SEE PAGE 156

Without veil
SEE PAGE 171

Inky with age
SEE PAGE 174

With gills joined to a collar
SEE PAGE 177

WITH PORES

With soft flesh
SEE PAGE 184

With tough flesh
SEE PAGE 202

OTHER FUNGI: MAIN TYPES

This part of the key features fungi that do not combine a cap and stem and are not, for the most part, the traditional mushroom shape. The best first clue to their identity is to decide on their shape and appearance, followed by other features such as texture or where they grow (see p.27). Compare your specimen with the shapes illustrated and choose the closest example, bearing in mind that there are many variations, some of which can be seen in the final part of the key on p.27. Do not expect to see the exact replica of what you have found illustrated here, and do not be put off by differences in color or details. Turn to the pages indicated to learn about variations in shapes and sizes within each section.

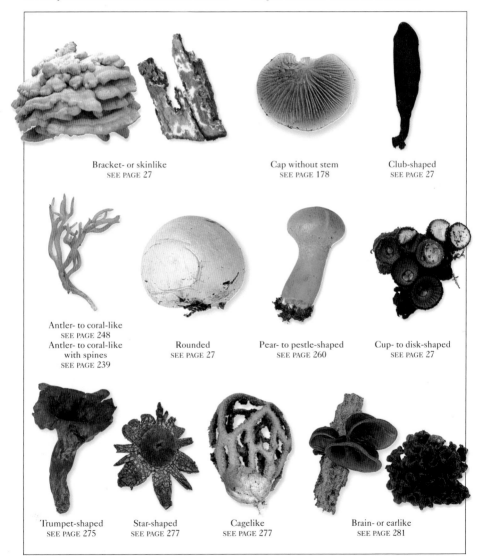

Bracket- or skinlike
SEE PAGE 27

Cap without stem
SEE PAGE 178

Club-shaped
SEE PAGE 27

Antler- to coral-like
SEE PAGE 248
Antler- to coral-like
with spines
SEE PAGE 239

Rounded
SEE PAGE 27

Pear- to pestle-shaped
SEE PAGE 260

Cup- to disk-shaped
SEE PAGE 27

Trumpet-shaped
SEE PAGE 275

Star-shaped
SEE PAGE 277

Cagelike
SEE PAGE 277

Brain- or earlike
SEE PAGE 281

OTHER FUNGI: OTHER CHARACTERISTICS

In this book, the sections that contain a wide variety of forms are further subdivided. The subsections for fungi that are not the familiar cap and stem shape are illustrated below. Pick the illustration and description most similar to the fruitbodies you have found, then turn to the page given. It is helpful to use a hand lens to check whether the underside of a bracket is smooth or has thousands of minute pores. **Note:** The illustrations here are not to scale.

BRACKET- OR SKINLIKE

| With pores | Wrinkled or smooth underneath | Skinlike, growing flat or crustlike |
| SEE PAGE 211 | SEE PAGE 228 | SEE PAGE 232 |

CLUB-SHAPED

Smooth or hairy
SEE PAGE 240

With pimples or a dusty surface
SEE PAGE 244

Phallus-shaped
SEE PAGE 246

ROUNDED

| Above ground | Below ground |
| SEE PAGE 253 | SEE PAGE 258 |

CUP- TO DISK-SHAPED

Without "eggs"
SEE PAGE 264

Cup-shaped containing "eggs"
SEE PAGE 274

CAP & STEM FUNGI WITH DECURRENT GILLS

*Mushrooms that have caps and stems,
with gills under the caps, are called
agarics. This section consists of agarics with
"decurrent" gills – gills that run down the stem.
Chanterelles are included in this section.*

• *decurrent
gills run
down stem*

FUNNEL-SHAPED WITH FIBROUS FLESH

T HIS SUBSECTION features agarics with funnel-shaped or depressed caps. They also have fibrous flesh, unlike the crumbly flesh of *Lactarius*

species (see pp.43–55) or russulas (see pp.120–31). The combination of fibrous flesh and funnel-shaped caps can also be found in distantly related families.

Family CANTHARELLACEAE	Species *Cantharellus cibarius*	Season Summer–winter

COMMON CHANTERELLE

Widely varied in color, but often yellow with a hint of red, most forms of this species smell like dried apricots, and all make very good edibles. The cap is depressed in the center and often has a wavy margin; it has thick, decurrent, forked, gill-like veins. The pale cap flesh often bruises orange to red.
• **OCCURRENCE** Mycorrhizal with spruce and pine, also with deciduous trees, such as oak. Widespread in cold- and warm-temperate areas of the Northern Hemisphere; very common to rare.
• **SIMILAR SPECIES** *Hygrophoropsis aurantiaca* (p.29) is not mycorrhizal. *Omphalotus olearius* (p.29) has a luminous quality and grows on dead wood.

*undulating
• cap margin*   SECTION

*depressed
cap center •*

• *smooth,
solid,
tapering
stem*

*firm, pale flesh •
smells of apricots*

FRUITING In troops on well-drained soil.

*decurrent,
forking,
gill-like
veins •*

△ *CANTHARELLUS SUBALBIDUS*
This fleshy, off-white to cream species is found in the Pacific Northwest coastal woods. ¡◎¡

Dimensions CAP ⊕ 2–12cm | STEM ↕ 2–10cm ↔ 0.4–1.5cm	Spores Pale cream	Edibility ¡◎¡

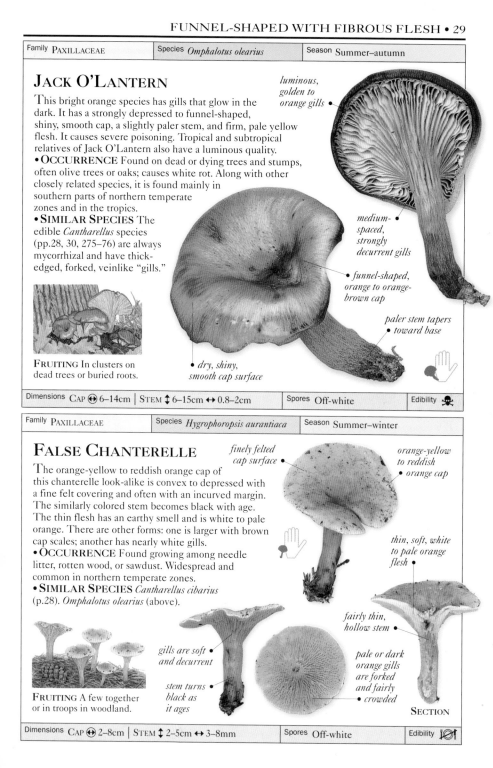

| Family PAXILLACEAE | Species *Omphalotus olearius* | Season Summer–autumn |

JACK O'LANTERN

This bright orange species has gills that glow in the dark. It has a strongly depressed to funnel-shaped, shiny, smooth cap, a slightly paler stem, and firm, pale yellow flesh. It causes severe poisoning. Tropical and subtropical relatives of Jack O'Lantern also have a luminous quality.

• **OCCURRENCE** Found on dead or dying trees and stumps, often olive trees or oaks; causes white rot. Along with other closely related species, it is found mainly in southern parts of northern temperate zones and in the tropics.

• **SIMILAR SPECIES** The edible *Cantharellus* species (pp.28, 30, 275–76) are always mycorrhizal and have thick-edged, forked, veinlike "gills."

luminous, golden to orange gills

medium-spaced, strongly decurrent gills

funnel-shaped, orange to orange-brown cap

paler stem tapers toward base

FRUITING In clusters on dead trees or buried roots.

dry, shiny, smooth cap surface

| Dimensions CAP ⊕ 6–14cm | STEM ↕ 6–15cm ↔ 0.8–2cm | Spores Off-white | Edibility ☠ |

| Family PAXILLACEAE | Species *Hygrophoropsis aurantiaca* | Season Summer–winter |

FALSE CHANTERELLE

The orange-yellow to reddish orange cap of this chanterelle look-alike is convex to depressed with a fine felt covering and often with an incurved margin. The similarly colored stem becomes black with age. The thin flesh has an earthy smell and is white to pale orange. There are other forms: one is larger with brown cap scales; another has nearly white gills.

• **OCCURRENCE** Found growing among needle litter, rotten wood, or sawdust. Widespread and common in northern temperate zones.

• **SIMILAR SPECIES** *Cantharellus cibarius* (p.28). *Omphalotus olearius* (above).

finely felted cap surface

orange-yellow to reddish orange cap

thin, soft, white to pale orange flesh

fairly thin, hollow stem

gills are soft and decurrent

stem turns black as it ages

pale or dark orange gills are forked and fairly crowded

FRUITING A few together or in troops in woodland.

SECTION

| Dimensions CAP ⊕ 2–8cm | STEM ↕ 2–5cm ↔ 3–8mm | Spores Off-white | Edibility |

Family CANTHARELLACEAE	Species *Cantharellus cinnabarinus*	Season Summer–autumn

CINNABAR CHANTERELLE

This very brightly colored species has a broadly convex cap that becomes funnel-shaped with a distinctly incurved and wavy margin as it matures. The cap emerges cinnabar-red and ages to pink-red. The pink to red stem is fairly short. The decurrent, pink, gill-like veins are forked with thick edges. The edible, fibrous flesh is fairly thin and red to off-white in the cap, thicker and white in the stem.
• **OCCURRENCE** Mycorrhizal, especially with oak trees, often appearing in moss. Widespread and common in eastern North America.
• **SIMILAR SPECIES** *Hygrocybe cantharellus* has comparatively sharp-edged, unforked gills.

cinnabar-red cap matures pink-red •

cap surface is matted and • fibrillose

convex cap ages to funnel- • shaped

incurved, wavy cap margin •

decurrent, thick-edged, forked "gills" •

FRUITING Appears in large troops of conspicuous fruitbodies on soil along paths in woodland.

Dimensions CAP ⊕ 1–4cm | STEM ↕ 1.5–4cm ↔ 0.3–1cm	Spores Pinkish cream	Edibility

Family CANTHARELLACEAE	Species *Cantharellus tubaeformis*	Season Autumn–winter

TRUMPET CHANTERELLE

This species, when young, has a domed cap that becomes funnel-shaped with a wavy margin with age. The cap is in shades of brown; the stem is chrome-yellow, fading to dull yellow in mature specimens. It has gill-like veins. Its thin flesh tastes bitter but has an aromatic smell. The dull coloring makes it fairly difficult to find, but when discovered it is normally abundant, enabling large quantities to be gathered for eating.
• **OCCURRENCE** Mycorrhizal with both deciduous and coniferous trees, especially in older spruce forests. Widespread throughout northern temperate zones.
• **SIMILAR SPECIES** *Cantharellus lutescens* (p.275) lacks veins under cap.

wavy, • irregular cap margin

funnel-shaped • mature cap

more or less hollow stem •

SECTION

pale gray veins • are decurrent

• chrome-yellow stem fades to dull yellow

cap occurs in shades of brown •

FRUITING In large troops among mosses in woodland.

wrinkled and • forked veins

Dimensions CAP ⊕ 1–6cm | STEM ↕ 3–8cm ↔ 3–8mm	Spores Cream	Edibility

Family TRICHOLOMATACEAE	Species *Lepista flaccida*	Season Summer–early winter

TAWNY FUNNEL CAP

The cap of this species is funnel-shaped, with an inrolled margin. It is tawny brown and may develop darker spots with age. Deeply decurrent gills run down the stem, which may be smooth or finely fibrillose. It is worthless as an edible.

• **OCCURRENCE** In woodland, especially near coniferous trees. Widespread and common in Europe; world distribution unknown.

• **SIMILAR SPECIES** Like most *Lepista* species, this mushroom is best distinguished from look-alikes, such as species of *Clitocybe* (pp.31, 33–34, 39–40) and *Tricholoma* (pp.59–64, 81), by microscopic features like its rough-walled spores. *Clitocybe gibba* (below) is less fleshy and has a paler spore deposit. *L. gilva* is more yellow with a margin that is distinctly spotted.

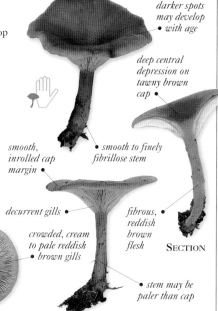

darker spots may develop with age •

deep central depression on tawny brown cap •

smooth, inrolled cap margin •

smooth to finely fibrillose stem

decurrent gills •

crowded, cream to pale reddish brown gills •

fibrous, reddish brown flesh

SECTION

stem may be paler than cap

FRUITING In troops or fairy rings on woodland litter.

Dimensions CAP ⊕ 4–12cm | STEM ↕ 3–7cm ↔ 0.5–1cm	Spores Cream	Edibility

Family TRICHOLOMATACEAE	Species *Clitocybe gibba*	Season Late summer–late autumn

COMMON FUNNEL CAP

The cap of this species is pale leather-brown, with a pink tinge, and is markedly depressed in the center, sometimes with a small umbo. The stem is smooth and paler than the cap. The deeply decurrent gills are almost pure white. The Common Funnel Cap is edible but is not recommended because it can be confused with other members of the genus (see also SIMILAR SPECIES).

• **OCCURRENCE** Found in a very wide range of wooded habitats, from lowland to alpine. Widespread and common in northern temperate zones.

• **SIMILAR SPECIES** *Lepista flaccida* (above). *L. gilva* is more fleshy and paler with a spotted cap margin.

smooth cap • surface

pink-tinged, leather-brown cap

deeply • decurrent gills

• stem is off-white

leaf litter adheres to stem base •

flesh is soft • and white with a fruity smell

SECTION

• closely spaced, pale gills

FRUITING In troops on woodland litter.

Dimensions CAP ⊕ 3–8cm | STEM ↕ 2.5–6cm ↔ 0.5–1cm	Spores White-cream	Edibility

| Family TRICHOLOMATACEAE | Species *Pseudoclitocybe cyathiformis* | Season Late autumn–early winter |

GOBLET FUNNEL CAP

This very distinctive species has a strongly funnel-shaped cap, very dark coloration, and a tall stem. The cap dries from dark gray-brown to pale grayish leather-brown and has an inrolled margin. The flesh is aromatic and mild tasting; although edible, it is not recommended. The genus *Pseudoclitocybe* differs from *Clitocybe* (pp.31, 33–34, 39–40) in that the spores produce a blue reaction in iodine reagents (amyloid).

• **OCCURRENCE** In woodland and open areas, on litter in tall grass, or on very decayed trunks of deciduous trees. Widespread in northern temperate zones; quite common.

• **SIMILAR SPECIES** Other *Pseudoclitocybe* species, on the whole smaller and paler, are often found in more open habitats. *Omphalina* species (p.36) are smaller.

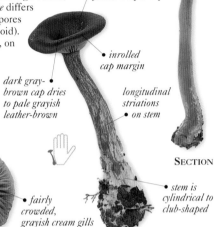

gills are strongly decurrent

smooth, deeply funnel-shaped cap

inrolled cap margin

dark gray-brown cap dries to pale grayish leather-brown

longitudinal striations on stem

SECTION

stem is cylindrical to club-shaped

fairly crowded, grayish cream gills age to pale brown

FRUITING Singly or in troops in a range of habitats.

| Dimensions CAP ⊕ 3–7cm \| STEM ↕ 6–10cm ↔ 0.5–1cm | Spores Cream-white | Edibility |

| Family TRICHOLOMATACEAE | Species *Leucopaxillus giganteus* | Season Late summer–autumn |

GIANT FUNNEL CAP

A large, funnel-shaped cap that is flat when young is characteristic of this species. The cap, gills, flesh, and comparatively short stem are off-white to cream. The spores turn blue in the presence of reagents containing iodine (amyloid) – a trait shared by all *Leucopaxillus* species. It can often cause stomach upsets.

• **OCCURRENCE** Borne from mycelia that may be hundreds of years old. The fruitbodies are found in grassland and also in parks and open woodland areas. Widespread in Europe; world distribution is poorly understood.

• **SIMILAR SPECIES** *Clitocybe geotropa* (p.33) has a longer stem.

margin is inrolled when young, splitting with age

huge, funnel-shaped cap up to 40cm across

crowded gills are decurrent and cream

dingy white to cream cap ages to pale brown

short stem hidden in grass

FRUITING Appears in fairy rings, which may be huge, mostly on nutrient-rich grassland.

| Dimensions CAP ⊕ 12–40cm \| STEM ↕ 4–8cm ↔ 2–4cm | Spores Whitish cream | Edibility |

Family TRICHOLOMATACEAE	Species *Clitocybe geotropa*	Season Autumn–early winter

STOUT-STALKED FUNNEL CAP

A funnel-shaped, fairly fleshy cap with a central umbo on a tall stem, pale leather-brown coloring, and a tendency to grow in fairy rings is typical of a closely related group of North American species. The genus *Clitocybe* is ridden with identification problems.

• **OCCURRENCE** Occurs mostly in woodland. In some parts it is found growing under deciduous trees, but it also thrives in certain types of coniferous woodland. Widespread and common in Europe, although not in cooler regions; worldwide distribution is poorly understood.

• **SIMILAR SPECIES** *Clitocybe nebularis* (p.40), often found in similar woodland habitats, is much grayer and has a bun-shaped cap. *Leucopaxillus giganteus* (p.32) has a shorter stem and fruits mostly in nutrient-rich grassland.

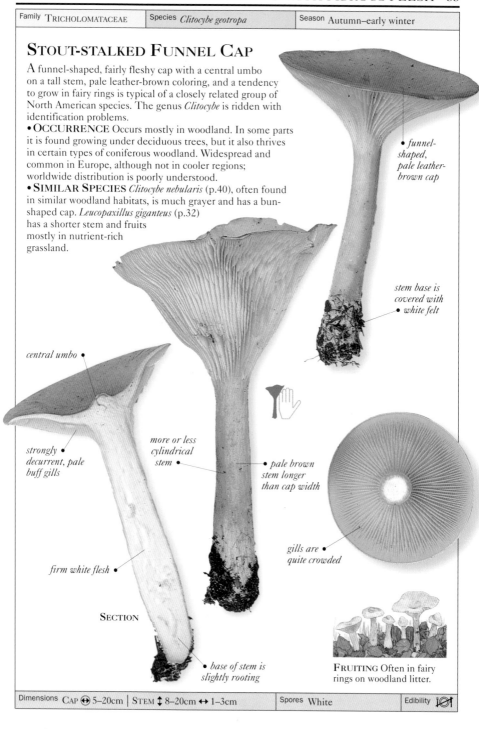

funnel-shaped, pale leather-brown cap

stem base is covered with white felt

central umbo

strongly decurrent, pale buff gills

more or less cylindrical stem

pale brown stem longer than cap width

gills are quite crowded

firm white flesh

SECTION

base of stem is slightly rooting

FRUITING Often in fairy rings on woodland litter.

Dimensions CAP ⊕ 5–20cm | STEM ↕ 8–20cm ↔ 1–3cm	Spores White	Edibility

| Family TRICHOLOMATACEAE | Species *Clitocybe metachroa* | Season Autumn–winter |

GRAY-BROWN FUNNEL CAP

*thin, striate
• cap margin* SECTION

Like many small members of this genus, this pale gray-brown species is difficult to identify with certainty. A very indistinct smell, which is not yeasty like many *Clitocybe* species, is perhaps its clearest characteristic. The flattened to deeply depressed cap dries with age, remaining darker at the center with a striate margin.

*decurrent,
• gray-white gills*

*faint smell from
• white flesh*

• **OCCURRENCE** Found growing among tree litter in deciduous and coniferous woodland. Widespread and common throughout Europe; worldwide distribution not known.

• **SIMILAR SPECIES** *Clitocybe vibecina* has a strong, rancid-yeast smell and taste.

*stem more •
or less hollow*

*very felty
white mycelium
at base of
smooth stem •*

FRUITING In troops on poor and more fertile soil.

*• cap dries out
to a paler shade
of brown*

*gills are •
crowded*

| Dimensions CAP ⊕ 2.5–6cm | STEM ↕ 3–6cm ↔ 3–7mm | Spores Off-white | Edibility ☠ |

| Family TRICHOLOMATACEAE | Species *Clitocybe dealbata* | Season Summer–autumn |

POISON LAWN FUNNEL CAP

*cap surface is thin
and develops
• cracks*

*often has dark
spots in
concentric rings
• on cap surface*

This is a highly poisonous mushroom, sometimes classed as two species: *Clitocybe rivulosa*, which has brown coloring, and *C. dealbata*, which is almost pure white. The convex to funnel-shaped cap has a mealy surface, often with dark spots in concentric rings; it cracks and dries even paler. The stem is off-white to pale brown. The white to buff-brown flesh has a somewhat yeasty smell.

*• stem is
off-white to
pale brown*

• **OCCURRENCE** In grassy areas, including parks, lawns, and sports fields; may be found growing with the edible *Marasmius oreades* (p.117), which is distinguished by its adnexed to almost free gills and rubbery stem. Widespread in northern temperate zones.

*mealy layer
• on cap*

FRUITING Often in fairy rings among grasses.

*• decurrent
gills are white
to pale gray*

| Dimensions CAP ⊕ 2–6cm | STEM ↕ 1.5–4cm ↔ 3–6mm | Spores White | Edibility ☠ |

Family PAXILLACEAE	Species *Paxillus involutus*	Season Summer–autumn

POISON PAX

SECTION

A strongly inrolled, yellow- to red-brown cap, with a downy margin and slightly depressed center, are particularly clear indicators of this very common poisonous species. So are the soft, crowded yellow gills that stain brown where touched and are removable with a knife tip. Colored like the cap, the stem is short and felty; the flesh is pale yellow to pale brown and darkens on cutting.

• **OCCURRENCE** Mycorrhizal mostly with coniferous trees and birch, in woodland, parks, and gardens. Widespread and common in northern temperate zones.

• **SIMILAR SPECIES** *Paxillus filamentosus* has a less incurved margin, yellow flesh, and occurs under alder.

decurrent gills are • soft and easy to remove

flesh is pale yellow • to pale brown

felty to smooth, • yellow- to red-brown cap

short, felt-covered stem •

• finely downy, inrolled cap margin

FRUITING In troops, rings, or a few together under trees.

Dimensions CAP ⊕ 6–15cm | STEM ↕ 4–8cm ↔ 1–2cm	Spores Yellowish brown	Edibility ☠

Family POLYPORACEAE	Species *Lentinus tigrinus*	Season Summer–autumn

TIGER LENTINUS

The funnel-shaped, off-white cap of this species has brown scales at the center and an incurved margin; the stem is also off-white, with brown scales that may appear to be stripes. The off-white gills are tough and decurrent. In one form the veil over the gills fails to open, making it look like it is parasitized by a mold.

• **OCCURRENCE** On deciduous trees, where it causes a white rot. Widespread and common in Europe and also in eastern North America.

• **SIMILAR SPECIES** *Lentinus lepideus* typically appears singly or in small clusters on conifers and produces a crumbly brown rot.

funnel-shaped cap is off-white •

toothed or torn gill • edges

thick, cobweb-like veil may • stick to gills

cap margin is incurved •

scales in • stripes on off-white stem

FRUITING In clusters on old branches or logs, particularly of poplar and willow, often near water.

Dimensions CAP ⊕ 1–10cm | STEM ↕ 1.5–7.5cm ↔ 0.5–1cm	Spores White	Edibility ⦿

| Family TRICHOLOMATACEAE | Species *Omphalina ericetorum* | Season Spring–late autumn |

LICHEN AGARIC

The yellow-brown cap of this small species has a central depression and radial striations, each one representing a gill beneath. The thin stem is smooth and is also yellow-brown, with a violet-gray tinge at the top. The flesh is very thin and off-white to ocher.

• **OCCURRENCE** This species is also a lichen, *Botrydina vulgaris*, living with an algal partner. The energy produced by the algae through photosynthesis enables it to colonize harsh acidic environments. It is found on turf or sphagnum moss, often at higher altitudes but also in lowlands. Widespread in cooler regions of northern temperate zones; widely distributed across northern North America.

• **SIMILAR SPECIES** *Omphalina alpina*, found growing in alpine and arctic areas, is a brighter yellow color.

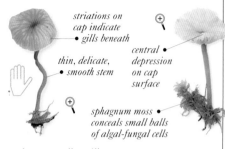

striations on cap indicate gills beneath

thin, delicate, smooth stem

central depression on cap surface

sphagnum moss conceals small balls of algal-fungal cells

pale creamy yellow gills

well-spaced, decurrent gills

FRUITING Appears singly or a few together.

| Dimensions CAP ⊕ 0.5–1.5cm | STEM ↕ 1–2cm ↔ 1–2mm | Spores White | Edibility |

| Family TRICHOLOMATACEAE | Species *Rickenella fibula* | Season Summer–autumn |

ORANGE MOSS AGARIC

Orange to pale yellow in color, this species is tiny, with a semi-spherical cap that is centrally depressed and has radial striations that fade as it dries. The stem is long and thin, and the gills are strongly decurrent. A hand lens reveals fine hairs all over the fruitbody. This and *Rickenella setipes* (inset, right) are the two most common species in the genus. *Rickenella* species have been classified under *Mycena*, *Omphalina*, and *Gerronema*.

• **OCCURRENCE** Parasitic on moss in a range of grassy habitats; a typical lawn mushroom. Widespread and common in northern temperate zones.

△ ***RICKENELLA SETIPES***
This tiny species is pale gray to gray-brown; the cap center (navel) is almost black. The top of the stem is tinged dark violet.

semispherical cap with central depression (navel)

orange to almost yellow cap

thin, orange-brown flesh

well-spaced gills are off-white and strongly decurrent

striations on cap are difficult to see when it dries

tiny hairs on pale orange stem

FRUITING Singly or in small groups or troops.

| Dimensions CAP ⊕ 0.3–1cm | STEM ↕ 3–5cm ↔ 1–2mm | Spores White | Edibility |

WITH CONVEX CAP AND FIBROUS FLESH

T HE SPECIES here have semi-spherical, convex, or umbonate caps and fibrous flesh. Unlike the species on pp.28–36, the caps very rarely develop a central depression. Those on pp.43–55 may have caps of a similar shape, but they are distinguished by their crumbly, cheeselike flesh.

Family GOMPHIDIACEAE	Species *Chroogomphus rutilus*	Season Autumn

PINE GOMPH

This agaric has a convex or umbonate, rusty brown cap with a wine-red flush; unlike species in the related *Gomphidius* genus (p.38), it is greasy only in wet weather. The rust-orange stem has zones of threadlike, reddish brown veil remains. The flesh is orange to wine-red or chrome-yellow at the stem base; it has no distinct taste or smell.
• OCCURRENCE Mycorrhizal with pine trees in woods and stands. Widespread and locally common in northern temperate zones.

wine-red flush on rusty brown cap surface •

decurrent gills are olive-brown becoming • gray-black

fairly broad, medium-spaced gills •

fibrillose, reddish brown remains of veil

stem tapers toward base •

soft gills can be loosened from cap flesh

FRUITING In small groups or troops on sandy soil.

Dimensions CAP ⊕ 4–8cm	STEM ↕ 4–12cm ↔ 0.5–1.5cm	Spores Almost black	Edibility

Family HYGROPHORACEAE	Species *Hygrophorus hypothejus*	Season Late autumn–early winter

LATE FALL WAX CAP

This late-fruiting species has a convex to funnel-shaped, slimy, brown to olive-brown cap, a slimy stem, and decurrent yellow gills. An orange form, known as *Hygrophorus aureus*, is occasionally found.
• OCCURRENCE Mycorrhizal with pine trees, preferring sandy soil; typically found following the first frosts. Widespread in northern temperate zones; locally common.
• SIMILAR SPECIES *H. lucorum* is bright yellow and is associated with larch. Several other *Hygrophorus* species that are also found with pine are all distinguished from *H. hypothejus* by their different coloring.

thick slime layer on • cap surface

well-spaced, pale to deep yellow gills •

• clearly decurrent gills

stem • top is not slimy

• brown to olive-brown cap with paler margin

• slimy, pale yellow stem

FRUITING In small groups among mosses and lichens.

Dimensions CAP ⊕ 3–5cm	STEM ↕ 4–7cm ↔ 0.5–1cm	Spores White	Edibility

Family GOMPHIDIACEAE	Species *Gomphidius roseus*	Season Late summer–autumn

ROSY GOMPH

This unmistakable species has a coral-red cap that is convex with an inrolled margin when young, becoming flattened with age. The stem is spindle-shaped and bears the remains of the slimy, colorless veil, which is often stained black by the falling spores. The flesh is off-white with a coral-red tint and has no distinctive smell or taste. It is edible but not recommended, due to its rarity.

• **OCCURRENCE** Under pine trees on sandy soil, among mosses, lichens, and pine litter. Widespread in northern temperate zones.

△ *GOMPHIDIUS GLUTINOSUS*
This gray-brown species is covered in a colorless, slimy veil. The stem has an indistinct ring zone, often stained black by spores, and its base is lemon-yellow. Mycorrhizal with spruce.

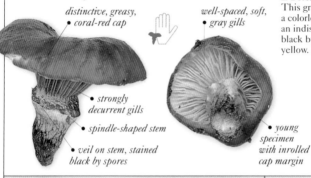

distinctive, greasy, coral-red cap

well-spaced, soft, gray gills

• *strongly decurrent gills*

• *spindle-shaped stem*

• *veil on stem, stained black by spores*

• *young specimen with inrolled cap margin*

FRUITING A few together with *Suillus bovinus* (p.200).

Dimensions CAP ⊕ 1.5–5cm	STEM ↕ 2–4cm ↔ 0.5–1cm	Spores Almost black	Edibility

Family HYGROPHORACEAE	Species *Hygrocybe pratensis*	Season Throughout autumn

BUFF WAX CAP

This orange species has a fleshy, dry to greasy, convex cap that flattens with age. It has a wavy margin and sometimes a central umbo. The faintly striated stem is paler than the cap and may taper toward the base. A popular edible, with fairly solid, buff flesh, it has an earthy smell and pleasant taste. Along with *Hygrocybe virginea* (p.39), it is often classified in the genera *Camarophyllus* or *Cuphophyllus*.

• **OCCURRENCE** Found in unimproved grassland, rarely in damp woodland. Widespread and fairly common in northern temperate zones.

• **SIMILAR SPECIES** *Hygrophorus nemoreus* has a dry cap and grows in oak woods.

greasy cap

• *decurrent gills are paler than cap surface*

• *dry stem with fine, longitudinal fibers*

stem may taper toward base

widely spaced, thick, waxy gills •

• *cap color is uniform orange or slightly frosted with white*

FRUITING In groups or rings with moss and grass.

Dimensions CAP ⊕ 2.5–6cm	STEM ↕ 2.5–6cm ↔ 0.5–1.5cm	Spores White	Edibility

Family HYGROPHORACEAE	Species *Hygrocybe virginea*	Season Autumn

SNOWY WAX CAP

The most obvious characteristics of this variable species are an absence of slime, a dry to greasy, ivory-white cap, which may be translucently striate at the margin, and well-spaced, decurrent gills. The white stem sometimes has a pink base due to an infection that may produce a smell of coconut. Two varieties occur: var. *fuscescens* has a yellow-ocher to brown cap center; var. *ochraceopallida* has a pale leather-brown cap. Slimy-capped specimens are sometimes classified as *H. nivea*.
• **OCCURRENCE** In grassland or open woods. Widespread and common in eastern and northern North America.
• **SIMILAR SPECIES** *H. russocoriacea* smells of leather, sandalwood, or pencil shavings. It is also widespread in northern temperate zones.

convex to flat cap, often with navel or • small umbo

ivory-white cap surface • is not slimy

well-spaced, • decurrent, thick, waxy, white to cream gills

• dry, solid, white stem

SECTION

FRUITING Found in troops or fairy rings among grass.

Dimensions CAP ⊕ 1.5–5cm	STEM ↕ 2–7cm ↔ 0.3–1cm	Spores White	Edibility |O|

Family TRICHOLOMATACEAE	Species *Clitocybe odora*	Season Summer–autumn

ANISE FUNNEL CAP

The convex or umbonate cap of this species matures from blue-green to gray or gray-brown; it is rarely funnel-shaped. The adnate or only slightly decurrent gills are unusual in this genus, but the strong anise smell of the marbled flesh is common to a number of *Clitocybe* species. It is edible, but see SIMILAR SPECIES.
• **OCCURRENCE** Among deciduous or coniferous litter in woodlands. Widespread in northern temperate zones.
• **SIMILAR SPECIES** A number of species that smell similar, including *C. fragrans*, are typically smaller, white or leather-brown, and have decurrent gills. They are not edible.

inrolled cap margin •

adnate to slightly decurrent gills

marbled flesh •

• green-blue cap surface, tinged brown with age

SECTION

• finely felted white mycelium

• crowded gills, paler than cap or stem

FRUITING In troops on soil; it prefers fertile soil.

Dimensions CAP ⊕ 3–6cm	STEM ↕ 3–6cm ↔ 0.4–1cm	Spores Dull pink	Edibility |O|

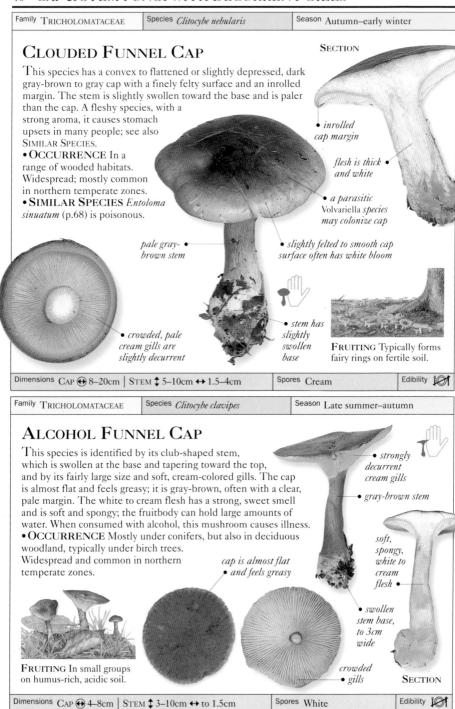

Family TRICHOLOMATACEAE	Species *Clitocybe nebularis*	Season Autumn–early winter

CLOUDED FUNNEL CAP

SECTION

This species has a convex to flattened or slightly depressed, dark gray-brown to gray cap with a finely felty surface and an inrolled margin. The stem is slightly swollen toward the base and is paler than the cap. A fleshy species, with a strong aroma, it causes stomach upsets in many people; see also SIMILAR SPECIES.
• **OCCURRENCE** In a range of wooded habitats. Widespread; mostly common in northern temperate zones.
• **SIMILAR SPECIES** *Entoloma sinuatum* (p.68) is poisonous.

• *inrolled cap margin*

flesh is thick and white •

• *a parasitic Volvariella species may colonize cap*

pale gray-brown stem •

• *slightly felted to smooth cap surface often has white bloom*

• *crowded, pale cream gills are slightly decurrent*

• *stem has slightly swollen base*

FRUITING Typically forms fairy rings on fertile soil.

Dimensions CAP ⊕ 8–20cm | STEM ↕ 5–10cm ↔ 1.5–4cm	Spores Cream	Edibility

Family TRICHOLOMATACEAE	Species *Clitocybe clavipes*	Season Late summer–autumn

ALCOHOL FUNNEL CAP

This species is identified by its club-shaped stem, which is swollen at the base and tapering toward the top, and by its fairly large size and soft, cream-colored gills. The cap is almost flat and feels greasy; it is gray-brown, often with a clear, pale margin. The white to cream flesh has a strong, sweet smell and is soft and spongy; the fruitbody can hold large amounts of water. When consumed with alcohol, this mushroom causes illness.
• **OCCURRENCE** Mostly under conifers, but also in deciduous woodland, typically under birch trees. Widespread and common in northern temperate zones.

• *strongly decurrent cream gills*

• *gray-brown stem*

soft, spongy, white to cream flesh •

cap is almost flat and feels greasy •

• *swollen stem base, to 3cm wide*

FRUITING In small groups on humus-rich, acidic soil.

crowded gills •

SECTION

Dimensions CAP ⊕ 4–8cm | STEM ↕ 3–10cm ↔ to 1.5cm	Spores White	Edibility

Family ENTOLOMATACEAE	Species *Clitopilus prunulus*	Season Autumn

BREAD DOUGH CLITOPILUS

A pale gray-white cap and decurrent, pale pink gills, combined with a strong smell of fresh bread dough, distinguish this species. The cap is convex to funnel-shaped; the stem is central or off-center and is similar in color to the cap. This species is a choice edible, with soft white flesh, but see also SIMILAR SPECIES.
• **OCCURRENCE** In mostly acidic woodland; also found growing in open, grassy places, but close to trees. Widespread and rather common in northern temperate zones.
• **SIMILAR SPECIES** Species of *Clitocybe* and *Entoloma* can look very similar and are poisonous.

dry, matte cap surface

pale pink to pinkish gray gills

convex to funnel-shaped cap may have inrolled margin

SECTION

off-white stem

gray-white cap

decurrent gills are crowded

FRUITING A few or in troops on humus-rich soil.

Dimensions CAP ⊕ 3–9cm | STEM ↕ 2–6cm ↔ 0.4–1cm	Spores Pale pink	Edibility ⦶

Family TRICHOLOMATACEAE	Species *Lyophyllum decastes*	Season Autumn, mostly late

SHIMEJI FUNNEL CAP

This is one of several fleshy *Lyophyllum* species that are apparently closely related and are difficult to separate. Its convex to flattened, gray-brown cap has a smooth margin and becomes wavy with age. The stem is off-white or pale gray-brown, as are the slightly decurrent, fairly crowded gills. It has no distinctive taste or smell, but is considered a good edible.
• **OCCURRENCE** Along woodland paths and in gardens and parks, but not in direct association with trees. Widespread and common in northern temperate zones.
• **SIMILAR SPECIES** *L. fumosum* has a stem fused into a trunklike base.

greasy to dry cap has smooth margin

SECTION

slightly decurrent gills are white to pale gray

fibrous, pale grayish brown flesh

FRUITING Often in dense clusters with fused stems.

pale gray or off-white stem

Dimensions CAP ⊕ 5–10cm | STEM ↕ 4–10cm ↔ 0.5–2.5cm	Spores White	Edibility ⦶

| Family TRICHOLOMATACEAE | Species *Lyophyllum connatum* | Season Autumn |

POISON ROADSIDE FUNNEL CAP

convex cap with wavy margin •

decurrent, pale gray to white gills •

The cap of this white mushroom is convex, often with a wavy margin, and the stem tapers toward the base. The rather crowded, white to pale gray gills are slightly decurrent; they stain violet when in contact with solid or dissolved ferrous sulfate ($FeSO_4$). The flesh is white and also stains violet.
• **OCCURRENCE** Mostly on disturbed soil on woodland edges. Widespread in northern temperate zones, including alpine areas.
• **SIMILAR SPECIES** Some of the white *Clitocybe* species are fairly similar in appearance. They are distinguished by their failure to stain violet.

FRUITING Singly or in clusters of fruitbodies on road edges in woodlands.

| Dimensions CAP ⊕ 3–10cm │ STEM ↕ 5–12cm ↔ 0.5–1.5cm | Spores White | Edibility ☠ |

| Family TRICHOLOMATACEAE | Species *Armillaria tabescens* | Season Autumn |

RINGLESS HONEY MUSHROOM

erect brown scales at cap center •

fibrous, off-white stem •

The convex to flat or depressed, dry, yellowish brown cap of this species has erect brown scales at the center. The stem is fibrous and off-white and is often fused with many others at its base. Black mycelial strands are present on the substrate. Its off-white flesh is edible after careful cooking.
• **OCCURRENCE** Attached to roots or near trees. Rare in warmer parts of Europe but widespread and common in eastern North America.
• **SIMILAR SPECIES** *Armillaria mellea* (p.80) has a stem ring. *Clitocybe* species (pp.31, 33–4, 39–40) lack the cap scales and the black mycelial strands.

FRUITING In clusters on the ground near trees such as oaks; it kills the host tree.

| Dimensions CAP ⊕ 2.5–10cm │ STEM ↕ 7.5–20cm ↔ 0.5–1.5cm | Spores Pale cream | Edibility |◎| |

| Family BOLETACEAE | Species *Phylloporus rhodoxanthus* | Season Summer–autumn |

GILLED BOLETE

convex to flat or depressed cap •

This species has a dry, reddish brown cap. Its stem is red to reddish yellow. This is a gilled bolete, but it may produce a tube layer and is more closely related to pored boletes, such as *Boletus pascuus* (p.192), than to agarics. The gills are easily separated from the yellow to red-tinged flesh.

bright yellow gills may bruise green or blue •

decurrent gills with interlinking veins

• **OCCURRENCE** Mycorrhizal with oak; also found under conifers. Widespread and common in northern temperate zones, except the far north.
• **SIMILAR SPECIES** *Phylloporus leucomycelinus* has a white mycelium at the base.

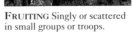

FRUITING Singly or scattered in small groups or troops.

| Dimensions CAP ⊕ 2.5–7.5cm │ STEM ↕ 4.5–10cm ↔ 0.5–1cm | Spores Ochre-yellow | Edibility |◎| |

CRUMBLY FLESH EXUDING MILK

BELONGING EXCLUSIVELY to the genus *Lactarius*, all species in this subsection have slightly decurrent gills and variable cap shapes, and almost all exude a white or colored fluid from cut or broken flesh. This "milk" may change color rapidly on exposure and is a good identification feature; the best way to see this is by testing one or two drops on a white handkerchief.

Family RUSSULACEAE	Species *Lactarius piperatus*	Season Summer–early autumn

PEPPERY LACTARIUS

This large, crumbly-fleshed species has an off-white fruitbody, very crowded gills, and an almost smooth cap that is depressed in the center. The white milk, which dries olive-green, has a very peppery taste. Although not edible, this species can be rendered safe by layering in salt and storing before cooking.

• **OCCURRENCE** Mycorrhizal with both deciduous and coniferous trees in woodlands on well-drained soil. Widespread and rather common in northern temperate zones.

• **SIMILAR SPECIES** The milk of *Lactarius glaucescens* dries grayish blue-green. *L. vellereus* (p.44). *L. deceptivus* has a cottony inrolled cap margin, and the milk does not change color.

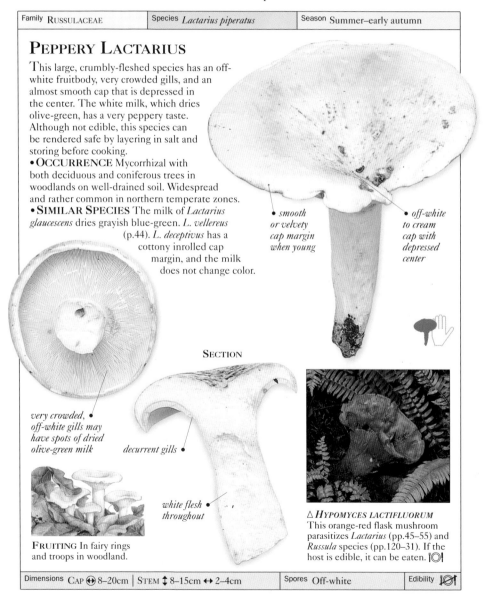

• *smooth or velvety cap margin when young*

• *off-white to cream cap with depressed center*

SECTION

very crowded, off-white gills may have spots of dried olive-green milk •

decurrent gills •

white flesh throughout •

FRUITING In fairy rings and troops in woodland.

△ *HYPOMYCES LACTIFLUORUM*
This orange-red flask mushroom parasitizes *Lactarius* (pp.45–55) and *Russula* species (pp.120–31). If the host is edible, it can be eaten.

Dimensions CAP ⊕ 8–20cm	STEM ↕ 8–15cm ↔ 2–4cm	Spores Off-white	Edibility

| Family RUSSULACEAE | Species *Lactarius vellereus* | Season Autumn |

FLEECY LACTARIUS

The white to cream cap of this very large species is densely felted and has a clear central depression. Its cream gills are fairly crowded, and it has a comparatively short, tapered stem. The white milk from its crumbly white flesh is copious and dries to brown on the gills; it does not stain with potassium hydroxide (KOH).

• **OCCURRENCE** Mycorrhizal with deciduous trees, such as beech, but also found with various conifers. Exact range unknown but widespread in northern temperate zones.

• **SIMILAR SPECIES** The milk in *Lactarius bertillonii* stains yellow then orange with KOH and has a hot taste. *L. piperatus* (p.43) is distinguished by more crowded gills, a longer stem, and a smooth cap.

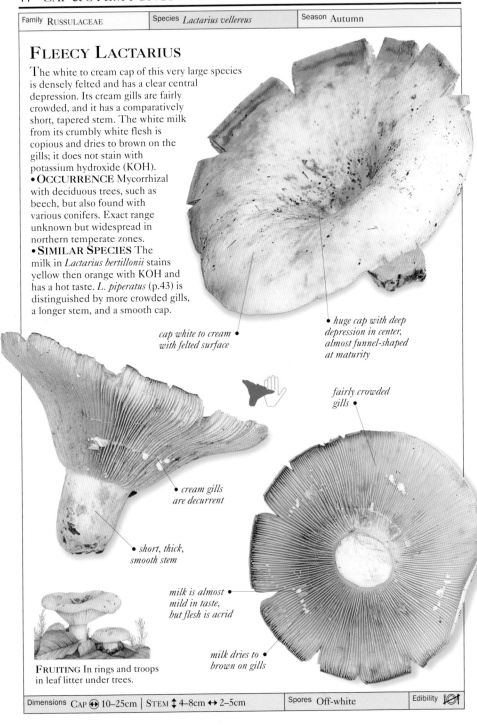

cap white to cream with felted surface

huge cap with deep depression in center, almost funnel-shaped at maturity

fairly crowded gills

cream gills are decurrent

short, thick, smooth stem

milk is almost mild in taste, but flesh is acrid

milk dries to brown on gills

FRUITING In rings and troops in leaf litter under trees.

| Dimensions CAP ⊕ 10–25cm | STEM ↕ 4–8cm ↔ 2–5cm | Spores Off-white | Edibility |

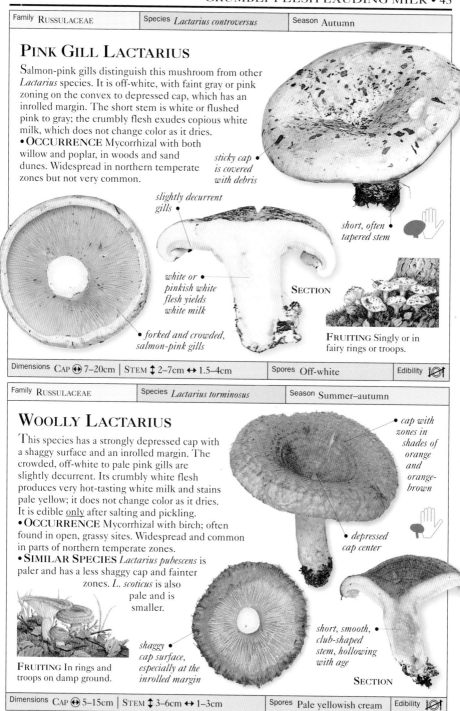

| Family RUSSULACEAE | Species *Lactarius controversus* | Season Autumn |

PINK GILL LACTARIUS

Salmon-pink gills distinguish this mushroom from other *Lactarius* species. It is off-white, with faint gray or pink zoning on the convex to depressed cap, which has an inrolled margin. The short stem is white or flushed pink to gray; the crumbly flesh exudes copious white milk, which does not change color as it dries.
• **OCCURRENCE** Mycorrhizal with both willow and poplar, in woods and sand dunes. Widespread in northern temperate zones but not very common.

sticky cap is covered with debris

slightly decurrent gills

short, often tapered stem

white or pinkish white flesh yields white milk

SECTION

forked and crowded, salmon-pink gills

FRUITING Singly or in fairy rings or troops.

| Dimensions CAP ⊕ 7–20cm | STEM ↕ 2–7cm ↔ 1.5–4cm | Spores Off-white | Edibility |

| Family RUSSULACEAE | Species *Lactarius torminosus* | Season Summer–autumn |

WOOLLY LACTARIUS

This species has a strongly depressed cap with a shaggy surface and an inrolled margin. The crowded, off-white to pale pink gills are slightly decurrent. Its crumbly white flesh produces very hot-tasting white milk and stains pale yellow; it does not change color as it dries. It is edible <u>only</u> after salting and pickling.
• **OCCURRENCE** Mycorrhizal with birch; often found in open, grassy sites. Widespread and common in parts of northern temperate zones.
• **SIMILAR SPECIES** *Lactarius pubescens* is paler and has a less shaggy cap and fainter zones. *L. scoticus* is also pale and is smaller.

cap with zones in shades of orange and orange-brown

depressed cap center

short, smooth, club-shaped stem, hollowing with age

FRUITING In rings and troops on damp ground.

shaggy cap surface, especially at the inrolled margin

SECTION

| Dimensions CAP ⊕ 5–15cm | STEM ↕ 3–6cm ↔ 1–3cm | Spores Pale yellowish cream | Edibility |

Family RUSSULACEAE	Species *Lactarius deliciosus*	Season Late summer–autumn

ORANGE LATEX LACTARIUS

This brownish orange species has a depressed cap with faint concentric zones and an inrolled margin; its short stem is covered with orange depressions. It has thick, crumbly, pale yellow to orange flesh yielding carrot-orange milk, which does not change color. A choice edible, it has the harmless, if slightly alarming, effect of making urine turn red.

• **OCCURRENCE** Mycorrhizal with pine trees, often on sandy, alkaline soil. Widespread in northern temperate zones, but distribution is unclear.

• **SIMILAR SPECIES** *Lactarius deterrimus* (inset, below left). *L. indigo* has blue flesh and milk in the cap and stem. It grows with pines. *L. salmonicolor*, which grows with firs, is larger. *L. semisanguifluus* (inset, below right).

pale yellow • to orange flesh

SECTION

• faint brownish orange zones on cap

orange dents mark • the short stem

cap is greasy or • dry and smooth

• fairly crowded, brownish orange, decurrent gills

cap margin • is inrolled

△ ***LACTARIUS DETERRIMUS***
Found with spruce trees, this has a smooth stem and exudes green-staining orange milk. Common and widespread in the Rockies. |⊙|

△ ***LACTARIUS SANGUIFLUUS***
This species is a popular edible, particularly in Spain. It has blood-red milk, staining green as it dries. It is mycorrhizal with pine. |⊙|

FRUITING In groups or troops in grass or pine litter.

Dimensions CAP ⊕ 5–15cm │ STEM ↕ 3–7cm ↔ 1–3cm	Spores Off-white	Edibility |⊙|

Family RUSSULACEAE	Species *Lactarius necator*	Season Summer–autumn

MUTAGEN LACTARIUS

Marked by its dark olive-green coloring, this species has a sticky cap with a depressed center and a felty margin, inrolled when young. The crumbly white flesh produces copious white milk, which dries in greenish brown spots on the off-white to pale green gills. Although eaten salted or marinated in eastern Europe, it may contain carcinogens.
• **OCCURRENCE** Mycorrhizal with birch and spruce, in woods, parks, and gardens. Widespread from Europe to east Asia; absent in North America.
• **SIMILAR SPECIES** *Lactarius blennius* (below) and *L. fluens* are paler and often more distinctly zoned or spotted on their caps.

shiny, dark olive-green cap

short stem, mostly paler than cap

crowded, narrow gills are slightly decurrent

FRUITING Singly, a few together, or in troops.

Dimensions CAP ⊕ 6–15cm	STEM ↕ 4–7cm ↔ 1–2.5cm	Spores Off-white	Edibility

Family RUSSULACEAE	Species *Lactarius blennius*	Season Summer–autumn

EURO SLIMY LACTARIUS

This species has a smooth cap with a central depression. Of varying shades, usually in a mixture or brown, gray, and olive, it is typically ringed with dark spots near the cap margin. Its firm white flesh produces white milk that dries to olive-gray on the white gills. Although considered inedible, it has been eaten after boiling or salting.
• **OCCURRENCE**
Mycorrhizal with beech. Widespread and very common in Europe and adjacent parts of Asia.
• **SIMILAR SPECIES** *Lactarius circellatus* grows only under hornbeam and has darker, ocher gills. *L. fluens* is larger and greener with cream gills and a zoned cap with a near white margin. *L. hortensis* (p.48). *L. trivialis* (p.49).

smooth cap is slimy when wet

smooth stem is paler than cap

spots of milk on crowded gills

slightly decurrent white gills

SECTION

FRUITING Mostly found in troops in beech litter.

Dimensions CAP ⊕ 4–9cm	STEM ↕ 3–7cm ↔ 1–2.5cm	Spores Pale yellow	Edibility

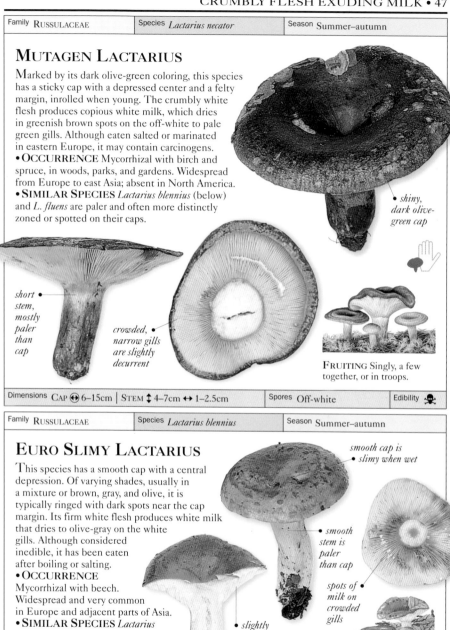

| Family RUSSULACEAE | Species *Lactarius fuliginosus* | Season Autumn |

VELVETY LACTARIUS

This species has a brown, slightly velvety cap, often with a central depression, and a tapering, pale brown to almost white stem. The firm, off-white flesh becomes pink-brown on exposure. White milk is exuded and slowly turns pink on the flesh. The ocher gills bruise pinkish brown. The spores are spherical, with crests and a netted surface.
- **OCCURRENCE** Mycorrhizal with deciduous trees, such as oak and beech, in woods. European, but world distribution unclear.
- **SIMILAR SPECIES** Other brown *Lactarius* species with white milk that turns pink are identified by the speed with which this occurs and by cap color and spore ornament: *L. acris* is pale and fast staining; *L. lignyotus*, found by conifers, is dark brown velvet, and slow reacting; *L. pterosporus* has a lighter colored cap and winged spores.

• *cap is mid- to dark brown*

where exposed, off-white flesh stains pink-brown •

• *pale brown to almost white stem with white base*

SECTION

• *velvety cap surface*

very slightly • decurrent gills

• *well-spaced gills*

young, inrolled • margin

FRUITING Appears singly or a few together.

| Dimensions CAP ⊕ 6–10cm | STEM ↕ 4–7cm ↔ 1–1.5cm | Spores Pale ocher | Edibility  |

| Family RUSSULACEAE | Species *Lactarius pyrogalus* | Season Summer–autumn |

ZEBRA-SPORED LACTARIUS

The pale gray-brown cap of this species is often wavy margined with a depressed center; it is faintly concentrically zoned and slightly greasy. The ocher gills are unusually well spaced for a *Lactarius* species. A tiny drop of the white milk yielded by the crumbly flesh produces a burning taste that lasts for hours.
- **OCCURRENCE** Mycorrhizal with hazel in woods or gardens. Widespread and fairly common in Europe and adjacent areas of Asia.
- **SIMILAR SPECIES** *L. circellatus* grows with hornbeam trees. It has more crowded gills and more dense, well-marked zones on the cap. *L. vietus*, which grows under birch trees, is more violet-gray, less zoned, and has yellowish white gills, gray-spotted with age. Its white milk dries lead-gray.

faint zones on • cap surface

short stem is white to • pale gray

greasy • cap with wavy margin

• *well-spaced, ocher gills*

adnate to slightly decurrent • gills

cap center • often depressed

stem base is often • pointed

FRUITING In troops or a few together on fertile soil.

SECTION

| Dimensions CAP ⊕ 4–10cm | STEM ↕ 3–7cm ↔ 0.5–2cm | Spores Pale ocher-yellow | Edibility |

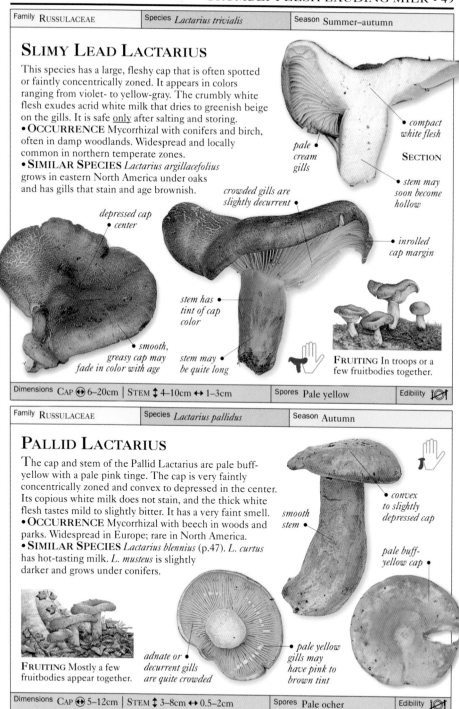

Family RUSSULACEAE	Species *Lactarius trivialis*	Season Summer–autumn

SLIMY LEAD LACTARIUS

This species has a large, fleshy cap that is often spotted or faintly concentrically zoned. It appears in colors ranging from violet- to yellow-gray. The crumbly white flesh exudes acrid white milk that dries to greenish beige on the gills. It is safe <u>only</u> after salting and storing.
• **OCCURRENCE** Mycorrhizal with conifers and birch, often in damp woodlands. Widespread and locally common in northern temperate zones.
• **SIMILAR SPECIES** *Lactarius argillacefolius* grows in eastern North America under oaks and has gills that stain and age brownish.

compact white flesh

pale cream gills

SECTION

stem may soon become hollow

crowded gills are slightly decurrent

inrolled cap margin

depressed cap center

stem has tint of cap color

smooth, greasy cap may fade in color with age

stem may be quite long

FRUITING In troops or a few fruitbodies together.

Dimensions CAP ⊕ 6–20cm	STEM ↕ 4–10cm ↔ 1–3cm	Spores Pale yellow	Edibility

Family RUSSULACEAE	Species *Lactarius pallidus*	Season Autumn

PALLID LACTARIUS

The cap and stem of the Pallid Lactarius are pale buff-yellow with a pale pink tinge. The cap is very faintly concentrically zoned and convex to depressed in the center. Its copious white milk does not stain, and the thick white flesh tastes mild to slightly bitter. It has a very faint smell.
• **OCCURRENCE** Mycorrhizal with beech in woods and parks. Widespread in Europe; rare in North America.
• **SIMILAR SPECIES** *Lactarius blennius* (p.47). *L. curtus* has hot-tasting milk. *L. musteus* is slightly darker and grows under conifers.

convex to slightly depressed cap

smooth stem

pale buff-yellow cap

FRUITING Mostly a few fruitbodies appear together.

adnate or decurrent gills are quite crowded

pale yellow gills may have pink to brown tint

Dimensions CAP ⊕ 5–12cm	STEM ↕ 3–8cm ↔ 0.5–2cm	Spores Pale ocher	Edibility

| Family RUSSULACEAE | Species *Lactarius mitissimus* | Season Autumn |

MILD LACTARIUS

convex to depressed cap center

This smallish lactarius has a convex orange cap that develops a central depression with age. Its crumbly, pale yellowish orange flesh has a mild taste and produces copious, nonstaining, white milk.

stem paler or same color as cap

smooth, dry, yellow-orange to orange cap

• **OCCURRENCE** Mycorrhizal with conifers and deciduous trees, often found with moss. Widespread in Europe; similar, closely related forms are found in other northern temperate zones.

• **SIMILAR SPECIES** Relatives of a similar size tend to be darker, less vividly orange, or with more or less hot-tasting milk. *Lactarius ichoratus* is slightly larger, reddish orange, and has an unpleasant, sickly smell. *L. volemus* (p.54) is larger.

off-white gills are slightly decurrent

gills are medium spaced

pale yellowish orange flesh

SECTION

FRUITING Typically, a few fruitbodies appear together.

| Dimensions CAP ⊕ 2–6cm | STEM ↕ 2–5cm ↔ 3–8mm | Spores Creamy pink | Edibility |

| Family RUSSULACEAE | Species *Lactarius theiogalus* | Season Autumn |

YELLOW-STAINING LACTARIUS

furrowed cap margin

The pale orange-tinted, gray-brown cap of this species has a central umbo; its margin is often furrowed. Its thin, pale flesh tastes mild, and the white milk stains yellow on a white handkerchief in 30 seconds or less. The stem is fairly long and is a similar color to the cap. The larger, more wrinkled form is sometimes regarded as a separate species, *Lactarius tabidus*.

orange-tinted, gray-brown surface

stem same color as cap or darker

stem is fairly long and thin

• **OCCURRENCE** Mycorrhizal with conifers and deciduous trees, often in damp, acid conditions among leaf litter. Widespread and common in many areas of northern temperate zones.

• **SIMILAR SPECIES** *L. lacunarum* also stains yellow but has a less wrinkled, non-striate, darker colored cap.

white milk stains yellow

somewhat decurrent gills

gills are crowded

pale flesh is fragile and thin

off-white to cream gills

FRUITING In troops or a few fruitbodies together.

SECTION

| Dimensions CAP ⊕ 2–5cm | STEM ↕ 3–8cm ↔ 0.4–1cm | Spores Off-white, tinged pink | Edibility |

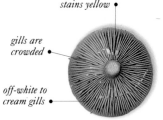

| Family RUSSULACEAE | Species *Lactarius hepaticus* | Season Autumn |

LIVER LACTARIUS

The smooth cap of this mushroom has a depressed or slightly raised center and is dull liver-brown. The stem is a similar color or paler. It has crumbly, cream to pale brown flesh, exuding white milk that turns yellow. The flesh tastes hot and is not recommended for eating.
• **OCCURRENCE** Mycorrhizal with pine trees in woods and stands on very acidic, sandy soil; it has become more common because of the increase in acid rain. Widespread and common in northern temperate zones.
• **SIMILAR SPECIES** *Lactarius badiosanguineus* is shinier and red-brown; its milk displays a faint yellow reaction. *L. rufus* (p.53) is often found in the same habitat and has unchanging milk. The much paler *L. theiogalus* (p.50) has the same yellow milk reaction.

dull liver-brown cap sometimes has faint olive-green sheen •

cap is smooth • with depressed or slightly umbonate center

adnate to • decurrent gills

thin, crumbly, • cream or pale brown flesh

• cylindrical stem

SECTION

fairly crowded, pink-tinged, brown or • ocher gills

FRUITING In small groups or troops on pine needles.

| Dimensions CAP ⊕ 3–6cm | STEM ↕ 4–6cm ↔ 0.6–1cm | Spores Cream | Edibility |

| Family RUSSULACEAE | Species *Lactarius subdulcis* | Season Summer–autumn |

DULL LACTARIUS

SECTION

This species is most easily identified by its negative characteristics. These include white milk that does not turn yellow and thin white flesh without a hot taste. The buff to dull brown cap is convex with a center that may be slightly depressed or umbonate. The stem is a similar color to the cap, and the slightly decurrent gills are off-white at first, becoming pale brown.
• **OCCURRENCE** Mycorrhizal with deciduous trees, chiefly beech. Widespread and common in Europe; world distribution unknown.

slightly • decurrent, pale brown gills

buff to • pale brown stem, darker toward base

flesh is thin • and white

fairly crowded gills •

white milk does • not stain

• convex cap may be slightly depressed or umbonate

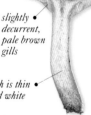

FRUITING Typically a few fruitbodies appear together.

| Dimensions CAP ⊕ 3–7cm | STEM ↕ 3–6cm ↔ 0.5–1cm | Spores Cream to pink-cream | Edibility |

| Family RUSSULACEAE | Species *Lactarius hygrophoroides* | Season Summer–autumn |

DISTANT-GILLED LACTARIUS

This orange-brown species has a convex to flat or depressed cap without any zoning. Both the cap and the stem have a dry surface. The crumbly flesh is white and exudes abundant, unchanging white milk, which has a mild taste.

• **OCCURRENCE**
Mycorrhizal, especially with oak trees in wooded areas. Widespread and common in eastern North America; not found in Europe.

• **SIMILAR SPECIES**
Lactarius corrugis has a reddish brown cap with a wrinkled margin, ocher gills, and milk that stains brown. See also *L. volemus* (p.54). Both are choice edibles, and all three species can be found in the same area at the same time of the year.

well-spaced, white to cream gills exuding milk drops

dry, orange-brown cap is convex to flat

gills are decurrent

stem is dry and orange-brown

FRUITING Appears in scattered but often abundant troops on the ground in open woodland.

| Dimensions CAP ⊕ 3–10cm | STEM ↕ 3–5cm ↔ 0.5–1.5cm | Spores White | Edibility |

| Family RUSSULACEAE | Species *Lactarius quietus* | Season Summer–autumn |

OAK LACTARIUS

This abundant species produces a variably zoned, dull gray- to red-brown cap, which has a slight depression when mature. It has crumbly, pale brown flesh and exudes sparse, creamy milk that does not change. Its characteristic oily smell is often likened to the smell of stinkbugs.

• **OCCURRENCE** Strictly mycorrhizal with oak trees, in mostly acidic woodland. Very common in Europe and neighboring parts of Asia.

• **SIMILAR SPECIES** *Lactarius chrysorrheus* is also mycorrhizal with oak but is paler and more yellow; it has copious white milk that quickly turns sulfur-yellow. *L. serifluus* has a similar but even stronger smell and a much darker cap.

adnate to slightly decurrent gills

pale brown flesh with sparse milk

older caps have small central depression

SECTION

dark spots or zones on cap

stem usually same length as cap diameter

club-shaped stem base

medium-spaced, pale brown gills, becoming redder with age

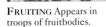

FRUITING Appears in troops of fruitbodies.

| Dimensions CAP ⊕ 4–8cm | STEM ↕ 3–7cm ↔ 0.5–1.5cm | Spores Cream to pink | Edibility |

| Family RUSSULACEAE | Species *Lactarius camphoratus* | Season Autumn |

FRAGRANT LACTARIUS

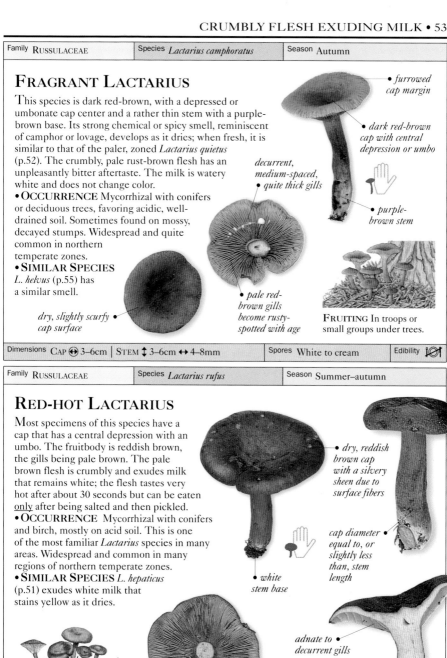

This species is dark red-brown, with a depressed or umbonate cap center and a rather thin stem with a purple-brown base. Its strong chemical or spicy smell, reminiscent of camphor or lovage, develops as it dries; when fresh, it is similar to that of the paler, zoned *Lactarius quietus* (p.52). The crumbly, pale rust-brown flesh has an unpleasantly bitter aftertaste. The milk is watery white and does not change color.

• **OCCURRENCE** Mycorrhizal with conifers or deciduous trees, favoring acidic, well-drained soil. Sometimes found on mossy, decayed stumps. Widespread and quite common in northern temperate zones.

• **SIMILAR SPECIES** *L. helvus* (p.55) has a similar smell.

• furrowed cap margin

• dark red-brown cap with central depression or umbo

decurrent, medium-spaced, • quite thick gills

• purple-brown stem

dry, slightly scurfy • cap surface

• pale red-brown gills become rusty-spotted with age

FRUITING In troops or small groups under trees.

| Dimensions CAP ⊕ 3–6cm │ STEM ↕ 3–6cm ↔ 4–8mm | Spores White to cream | Edibility |

| Family RUSSULACEAE | Species *Lactarius rufus* | Season Summer–autumn |

RED-HOT LACTARIUS

Most specimens of this species have a cap that has a central depression with an umbo. The fruitbody is reddish brown, the gills being pale brown. The pale brown flesh is crumbly and exudes milk that remains white; the flesh tastes very hot after about 30 seconds but can be eaten only after being salted and then pickled.

• **OCCURRENCE** Mycorrhizal with conifers and birch, mostly on acid soil. This is one of the most familiar *Lactarius* species in many areas. Widespread and common in many regions of northern temperate zones.

• **SIMILAR SPECIES** *L. hepaticus* (p.51) exudes white milk that stains yellow as it dries.

• dry, reddish brown cap with a silvery sheen due to surface fibers

cap diameter • equal to, or slightly less than, stem length

• white stem base

adnate to • decurrent gills

SECTION

FRUITING In troops or a few fruitbodies together.

• fairly crowded, pale brown gills

pale brown flesh •

| Dimensions CAP ⊕ 3–10cm │ STEM ↕ 5–10cm ↔ 0.5–2cm | Spores Off-white | Edibility |

Family RUSSULACEAE	Species *Lactarius glyciosmus*	Season Summer–autumn

COCONUT-SCENTED LACTARIUS

A smell like freshly baked coconut cookies exudes from this species, which has subtle gray to ocher coloring, with pink-tinged, pale cream gills. The cap may have a central depression and an upward-flaring margin. The thin white flesh produces sparse amounts of mild- or slightly acrid-tasting white milk that does not stain on exposure to air.
• **OCCURRENCE** Mycorrhizal with birch, often in damp places. Widespread and common in many areas of northern temperate zones.
• **SIMILAR SPECIES** *Lactarius hibbardae* in northeastern North America has the same odor but is much darker and grows with conifers.

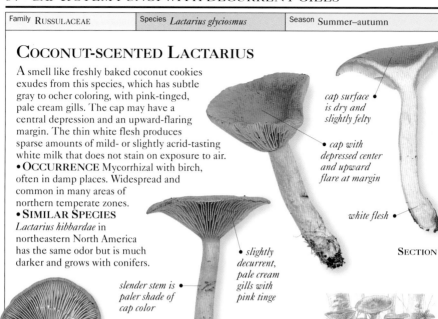

cap surface is dry and slightly felty

cap with depressed center and upward flare at margin

white flesh

SECTION

slightly decurrent, pale cream gills with pink tinge

slender stem is paler shade of cap color

fairly crowded gills

FRUITING Appears in troops among leaf litter.

Dimensions CAP ⊕ 2–6cm	STEM ↕ 2–7cm ↔ 0.5–1cm	Spores Pale yellow	Edibility 🚫🍴

Family RUSSULACEAE	Species *Lactarius volemus*	Season Autumn

LUSCIOUS LACTARIUS

This very fleshy, matte orange species has a thin, cracking skin on its cap and a thick, paler orange stem with a velvety surface. When cut, its off-white, mild-tasting flesh produces copious white milk, which stains brown, and it smells strongly of shellfish, especially in mature specimens. The crowded, slightly decurrent gills are pale golden yellow.
• **OCCURRENCE** Mycorrhizal, mostly with oak and beech. Widespread but mostly uncommon in northern temperate zones.
• **SIMILAR SPECIES** *Lactarius hygrophoroides* (p.52), an equally common and choice edible in eastern North America, lacks the odor, does not stain, and has distant gills.

skin is thin and cracking on convex, matte orange cap

crowded gills are slightly decurrent

thick stem is pale orange

FRUITING In troops or a few together under deciduous trees, more rarely conifers.

Dimensions CAP ⊕ 6–12cm	STEM ↕ 4–12cm ↔ 1–4cm	Spores Off-white	Edibility 🍴

Family RUSSULACEAE	Species *Lactarius helvus*	Season Summer–autumn

POISON LACTARIUS

A strong, spicy smell, similar to curry or the herbs lovage and fenugreek, characterizes this yellow-ocher to gray-brown species. Fairly large, it becomes funnel-shaped, with a central umbo, as it matures. Its crumbly flesh is yellow, white, or pale pink, and its mild-tasting milk is more sparse and watery than in most *Lactarius* species.
• **OCCURRENCE** Mycorrhizal with birch, pine, and spruce trees; often found growing among sphagnum moss. Widespread in northern temperate zones.
• **SIMILAR SPECIES** *L. aquifluus* is very similar in appearance and occurs in North America.

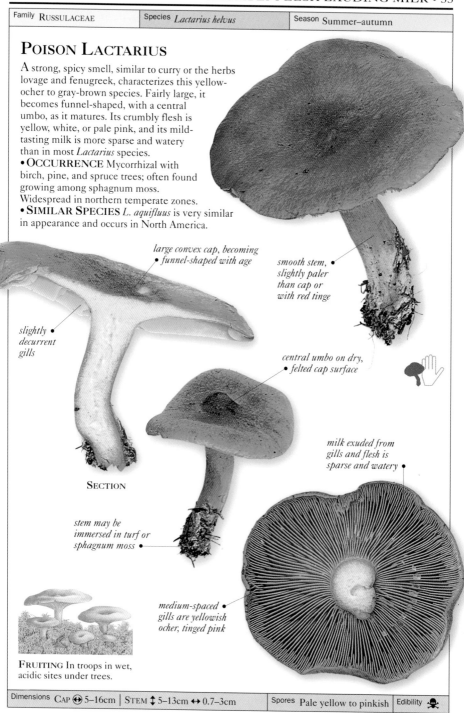

large convex cap, becoming
• funnel-shaped with age

smooth stem,
slightly paler
than cap or
with red tinge

slightly •
decurrent
gills

central umbo on dry,
• felted cap surface

milk exuded from
gills and flesh is
sparse and watery •

SECTION

stem may be
immersed in turf or
sphagnum moss •

medium-spaced •
gills are yellowish
ocher, tinged pink

FRUITING In troops in wet,
acidic sites under trees.

Dimensions CAP ⊕ 5–16cm │ STEM ↕ 5–13cm ↔ 0.7–3cm	Spores Pale yellow to pinkish	Edibility ☠

CAP & STEM FUNGI WITH ADNEXED TO ADNATE GILLS

This section consists of agarics in which the gill attachment to the stem varies from very narrow (adnexed) to very broad (broadly adnate). Some gills have a sharp indentation close to the stem; this is known as a notch (see p.15). The gill edge may be straight or curved.

gills • adnate

gills adnexed

FLESHY WITH NO OBVIOUS VEIL

THIS SUBSECTION features agarics with fruitbodies that are fleshy but which, unlike other fleshy species, do not have obvious veil remains either on the cap, the cap margin, or the stem (pp.69–97). It includes the blewits and most of the mycorrhizal trichs, as well as a range of other groups.

Family HYGROPHORACEAE	Species *Hygrocybe punicea*	Season Autumn

CRIMSON WAX CAP

This large, fleshy mushroom has a broadly conical to almost flat, slightly moist, crimson-red cap and pale crimson-red to orange gills. The yellow stem is red flushed with a dry surface and a covering of fine, longitudinal fibers. Its taste and smell are unremarkable; it should not be eaten.

• **OCCURRENCE**
In open deciduous and coniferous woods on the East and West coasts. Usually found growing with other species of *Hygrocybe*, *Geoglossum*, and *Clavulinopsis*; also in humus under coastal redwood trees in California.
• **SIMILAR SPECIES** *H. coccinea* (p.105). *H. splendidissima* is brighter vermilion-red with a dry cap and a sweet, sickly smell.

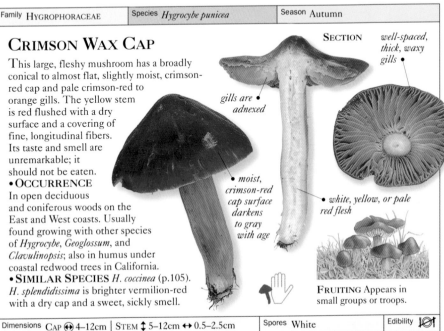

SECTION — well-spaced, thick, waxy gills •

gills are • adnexed

• moist, crimson-red cap surface darkens to gray with age

• white, yellow, or pale red flesh

FRUITING Appears in small groups or troops.

Dimensions CAP ⊕ 4–12cm	STEM ↕ 5–12cm ↔ 0.5–2.5cm	Spores White	Edibility

Family TRICHOLOMATACEAE	Species *Lepista irina*	Season Autumn

PUNGENT FALSE BLEWIT

This species is gray-brown all over, although the mature gills are pink tinged. The convex cap becomes flattened with age, and the stem has a fibrillose surface. The strongly perfumed, off-white flesh is edible in Europe, but the common American form makes some people ill.

• **OCCURRENCE** Typically on calcareous soil in leaf litter, sometimes in mass fruitings late in the season. Widespread in Europe; found in northern North America and the Rockies.

• **SIMILAR SPECIES** *Lepista nuda* (below) and *L. personata* (p.58) are of similar stature but have violet or lilac tints and fainter smells.

• pink stain from spores

• pale gray-brown cap

• cylindrical, fibrillose stem

crowded gills •

adnate, notched, and sinuate gills

SECTION

convex cap is often wavy-margined •

perfumed • flesh is off-white

FRUITING Often in fairy rings on leaf litter in forests.

Dimensions CAP ⊕ 5–15cm	STEM ↕ 5–10cm ↔ 1–2cm	Spores Dingy pink	Edibility

Family TRICHOLOMATACEAE	Species *Lepista nuda*	Season Mainly autumn

TRUE BLEWIT

The violet-brown cap of this easily identified, choice edible emerges dark and bun-shaped, becoming convex then flattened; its color becomes paler from the margin as the cap surface dries. The stem, with a club-shaped base, is a similar violet-brown; the sinuate gills are brighter violet, aging to buff-brown; the perfumed, firm flesh is marbled lilac-blue.

• **OCCURRENCE** Nutrient-rich woodland and garden habitats, such as in compost and thick leaf litter. Widespread and common in Europe and North America.

• **SIMILAR SPECIES** Unrelated poisonous look-alikes include species of *Entoloma* (p.68, 109–10, 144), *Cortinarius* (p.69–77), and *Hebeloma* (p.67, 82, 93).

• cap may be bluer than shown

firm flesh • marbled lilac-blue

fibrillose stem surface •

SECTION

• club-shaped stem base

crowded gills •

bun-shaped, • dark young cap

FRUITING Appears in small groups and fairy rings.

Dimensions CAP ⊕ 5–20cm	STEM ↕ 4–10cm ↔ 1.5–3cm	Spores Dingy pink	Edibility

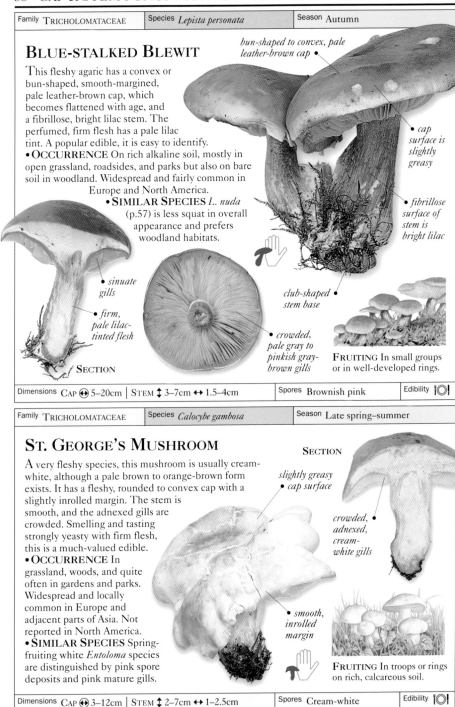

Family TRICHOLOMATACEAE	Species *Lepista personata*	Season Autumn

BLUE-STALKED BLEWIT

This fleshy agaric has a convex or bun-shaped, smooth-margined, pale leather-brown cap, which becomes flattened with age, and a fibrillose, bright lilac stem. The perfumed, firm flesh has a pale lilac tint. A popular edible, it is easy to identify.

• OCCURRENCE On rich alkaline soil, mostly in open grassland, roadsides, and parks but also on bare soil in woodland. Widespread and fairly common in Europe and North America.

• SIMILAR SPECIES *L. nuda* (p.57) is less squat in overall appearance and prefers woodland habitats.

bun-shaped to convex, pale leather-brown cap •

• cap surface is slightly greasy

• fibrillose surface of stem is bright lilac

• sinuate gills

• firm, pale lilac-tinted flesh

SECTION

club-shaped • stem base

• crowded, pale gray to pinkish gray-brown gills

FRUITING In small groups or in well-developed rings.

Dimensions CAP ⊕ 5–20cm | STEM ↕ 3–7cm ↔ 1.5–4cm	Spores Brownish pink	Edibility ⦿

Family TRICHOLOMATACEAE	Species *Calocybe gambosa*	Season Late spring–summer

ST. GEORGE'S MUSHROOM

SECTION

A very fleshy species, this mushroom is usually cream-white, although a pale brown to orange-brown form exists. It has a fleshy, rounded to convex cap with a slightly inrolled margin. The stem is smooth, and the adnexed gills are crowded. Smelling and tasting strongly yeasty with firm flesh, this is a much-valued edible.

• OCCURRENCE In grassland, woods, and quite often in gardens and parks. Widespread and locally common in Europe and adjacent parts of Asia. Not reported in North America.

• SIMILAR SPECIES Spring-fruiting white *Entoloma* species are distinguished by pink spore deposits and pink mature gills.

slightly greasy • cap surface

crowded, • adnexed, cream-white gills

• smooth, inrolled margin

FRUITING In troops or rings on rich, calcareous soil.

Dimensions CAP ⊕ 3–12cm | STEM ↕ 2–7cm ↔ 1–2.5cm	Spores Cream-white	Edibility ⦿

| Family TRICHOLOMATACEAE | Species *Tricholoma terreum* | Season Autumn |

DARK GRAY TRICH

The subtle colors of the Dark Gray Trich blend with the soil. It has an umbonate, dark gray cap with radial fibers and a smooth margin, and a silky-fibrillose, gray-white stem. The gills are sinuate, notched, and pale gray; unlike those of *Tricholoma sculpturatum* (below), they do not stain yellow. The pale flesh smells and tastes mild. It is edible, but see SIMILAR SPECIES.
• **OCCURRENCE** Mycorrhizal with conifers on rich, calcareous soil. Widespread and common in northern temperate zones.
• **SIMILAR SPECIES** *T. pardinum* (p.60), is poisonous, bigger, scaly, and smells yeasty. *T. sculpturatum* (below).

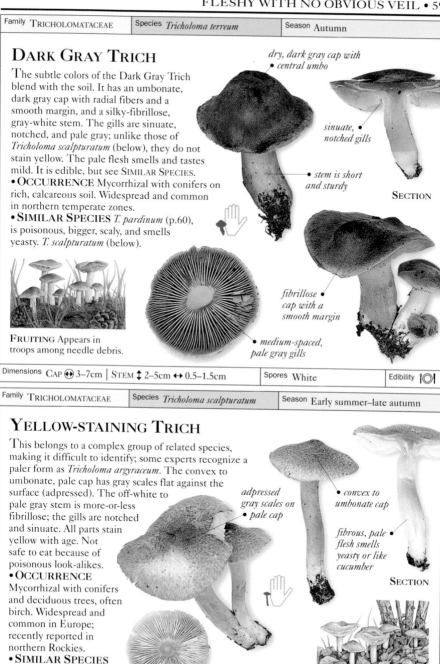

dry, dark gray cap with central umbo

sinuate, notched gills

stem is short and sturdy

SECTION

fibrillose cap with a smooth margin

medium-spaced, pale gray gills

FRUITING Appears in troops among needle debris.

| Dimensions CAP ⊕ 3–7cm | STEM ↕ 2–5cm ↔ 0.5–1.5cm | Spores White | Edibility |

| Family TRICHOLOMATACEAE | Species *Tricholoma sculpturatum* | Season Early summer–late autumn |

YELLOW-STAINING TRICH

This belongs to a complex group of related species, making it difficult to identify; some experts recognize a paler form as *Tricholoma argyraceum*. The convex to umbonate, pale cap has gray scales flat against the surface (adpressed). The off-white to pale gray stem is more-or-less fibrillose; the gills are notched and sinuate. All parts stain yellow with age. Not safe to eat because of poisonous look-alikes.
• **OCCURRENCE** Mycorrhizal with conifers and deciduous trees, often birch. Widespread and common in Europe; recently reported in northern Rockies.
• **SIMILAR SPECIES** Poisonous *T. pardinum* (p.60). *T. terreum* (above).

adpressed gray scales on pale cap

convex to umbonate cap

fibrous, pale flesh smells yeasty or like cucumber

SECTION

white to pale gray gills stain yellow

FRUITING Often in large troops of several hundred.

| Dimensions CAP ⊕ 2–8cm | STEM ↕ 3–7cm ↔ 0.5–1cm | Spores White | Edibility |

| Family TRICHOLOMATACEAE | Species *Tricholoma atrosquamosum* | Season Autumn–late autumn |

DIRTY TRICH COMPLEX

This complex has a convex or umbonate, pale gray cap, with radially arranged upturned, dark, threadlike, fibrous scales and an inrolled margin. The pale stem is covered with black scales, and the flesh is pale and fibrous with a spicy fragrance like geranium (*Pelargonium*). It can be hard to identify (see SIMILAR SPECIES), so eating it is not recommended.

• **OCCURRENCE** Mycorrhizal with conifers and deciduous trees. Widespread but local in Europe; world distribution not clear.

• **SIMILAR SPECIES** *Tricholoma orirubens* stains green and pink. *T. pardinum* (inset, right) is poisonous. *T. squarrulosum* is even more scaly.

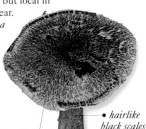

sinuate, notched, pale gray gills stain black at or near edge

SECTION

gills are medium spaced

pale flesh smells of spice

club-shaped stem base

dark radial fibers and scales on pale gray cap surface

hairlike black scales on stem

△ *TRICHOLOMA PARDINUM*
This species has a black-scaly cap and flesh that smells and tastes yeasty. It is found growing in mixed woods. ☠

FRUITING Singly or in small groups on alkaline soil.

| Dimensions CAP ⊕ 3–12cm | STEM ↕ 4–8cm ↔ 0.5–1.5cm | Spores White | Edibility |

| Family TRICHOLOMATACEAE | Species *Tricholoma sciodes* | Season Autumn |

SPOTTED GILL TRICH

This species has an off-white cap partially concealed by dark scales flattened against the surface (adpressed); it has a fairly prominent umbo. The gills have distinctive black spots, and the more or less cylindrical, pale stem is clad in hairlike gray scales; both may be pink flushed. It has earthy-smelling, sharp-tasting flesh, and is inedible.

• **OCCURRENCE** Mycorrhizal with deciduous trees, often beech, on fertile soil. Widespread and common in Europe, except the boreal-arctic; world distribution not clear.

• **SIMILAR SPECIES** *Tricholoma orirubens* stains green and pink. *T. virgatum*, found in rich conifer forests, is silvery gray and conical.

adpressed dark scales on off-white cap surface

umbo in cap center

fairly crowded, sinuate, notched gills

pale gray gills have dark edges

fibrous, pale flesh with earthy smell

SECTION

FRUITING A few specimens together in leaf litter.

| Dimensions CAP ⊕ 4–8cm | STEM ↕ 4–10cm ↔ 1–2cm | Spores White | Edibility |

| Family TRICHOLOMATACEAE | Species *Tricholoma saponaceum* | Season Late summer–late autumn |

SOAPY TRICH

An extremely variable species, the Soapy Trich is often divided into a number of varieties. All forms are fleshy and smell strongly of soap. Some have dark scales on the stem. The gills are cream to gray-green, staining in shades of red or becoming pale green with age. The flattened to umbonate cap is gray-green here but is variable in color and lacks the streaking of *Tricholoma portentosum* (below) and *T. sejunctum* (p.63). Its surface is greasy when damp, becoming scaly when dry.
• **OCCURRENCE** Mycorrhizal with deciduous trees, it is also found with conifers. Widespread throughout northern temperate zones.

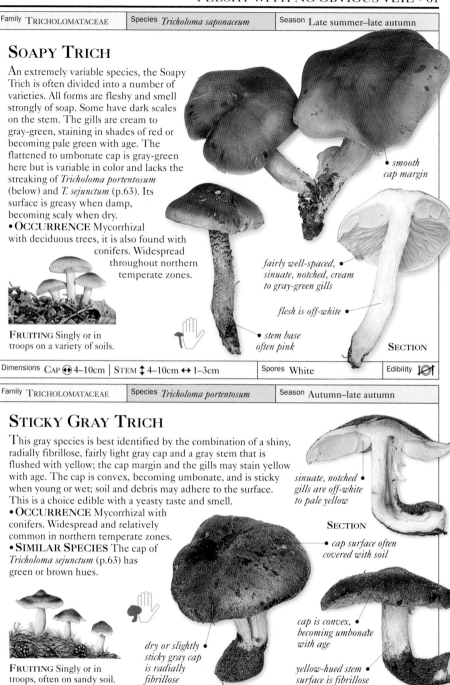

smooth cap margin

fairly well-spaced, sinuate, notched, cream to gray-green gills

flesh is off-white

FRUITING Singly or in troops on a variety of soils.

stem base often pink

SECTION

| Dimensions CAP ⊕ 4–10cm | STEM ↕ 4–10cm ↔ 1–3cm | Spores White | Edibility |

| Family TRICHOLOMATACEAE | Species *Tricholoma portentosum* | Season Autumn–late autumn |

STICKY GRAY TRICH

This gray species is best identified by the combination of a shiny, radially fibrillose, fairly light gray cap and a gray stem that is flushed with yellow; the cap margin and the gills may stain yellow with age. The cap is convex, becoming umbonate, and is sticky when young or wet; soil and debris may adhere to the surface. This is a choice edible with a yeasty taste and smell.
• **OCCURRENCE** Mycorrhizal with conifers. Widespread and relatively common in northern temperate zones.
• **SIMILAR SPECIES** The cap of *Tricholoma sejunctum* (p.63) has green or brown hues.

sinuate, notched gills are off-white to pale yellow

SECTION

cap surface often covered with soil

FRUITING Singly or in troops, often on sandy soil.

dry or slightly sticky gray cap is radially fibrillose

cap is convex, becoming umbonate with age

yellow-hued stem surface is fibrillose

| Dimensions CAP ⊕ 5–12cm | STEM ↕ 5–10cm ↔ 1–3cm | Spores White | Edibility |

Family TRICHOLOMATACEAE	Species *Tricholoma ustale*	Season Autumn–late autumn

BURNT TRICH

flattened brown cap with smooth margin

This species lacks unique identification features. The convex then flat brown cap is greasy when wet; the stem is pale brown with red-brown marking; and the off-white gills stain red-brown with age.

cap surface is greasy in wet weather

• **OCCURRENCE** Mycorrhizal with deciduous trees on neutral to alkaline soil – often found with beech on rich soil. Widespread and common throughout European temperate regions.

• **SIMILAR SPECIES** *Tricholoma populinum* is similar but occurs with poplar trees. *T. ustaloides* has a distinct pale zone at the top of the stem.

sinuate, notched gills stain red-brown with age

stem is pale with red-brown markings

SECTION

gills are off-white

△ **TRICHOLOMA AURANTIUM**
Mainly found with conifers, this species is orange with white showing on the stem. The cap may be sticky or almost velvety, depending on the weather. 🍴

pale flesh becomes darker at stem base

gills are fairly crowded

FRUITING Appears singly or in troops of fruitbodies.

Dimensions CAP ⊕ 3–10cm | STEM ↕ 4–10cm ↔ 0.5–2cm	Spores White	Edibility 🍴

Family TRICHOLOMATACEAE	Species *Tricholoma lascivum*	Season Autumn–late autumn

OAK TRICH

gills are white to pale brown, notched, and crowded

This small to medium-sized *Tricholoma* species is recognized by its preference for a particular habitat and then by its sweet or yeasty to gaslike smell, which some people find pleasant and others dislike. It has a convex then flattened, pale leather-brown cap and a solid, cylindrical, off-white stem that becomes pale brown. It may be poisonous.

cap margin is smooth

strongly aromatic white flesh

SECTION

• **OCCURRENCE** Mycorrhizal with oak, beech, and hornbeam in woodland. Widespread and common throughout Europe.

gray- to pale leather-brown cap

• **SIMILAR SPECIES** Among other pale *Tricholoma* species, *T. album* is almost pure white and found only with birch. *Calocybe gambosa* (p.58) occurs mostly in spring.

cylindrical, solid stem

stem is white or similar in color to cap

FRUITING In troops on soil that is acidic to neutral.

Dimensions CAP ⊕ 4–8cm | STEM ↕ 5–8cm ↔ 1–1.5cm	Spores White	Edibility 🍴

| Family TRICHOLOMATACEAE | Species *Tricholoma sejunctum* | Season Autumn |

FALSE EDIBLE TRICH

The green or brown cap of this species is moist and domed, flattening with age. Its surface has dark fibrils and is greasy in wet weather. The white stem develops yellow flushes with age, and the flesh is off-white, tinted yellow under the cap skin. It causes nausea if eaten; see also SIMILAR SPECIES.

• **OCCURRENCE** Mycorrhizal with deciduous trees, such as beech, and conifers. It is found in woodland or large stands, usually on acidic soil; the beech form occurs on alkaline soil. Widespread throughout northern temperate regions.

• **SIMILAR SPECIES** *Tricholoma portentosum* (p.61). The poisonous *Amanita phalloides* (p.151) is distinguished by its volva, stem ring, and free gills.

pale brown cap with radiating, dark fibrils

pointed stem base

cap surface is greasy when wet

cap is domed, flattening with age

sinuate, notched, white, cream, or pale gray gills

firm, off-white flesh

FRUITING Appears in small groups or troops.

white stem develops yellow flushes with age

SECTION

| Dimensions CAP ⊕ 5–10cm │ STEM ↕ 5–8cm ↔ 1–1.5cm | Spores White | Edibility |

| Family TRICHOLOMATACEAE | Species *Tricholoma flavovirens* | Season Autumn–early winter |

EDIBLE YELLOW TRICH

There are several forms of this species, which is also known as *Tricholoma auratum* or *T. equestre*. They are all yellow, with an expanded convex cap and pale yellow stem, but differ in fruitbody size, being slender or more robust depending on location. The flesh is a whitish yellow and has a faint to strong yeasty smell, differing in the various forms and strongest in the form associated with pine (shown here). It is a choice edible, but the pine form can be difficult to clean because it is ingrained with grit.

• **OCCURRENCE** Mycorrizal; robust forms occur in pine woods; slender forms are mostly found under spruce and aspen. Widespread and fairly common throughout northern temperate zones.

medium-spaced, sinuate, notched gills

expanded-convex, yellow-brown cap

dirt sticks to cap and stem

pale yellow stem

gills are bright yellow

FRUITING In troops; different forms are found with pine, on sandy soil, or with spruce or aspen.

| Dimensions CAP ⊕ 5–14cm │ STEM ↕ 5–10cm ↔ 1.5–2.5cm | Spores White | Edibility |

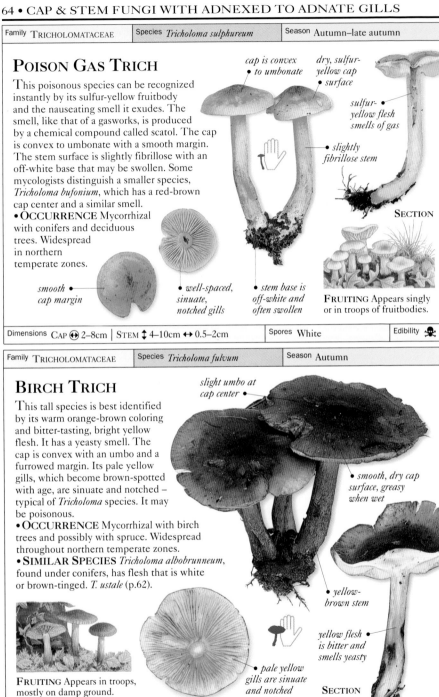

| Family TRICHOLOMATACEAE | Species *Tricholoma sulphureum* | Season Autumn–late autumn |

POISON GAS TRICH

This poisonous species can be recognized instantly by its sulfur-yellow fruitbody and the nauseating smell it exudes. The smell, like that of a gasworks, is produced by a chemical compound called scatol. The cap is convex to umbonate with a smooth margin. The stem surface is slightly fibrillose with an off-white base that may be swollen. Some mycologists distinguish a smaller species, *Tricholoma bufonium*, which has a red-brown cap center and a similar smell.

• **OCCURRENCE** Mycorrhizal with conifers and deciduous trees. Widespread in northern temperate zones.

cap is convex to umbonate

dry, sulfur-yellow cap surface

sulfur-yellow flesh smells of gas

slightly fibrillose stem

SECTION

smooth cap margin

well-spaced, sinuate, notched gills

stem base is off-white and often swollen

FRUITING Appears singly or in troops of fruitbodies.

| Dimensions CAP ⊕ 2–8cm | STEM ↕ 4–10cm ↔ 0.5–2cm | Spores White | Edibility ☠ |

| Family TRICHOLOMATACEAE | Species *Tricholoma fulvum* | Season Autumn |

BIRCH TRICH

This tall species is best identified by its warm orange-brown coloring and bitter-tasting, bright yellow flesh. It has a yeasty smell. The cap is convex with an umbo and a furrowed margin. Its pale yellow gills, which become brown-spotted with age, are sinuate and notched – typical of *Tricholoma* species. It may be poisonous.

• **OCCURRENCE** Mycorrhizal with birch trees and possibly with spruce. Widespread throughout northern temperate zones.

• **SIMILAR SPECIES** *Tricholoma albobrunneum*, found under conifers, has flesh that is white or brown-tinged. *T. ustale* (p.62).

slight umbo at cap center

smooth, dry cap surface, greasy when wet

yellow-brown stem

yellow flesh is bitter and smells yeasty

FRUITING Appears in troops, mostly on damp ground.

pale yellow gills are sinuate and notched

SECTION

| Dimensions CAP ⊕ 4–10cm | STEM ↕ 7–15cm ↔ 1–2.5cm | Spores White | Edibility |

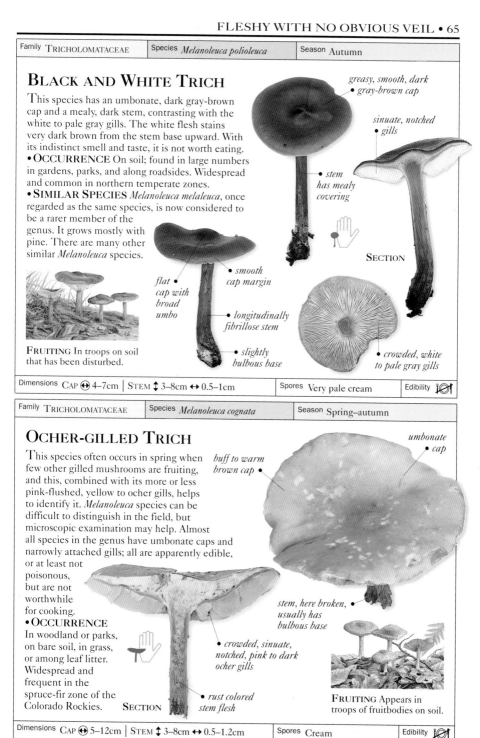

| Family | TRICHOLOMATACEAE | Species | *Melanoleuca polioleuca* | Season | Autumn |

BLACK AND WHITE TRICH

This species has an umbonate, dark gray-brown cap and a mealy, dark stem, contrasting with the white to pale gray gills. The white flesh stains very dark brown from the stem base upward. With its indistinct smell and taste, it is not worth eating.
• **OCCURRENCE** On soil; found in large numbers in gardens, parks, and along roadsides. Widespread and common in northern temperate zones.
• **SIMILAR SPECIES** *Melanoleuca melaleuca*, once regarded as the same species, is now considered to be a rarer member of the genus. It grows mostly with pine. There are many other similar *Melanoleuca* species.

greasy, smooth, dark gray-brown cap

sinuate, notched gills

stem has mealy covering

SECTION

flat cap with broad umbo

smooth cap margin

longitudinally fibrillose stem

slightly bulbous base

crowded, white to pale gray gills

FRUITING In troops on soil that has been disturbed.

| Dimensions | CAP ⊕ 4–7cm | STEM ↕ 3–8cm ↔ 0.5–1cm | Spores | Very pale cream | Edibility |

| Family | TRICHOLOMATACEAE | Species | *Melanoleuca cognata* | Season | Spring–autumn |

OCHER-GILLED TRICH

This species often occurs in spring when few other gilled mushrooms are fruiting, and this, combined with its more or less pink-flushed, yellow to ocher gills, helps to identify it. *Melanoleuca* species can be difficult to distinguish in the field, but microscopic examination may help. Almost all species in the genus have umbonate caps and narrowly attached gills; all are apparently edible, or at least not poisonous, but are not worthwhile for cooking.
• **OCCURRENCE** In woodland or parks, on bare soil, in grass, or among leaf litter. Widespread and frequent in the spruce-fir zone of the Colorado Rockies.

umbonate cap

buff to warm brown cap

stem, here broken, usually has bulbous base

crowded, sinuate, notched, pink to dark ocher gills

rust colored stem flesh

SECTION

FRUITING Appears in troops of fruitbodies on soil.

| Dimensions | CAP ⊕ 5–12cm | STEM ↕ 3–8cm ↔ 0.5–1.2cm | Spores | Cream | Edibility |

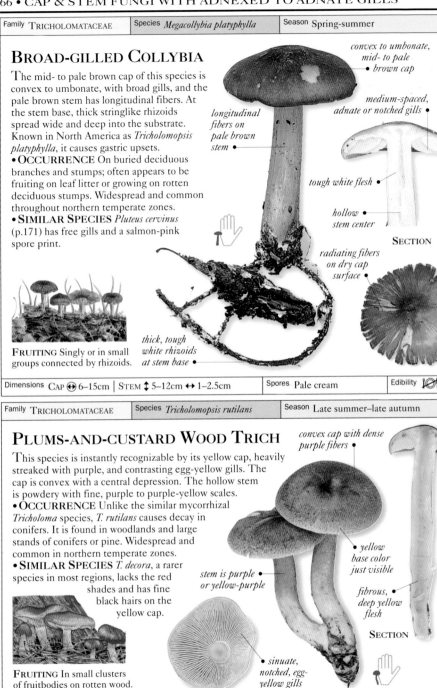

| Family TRICHOLOMATACEAE | Species *Megacollybia platyphylla* | Season Spring-summer |

BROAD-GILLED COLLYBIA

The mid- to pale brown cap of this species is convex to umbonate, with broad gills, and the pale brown stem has longitudinal fibers. At the stem base, thick stringlike rhizoids spread wide and deep into the substrate. Known in North America as *Tricholomopsis platyphylla*, it causes gastric upsets.
• **OCCURRENCE** On buried deciduous branches and stumps; often appears to be fruiting on leaf litter or growing on rotten deciduous stumps. Widespread and common throughout northern temperate zones.
• **SIMILAR SPECIES** *Pluteus cervinus* (p.171) has free gills and a salmon-pink spore print.

convex to umbonate, mid- to pale brown cap

medium-spaced, adnate or notched gills •

longitudinal fibers on pale brown stem •

tough white flesh •

hollow • stem center

SECTION

radiating fibers on dry cap surface •

FRUITING Singly or in small groups connected by rhizoids.

thick, tough white rhizoids at stem base •

| Dimensions CAP ⊕ 6–15cm | STEM ↕ 5–12cm ↔ 1–2.5cm | Spores Pale cream | Edibility 🖐️🍴 |

| Family TRICHOLOMATACEAE | Species *Tricholomopsis rutilans* | Season Late summer–late autumn |

PLUMS-AND-CUSTARD WOOD TRICH

This species is instantly recognizable by its yellow cap, heavily streaked with purple, and contrasting egg-yellow gills. The cap is convex with a central depression. The hollow stem is powdery with fine, purple to purple-yellow scales.
• **OCCURRENCE** Unlike the similar mycorrhizal *Tricholoma* species, *T. rutilans* causes decay in conifers. It is found in woodlands and large stands of conifers or pine. Widespread and common in northern temperate zones.
• **SIMILAR SPECIES** *T. decora*, a rarer species in most regions, lacks the red shades and has fine black hairs on the yellow cap.

convex cap with dense purple fibers •

yellow base color just visible

stem is purple • or yellow-purple

fibrous, • deep yellow flesh

SECTION

FRUITING In small clusters of fruitbodies on rotten wood.

• sinuate, notched, egg-yellow gills

| Dimensions CAP ⊕ 5–10cm | STEM ↕ 4–10cm ↔ 1–2.5cm | Spores White | Edibility 🖐️🍴 |

| Family TRICHOLOMATACEAE | Species *Collybia maculata* | Season Autumn |

RUST-SPOTTED COLLYBIA

SECTION

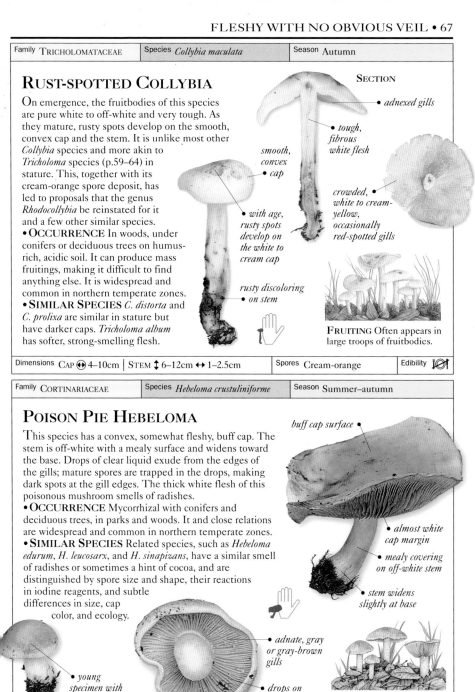

On emergence, the fruitbodies of this species are pure white to off-white and very tough. As they mature, rusty spots develop on the smooth, convex cap and the stem. It is unlike most other *Collybia* species and more akin to *Tricholoma* species (p.59–64) in stature. This, together with its cream-orange spore deposit, has led to proposals that the genus *Rhodocollybia* be reinstated for it and a few other similar species.
• **OCCURRENCE** In woods, under conifers or deciduous trees on humus-rich, acidic soil. It can produce mass fruitings, making it difficult to find anything else. It is widespread and common in northern temperate zones.
• **SIMILAR SPECIES** *C. distorta* and *C. prolixa* are similar in stature but have darker caps. *Tricholoma album* has softer, strong-smelling flesh.

• adnexed gills

• tough, fibrous white flesh

smooth, convex • cap

crowded, • white to cream-yellow, occasionally red-spotted gills

• with age, rusty spots develop on the white to cream cap

rusty discoloring • on stem

FRUITING Often appears in large troops of fruitbodies.

| Dimensions CAP ⊕ 4–10cm | STEM ↕ 6–12cm ↔ 1–2.5cm | Spores Cream-orange | Edibility |

| Family CORTINARIACEAE | Species *Hebeloma crustuliniforme* | Season Summer–autumn |

POISON PIE HEBELOMA

This species has a convex, somewhat fleshy, buff cap. The stem is off-white with a mealy surface and widens toward the base. Drops of clear liquid exude from the edges of the gills; mature spores are trapped in the drops, making dark spots at the gill edges. The thick white flesh of this poisonous mushroom smells of radishes.
• **OCCURRENCE** Mycorrhizal with conifers and deciduous trees, in parks and woods. It and close relations are widespread and common in northern temperate zones.
• **SIMILAR SPECIES** Related species, such as *Hebeloma edurum*, *H. leucosarx*, and *H. sinapizans*, have a similar smell of radishes or sometimes a hint of cocoa, and are distinguished by spore size and shape, their reactions in iodine reagents, and subtle differences in size, cap color, and ecology.

buff cap surface •

• almost white cap margin

• mealy covering on off-white stem

• stem widens slightly at base

• young specimen with convex cap

• adnate, gray or gray-brown gills

• drops on gills turn dark as they dry

FRUITING In troops or fairy rings, often among grass.

| Dimensions CAP ⊕ 4–9cm | STEM ↕ 3–8cm ↔ 0.8–2cm | Spores Brown | Edibility ☠ |

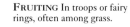

Family ENTOLOMATACEAE	Species *Entoloma sinuatum*	Season Autumn

LEAD POISON ENTOLOMA

A convex, pale gray-brown to ocher-cream cap with medium-spaced, sinuate, notched, pale yellow young gills, which become the typical *Entoloma*-pink with age, are good indicators of this mushroom. It also has a white to grayish cream stem and a yeasty to nauseating smell. It is important to get to know this *Lepista* look-alike because it is responsible for a high percentage of mushroom poisonings.
• **OCCURRENCE** In mature deciduous woodlands, often on clay soil. Widespread but local in Europe. Replaced by close relatives in North America and East Asia.
• **SIMILAR SPECIES** *Lepista irina* (p.57) is strongly perfumed, and its gray-brown stem is fibrillose.

sinuate, notched, medium-spaced gills •

cap is pale gray-brown to ocher-cream •

convex cap with central umbo •

FRUITING Appears in small groups often under deciduous trees, such as oak or beech, in woods.

Dimensions CAP ⊕ 8–20cm │ STEM ↕ 10–18cm ↔ 2–4cm	Spores Pale pink	Edibility ☠

Family ENTOLOMATACEAE	Species *Entoloma rhodopolium*	Season Autumn–late autumn

BEECH WOODS ENTOLOMA

This very varied species is difficult to identify. The gray or gray-brown cap is convex with an umbo, or slightly depressed. The gray stem is often long and slender with pale gray to pale brown flesh, odorless or smells of gas. The gaslike form is more slender and was once considered a separate species, *Entoloma nidorosum*. All forms are poisonous.
• **OCCURRENCE** In deciduous woodlands, especially beech woods, on rich soil. Widespread and locally common in northern temperate zones; world distribution unclear.
• **SIMILAR SPECIES** A number of similar species differ subtly in coloring and various microscopic characteristics.

broad, thick gills are sinuate and notched •

cap margin may have radial striations •

slender, silky gray stem with longitudinal fibers •

soft, pale gray to pale brown flesh •

SECTION

crowded, whitish gray then dirty pink gills •

△ ***ENTOLOMA CLYPEATUM***
This spring-fruiting species has a gray-brown cap, a brown-tinged, white stem, and sinuate, notched, pale gray gills aging to pink. ✋

FRUITING Appears in troops among leaf litter.

Dimensions CAP ⊕ 4–12cm │ STEM ↕ 6–15cm ↔ 0.5–2cm	Spores Dirty pink	Edibility ☠

| Family ENTOLOMATACEAE | Species *Entoloma porphyrophaeum* | Season Summer–autumn |

PURPLISH ENTOLOMA

Gray-purple coloring and a tall stature, along with a grassland habitat, make this species easily recognizable. The cap is umbonate, becoming conical with age. It has white flesh, with no distinctive smell, and may be poisonous.

• OCCURRENCE In unimproved grassland, often associated with Hygrophoraceae and Clavariaceae; also in alpine areas. Widespread but uncommon in Europe and eastern North America; it has suffered from the farming practice of using commercial fertilizer on pastures.

FRUITING Singly or in small groups of fruitbodies.

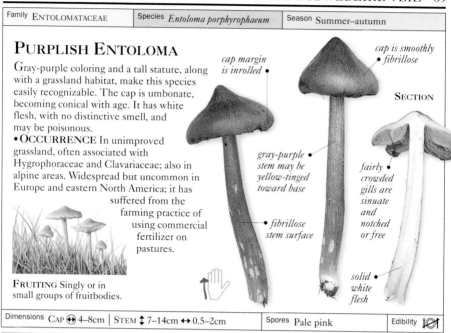

cap margin is inrolled •

cap is smoothly • fibrillose

SECTION

gray-purple • stem may be yellow-tinged toward base

fairly • crowded gills are sinuate and notched or free

• fibrillose stem surface

solid • white flesh

| Dimensions CAP ⊕ 4–8cm \| STEM ↕ 7–14cm ↔ 0.5–2cm | Spores Pale pink | Edibility 🚫🍴 |

WITH COBWEBLIKE VEIL

S PECIES OF *CORTINARIUS*, which are featured in this subsection, are highly variable in size and shape. However, they all have a partial veil, resembling a fine spider's web, which protects the young gills. They also have rusty brown spore deposits, often seen as a rusty smudge on the veil remains.

| Family CORTINARIACEAE | Species *Cortinarius bolaris* | Season Summer–autumn |

MOTTLED POISON CORT

Distinctive red scales covering the cap and stem readily identify this species. A fairly short stem makes it look sturdy, and the fleshy cap is broadly convex with remains of the veil visible as fine threads at the margin. Thick, off-white flesh in the cap becomes yellow to orange toward the stem base.

• OCCURRENCE Mycorrhizal with deciduous trees, especially oak and birch, on acidic soil. Widespread and locally common in northern temperate zones in eastern North America.

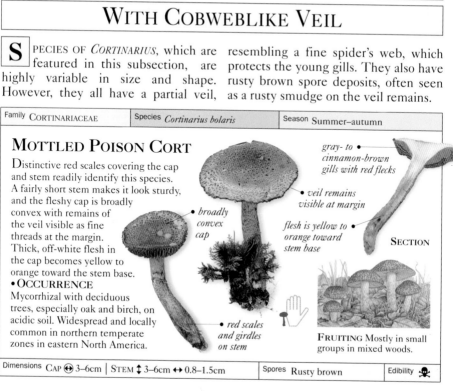

gray- to • cinnamon-brown gills with red flecks

• veil remains visible at margin

• broadly convex cap

flesh is yellow to • orange toward stem base

SECTION

• red scales and girdles on stem

FRUITING Mostly in small groups in mixed woods.

| Dimensions CAP ⊕ 3–6cm \| STEM ↕ 3–6cm ↔ 0.8–1.5cm | Spores Rusty brown | Edibility ☠️ |

| Family CORTINARIACEAE | Species *Cortinarius pholideus* | Season Autumn |

SCALY CORT

A brown-scaled cap and a long stem ringed with brown veil girdles characterize this web-cap. The cap is more or less convex when young, flat with a central umbo when mature. When young, the adnate gills are violet-blue; they age to violet-brown as the spores mature to rusty brown. A faint smell reminiscent of fresh tangerines exudes from the violet-tinged, pale brown flesh.
• OCCURRENCE Typically mycorrhizal with birch but may also be found with other trees in mixed woodlands. It prefers acidic soil. Widespread and quite common in northern temperate zones.

thin, pointed brown scales on cap

violet to violet-brown gills

fibrous brown girdles on stem

cap is pointed to umbonate

stem is violet at top

solid stem with violet-brown flesh

SECTION

FRUITING Appears in small groups on mossy soil.

| Dimensions CAP ⊕ 3–8cm | STEM ↕ 5–12cm ↔ 0.5–1cm | Spores Rusty brown | Edibility |

| Family CORTINARIACEAE | Species *Cortinarius semisanguineus* | Season Summer–autumn |

POISON DYE CORT

SECTION

The uniform red-brown coloring and blood-red gills are the best aid to identification of this species. It has a convex, olive- to red-brown cap, becoming umbonate with age; the paler stem exhibits threadlike veil remnants. The flesh of the cap is a paler red-brown than that of the stem. The Poison Dye Cort is an excellent source of a dye used for coloring wool.
• OCCURRENCE Almost exclusively mycorrhizal with conifers, it is often abundant under young spruce trees in large stands. Widespread in northern temperate zones.
• SIMILAR SPECIES
Cortinarius phoeniceus has a redder cap and more distinct red veil girdles around the stem.

blood-red gills are fairly crowded

adnate, sinuate gills

stem surface paler than cap

stem flesh darker red-brown than cap flesh

olive- to dark reddish brown cap

convex to umbonate cap

threadlike remnants of veil

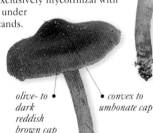

△ CORTINARIUS CINNAMOMEUS
This close relative occurs with deciduous trees and conifers. It has orange or orange-yellow gills aging to cinnamon-brown.

FRUITING In troops under conifers, often in moss.

| Dimensions CAP ⊕ 2–7cm | STEM ↕ 4–10cm ↔ 0.5–1cm | Spores Rusty brown | Edibility |

Family CORTINARIACEAE	Species *Cortinarius paleaceus*	Season Summer–autumn

GERANIUM CORT

Fine, white to off-white veil scales on an umbonate or pointed, dark brown cap and a geranium-like fragrance (*Pelargonium*) help identify this species. On some specimens, the scales are almost absent, or the cap margin may be striate. The margin usually also displays veil remnants, and the slender stem has a thin ring and often white veil bands (forms with lilac on the stem are sometimes distinguished as a separate species called *Cortinarius paleifer*). The widely spaced gills, which may be violet-tinged when young, age to cinnamon-brown.
• **OCCURRENCE** Mycorrhizal mainly with conifers in damp woods, but also found under deciduous trees in a wide range of woodland habitats. Widespread in northern temperate zones.
• **SIMILAR SPECIES** There is a wide range of similar but not very distinctive small *Cortinarius* species.

umbonate, dark brown cap dries to pale brown

thin ring on stem

broad, notched gills become cinnamon-brown with age

umber flesh

fine, pointed, off-white veil scales on cap surface

FRUITING In troops, often among moss and pine litter.

remnants of veil on cap margin

SECTION

Dimensions CAP ⊕ 1–3cm | STEM ↕ 4–7cm ↔ 3–5mm	Spores Rusty brown	Edibility

Family CORTINARIACEAE	Species *Cortinarius violaceus*	Season Summer–autumn

EDIBLE CORT

A deep violet-blue coloring sets this species apart. The convex to umbonate cap has fine radial fibers, and the stem bears the cobwebby remains of the veil on top of longitudinal fibers. The thick, broad gills are adnexed and become violet-brown as the spores mature. There are two forms, distinguished by their mycorrhizal associations (see OCCURRENCE). The scaly-capped, dark violet Corts are the only safe edibles in this genus in North America.
• **OCCURRENCE** Mycorrhizal with conifers and deciduous trees; the coniferous form may be a separate species, *Cortinarius hercynicus*. Widespread but local in northern temperate zones.

fine radial fibers cover dry, violet-blue cap

fibers on stem are mixed with remains of veil

SECTION

weblike white veil at cap margin

deep violet-blue stem

club-shaped stem base

paler flesh at stem base

FRUITING In small groups in damp woods or by bogs.

Dimensions CAP ⊕ 6–15cm | STEM ↕ 6–14cm ↔ 1–2.5cm	Spores Rusty brown	Edibility

Family CORTINARIACEAE	Species *Cortinarius armillatus*	Season Summer–autumn

RED-BANDED CORT

This web-cap has a large, thick-fleshed, convex, orange-brown cap, the surface of which is covered with fine fibers. The tall, sturdy stem is girdled with prominent cinnamon-red veil remains. The cap margin also bears the remains of the veil.

• **OCCURRENCE** Mycorrhizal with birch and possibly other trees, in damp woods and boggy areas. Widespread and rather common in northern temperate zones.

• **SIMILAR SPECIES** *Cortinarius paragaudis* is slightly smaller, with stem girdles of a more dirty red. It is associated with conifers.

SECTION

adnate gills are pale brown, darkening with age

fine scales and fibers cover cap surface

firm, lilac to pale brown flesh

convex cap

margin of cap has red veil remains

club-shaped stem base

cinnamon-red veil girdles on stem

some stems may be joined at the base

FRUITING Appears in troops or a few together.

Dimensions CAP ⊕ 5–12cm | STEM ↕ 7–15cm ↔ 1–3cm	Spores Rusty brown	Edibility

Family CORTINARIACEAE	Species *Cortinarius rubellus*	Season Summer–autumn

DEADLY CONIFER CORT

This deadly poisonous mushroom, which smells of radishes, is reddish orange with a pointed, umbonate cap covered with fibrils. The cylindrical to club-shaped, orange-brown stem has pale yellow to ocher bands indicating the veil remnants. The medium-spaced, adnexed to adnate gills are pale ocher-brown, darkening to deep rust-brown with age.

• **OCCURRENCE** Mycorrhizal, mostly with coniferous trees, on acidic soil. Widespread and locally common in Europe and parts of Asia.

• **SIMILAR SPECIES** *C. limonius*, also poisonous, has more vivid orange coloring. *C. orellanus* (p.73) has a less conical cap and grows near deciduous trees.

pointed, umbonate cap with fibrils

pale veil girdles on pale orange-brown stem

stem base is up to 2cm wide

FRUITING Appears singly or in troops of fruitbodies on acid soil.

Dimensions CAP ⊕ 3–8cm | STEM ↕ 5–11cm ↔ 0.8–1.5cm	Spores Rusty brown	Edibility ☠

Family CORTINARIACEAE	Species *Cortinarius orellanus*	Season Autumn

DEADLY CORT

This deadly poisonous species has an umbonate to flattened, red-brown cap with a strongly fibrillose surface. The thick, adnexed to adnate gills are rusty yellow and well spaced, whereas the cylindrical stem is pale yellow-brown. The stem also bears darker, threadlike traces of the universal veil, but it has no girdles, unlike *Cortinarius rubellus* (p.72). Ingestion of this deadly mushroom causes severe kidney damage; the symptoms typically appear a long time after eating.
• OCCURRENCE Mostly associated with deciduous trees, such as oak, on acidic soils. Widespread in warm-temperate parts of Europe; absent from North America.

umbonate to flattened cap with fibrillose surface •

cap surface is • orange-red

adnexed to adnate gills are rusty • yellow

cylindrical stem may taper toward base •

stem base is yellow-orange without obvious girdles •

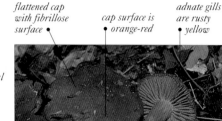

FRUITING Appears mainly in small groups of fruitbodies on acid soil under deciduous trees.

Dimensions CAP ⊕ 3–6cm │ STEM ↕ 4–9cm ↔ 1–2cm	Spores Rusty brown	Edibility ☠

Family CORTINARIACEAE	Species *Cortinarius alboviolaceus*	Season Autumn

SILVERY VIOLET CORT

This species has a convex to umbonate, fleshy, silvery violet cap. The twisted, often club-shaped stem is also silvery violet and is sometimes marked rust-brown around the veil zone by deposited spores. The rather broad, sinuate, notched gills are medium spaced and light gray-blue to cinnamon-brown.
• OCCURRENCE Mycorrhizal, usually with deciduous trees, but also found with conifers, often on acidic soil. Widespread in northern temperate zones; common in eastern North America.
• SIMILAR SPECIES *Cortinarius malachius* has a slightly scaly cap. It is associated with conifers, as are *C. camphoratus* and *C. traganus*, which are noted for their penetrating smells: the former reminiscent of half-rotten potatoes, the latter sweet and sickly.

convex, dry, silvery violet cap •

SECTION

light gray-blue or cinnamon-brown gills

off-white flesh • with violet tinge

• remains of white veil, often rust-brown from spores

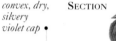

twisted, silvery violet stem •

club-shaped stem base •

medium-spaced gills

FRUITING Singly or in small groups in leaf litter.

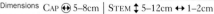

Dimensions CAP ⊕ 5–8cm │ STEM ↕ 5–12cm ↔ 1–2cm	Spores Rusty brown	Edibility

Family CORTINARIACEAE	Species *Cortinarius torvus*	Season Autumn–late autumn

SHEATHED CORT

Comparatively pale coloring, along with a "stocking" on the stem and a fleshy cap with widely spaced gills, help identify this mushroom. The cap is bun-shaped and grayish brown, with white veil remnants (violet when young) at the margin, and radiating fibers on the surface. The buff-brown flesh may be tinged violet in the upper stem.
• **OCCURRENCE** Mycorrhizal with beech or pine, in woodlands on a variety of soil types. Widespread in Europe and eastern North America.
• **SIMILAR SPECIES** *Cortinarius subtorvus* is darker and grows with willow and the woody perennial Mountain Avens (*Dryas octopetala*) in mountain areas. There are several other similar species that differ mostly in coloring or in habitat preference.

bun-shaped, grayish brown cap

thick, firm, sinuate, notched gills

"stocking" rim on stem

club-shaped stem base

widely spaced, violet gills age to rusty brown

SECTION

FRUITING Singly or a few together among leaf litter.

Dimensions CAP ⊕ 4–8cm | STEM ↕ 4–9cm ↔ 0.5–1.5cm	Spores Rusty brown	Edibility

Family CORTINARIACEAE	Species *Cortinarius anserinus*	Season Autumn

PLUM-SCENTED CORT

This is a fleshy species with a convex, yellow-brown cap and a sturdy stem with a bulbous base. As its common name suggests, it smells of plums. It is inedible; the lilac to off-white flesh is mild tasting, but the cap skin is bitter.
• **OCCURRENCE** Mycorrhizal with beech on alkaline soil. Widespread and locally common in Europe. World distribution not clear.
• **SIMILAR SPECIES** A host of other related species, such as *Cortinarius calochrous* (below), occur in similar habitats.

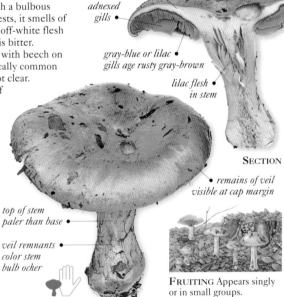

thick, firm flesh is off-white in cap

adnexed gills

gray-blue or lilac gills age rusty gray-brown

lilac flesh in stem

SECTION

remains of veil visible at cap margin

top of stem paler than base

veil remnants color stem bulb ocher

△ **CORTINARIUS CALOCHROUS**
This species has a yellow-green cap with a dark center, lilac gills, and a stem bulb. Both its flesh and its cap skin taste mild.

FRUITING Appears singly or in small groups.

Dimensions CAP ⊕ 6–12cm | STEM ↕ 6–12cm ↔ 1–2.5cm	Spores Rusty brown	Edibility

| Family CORTINARIACEAE | Species *Cortinarius triumphans* | Season Summer–autumn |

YELLOW-BANDED CORT

This impressive species has a greasy, convex,
orange-yellow cap, often with veil remnants
at the margin, and prominent yellow veil
girdles on the sturdy stem. The thick,
yellow-cream flesh tastes bitter and
has a faint, pleasant smell.
• **OCCURRENCE** Mycorrhizal with
birch, in woods and on damp lawns in
gardens and parks. Widespread but
local in Europe and parts of Asia;
reported in northeastern North America.
• **SIMILAR SPECIES** *Cortinarius cliduchus*
has a darker cap and grows on alkaline soil
among deciduous trees.
C. olidus has a darker
cap and a brown-olive
veil. It smells strongly
earthy and is not found
with birch. *C. saginus*
has a redder cap and
is found growing
among pines.

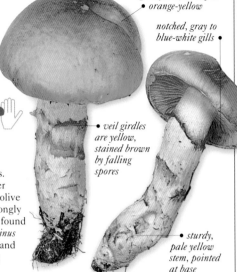

greasy, convex cap is
orange-yellow •

notched, gray to
blue-white gills •

• veil girdles
are yellow,
stained brown
by falling
spores

• sturdy,
pale yellow
stem, pointed
at base

FRUITING In troops in
grass under birch trees.

| Dimensions CAP ⊕ 8–15cm | STEM ↕ 10–15cm ↔ 1–3cm | Spores Rusty brown | Edibility |

| Family CORTINARIACEAE | Species *Cortinarius mucosus* | Season Summer–autumn |

ORANGE SLIME CORT

A fairly dark reddish to orange-brown cap, which
is convex or has a wavy margin, and a sturdy
white stem are good indicators of this
species. Both the cap and the white stem
are covered in the slimy remains of the
veil. The flesh is thick and white, and
the gills are gray- to cinnamon-brown.
• **OCCURRENCE** Mycorrhizal with two-needled
pines, usually on sandy soil. Widespread and
locally common in northern temperate zones.
• **SIMILAR SPECIES** *Cortinarius collinitus*
occurs with spruce and has blue-tinged slime
on its stem. Other similar species
grow under different host trees.

convex or
wavy-margined
cap

sinuate,
adnate gills
are gray- to
cinnamon-
brown

slimy veil •
covers white
stem

thick
pale flesh

FRUITING Singly or a few
together beneath pines.

• *extremely slimy cap surface*

• cap darkens in
color at its center

SECTION

| Dimensions CAP ⊕ 6–10cm | STEM ↕ 7–12cm ↔ 1–2.5cm | Spores Rusty brown | Edibility |

| Family CORTINARIACEAE | Species *Cortinarius sodagnitus* | Season Autumn |

BITTER LILAC CORT

The convex cap of this species is bright violet, as is the slender stem, which has a prominent bulb at the base. The coloring becomes ocher-buff from the cap center with age. The cap skin is bitter tasting, but the flesh is mild; this mushroom is not recommended for eating.
• **OCCURRENCE** Mycorrhizal, mainly with beech trees. Widespread but locally common in northern temperate zones.
• **SIMILAR SPECIES** *Cortinarius dibaphus* is slightly larger and even more colorful. It has a similar distribution in northern temperate zones.

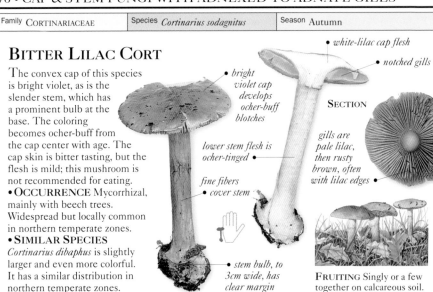

• *white-lilac cap flesh*

• *notched gills*

• *bright violet cap develops ocher-buff blotches*

SECTION

lower stem flesh is ocher-tinged •

gills are pale lilac, then rusty brown, often with lilac edges •

fine fibers cover stem •

• *stem bulb, to 3cm wide, has clear margin*

FRUITING Singly or a few together on calcareous soil.

| Dimensions CAP ⊕ 4–10cm | STEM ↕ 6–10cm ↔ 0.5–1.5cm | Spores Rusty brown | Edibility |

| Family CORTINARIACEAE | Species *Cortinarius rufoolivaceus* | Season Autumn |

RED AND GREEN CORT

This large species, belonging to the subgenus *Phlegmacium*, is identified by a unique color combination: its convex to umbonate cap is rich copper with rhubarb-pink or olive-green at the margin. The typically long, slender but bulbous stem is many-colored; the gills can be tinged olive-green or lilac. The white flesh is purple-tinged in the cap and upper stem.
• **OCCURRENCE** Mycorrhizal, especially with beech and oak trees. Widespread but local in Europe; not reported in North America.
• **SIMILAR SPECIES** Several other subgenus *Phlegmacium* species have olive coloring, including *Cortinarius atrovirens*, which has a fleshy, dark olive cap, a sulfur-yellow stem, and olive to rusty brown gills.

△ **CORTINARIUS CAERULESCENS**
This fleshy species has a gray-blue cap and stem with white veil patches and purple gills. It ages to yellow-ocher.

SECTION

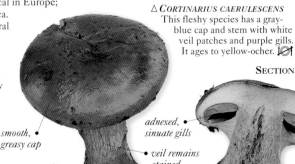

smooth, greasy cap •

adnexed, sinuate gills •

• *veil remains stained rust-brown*

FRUITING In small groups in leaf litter on soil.

stem bulb to 3cm wide •

stem base flesh may be rusty brown •

| Dimensions CAP ⊕ 6–10cm | STEM ↕ 7–12cm ↔ 1.5–2cm | Spores Rusty brown | Edibility |

Family CORTINARIACEAE	Species *Cortinarius splendens*	Season Autumn

LOVELY POISON CORT

A striking species with a convex, wavy-margined yellow cap. The stem has fibrous, sulfur-yellow veil remains and a bulbous base. Potassium hydroxide (KOH) turns the yellow flesh reddish pink. This is a relatively small member of the *Phlegmacium* subgenus.
• **OCCURRENCE** Mycorrhizal, often with beech. Widespread and common in Europe; not reported in North America.
• **SIMILAR SPECIES** *Cortinarius citrinus* has a greenish yellow tinge. Similar-looking edible *Tricholoma* species (pp.63–4) have white spore deposits and lack the cobwebby veil.

shiny cap surface

orange-brown in cap center

SECTION

bright yellow flesh

prominent stem bulb

adnexed, sinuate, bright yellow gills age to rusty yellow

FRUITING Singly or a few together on alkaline soil.

Dimensions CAP ⊕ 3–7cm	STEM ↕ 4–9cm ↔ 0.7–1.4cm	Spores Rusty brown	Edibility ☠

Family CORTINARIACEAE	Species *Cortinarius elegantissimus*	Season Autumn

ELEGANT CORT

convex, orange-yellow cap

SECTION

The convex, orange-yellow cap of this species is greasy, as in other subgenus *Phlegmacium* species. The stem is yellow and smooth, although covered with threads remaining from the veil. The flesh is very pale yellow, with a blue tinge in the upper stem, darker yellow in the bulbous stem base. This fungus has a fruity smell and mild-tasting flesh and cap skin.
• **OCCURRENCE** Mycorrhizal with beech. Widespread but local in Europe; not reported in North America.
• **SIMILAR SPECIES** Other similar subgenus *Phlegmacium* species, including *Cortinarius aureofulvus* and *C. osmophorus*, differ in smell and taste, and in the amount of green in the cap.

sinuate, notched gills

veil threads on smooth yellow stem

greenish yellow bulb to 5cm across

shiny, greasy cap surface

vivid yellow to cinnamon-yellow gills

FRUITING Singly or a few together on calcareous soil.

Dimensions CAP ⊕ 6–10cm	STEM ↕ 6–10cm ↔ 2–3cm	Spores Rusty brown	Edibility ☠

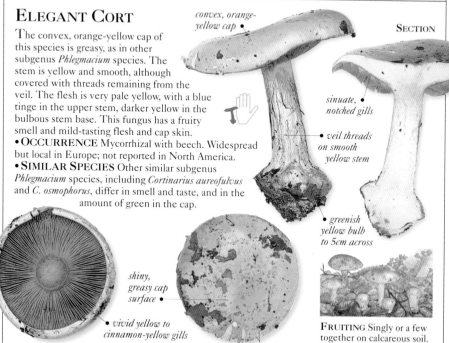

WITH STEM RING OR RING ZONE

THE FUNGI in this subsection have a veil that protects the young gills. As the cap expands to its mature size, the veil, or part of it, remains attached to the stem, either as a distinct ring around the stem or as a fibrillose zone. (See also pp.69–77 for species that have cobweblike veil remains.)

Both the rings and the zones are often stained by falling spores, thus the true veil color can be difficult to see on mature specimens. Agarics from the mainly white-spored Tricholomataceae, and families with colored spores, including Strophariaceae, Cortinariaceae, and Coprinaceae, are featured here.

Family STROPHARIACEAE	Species *Pholiota aurivella*	Season Autumn, rarely spring

ONION-BAGEL PHOLIOTA

The convex to broadly umbonate, slimy, bright yellow cap of this species has a striking pattern of dark rust-brown veil scales, and its inrolled margin also bears veil remnants. The stem is also slimy and scaly. The inedible but pleasant-smelling flesh is very pale in the cap, darker in the stem.

• **OCCURRENCE** Typically found growing high in living but damaged deciduous trees, for example, where branches have been broken. It has a preference for beech trees, although it is also found on linden and willow. Widespread in northern temperate zones.

• **SIMILAR SPECIES** *Pholiota jahnii* has more upturned, black-tipped cap scales and smaller spores (5.5 x 3.5µm compared to 9 x 5.5µm for *L. aurivella*). *P. limonella* also has smaller spores (7 x 4.5µm).

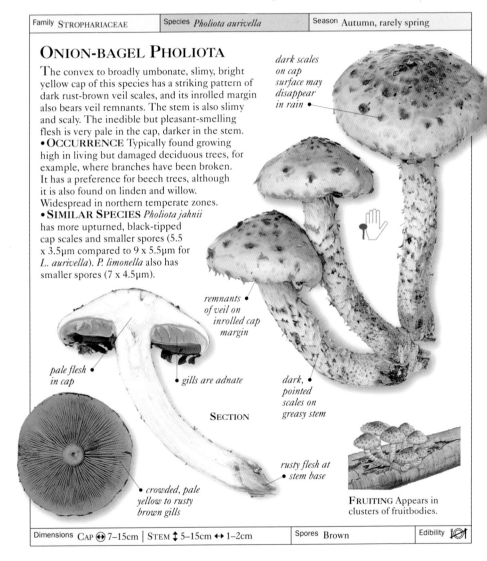

dark scales on cap surface may disappear in rain •

remnants • of veil on inrolled cap margin

pale flesh • in cap

• gills are adnate

dark, pointed scales on greasy stem

SECTION

rusty flesh at • stem base

• crowded, pale yellow to rusty brown gills

FRUITING Appears in clusters of fruitbodies.

Dimensions CAP ⊕ 7–15cm	STEM ↕ 5–15cm ↔ 1–2cm	Spores Brown	Edibility

| Family STROPHARIACEAE | Species *Pholiota squarrosa* | Season Autumn–early winter |

DRY SCALY PHOLIOTA

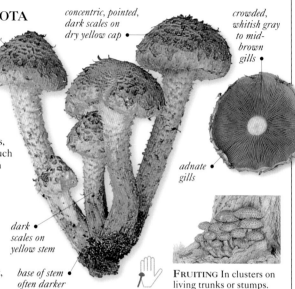

This dry-skinned species has dense, upturned scales on its convex to umbonate cap. Veil remnants are visible at the cap margin. The pale yellow flesh smells of onions and, if eaten, can cause stomach upsets.
• **OCCURRENCE** Found in built-up areas as well as in woods, at the base of deciduous trees, such as elm and rowan. Widespread in northern temperate zones.
• **SIMILAR SPECIES** Smaller and paler *Pholiota squarrosoides* is highly sticky-slimy beneath the scales. It also occurs on deciduous trees but is rare in Europe, more common in North America. *Gymnopilus junonius* (p.83), found in the same habitat, lacks the distinctive cap scales.

concentric, pointed, dark scales on dry yellow cap

crowded, whitish gray to mid-brown gills

adnate gills

dark scales on yellow stem

base of stem often darker

FRUITING In clusters on living trunks or stumps.

| Dimensions CAP ⊕ 5–15cm | STEM ↕ 6–15cm ↔ 1–2cm | Spores Brown | Edibility |

| Family TRICHOLOMATACEAE | Species *Oudemansiella mucida* | Season Autumn, rarely summer |

EURO PORCELAIN MUSHROOM

This unmistakable species has a convex, thickly slimy, pale gray to ivory-white cap and a prominent gray to gray-brown ring on the off-white stem. Above the ring, the stem is dry; below, it is slimy and often gray. These features, combined with its habitat, make it easy to identify. It is edible but not worth eating.
• **OCCURRENCE** On beech or, more rarely, on oak. On living trees, it will often appear high up where the tree has been damaged, such as where a branch has been broken off. Widespread in northern temperate zones but absent in North America.

broadly adnate, sinuate gills

slimy, pale gray to ivory-white cap

SECTION

stem dry above stem ring

bulbous stem base

tough white gills are medium- to well spaced

prominent stem ring, gray or brown underneath

thick slime on cap surface

FRUITING In clusters or singly on standing or fallen trees.

| Dimensions CAP ⊕ 2–15cm | STEM ↕ 3–8cm ↔ 0.3–1cm | Spores Pale cream | Edibility |

Family TRICHOLOMATACEAE	Species *Armillaria mellea*	Season Autumn

HONEY MUSHROOM

This large agaric has a convex, flattened, or wavy, olive-tinged, pale yellow-brown cap with a darker center and sparse pale scales. There is a black, stringlike, luminescent mycelium on the host wood. The well-spaced, adnate gills begin white and become pink-brown, often with some dark spotting, with age. *Armillaria mellea* once included a range of species with similar features and they have now been reclassified separately (see *A. cepistipes*, below). The Honey Mushroom is collected in quantities as a popular fall edible even though it can cause stomach upsets.

• **OCCURRENCE** Found in woods, mainly with beech, often on fallen stumps and logs. Widespread but local in northern temperate zones.

stems joined in groups at their bases •

white ring has yellow margin •

cap is convex, flattened, or wavy •

slender, pale ocher-yellow stem is long and tapers to point •

center of cap is darker brown than edge •

pale yellow-brown cap with ocher tinges •

FRUITING Almost always found growing in dense tufts with stems joined at the base.

Dimensions CAP ⊕ 3–10cm	STEM ↕ 8–10cm ↔ 1–2cm	Spores White	Edibility

Family TRICHOLOMATACEAE	Species *Armillaria cepistipes*	Season Autumn

FINE-SCALY HONEY MUSHROOM

SECTION

This species has a sturdy, fibrous stem, with a pendent, thin, white to pale gray ring, and a convex to umbonate, tawny to ocher cap with sparse, fibrous scales. The adnate gills are pale yellow to pale tan and well spaced. Scaly capped Honey Mushrooms are more apt to cause stomach upsets than the smooth capped species.

• **OCCURRENCE** Mostly with dead or dying deciduous trees, but also on conifers, in woods, parks, and gardens. Widespread; common in northern temperate zones; throughout Pacific Northwest.

• **SIMILAR SPECIES** The young cap of *A. gallica* has a pale center, and the stem ring is white to yellow. *A. ostoyae* has a thicker stem, turning brown from the base, a big, brown-edged ring, and coarser cap scales.

fine, pointed, dark scales on tawny-ocher cap •

• thin white to pale gray stem ring is pendent and short lived

thick • white flesh

FRUITING Clustered or scattered near deciduous trees.

swollen • stem base

Dimensions CAP ⊕ 3–12cm	STEM ↕ 4–12cm ↔ 1–3cm	Spores White	Edibility

| Family TRICHOLOMATACEAE | Species *Tricholoma caligatum* | Season Late summer–autumn |

BROWN MATSUTAKE

The convex to flat cap of this species has a brown-scaled, dry surface. The slender stem is white above the flaring ring and has brown veil zones and patches below. The flesh is white. The name actually encompasses a widespread complex of very similar mushrooms, which range from spicy-fragrant, choice edibles with a nutty flavor to forms that smell foul and are unpalatable.

• **OCCURRENCE** Found growing under deciduous trees, like oaks, in eastern North America; with conifers, like spruce, in the Rockies and Pacific Northwest; widespread and common across northern North America. Associated with atlas cedar (*Cedrus atlantica*) in parts of southern Europe and North Africa.

cap surface is pale cream under the brown scales

convex to flat cap with a dry surface

crowded gills are sinuate, notched, each with a tooth

stem is white above ring

stem sheathed by flaring white ring

brown zones and patches below ring

FRUITING Singly or a few fruitbodies together under deciduous and coniferous trees.

| Dimensions CAP ⊕ 5–12.5cm | STEM ↕ 5–10cm ↔ 2–3cm | Spores White | Edibility ¡○¡ |

| Family TRICHOLOMATACEAE | Species *Tricholoma magnivelare* | Season Late summer–autumn |

WHITE MATSUTAKE

This choice edible, with firm white flesh, has a distinctive smell of cinnamon and pine. Its convex white cap has an inrolled margin and is tacky when moist. It becomes flat with age and develops yellow to rusty brown scales and spots. A flaring ring sheaths the stem, which is white above the ring, aging light brown below it.

• **OCCURRENCE** Under conifers. Widespread and common across northern North America and in the south in the Rocky Mountains; most common on the Pacific Northwest coast.

• **SIMILAR SPECIES** *Amanita* species such as *A. smithiana* (p.148) lack the spicy smell and have free gills. They also have loose veil patches on their caps.

cottony, threadlike veil remains at cap margin

ring on stem is prominent and flaring

white gills stain pinkish brown with age

crowded, notched gills

cap is white with light brown scales

FRUITING Appear singly or in groups of a few fruitbodies together under coniferous trees.

| Dimensions CAP ⊕ 5–20cm | STEM ↕ 5–15cm ↔ 2–4cm | Spores White | Edibility ¡○¡ |

Family CORTINARIACEAE	Species *Hebeloma radicosum*	Season Autumn

ROOTING HEBELOMA

The convex, cream to pale yellow-brown cap of this large *Hebeloma* species is covered with distinct brown scales that lie flat against its surface (adpressed). The similarly scaly stem has a "root" that goes deep underground. The prominent stem ring is unusual in this genus. The firm white flesh has a strong smell of marzipan or bitter almonds and a bitter taste, both of which also help in its identification.

• **OCCURRENCE** Mycorrhizal with deciduous trees, it is associated with vole nests and latrines underground, in well-drained soil in woods. Widespread but uncommon in northern temperate zones; not reported in North America.

• **SIMILAR SPECIES** Some smaller, nonscaly *Hebeloma* species, including *H. pallidoluctuosum*, have a similar sweet smell. *Pholiota* species (pp.78–9, 91–2) are similar in appearance, but none smell of marzipan and all are associated with dead wood.

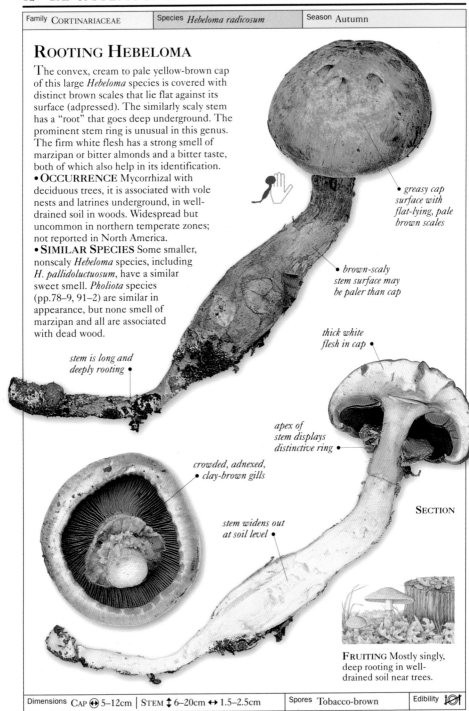

greasy cap surface with flat-lying, pale brown scales

brown-scaly stem surface may be paler than cap

thick white flesh in cap

stem is long and deeply rooting

apex of stem displays distinctive ring

crowded, adnexed, clay-brown gills

SECTION

stem widens out at soil level

FRUITING Mostly singly, deep rooting in well-drained soil near trees.

Dimensions CAP ⊕ 5–12cm	STEM ↕ 6–20cm ↔ 1.5–2.5cm	Spores Tobacco-brown	Edibility

| Family TRICHOLOMATACEAE | Species *Phaeolepiota aurea* | Season Summer–autumn |

GOLDEN PHAEOLEPIOTA

This large, golden yellow agaric, which smells of bitter almonds, has a convex cap with a fringed margin and granular surface, and a flaring stem ring beneath which the stem is very wrinkled. The adnexed gills are crowded and off-white, becoming russet-brown. It is sometimes classified within the Cortinariaceae family due to its ocher-brown spore deposit. It is reported as edible but can cause stomach upsets.

golden yellow cap surface is granular •

cap margin • is fringed with veil remains

large, flaring • stem ring is stained ocher-brown by falling spores

• **OCCURRENCE** In woods, along bridle paths or in other disturbed sites; it prefers rich soil. Widespread and locally common in northern temperate zones; found in Pacific Northwest.
• **SIMILAR SPECIES** *Gymnopilus spectabilis* (below) occurs on rotting wood and has a streaked cap and stem.

FRUITING Appears in large groups of fruitbodies on nutrient-rich soil.

| Dimensions CAP ⊕ 10–25cm | STEM ↕ 10–30cm ↔ 1.5–4cm | Spores Ocher-brown | Edibility |

| Family CORTINARIACEAE | Species *Gymnopilus spectabilis* | Season Autumn |

BIG LAUGHING GYM

A tuft-forming habit, prominent stem ring, and threadlike veil at the margin of the convex to umbonate cap help to identify this variable mushroom. The cap is dry and orange-yellow with a thread-like veil at the margin; the fibrillose stem is a similar color but stained darker near the ring by falling spores. The fleshiest *Gymnopilus* species, it is bitter, inedible, and contains hallucinogens.

convex to umbonate, orange-yellow cap is radially • streaked and dry

• ring near stem top

• **OCCURRENCE** Grows on rotten deciduous trees and stumps, rarely on conifers. Widespread in northern temperate zones.
• **SIMILAR SPECIES** The Honey Mushroom, *Armillaria mellea* complex (p.80), is similar in color, shape, and habitat. It has a white spore deposit and print. **SECTION**

• close, notched to adnate gills are yellow, aging to rust-brown

flesh is pale • yellow

grows in tufts • but may occur singly

• base of stem widens slightly

FRUITING In tufts on dead wood, mostly at soil level.

| Dimensions CAP ⊕ 5–15cm | STEM ↕ 5–15cm ↔ 1–3.5cm | Spores Rust-brown | Edibility |

Family STROPHARIACEAE	Species *Psilocybe cubensis*	Season All year

SAN ISIDRO PSILOCYBE

This large *Psilocybe* species has a bell-shaped to umbonate, sticky, yellow-brown cap, the surface of which may be covered with small white scales – the remains of the veil. The stem is off-white with a pendent ring that soon becomes black from falling spores. The white to cream flesh bruises blue. The fairly crowded, adnate gills are purple-brown with white edges when mature. It is a hallucinogen.

• **OCCURRENCE** In subtropical to tropical grassland, where animals graze. Widespread and common in Caribbean and Gulf coastal areas of North America and elsewhere in the tropics. It has been introduced into Europe, where it can be cultivated.

• **SIMILAR SPECIES** *Panaeolus semiovatus* (p.95) does not stain blue.

dark purple-brown gills with white edge •

bell-shaped to umbonate cap •

white veil scales on • surface

off-white stem with pendent ring •

FRUITING Appears singly or in small groups on cow and horse dung in grassland.

Dimensions CAP ⊕ 2–12cm	STEM ↕ 5–15cm ↔ 0.5–1.2cm	Spores Dark purple-brown	Edibility ☠

Family STROPHARIACEAE	Species *Psilocybe squamosa*	Season Autumn–late autumn

SCALY-STALKED PSILOCYBE

Short-lived, concentric cap scales and a distinctive stem ring characterize this large *Psilocybe* species. The umbonate cap is yellowish white with white-edged, gray or purple-brown to almost black gills; the stem is scaly and off-white, turning brown with age. It is not edible; the flesh has a slight aroma and a mild to slightly bitter taste.

• **OCCURRENCE** In woods, emerging from buried or half-buried deciduous debris, wood chips, or sawdust. Widespread and fairly common in northern temperate zones.

• **SIMILAR SPECIES** A varient found in northern North America is *P. thrausta*, which has a brick-red cap.

• bell-shaped to umbonate cap

white-edged, gray or purple-brown to almost black • gills

• pendent, furrowed stem ring, stained by spores

broad, adnate • to slightly decurrent gills

• long, slender stem is quite sturdy

scaly, off-white stem ages to brown toward base •

SECTION

• pale brown flesh, darker toward base

FRUITING Appears singly or in small groups.

Dimensions CAP ⊕ 2–5cm	STEM ↕ 10–15cm ↔ 3–5mm	Spores Purple-brown	Edibility

| Family BOLBITIACEAE | Species *Agrocybe cylindracea* | Season Late spring–autumn |

POPLAR AGROCYBE

This fleshy mushroom has a convex, ocher-tinged, white cap; as with most *Agrocybe* species, the smooth surface cracks in dry weather. The stem has a well-developed ring and is off-white, becoming brown with age. Widely cultivated and eaten in southern Europe, it has pale flesh with a rather strong, yeasty smell and taste.
• OCCURRENCE On or inside dead or pollarded willows and poplars. Widespread in warm northern temperate to subtropical zones.
• SIMILAR SPECIES *A. praecox* (below) grows on wood chips or in grass and is usually smaller.

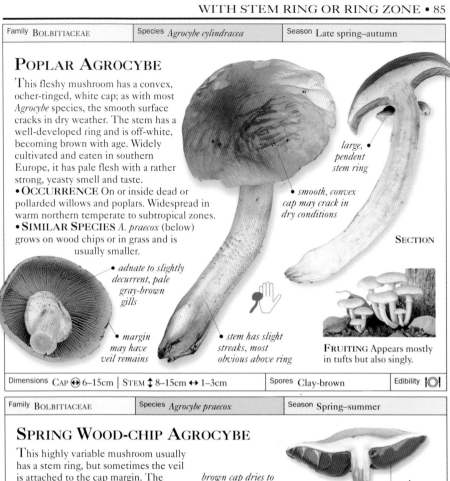

large, pendent stem ring

smooth, convex cap may crack in dry conditions

SECTION

adnate to slightly decurrent, pale gray-brown gills

margin may have veil remains

stem has slight streaks, most obvious above ring

FRUITING Appears mostly in tufts but also singly.

| Dimensions CAP ⊕ 6–15cm | STEM ↕ 8–15cm ↔ 1–3cm | Spores Clay-brown | Edibility |

| Family BOLBITIACEAE | Species *Agrocybe praecox* | Season Spring–summer |

SPRING WOOD-CHIP AGROCYBE

This highly variable mushroom usually has a stem ring, but sometimes the veil is attached to the cap margin. The convex to umbonate cap dries very quickly from light brown to yellowish gray-white; its smooth surface may crack. The base of the stem may be swollen. The pale, yeasty-smelling flesh often has a bitter aftertaste.
• OCCURRENCE In woods, parks, and gardens, among rotting wood chips or in grass. Widespread and common in northern temperate zones.
• SIMILAR SPECIES There is a complex of grass and wood-chip *Agrocybe* species that cannot be recognized easily.

brown cap dries to yellowish gray-white

pale gray to brown gills

SECTION

pendent ring stained brown by spores

fairly solid stem

streaks along slender stem

veil remains at cap margin

white to buff flesh

SECTION

FRUITING Appears in small groups or troops of fruitbodies.

| Dimensions CAP ⊕ 3–7cm | STEM ↕ 4–10cm ↔ 0.6–1cm | Spores Tobacco-brown | Edibility |

Family STROPHARIACEAE	Species *Hypholoma capnoides*	Season Summer–autumn

CONIFER TUFT PSILOCYBE

The convex cap of this agaric is yellowish orange, drying to pale orange-brown, and has veil remnants visible at the pale margin. It is greasy when wet. The stem is pale yellow at the top and rusty brown at the bottom. This mushroom has mild-tasting, pale yellow flesh.

• **OCCURRENCE** One of the few agarics found almost all year, except in cold winters, on strongly decayed conifer stumps. Widespread and common in northern temperate zones.

• **SIMILAR SPECIES** *H. radicosum* is much rarer but is found in similar sites. *Hypholoma*s and *Stropharia*s are now often called *Psilocybe*s.

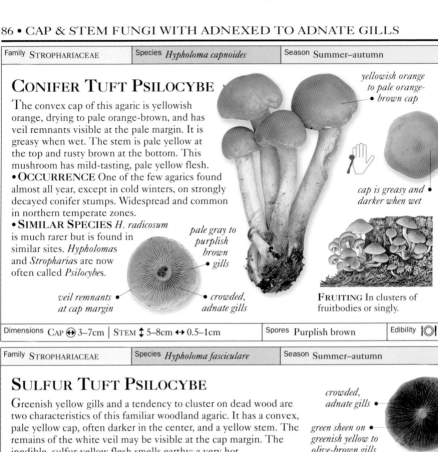

yellowish orange to pale orange-brown cap

cap is greasy and darker when wet

pale gray to purplish brown gills

veil remnants at cap margin

crowded, adnate gills

FRUITING In clusters of fruitbodies or singly.

Dimensions CAP ⊕ 3–7cm | STEM ↕ 5–8cm ↔ 0.5–1cm	Spores Purplish brown	Edibility 🍽

Family STROPHARIACEAE	Species *Hypholoma fasciculare*	Season Summer–autumn

SULFUR TUFT PSILOCYBE

Greenish yellow gills and a tendency to cluster on dead wood are two characteristics of this familiar woodland agaric. It has a convex, pale yellow cap, often darker in the center, and a yellow stem. The remains of the white veil may be visible at the cap margin. The inedible, sulfur-yellow flesh smells earthy; a very hot, bitter taste is another identification mark. Species referred to as *Hypholoma* were until recently, *Naematolomas* and are now *Psilocybe*s.

• **OCCURRENCE** On rotten deciduous stumps and upturned roots, rarely on conifers. Widespread and common in northern temperate zones.

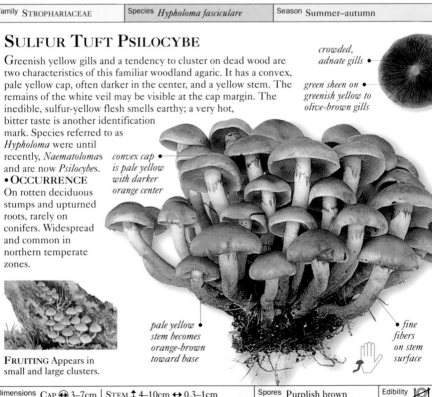

crowded, adnate gills

green sheen on greenish yellow to olive-brown gills

convex cap is pale yellow with darker orange center

pale yellow stem becomes orange-brown toward base

fine fibers on stem surface

FRUITING Appears in small and large clusters.

Dimensions CAP ⊕ 3–7cm | STEM ↕ 4–10cm ↔ 0.3–1cm	Spores Purplish brown	Edibility

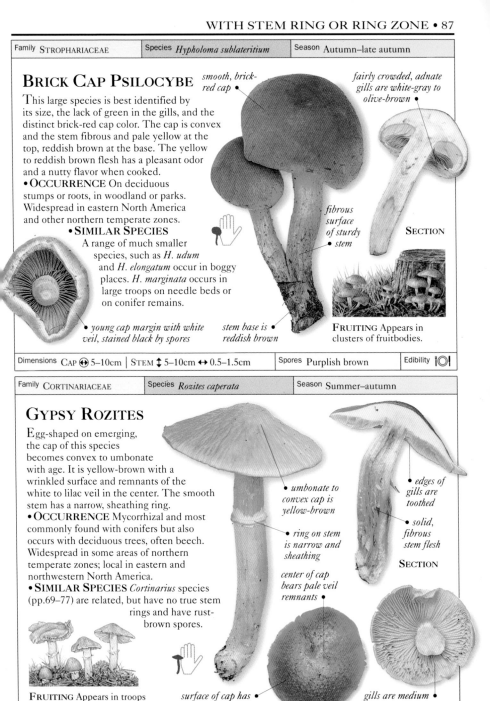

| Family STROPHARIACEAE | Species *Hypholoma sublateritium* | Season Autumn–late autumn |

BRICK CAP PSILOCYBE

smooth, brick-red cap •

fairly crowded, adnate gills are white-gray to olive-brown •

This large species is best identified by its size, the lack of green in the gills, and the distinct brick-red cap color. The cap is convex and the stem fibrous and pale yellow at the top, reddish brown at the base. The yellow to reddish brown flesh has a pleasant odor and a nutty flavor when cooked.

• **OCCURRENCE** On deciduous stumps or roots, in woodland or parks. Widespread in eastern North America and other northern temperate zones.

• **SIMILAR SPECIES** A range of much smaller species, such as *H. udum* and *H. elongatum* occur in boggy places. *H. marginata* occurs in large troops on needle beds or on conifer remains.

fibrous surface of sturdy • stem

SECTION

• young cap margin with white veil, stained black by spores

stem base is • reddish brown

FRUITING Appears in clusters of fruitbodies.

| Dimensions CAP ⊕ 5–10cm | STEM ↕ 5–10cm ↔ 0.5–1.5cm | Spores Purplish brown | Edibility |

| Family CORTINARIACEAE | Species *Rozites caperata* | Season Summer–autumn |

GYPSY ROZITES

Egg-shaped on emerging, the cap of this species becomes convex to umbonate with age. It is yellow-brown with a wrinkled surface and remnants of the white to lilac veil in the center. The smooth stem has a narrow, sheathing ring.

• **OCCURRENCE** Mycorrhizal and most commonly found with conifers but also occurs with deciduous trees, often beech. Widespread in some areas of northern temperate zones; local in eastern and northwestern North America.

• **SIMILAR SPECIES** *Cortinarius* species (pp.69–77) are related, but have no true stem rings and have rust-brown spores.

• umbonate to convex cap is yellow-brown

• ring on stem is narrow and sheathing

center of cap bears pale veil remnants •

• edges of gills are toothed

• solid, fibrous stem flesh

SECTION

FRUITING Appears in troops or small groups on acidic soil.

surface of cap has • furrows or wrinkles

gills are medium • spaced and adnexed

| Dimensions CAP ⊕ 5–12cm | STEM ↕ 5–15cm ↔ 1–2cm | Spores Pale brown | Edibility |

Family STROPHARIACEAE	Species *Stropharia cyanea*	Season Autumn

BLUE-GREEN PSILOCYBE

This mushroom is distinguished from other blue-green *Stropharia* species by its gills, which are not white edged. The convex, greasy cap is blue-green, soon fading and developing yellow spots. Its margin has pale veil remnants, but the ring on the scaly, fibrous, blue-green stem is inconspicuous. The off-white flesh has an indistinct smell. All *Stropharia*s and *Hypholoma*s are referred to by some as *Psilocybe*.
• OCCURRENCE Among leaf litter on fertile soil; often in European beech woods on alkaline soil.
• SIMILAR SPECIES *S. aeruginosa* has darker spores and gills with white edges. *S. pseudocyanea* smells of freshly ground black pepper.

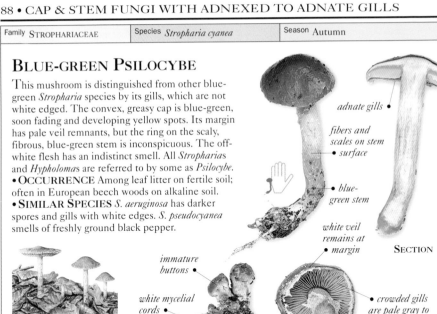

• adnate gills

fibers and scales on stem surface

• blue-green stem

white veil remains at margin

SECTION

immature buttons •

white mycelial cords •

crowded gills are pale gray to brown, with no white edges

FRUITING Appears in small groups or singly.

Dimensions CAP ⊕ 3–7cm	STEM ↕ 4–8cm ↔ 0.4–1cm	Spores Purplish brown	Edibility

Family STROPHARIACEAE	Species *Stropharia aurantiaca*	Season Summer–autumn

RED-CAP PSILOCYBE

This is a distinctive species, best recognized by its sturdy, bright orange-capped fruitbodies and its occurrence on wood chips. The cap is convex then flat. The stem is off-white with a fibrous surface and is often hollow. The flesh is off-white, sometimes with an orange flush, and has an indistinct smell; its edibility is unknown.
• OCCURRENCE Mostly on decaying wood chips or sawdust mixed with soil. Widespread and spreading in Europe; reported from California.
• SIMILAR SPECIES An orange variety of *Psilocybe squamosa* (var. *thrausta*) has an umbonate cap and thinner flesh.

gills have white edge •

• adnate to adnexed or notched gills

SECTION

slimy, bright • orange-red cap

medium-spaced, cream to olive- or purple-brown gills •

pale veil • remnants may be visible at cap margin

fibers cover surface of off-• white stem

FRUITING In troops, often in mulched flowerbeds.

• stem base often swollen

Dimensions CAP ⊕ 1.5–6cm	STEM ↕ 2–6cm ↔ 2–8mm	Spores Purplish brown	Edibility

| Family STROPHARIACEAE | Species *Stropharia rugoso-annulata* | Season Spring and autumn |

BURGUNDY CAPS

The smooth, dry cap of this species is red to tan, depending on its exposure to light. It is bell-shaped, becoming convex to flat with age. The off-white stem has a ring with dark lines above and coglike structures below. The stem base is widened or bulbous and has a conspicuous, cordlike white mycelium. The flesh is white and tastes good if eaten when young.

• **OCCURRENCE** In wood-chip mulch. Widespread in southern Europe, rare farther north; also found in North America.

• **SIMILAR SPECIES** *Stropharia aurantiaca* (p.88) is smaller and more bright orange-red. *Agaricus* species (pp.156–163) have free gills.

gills are purplish gray and fairly crowded

stem is firm and off-white

coglike structures on underside of ring

dark lines from spores on top of stem ring

bell-shaped to convex then flat cap is red to tan

FRUITING In abundant troops in wood-chip mulch; it has two distinct fruiting seasons.

| Dimensions CAP ⊕ 5–15cm | STEM ↕ 10–15cm ↔ 1–2cm | Spores Purplish gray-black | Edibility |

| Family STROPHARIACEAE | Species *Stropharia coronilla* | Season Autumn |

POISON LAWN PSILOCYBE

This fairly small but sturdy species has extremely thick white flesh, particularly in the convex, ocher-yellow cap. The narrow ring may be attached to the white stem. The gills are violet-gray, turning dark purple-brown. This species smells strongly of radishes. Recent reports suggest it could be poisonous.

• **OCCURRENCE** Common in grassy areas in drier situations, including gardens, parks, heathland, and sand dunes. Widespread in northern temperate zones.

• **SIMILAR SPECIES** Some forms, which have different spore sizes and coloring, are regarded as distinct species, including *Stropharia halophila* and *S. melasperma*.

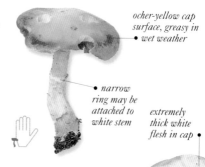

ocher-yellow cap surface, greasy in wet weather

narrow ring may be attached to white stem

extremely thick white flesh in cap

violet-gray to purple-brown gills

gills have white edges

stem has solid white flesh

medium-spaced gills

SECTION

FRUITING Singly or a few together in grass or on sandy soil.

| Dimensions CAP ⊕ 1.5–6cm | STEM ↕ 2.5–4cm ↔ 0.4–1cm | Spores Dark purplish brown | Edibility |

Family STROPHARIACEAE	Species *Stropharia semiglobata*	Season Late spring–autumn

DUNG PSILOCYBE

This elegant, slender species has a smooth, often hemispherical, light yellow cap and a long, slender, slimy, off-white stem. In common with many of its close relatives, its cap is greasy when wet, and it has an inconspicuous, tiny stem ring, which is frequently stained black by deposited spores. The inedible, thin, pale flesh has a yeasty smell.

• **OCCURRENCE** In grassland and pastures on old horse, cow, and sheep manure. A range of fungi fruit on herbivore dung at different stages of decay. Widespread in northern temperate zones and elsewhere.

• **SIMILAR SPECIES** *Stropharia umbonatescens* has a pimple or umbo at the cap center and basidia with only 2 spores; those of *S. semiglobata* have 4.

smooth cap surface, greasy in wet weather •

SECTION

• *convex or hemispherical cap*

white edge • on olive-gray gills

broad, • adnate, medium-spaced gills

hollow • stem

long, slender stem

stem base slightly swollen •

FRUITING Appears in small groups on dung.

Dimensions CAP ⊕ 0.5–4cm	STEM ↕ 2–8cm ↔ 2–5mm	Spores Purplish black	Edibility

Family STROPHARIACEAE	Species *Galerina mutabilis*	Season Summer–autumn

SCALY-VEILED GALERINA

Formerly known as *Kuehneromyces mutabilis*, this species has an umbonate, honey-brown to yellow cap, which dries from the center, producing a two-tone effect. The distinct stem ring is often stained ocher-brown by falling spores; below the ring, the stem is covered with pointed scales. Although edible, it would prove fatal to confuse it with the Deadly Galerina (p.91).

two-toned cap dries *from center* •

• **OCCURRENCE** On rotten deciduous trees and, rarely, conifers, in deep woods. Widespread and common in western North America.

• **SIMILAR SPECIES** A group of poisonous *Galerina* species are similar: *G. unicolor* (p.91) and *G. marginata* have fibers and no stem scales.

• *broadly adnate to decurrent gills*

medium-spaced, pale to rusty brown gills •

stem above • ring is pale and smooth

pale • brown, aromatic flesh

SECTION

• *stem is dark and scaly below ring*

FRUITING In dense troops of individual clusters.

Dimensions CAP ⊕ 2–7cm	STEM ↕ 3–7cm ↔ 0.4–1cm	Spores Ocher-brown	Edibility

| Family CORTINARIACEAE | Species *Galerina unicolor* | Season Summer–winter, into spring |

DEADLY GALERINA

The convex to broadly umbonate, wavy-margined cap of this species is rich brown; it changes to pale yellow-brown as it dries. The off-white to basally brown stem has a ring toward the top and is fibrous below. The narrow gills are adnate to slightly decurrent and are medium spaced. *Galerina* species need careful identification; there are seven others that can cause severe poisoning.

• **OCCURRENCE** On dead and rotten stumps and trunks, often on moss and leaf litter in damp, boggy deciduous woodland. Widespread in northern temperate zones.

• **SIMILAR SPECIES** *Armillaria mellea*, the Honey Mushroom (p.80), is typically larger with a white spore print.

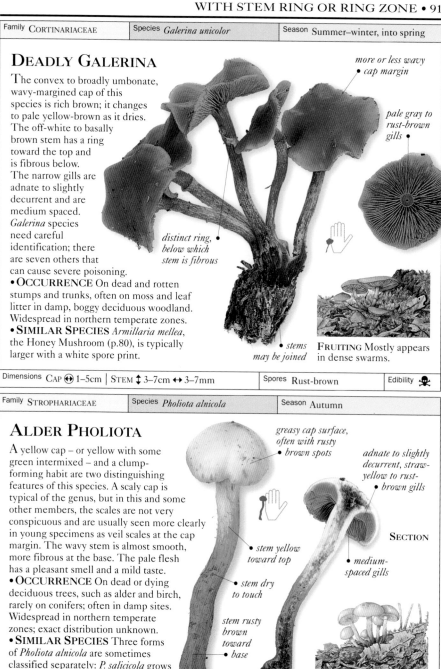

more or less wavy
• cap margin

pale gray to
rust-brown
gills •

distinct ring,
below which
stem is fibrous

• stems
may be joined

FRUITING Mostly appears in dense swarms.

| Dimensions CAP ⊕ 1–5cm | STEM ↕ 3–7cm ↔ 3–7mm | Spores Rust-brown | Edibility ☠ |

| Family STROPHARIACEAE | Species *Pholiota alnicola* | Season Autumn |

ALDER PHOLIOTA

A yellow cap – or yellow with some green intermixed – and a clump-forming habit are two distinguishing features of this species. A scaly cap is typical of the genus, but in this and some other members, the scales are not very conspicuous and are usually seen more clearly in young specimens as veil scales at the cap margin. The wavy stem is almost smooth, more fibrous at the base. The pale flesh has a pleasant smell and a mild taste.

• **OCCURRENCE** On dead or dying deciduous trees, such as alder and birch, rarely on conifers; often in damp sites. Widespread in northern temperate zones; exact distribution unknown.

• **SIMILAR SPECIES** Three forms of *Pholiota alnicola* are sometimes classified separately: *P. salicicola* grows on willow and tastes bitter; *P. flavida* and *P. pinicola* grow on conifers.

greasy cap surface,
often with rusty
• brown spots

adnate to slightly
decurrent, straw-
yellow to rust-
• brown gills

SECTION

• medium-
spaced gills

• stem yellow
toward top

• stem dry
to touch

stem rusty
brown
toward
• base

FRUITING Appears in clusters of fruitbodies.

| Dimensions CAP ⊕ 3–7cm | STEM ↕ 8–15cm ↔ 0.6–1cm | Spores Brown | Edibility 🍴 |

| Family STROPHARIACEAE | Species *Pholiota gummosa* | Season Autumn–late autumn |

OCHER-GREEN PHOLIOTA

The key identification points of this species are a convex then flattened cap with a slightly scaly, straw-yellow surface, flushed pale ocher-green; yellow to brown gills; and a dirty yellow to off-white, scaly stem. The cap is slimy only when wet and quickly dries out. The white to yellow flesh becomes rusty brown at the stem base. It has no distinct smell or taste.

• **OCCURRENCE** Often along roads, mostly from wood underground. Not reported in North America.

• **SIMILAR SPECIES** *Pholiota scamba* is smaller and grows on conifers.

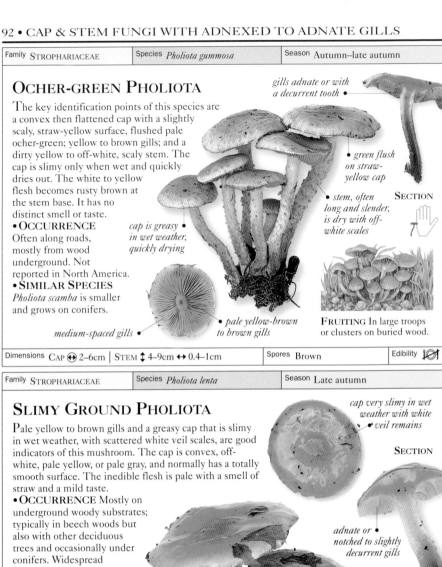

gills adnate or with a decurrent tooth

green flush on straw-yellow cap

stem, often long and slender, is dry with off-white scales

SECTION

cap is greasy in wet weather, quickly drying

medium-spaced gills

pale yellow-brown to brown gills

FRUITING In large troops or clusters on buried wood.

| Dimensions CAP ⊕ 2–6cm | STEM ↕ 4–9cm ↔ 0.4–1cm | Spores Brown | Edibility |

| Family STROPHARIACEAE | Species *Pholiota lenta* | Season Late autumn |

SLIMY GROUND PHOLIOTA

Pale yellow to brown gills and a greasy cap that is slimy in wet weather, with scattered white veil scales, are good indicators of this mushroom. The cap is convex, off-white, pale yellow, or pale gray, and normally has a totally smooth surface. The inedible flesh is pale with a smell of straw and a mild taste.

• **OCCURRENCE** Mostly on underground woody substrates; typically in beech woods but also with other deciduous trees and occasionally under conifers. Widespread in northern temperate zones.

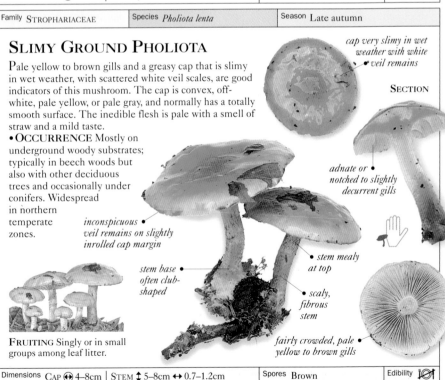

cap very slimy in wet weather with white veil remains

SECTION

adnate or notched to slightly decurrent gills

inconspicuous veil remains on slightly inrolled cap margin

stem base often club-shaped

stem mealy at top

scaly, fibrous stem

fairly crowded, pale yellow to brown gills

FRUITING Singly or in small groups among leaf litter.

| Dimensions CAP ⊕ 4–8cm | STEM ↕ 5–8cm ↔ 0.7–1.2cm | Spores Brown | Edibility |

Family STROPHARIACEAE	Species *Pholiota highlandensis*	Season Almost all year

CHARCOAL PHOLIOTA

Apart from its distinctive habitat – on bonfire sites – this mushroom is notable for having a fairly fleshy, orange-brown fruitbody with a convex to somewhat wavy, slimy cap. It has a dry stem, which is fibrous toward the base, and the inedible flesh is pale yellow to rusty brown with a mild taste; the smell is not distinctive.
• OCCURRENCE On bonfire sites or in woods and tree stands where a fire has occurred. Widespread in northern temperate zones.
• SIMILAR SPECIES Other gilled mushrooms found on charred sites, including *Mycena galopus* (p.137) and *Tephrocybe anthracophilum*, are usually smaller; *Myxomphalia maura* is a darker shade.

yellow-brown to dark orange-brown cap with
• paler margin

• surface slimy when wet, shiny when dry

adnate, sometimes notched gills

pale yellow • flesh, rusty brown at stem base

dry stem • surface

SECTION

• lower stem has fibrous, woolly covering

• medium-spaced, pale gray-brown to brown gills

FRUITING Appears in swarms or small clusters.

Dimensions CAP ⊕ 2–6cm	STEM ↕ 2–6cm ↔ 0.4–1cm	Spores Brown	Edibility 🚫🍴

Family CORTINARIACEAE	Species *Hebeloma mesophaeum*	Season Autumn–late autumn

VEILED HEBELOMA

This species has a convex to broadly umbonate, gray-brown cap, with a paler margin and a pale brown stem. Belonging to a group of *Hebeloma* species that have veils, its veil is visible as fine, off-white threads and patches near the cap margin and on the upper stem. The flesh is pale brown, and, like most *Hebeloma* species, it smells of radishes.
• OCCURRENCE Mycorrhizal with trees in mixed woods, parks, and gardens; sometimes found on burned ground. Widespread and very common in northern temperate zones.
• SIMILAR SPECIES Relatives such as *H. candidipes* are distinguished by microscopic examination.

surface of cap is dry • or slightly greasy

pale • brown gills

• cylindrical stem is pale brown with white veil fibers

flesh is • pale brown

SECTION

notched gills are medium spaced •

• white veil remains at cap margin

• slight widening at stem base

• gray-brown cap, darker toward center

FRUITING Appears in troops under trees.

Dimensions CAP ⊕ 2–5cm	STEM ↕ 2–6cm ↔ 3–7mm	Spores Tobacco-brown	Edibility ☠️

| Family CORTINARIACEAE | Species *Gymnopilus penetrans* | Season Autumn |

FRECKLE-GILLED GYM

This is a fairly uniformly orange-brown species with a convex to flattened or umbonate cap and a paler stem with an indistinct veil zone. The pale yellow gills have rusty flecks. It is sometimes divided into two more species: *Gymnopilus hybridus* and *G. sapineus*. All *Gymnopilus* species occur on dead wood or plant remains, unlike related *Cortinarius* species (pp.69–77), which are mycorrhizal.
• OCCURRENCE On dead wood, mostly conifers, in woods and tree stands. Widespread in northern temperate zones.

• SIMILAR SPECIES
G. picreus has a dark stem and vivid yellow gills.

FRUITING Appears mostly in small groups or singly.

• smooth, dry cap

• cap slightly greasy in wet weather

• stem paler orange-brown than cap

notched • to slightly decurrent gills

white-felted • stem base, often with rhizoids

SECTION

pale yellow • gills age to cinnamon-brown with rusty flecks

| Dimensions CAP ⊕ 3–8cm | STEM ↕ 4–7cm ↔ 0.4–1cm | Spores Rust-brown | Edibility |

| Family COPRINACEAE | Species *Psathyrella piluliformis* | Season Autumn |

COMMON STUMP PSATHYRELLA

In the large genus *Psathyrella*, consisting mainly of little brown mushrooms – so-called LBMs – among which it is difficult to distinguish, this species has some helpful characteristics: it occurs in clusters and has a distinct white veil, stained brown by spores, at the cap margin. The convex to bell-shaped cap is dark red-brown when wet, drying to paler yellowish brown. Details such as spore size ultimately ensure correct identification.
• OCCURRENCE In woods on rotten deciduous stumps; rarely on conifers. Widespread and common in northern temperate zones.

red-brown cap • dries yellowish brown

convex to bell- shaped cap •

almost • smooth white stem

gills adnexed with pale edges

FRUITING In dense clusters on and near deciduous stumps.

• fairly crowded, off- white to reddish brown gills

stem is • hollow but fairly sturdy

SECTION

| Dimensions CAP ⊕ 1.5–6cm | STEM ↕ 3–10cm ↔ 3–9mm | Spores Dark purplish brown | Edibility |

Family COPRINACEAE	Species *Psathyrella candolleana*	Season Late spring–autumn

COMMON PARK PSATHYRELLA

An early fruiting species, and perhaps one of the most common in this difficult genus of mostly little brown mushrooms, *Psathyrella candolleana* has a convex to umbonate, yellow-brown cap, which rapidly dries to ivory-white, and a threadlike veil that disappears with age, leaving an almost smooth surface. The fruitbody is extremely brittle when dry. As the spores mature, the gills change color from white through lilac to brown.
• OCCURRENCE In gardens, parks, and woods; it is found close to rotten deciduous trees. Widespread and common in northern temperate zones.
• SIMILAR SPECIES The much darker *P. spadiceogrisea* occurs along forest paths and in similar sites in late spring and early summer.

gray- to chocolate-brown mature gills

convex to umbonate cap dries to ivory-white

stem is hollow

SECTION

cap margin thin and with veil remains when young

fragile, smooth stem

crowded gills are adnexed

FRUITING In troops on and around rotten wood.

Dimensions CAP ⊕ 1.5–7cm | STEM ↕ 3–9cm ↔ 2–6mm	Spores Brownish purple	Edibility

Family COPRINACEAE	Species *Panaeolus semiovatus*	Season Late spring–autumn

COMMON RINGED PANAEOLUS

A distinguishing feature of this species is its cap, which is sticky when wet and shiny, often with wrinkles, when dry. White to ivory or beige, it is egg- to bell-shaped with a margin that is smooth or has white veil remnants. The stem has a white ring that is typically stained black from falling spores. The white to pale straw-yellow flesh may contain a hallucinogen.
• OCCURRENCE In pastures on dung or straw mixed with dung. Widespread in northern temperate zones.
• SIMILAR SPECIES *P. antillarum* lacks a stem ring.

cap margin smooth or with veil remnants

broad, adnate gills are mottled black and white

bell-shaped cap is sticky when wet, shiny when dry

erect then pendent, white stem ring with black staining from spores

fragile beige to brown stem

white stem base

cap is egg-shaped on young specimens

FRUITING Singly or a few on each dropping of dung.

SECTION

Dimensions CAP ⊕ 1–6cm | STEM ↕ 6–10cm ↔ 3–5mm	Spores Black	Edibility

| Family BOLBITIACEAE | Species *Conocybe arrhenii* | Season Late summer–late autumn |

DEADLY CONOCYBE COMPLEX

This is one of the most common members of a subgroup of *Conocybe* species often called *Pholiotina*. Members are so similar that they are best distinguished by their spores. They have scaly veil remnants at the cap margin or a stem ring. The ring tends to be loose and is easily lost. The gills are fairly crowded and adnexed, often with a white margin. All members are suspected to be poisonous.
• OCCURRENCE Typically on nutrient-rich soil in disturbed sites. Often occurs alongside other *Conocybe* species and with species of *Lepiota* and *Psathyrella*. Widespread in Asia and Europe; world distribution not clear.
• SIMILAR SPECIES *C. blattaria* and *C. percincta* have 2-spored basidia; those of *C. arrhenii* are 4-spored.

cap is initially brick-red at center, drying pale ocher •

cap is striate at margin when moist •

cufflike white ring is striate on top •

stem is pale brown, paler toward top •

FRUITING Often singly or just a few fruitbodies, along roads and beside paths.

| Dimensions CAP ⊕ 1–3cm \| STEM ↕ 1.5–5cm ↔ 1.5–3mm | Spores Rusty brown | Edibility 🕱 |

| Family TRICHOLOMATACEAE | Species *Cystoderma terrei* | Season Autumn |

CINNABAR CYSTODERMA

A convex to umbonate, brick-red cap with a mealy surface and a club-shaped stem with red scales on the lower part are the main features of this species. It has fairly crowded, adnexed, pale gills. When examined with a hand lens, the gills can be seen to be fimbriate. A microscope reveals cystidia (special sterile cells) on the edges of the gills.
• OCCURRENCE Woodland areas and in planted areas on humus-rich, acidic soil. The world distribution of this species is not fully understood, but it is widespread in Europe, Japan, and North America.
• SIMILAR SPECIES There are several similar *Cystoderma* species found in similar habitats. *C. granulosum* has more dirty, rusty brown coloring. Close relative *C. adnatifolium* lacks cystidia and is brighter in color.

edges of pale gills are fimbriate (visible through hand lens) •

pale pink to orange flesh •

SECTION

• mealy, brick-red cap surface

• convex to umbonate cap

stem is swollen at base •

• small red scales on lower stem

FRUITING Appears singly or a few together.

| Dimensions CAP ⊕ 2–8cm \| STEM ↕ 3–7cm ↔ 4–8mm | Spores Off-white | Edibility 🍴 |

Family TRICHOLOMATACEAE	Species *Cystoderma amianthinum*	Season Autumn

SAFFRON CYSTODERMA

This bright ocher-yellow species has a bell-shaped to flat cap with a mealy surface and a fringed margin. Below the short-lived ring, the stem surface is mealy or granular. The crowded, adnexed gills are white, becoming creamy yellow with age; the pale yellow flesh is thin and has a musty, pungent odor. The identity of *Cystoderma* species is best confirmed by microscopic comparison of spore size: those of *C. amianthinum* are generally 6 x 3µm.
• **OCCURRENCE** In varied sites – in moss in woodland, with willow, or with grasses or bracken. Widespread and common in northern temperate zones.
• **SIMILAR SPECIES** *Cystoderma amianthinum* var. *rugoso-reticulatum* has a deeply wrinkled cap and pungent odor. *Cystoderma jasonis* is darker with a coarser cap surface; its spores are larger (7 x 4µm).

mealy or granular surface below stem ring •

ocher-yellow cap has fringe • at margin

bell-shaped to flat cap with • mealy surface

FRUITING Appears singly or a few fruitbodies together among mosses in damp, acidic woodland.

Dimensions CAP ⊕ 1–4cm	STEM ↕ 2.5–6cm ↔ 3–7mm	Spores Off-white	Edibility

Family TRICHOLOMATACEAE	Species *Cystoderma carcharias*	Season Autumn–late autumn

PINK-GRAY CYSTODERMA

Besides the pinkish gray color of both cap and stem, this species is characterized by a prominent, cufflike, pink-gray stem ring. The surfaces of the cap and stem are powdery, as in other members of the genus *Cystoderma*. The adnexed gills are white and medium spaced. The white flesh has an unpleasant, rancid smell.
• **OCCURRENCE** In woods and on wasteland. Widespread in parts of northern temperate zones but not as common as *C. amianthinum* (above).
• **SIMILAR SPECIES** *C. ambrosii* has fruitbodies that are almost pure white and become slightly brown with age. The fruitbodies of *C. fallax* are yellow-brown. *Lepiota* species have free gills.

center of pinkish gray cap is umbonate •

distinctive, cufflike stem ring •

white gills are adnexed and medium • spaced

cap has fringed margin •

stem is pinkish gray and powdery, particularly below ring •

FRUITING Typically in small groups or singly, always on acidic soil and humus among leaf litter and moss.

Dimensions CAP ⊕ 2–5cm	STEM ↕ 4–8cm ↔ 2–7mm	Spores Off-white	Edibility

WITH FIBROUS CAP AND DARK SPORES

T HIS SUBSECTION comprises agarics that, in addition to having adnate to adnexed gills (see p.56), have a cap with a distinctly fibrous or scaly surface. The spore deposits of all the species featured here are in various shades of brown, although not rust-colored (see pp.69–77 for species with rusty brown spores). The species that belong in this subsection are members of the genera *Inocybe* and *Lacrymaria*. Some have veils; others do not. Those *Inocybe* species that lack veils have very fine hairs covering the entire stems. A hand lens is needed in order to see these hairs, which are called cystidia.

Family CORTINARIACEAE	Species *Inocybe haemacta*	Season Autumn

GREEN AND PINK INOCYBE

The fruitbodies of this species have green tones, rare in this usually dull-colored genus. The convex to umbonate, gray- to greenish brown cap has a fibrous or scaly center. Both the cap and the pale gray flesh become redder with age. The greenish gray stem is fibrous toward the base and has a mealy covering at the top, which is paler in color. The Green and Pink Inocybe smells similar to urine or a stable.

• **OCCURRENCE** Mycorrhizal with deciduous trees on rich soil, in parks and woods or on roadsides. Widespread but local to rare in Europe; not reported in North America.

• **SIMILAR SPECIES** *Inocybe corydalina*, which has a ciderlike smell, may have green hues on the cap.

gray- or greenish brown cap reddens with age •

• convex or umbonate cap

greenish gray stem, paler at top •

adnexed, gray to gray-brown gills become pinker then • brown with age

paler flesh visible • beneath fibers

flesh ages from • pale gray to redder hue

• meal covers upper stem

• fibrous or scaly cap center

SECTION

gills are fairly crowded •

FRUITING Appears singly or a few together.

Dimensions CAP ⊕ 3–6.5cm | STEM ↕ 2–8cm ↔ 4–6mm	Spores Tobacco-brown	Edibility ☠

| Family CORTINARIACEAE | Species *Inocybe erubescens* | Season Spring–autumn |

DEADLY INOCYBE

The early appearance of this fleshy species, which is known to be involved in poisonings (see SIMILAR SPECIES), is a noteworthy characteristic, as is the fact that the fruitbody stains red when older or if handled. It has a bell-shaped to broadly conical or umbonate cap, the surface of which has distinct radial fibers, common to the genus. The squat stem, which is rarely longer than the diameter of the cap, is sturdy, and its surface has a mealy covering.

• **OCCURRENCE** Mycorrhizal with trees such as beech and linden, on clay or calcareous soil. Widespread but local in Europe and parts of Asia.

• **SIMILAR SPECIES** It has been mistaken for edible fungi, such as *Calocybe gambosa* (p.58). *Inocybe pudica* stains red, but has more slender, whiter fruitbodies.

cap often has inrolled margin

nearly free gills are off-white to dirty olive-brown

red bruising on gills

white flesh stains red when cut or bruised

SECTION

mealy covering at top of stem

FRUITING In troops on fruitbodies on rich soil.

| Dimensions CAP ⊕ 3–9cm | STEM ↕ 4–7cm ↔ 1–2cm | Spores Snuff-brown | Edibility ☠ |

| Family CORTINARIACEAE | Species *Inocybe godeyi* | Season Autumn |

RED-STAINING INOCYBE

The conical to bell-shaped cap of this species is creamy white to pale ocher, soon turning bright orange-red. The off-white stem is covered with fine meal and has a bulbous base; it also develops red tones with age, as does the faintly scented flesh.

• **OCCURRENCE** Mycorrhizal with deciduous trees, especially beech, on alkaline soil. Widespread but rather local in Europe; reported in eastern North America.

• **SIMILAR SPECIES** *I. pudica*, found in Pacific Northwest, is also white, aging pale pink, but lacks the stem bulb.

cap ages and stains orange-red

adnexed gills

white flesh, staining red

SECTION

conical to bell-shaped cap is creamy white to pinkish buff

stem covered with fine meal

bulbous stem base

medium-spaced gills are cream to reddish brown

FRUITING Typically a few together on soil beside paths.

| Dimensions CAP ⊕ 1.5–5cm | STEM ↕ 2–7cm ↔ 3–6mm | Spores Tobacco-brown | Edibility ☠ |

| Family CORTINARIACEAE | Species *Inocybe geophylla* | Season Autumn |

WHITE OR LILAC INOCYBE

This species, which smells strongly spermatic, has a conical to umbonate, silky, streaked cap. The upper stem has a mealy covering; the lower stem is more fibrous. There is no stem bulb. It occurs in two main color forms: white, sometimes with ocher tinges, and lilac with brown gills. This is one of the most common *Inocybe* species.

• **OCCURRENCE** Mycorrhizal with conifers and deciduous trees, among pine needles or on rich soil, often bare and disturbed, such as along ditches or beside roads. It is widespread and common in northern temperate zones.

• **SIMILAR SPECIES** *I. sindonia* is also white, but it is more robust. It is found only under conifers. Other pale species tend to be bigger or have more fibrillose or scaly caps.

upper stem has mealy covering

lower stem is fibrous

LILAC FORM

• *umbonate cap with silky, streaky covering of radial fibers*

SECTION

• *adnexed gills are pale gray to gray-brown*

white flesh is slightly watery and smells spermatic •

• *umbo on lilac cap*

gills are fairly crowded •

WHITE FORM

FRUITING A few together or in troops near trees.

| Dimensions CAP ⊕ 1–4cm | STEM ↕ 2–5cm ↔ 3–5mm | Spores Brown | Edibility ☠ |

| Family CORTINARIACEAE | Species *Inocybe rimosa* | Season Summer–autumn |

STRAW-COLORED INOCYBE

This common, variable mushroom has a distinctive, pointed cap with coarse, radiating fibers and, with age, an upturned margin that tears very easily. The fruitbody is more or less yellow in color. The upper stem is finely downy; the base is wider but not bulbous. Typically, the gills will have a yellowish flush.

• **OCCURRENCE** Mycorrhizal, mostly with deciduous trees on more fertile, often disturbed soil along bridle paths. Widespread and common in northern temperate zones.

• **SIMILAR SPECIES** The equally common *Inocybe maculata* has a darker reddish brown cap with patches of off-white veil. Its pale stem may have a small basal bulb. The hundreds of other *Inocybe* species are accurately identified only by using very specialized literature.

SECTION

cap is covered with coarse, radial fibers •

• *narrow, adnate, yellowish gray to yellowish brown gills*

• *flesh is pale and smells spermatic*

• *cap margins flare upward and split with age*

• *stem is off-white or flushed yellow*

• *thicker stem base, but no bulb*

FRUITING Appears mostly in small groups on soil.

| Dimensions CAP ⊕ 3–7cm | STEM ↕ 6–10cm ↔ 0.5–1cm | Spores Tobacco-brown | Edibility ☠ |

| Family CORTINARIACEAE | Species *Inocybe griseolilacina* | Season Autumn |

GRAY AND LILAC INOCYBE

SECTION

Small brown scales cover the convex, ocher-brown cap of this species. The scaly, fibrous stem is pale lilac, and a lilac flush may be visible on the cap. There is no basal stem bulb.
• **OCCURRENCE**
Mycorrhizal with deciduous trees on more fertile soil; often found along road edges, like other close relatives. Widespread in northern temperate zones, but exact distribution is not known.
• **SIMILAR SPECIES**
Inocybe cincinnata has a darker cap, and the lilac stem color is stronger near the top. *I. pusio* also has lilac stem coloring but is less scaly on the cap.

small brown scales on convex cap

pale cap color under scales

pale flesh may be lilac-flushed

scaly, fibrous, lilac-tinted stem surface

cap is ocher-brown, sometimes lilac tinted at margin

stem darker in color toward base

adnate, ocher to pale brown gills have white edges

FRUITING Appears in troops or small groups.

| Dimensions CAP ⊕ 0.8–4cm | STEM ↕ 4–7cm ↔ 2–6mm | Spores Brown | Edibility ☠ |

| Family CORTINARIACEAE | Species *Inocybe lacera* | Season Spring–autumn |

TORN-CAP INOCYBE

Fine fibers and scales cover the convex cap of this dull brown to dark brown species. Young specimens display a veil at the cap margin. The brown fibrous stem does not have a basal bulb. The flesh is typically pale in the cap and becomes darker toward the stem base. A microscope will reveal smooth, cylindrical spores and thick-walled cystidia of this variable species.
• **OCCURRENCE** Mycorrhizal with various trees, including willow and conifers; found on hard-packed forest trails. Widespread and common in northern temperate zones.
• **SIMILAR SPECIES** *Inocybe lanuginosa* has a more woolly stem and spores with nodules.

surface of cap covered in scales and fine fibers

flesh is pale in cap

brown fibers on stem surface

flesh is dark in stem base

convex, dull to dark brown cap

SECTION

FRUITING A few together or in troops, often on poor soil.

adnexed gills are gray-brown with white edges

| Dimensions CAP ⊕ 1–4.5cm | STEM ↕ 2.5–6cm ↔ 2–6mm | Spores Tobacco-brown | Edibility |

Family CORTINARIACEAE	Species *Inocybe asterospora*	Season Autumn

STAR-SPORED INOCYBE

A distinctive, flattened bulb at the base of a slender, downy stem and a slightly umbonate, pale cap thickly covered with radiating, coarse, dark red-brown fibers characterize this species. Microscopic examination reveals star-shaped spores: the spores of *Inocybe* species are usually either smooth or have nodules (a star shape is an extreme form of the latter type).
• **OCCURRENCE** Mycorrhizal with deciduous trees, especially hazel or beech; often on bare soil. Widespread in northern temperate zones, locally common in eastern North America.
• **SIMILAR SPECIES** *I. margaritispora* has star-shaped spores but a paler, yellower cap. *I. napipes* has a less marked bulb, is smaller, and has ordinary noduled spores.

slightly umbonate cap is • pale beneath fibers

pale cap flesh, • darker in stem

radiating, coarse, dark red-brown • fibers on cap

SECTION

• flattened, rimmed bulb at stem base

• stem downy along its length

• adnexed, tobacco-brown gills

FRUITING Appears singly or a few fruitbodies together.

Dimensions CAP ⊕ 3–7cm | STEM ↕ 4–9cm ↔ 0.5–1.2cm	Spores Tobacco-brown	Edibility ☠

Family COPRINACEAE	Species *Psathyrella velutina*	Season Autumn

WEEPING GILLED PSATHYRELLA

The convex or umbonate cap of this species is brownish gray to ocher with a felted surface. The similarly colored stem is fibrillose and fragile. Gray becoming black, the gills are well spaced and adnate. Milky drops can be seen along the gill edges when they are young – hence the common name; these droplets fill with spores and dry as black spots.
• **OCCURRENCE** Saprotrophic; on nutrient-rich, disturbed soil. Widespread in northern temperate zones.
• **SIMILAR SPECIES** There are several similar species, including *Psathyrella glareosa* and *P. pyrotricha*. These are distinguished by their size and cap color and by spore characteristics.

cap is convex or with an • umbo

brownish gray to ocher cap • is felted

gills are gray with droplets at the edge •

well-spaced, • adnate gills

FRUITING Appears in large troops of fruitbodies along roads and paths, often near nettles.

Dimensions CAP ⊕ 2–10cm | STEM ↕ 4–12cm ↔ 0.5–2cm	Spores Blackish	Edibility 🍽

MEDIUM-SIZED WITH SMOOTH CAP

IN THIS SUBSECTION, species with adnate, adnexed, or notched gills (see pp.15 and 56) have been grouped together according to their size and cap characteristics. Medium-sized refers to the fruitbodies that have caps typically in the range of 1.5 to 6cm in diameter. The smooth surface of the caps is one of the most readily visible characteristics. The color of the spore deposits of species featured here varies widely from white, which is common to *Hygrocybe* species, through cream (found in species of *Collybia)* to pink (produced by *Entoloma* species) and black (which occurs in many *Psathyrella* species).

Family HYGROPHORACEAE	Species *Hygrocybe calyptraeformis*	Season Throughout autumn

PINK WAX CAP

The elegant and fragile, dusky pink fruitbodies of this rare species are quite unmistakable. Each has a cap that begins conical and opens out fully as it matures, eventually splitting radially. The stem is very brittle and is difficult to pull out of the substrate. It has mild-tasting, pale pink to white flesh. It is not recommended for eating because of concern about its conservation, and its edibility has not been very well documented.
• OCCURRENCE Long-established areas of grassland where commercial fertilizers have not been applied, often on alkaline soil. Widespread throughout Europe, including the islands of the North Atlantic.
• SIMILAR SPECIES *Hygrocybe citrinovirens* is similar in shape but is yellow-green and orange; it is also rare. Other *Hygrocybe* species have conical caps, but *H. calyptraeformis* and *H. citrinovirens* are the only ones that split so widely. *H. conica* (p.104) blackens with age. *H. spadicea* has a dark cap and yellow gills. It does not blacken.

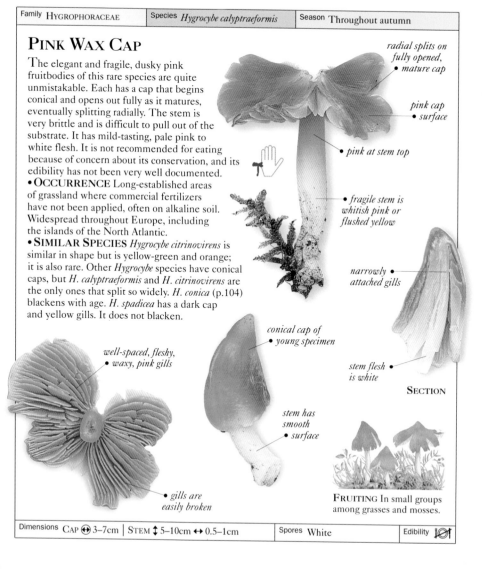

radial splits on fully opened, • mature cap

pink cap • surface

• pink at stem top

• fragile stem is whitish pink or flushed yellow

narrowly • attached gills

well-spaced, fleshy, • waxy, pink gills

conical cap of • young specimen

stem flesh • is white

SECTION

stem has smooth • surface

• gills are easily broken

FRUITING In small groups among grasses and mosses.

Dimensions CAP ⊕ 3–7cm	STEM ↕ 5–10cm ↔ 0.5–1cm	Spores White	Edibility

Family HYGROPHORACEAE	Species *Hygrocybe conica*	Season Summer–late autumn

BLACKENING WAX CAP

The slightly conical cap of this variable fungus is dry and fibrillose; the stem is yellow to red with longitudinal lines. This species occurs in a wide variety of colors, sizes, and shapes, and, among *Hygrocybe* species, it probably has the broadest range of habitats (leading some mycologists to suggest it is a range of species and varieties). It blackens with age or when handled. It may be slightly poisonous.

• OCCURRENCE In grassy areas, and open woods. Widespread in northern temperate zones.

• SIMILAR SPECIES *H. acutoconica* does not stain black nor does *Entoloma salmoneum*, which has a pink spore print and angular spores.

pale gray, yellow, or red gills •

SECTION

yellow to • red cap

• crowded gills are sinuate, almost free to adnexed

mostly dry, fibrillose cap surface

• *paler stem base, unless stained black*

fruitbody turns • black with age or when handled

• *stem is yellow to red*

longitudinal • fibers on stem

FRUITING Appears mostly in small groups of fruitbodies.

Dimensions CAP ⊕ 1–5cm │ STEM ↕ 2–10cm ↔ 0.4–1.5cm	Spores White	Edibility ☠

Family HYGROPHORACEAE	Species *Hygrocybe chlorophana*	Season Autumn–late autumn

GOLDEN WAX CAP

This fairly large *Hygrocybe* species, ranging from rich orange-yellow to shades of pale yellow, has a slimy, convex to flattened cap, aging grayish yellow and with a more or less striate margin. The stem can be slimy but tends to have a powdery top. Edible, but not recommended, it has mild, pale yellow flesh.

• OCCURRENCE In various unimproved grassy areas, mostly with other *Hygrocybe* species. Widespread and common in eastern North America, Texas, and Pacific Northwest.

• SIMILAR SPECIES *H. ceracea* is smaller and less slimy on the cap, with adnate or decurrent gills. *H. flavescens* has a similarly colored slimy cap but has a white stem base. *H. glutinipes.*

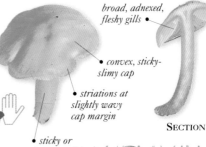

broad, adnexed, fleshy gills •

• *convex, sticky-slimy cap*

• *striations at slightly wavy cap margin*

SECTION

• *sticky or dry stem with powdery top*

• *well-spaced gills are paler than cap*

FRUITING Appears in troops and fairy rings.

Dimensions CAP ⊕ 1.5–7cm │ STEM ↕ 2.5–10cm ↔ 3–8mm	Spores White	Edibility ▢

Family HYGROPHORACEAE	Species *Hygrocybe coccinea*	Season Late summer–late autumn

SCARLET WAX CAP

A slightly grainy surface on the bell-shaped cap, which is dry but becomes sticky in wet weather, and adnate gills help to distinguish this mushroom from other red *Hygrocybe* species. It is edible, but not choice, with a faint smell and taste. Small and more orange forms of *H. coccinea* can be difficult to distinguish and need to be studied with a microscope and identified using very specialized literature.

• **OCCURRENCE** In unimproved grassy areas. Widespread and fairly common in eastern North America and California.
• **SIMILAR SPECIES** *H. punicea* (p.56) and *H. splendidissima* are fleshier and have adnexed gills. The latter has an almost smooth stem and smells of honey.

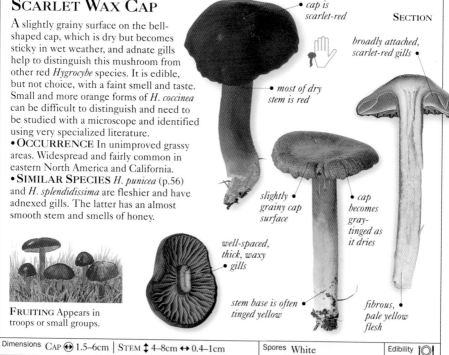

• *cap is scarlet-red*

SECTION

• *broadly attached, scarlet-red gills*

• *most of dry stem is red*

• *slightly grainy cap surface*

• *cap becomes gray-tinged as it dries*

well-spaced, thick, waxy • *gills*

stem base is often tinged yellow

fibrous, • *pale yellow flesh*

FRUITING Appears in troops or small groups.

Dimensions CAP ⊕ 1.5–6cm	STEM ↕ 4–8cm ↔ 0.4–1cm	Spores White	Edibility

Family HYGROPHORACEAE	Species *Hygrocybe psittacina*	Season Summer–late autumn

PARROT WAX CAP

This spectacular species may be difficult to identify because of the vast range of colors exhibited by specimens of different ages. When young, the convex or bell-shaped cap is deep bottle-green; with age, purple, orange, and yellow develop. The stem is yellow, tinged blue-green. The fruitbody has a slimy surface when young and is almost odorless. It is inedible.

• **OCCURRENCE** In meadows, roadsides, and woods on rich soil, with species of *Geoglossum* (p.242) and *Clavulinopsis* (p.240), and other members of the Clavariaceae. Widespread and common in northern temperate zones; common in eastern North America.
• **SIMILAR SPECIES** *Hygrocybe psittacina* var. *perplexa* lacks green color and is somewhat brick-red.

• *slimy, green to orange-pink cap*

top of stem is • *usually tinged blue-green*

• *bottle-green cap in young specimen*

• *slimy yellow and/or green stem*

• *adnexed, green to orange-yellow gills*

• *fragile flesh is white, tinged pale green and yellow*

SECTION

FRUITING In small groups, mostly in meadows.

Dimensions CAP ⊕ 1–4cm	STEM ↕ 3–7cm ↔ 4–8mm	Spores White	Edibility

| Family HYGROPHORACEAE | Species *Hygrophorus eburneus* | Season Autumn–early winter |

SATIN WAX CAP

The convex to flattened, sparkling white cap of this species drips with slime in wet weather. The stem is also slimy and white. Both stain slightly yellow with age. The gills are thick and waxy, and the white flesh smells pleasantly aromatic but is not worth eating.
• **OCCURRENCE** Mycorrhizal with beech trees on fertile soil. Widespread in northern temperate regions where beech grows; found in eastern North America and California.
• **SIMILAR SPECIES** *Hygrophorus discoxanthus* stains deep orange.

• satin-white cap slowly turns slightly yellow with age

more or less • decurrent gills

• slimy white stem is powdery at the top

SECTION

white flesh • smells aromatic

FRUITING In small clusters among leaf litter on soil.

• slimy cap surface

thick, waxy • white gills are medium spaced

| Dimensions CAP ⊕ 3–8cm | STEM ↕ 4–10cm ↔ 0.5–1cm | Spores White | Edibility |

| Family BOLBITIACEAE | Species *Agrocybe pediades* | Season Summer–autumn |

COMMON LAWN AGROCYBE

Normally completely smooth with a gently convex, yellowish ocher cap and no veil, this species is not particularly distinctive. The stem is solid, cylindrical, and straight, and the flesh is pale with a yeasty smell and taste. Some experts divide *Agrocybe pediades* into several species, mainly by habitat and microscopic features, such as spore size.
• **OCCURRENCE** Typically in lawns and other types of grassland but can also grow on mulch containing horse manure. Widespread and common in northern temperate zones.
• **SIMILAR SPECIES** *A. arvalis* has a downy stem that springs from a black sclerotium. Related *A. dura* is paler and fleshier, with a veil at the cap margin.

• convex, ocher-yellow cap becomes greasy when wet

• smooth cap surface cracks in dry conditions

adnate • brown gills

• grows in grass turf

well-spaced • gills

solid stem has a • few surface hairs

FRUITING Appears singly or in troops of fruitbodies.

• gills have off-white edge

SECTION

| Dimensions CAP ⊕ 1–3.5cm | STEM ↕ 2.5–5cm ↔ 3–5mm | Spores Tobacco-brown | Edibility |

Family COPRINACEAE	Species *Panaeolus papilionaceus*	Season Summer–late autumn

FRINGED PANAEOLUS

Triangular veil remnants at the cap margin are characteristic of this species. The cap is convex or bell-shaped and varies from dark gray to brownish gray; older specimens may have pale caps contrasting with the dark brown stems. Marbled gills caused by uneven ripening of the spores are typical of *Panaeolus* species. The flesh is dark brown in the stem, paler in the cap, and has no distinct smell. A form with a strongly veined cap was previously regarded as a separate species, *P. retirugis*. Because of conflicting reports on toxicity, this species should not be eaten.
• **OCCURRENCE** On old dung or in manured, grazed fields. Widespread in northern temperate zones and elsewhere.

convex or bell-shaped, • smooth cap

SECTION

• triangular veil remnants just visible at cap margin

broad, adnate gills are mottled black and gray

rather fragile • stem is gray to dark brown

stem is • hollow

FRUITING Singly or a few together on or near manure.

• sooty gray-brown cap indicates an older specimen

medium-spaced, • nearly black gills with white edges

Dimensions CAP ⊕ 1–4cm | STEM ↕ 4–10cm ↔ 2–3mm	Spores Black	Edibility ☠

Family STROPHARIACEAE	Species *Psilocybe cyanescens*	Season Autumn–early winter

COMMON WOOD-CHIP PSILOCYBE

This hallucinogenic agaric has a flattened cap with a wavy margin; reddish buff at first, it dries to creamy ocher and develops dark blue discoloration when handled. It becomes greasy in wet weather. The off-white to gray stem, which also stains blue, has no ring. Several stems are frequently joined at the base. The white flesh has a faint yeasty smell.
• **OCCURRENCE** Mostly in disturbed sites, such as a flower bed mulch that contains coniferous wood chips. Widespread but rather local, in northern temperate zones.
• **SIMILAR SPECIES** The many blue-staining *Psilocybe*s in North America can be reliably identified to species only with technical literature.

• adnate to slightly decurrent gills

SECTION

• pale flesh and stem surface stain blue

cap margin • may be wavy and upturned when old

fairly well-spaced gills •

blue most obvious • at cap margin

• silky, fibrillose, off-white to gray stem

FRUITING In troops or clusters in disturbed sites.

• gills are whitish gray to dark purplish brown with white edges

Dimensions CAP ⊕ 2–4cm | STEM ↕ 3–6cm ↔ 3–8mm	Spores Dark purplish brown	Edibility ☠

| Family TRICHOLOMATACEAE | Species *Macrocystidia cucumis* | Season Late summer–autumn |

CUCUMBER-SCENTED MUSHROOM

This agaric has a strong, rancid smell of rotten cucumbers or pickled herrings. The dark brown or orange-brown cap has a pale yellow margin and velvety surface. The fairly tough stem is also densely velvety; it is dark at the base and paler near the top. The spore print is sometimes off-white to pale pink, indicating a complex of species.

• OCCURRENCE In gardens, parks, or along roads, on rich soil mixed with leaf litter or sawdust. Widespread but local in northern temperate zones; widespread in Europe but more local in the Pacific Northwest.

adnexed gills are pale cream to pale reddish brown

fine down on cap surface, which may be striated

SECTION

yellow cap margin

fairly crowded, medium to very broad gills

cap may be convex, conical, or bell-shaped

black to dark brown stem base

FRUITING A few fruitbodies together or in troops.

| Dimensions CAP ⊕ 0.5–5cm | STEM ↕ 3–7cm ↔ 2–5mm | Spores Rusty ocher or off-white | Edibility |

| Family COPRINACEAE | Species *Psathyrella multipedata* | Season Autumn |

TUFTED PSATHYRELLA

The bell-shaped to conical, gray- or red-brown cap of this cluster-forming species has striations halfway to the center. It dries to pale yellow-brown and has no obvious veil. Clusters of up to 80 smooth white stems are joined at the base and extend, rootlike, deep into the soil. This is among the very few *Psathyrella* species with clear identification features, distinguishing it from most other little brown mushrooms (LBMs).

• OCCURRENCE On rich, loamy, or clay soil, often in urban areas such as city parks and on roadsides. Widespread in Europe; reported in the Midwest.

• SIMILAR SPECIES *P. piluliformis* (p.94). Other tufted agarics in open areas include *Lyophyllum decastes* (p.41) and other species of *Lyophyllum* (p.132), which all have white spore deposits.

moist, gray- or red-brown cap, striated at margin

hollow stems

SECTION

pale gray to dark purple-brown gills are white edged

smooth cap dries from center to pale yellow-brown

crowded, narrow, adnexed gills

FRUITING Always in tight clusters, rooted deeply in turf.

| Dimensions CAP ⊕ 0.8–4cm | STEM ↕ 8–14cm ↔ 2–4mm | Spores Brownish black | Edibility |

Family COPRINACEAE	Species *Psathyrella conopilus*	Season Late summer–late autumn

DARK CONE PSATHYRELLA

Known for its elegant stature and dark reddish brown cap, which dries to pale ocher-yellow, this is a distinctive, if fragile, *Psathyrella* species. The conical cap is smooth with marginal striations. When examined with a hand lens, thick-walled dark hairs are visible on the cap surface and in the thin flesh – a unique feature in the genus.
• **OCCURRENCE** Along roadsides, bridle paths, and in parks on disturbed soil, especially among wood chips and debris. Widespread and common in Europe and North America.
• **SIMILAR SPECIES** A number of similar species are smaller, paler, and often have pink tinges. In sand dunes, one of the most common gilled mushrooms is *P. ammophila*, which grows on marram grass.

• *conical cap with marginal striations but no veil*

white edge to • adnexed gills

SECTION

• *quite crowded, fragile gills are gray to black*

FRUITING In scattered fruitbodies or in troops.

• *orange-brown cap dries to pale ocher-yellow*

• *base, to 5mm wide, has tints of cap color*

• *very tall, fragile, hollow white stem*

Dimensions CAP ⊕ 2–6cm	STEM ↕ 9–19cm ↔ 2–3mm	Spores Black	Edibility

Family ENTOLOMATACEAE	Species *Entoloma cetratum*	Season Early summer–late autumn

HONEY-COLORED ENTOLOMA

This is an elegant species, identifiable by its warm honey-brown coloring, the clear striations on its cap, and its tall stature. The cap is bell-shaped to convex, and the stem is fibrillose. Examination under a microscope reveals its two-spored basidia. This and other *Collybia*-like *Entoloma* species are also sometimes classified in the genus, or subgenus, *Nolanea*.
• **OCCURRENCE** Under conifers on humus-rich soil but also in acidic, deciduous woods and bogs. Widespread and common in Europe; not reported in North America.
• **SIMILAR SPECIES** *E. lanuginosipes* and *E. pallescens* are distinguished by heavily powdered stem surfaces and four-spored basidia.

darker center on honey-brown • cap surface

• *lines at cap margin*   SECTION

• *young stem is powdered at the top*

• *fine fibers run lengthwise on stem*

FRUITING A few fruitbodies appear together or singly.

adnexed, honey-toned gills • turn pink with age

• *well-spaced gills*

• *thin, fragile, pale flesh*

Dimensions CAP ⊕ 0.5–3cm	STEM ↕ 5–8cm ↔ 2–4mm	Spores Pale pink	Edibility

Family ENTOMATACEAE	Species *Entoloma conferendum*	Season Spring–late autumn

STAR-SPORED ENTOLOMA

Despite an elegant stature and a strongly fibrillose, silvery stem, this species is not easy to identify. A microscope reveals its key identification feature: star-shaped spores. The reddish brown to gray-brown cap tends to be conical, aging to convex or umbonate; darker striations on the surface fade as it dries to pale gray-brown. The crowded gills are adnate, and the pale flesh smells and tastes yeasty.

• **OCCURRENCE** Mostly in grassy places in parks and playing fields but also in grass or moss in open woods. Widespread and common in northern temperate zones.

• **SIMILAR SPECIES** There are several *Entoloma* species that are similar in appearance, such as *E. cetratum* (p.109), which is warmer honey-brown, and *E. sericeum* (inset, right). All have spores that are angular and not star-shaped.

cap dries from reddish brown or gray-brown to pale gray-brown

pale gray then pink-tinged gills

margin has darker striations when moist

fine silvery fibers on elegant stem

△ **ENTOLOMA SERICEUM**
Short-stemmed, with a dark sepia-brown to horn-gray cap, this common European species has a very strong rancid-yeasty smell. The spores are angular but not star-shaped. ☠

young cap is conical

stem slightly swollen and paler at base

FRUITING Appears singly or in small groups.

Dimensions CAP ⊕ 2–4cm | STEM ↕ 3–6cm ↔ 3–7mm	Spores Pale pink	Edibility ☠

Family ENTOMATACEAE	Species *Entoloma nitidum*	Season Autumn

STEEL-BLUE ENTOLOMA

This is among the very few blue *Entoloma* species that are quite large and fleshy. It is very dark gray-blue with a convex to umbonate, smooth to fibrillose cap and a slender, twisted stem. The well-spaced, adnate gills are white, becoming pale pink with age. The white cap flesh has a blue tinge near the skin and has a faint smell. This species should not be eaten.

• **OCCURRENCE** Among moss in damp, acidic coniferous woods or tree stands. Widespread but mostly in northern Europe and adjacent parts of Asia; not reported in North America.

• **SIMILAR SPECIES** *E. bloxamii* is fleshier and prefers alkaline grassland. *E. euchroum* is smaller, bluer, and grows on deciduous trees.

dark gray-blue cap is smooth to fibrillose

cap is convex to umbonate

well-spaced, white gills age to pink

slender, twisted stem is dark gray-blue

FRUITING Appears singly or in small groups of fruitbodies in damp woods.

Dimensions CAP ⊕ 1–2.5cm | STEM ↕ 2–6cm ↔ 2–4mm	Spores Pale pink	Edibility

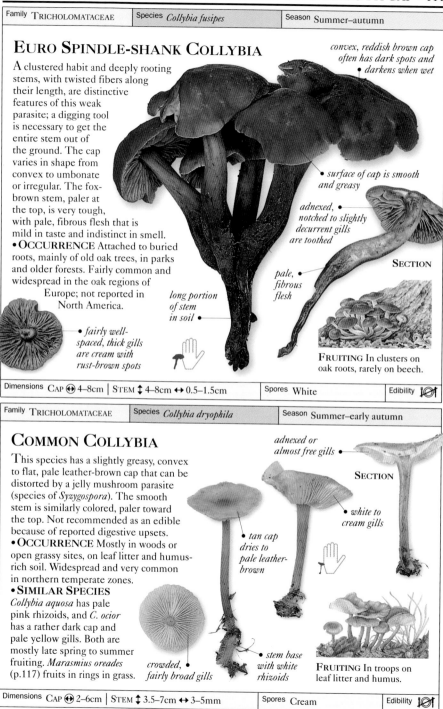

Family TRICHOLOMATACEAE	Species *Collybia fusipes*	Season Summer–autumn

EURO SPINDLE-SHANK COLLYBIA

A clustered habit and deeply rooting stems, with twisted fibers along their length, are distinctive features of this weak parasite; a digging tool is necessary to get the entire stem out of the ground. The cap varies in shape from convex to umbonate or irregular. The fox-brown stem, paler at the top, is very tough, with pale, fibrous flesh that is mild in taste and indistinct in smell.
• OCCURRENCE Attached to buried roots, mainly of old oak trees, in parks and older forests. Fairly common and widespread in the oak regions of Europe; not reported in North America.

convex, reddish brown cap often has dark spots and • darkens when wet

• surface of cap is smooth and greasy

adnexed, notched to slightly decurrent gills are toothed

SECTION

pale, fibrous flesh

long portion of stem in soil •

• fairly well-spaced, thick gills are cream with rust-brown spots

FRUITING In clusters on oak roots, rarely on beech.

Dimensions CAP ⊕ 4–8cm | STEM ‡ 4–8cm ↔ 0.5–1.5cm	Spores White	Edibility

Family TRICHOLOMATACEAE	Species *Collybia dryophila*	Season Summer–early autumn

COMMON COLLYBIA

This species has a slightly greasy, convex to flat, pale leather-brown cap that can be distorted by a jelly mushroom parasite (species of *Syzygospora*). The smooth stem is similarly colored, paler toward the top. Not recommended as an edible because of reported digestive upsets.
• OCCURRENCE Mostly in woods or open grassy sites, on leaf litter and humus-rich soil. Widespread and very common in northern temperate zones.
• SIMILAR SPECIES
Collybia aquosa has pale pink rhizoids, and *C. ocior* has a rather dark cap and pale yellow gills. Both are mostly late spring to summer fruiting. *Marasmius oreades* (p.117) fruits in rings in grass.

adnexed or almost free gills •

SECTION

• white to cream gills

• tan cap dries to pale leather-brown

crowded, • fairly broad gills

• stem base with white rhizoids

FRUITING In troops on leaf litter and humus.

Dimensions CAP ⊕ 2–6cm | STEM ‡ 3.5–7cm ↔ 3–5mm	Spores Cream	Edibility

Family TRICHOLOMATACEAE	Species *Collybia erythropus*	Season Autumn–late autumn

STALKED COLLYBIA

The convex to flat, cream to pale leather-brown cap of this species is more or less striate at the margin and has a slightly greasy surface. The smooth stem is fox-red. The flesh is white in the cap and red-brown in the stem. It has an indistinct smell and taste and is not a worthwhile edible.
• **OCCURRENCE** In deciduous woods, it grows on mossy tree trunks or emerges from half-buried, very decayed wood. Fairly common and widespread in Europe; not reported in North America.
• **SIMILAR SPECIES** *Collybia acervata* grows in clusters of fruitbodies on or under conifers. *C. dryophila* (p.111). *Marasmius* species (pp.114, 117, 138, 177) are also similar.

smooth, cream to pale leather-brown cap is slightly greasy

flesh is paler in cap

adnexed, white to cream gills

striations at cap margin   **SECTION**

smooth, fox-red stem

fairly broad gills often interconnect

FRUITING In clusters or, more rarely, singly.

Dimensions CAP ⊕ 1–4cm | STEM ↕ 3–7cm ↔ 2–5cm	Spores Pale cream	Edibility IOI

Family TRICHOLOMATACEAE	Species *Collybia butyracea*	Season Late summer–early winter

BUTTERY COLLYBIA

This species is recognized by its greasy, umbonate cap, which changes color as it dries, creating zones of light and dark, and by its distinctly club-shaped stem base. The flesh is tough and fibrous and is hollow or has a soft pith in the stem; although edible, it is not worthwhile.
• **OCCURRENCE** In deciduous woods, mostly on humus-rich soil and in leaf litter. Widespread and common to abundant in northern temperate zones.
• **SIMILAR SPECIES** A darker form, *Collybia filamentosa*, grows in acidic woods and is sometimes regarded as a separate species.

greasy cap surface

slightly striate, dark brown to horn-gray cap

gills are adnexed, but appear almost free

fibrillose, club-shaped stem base

crowded white gills

tough, fibrous flesh

FRUITING In troops on leaf litter and soil.

SECTION

Dimensions CAP ⊕ 3–6cm | STEM ↕ 4–7cm ↔ 0.5–2cm	Spores Pale cream	Edibility IOI

| Family TRICHOLOMATACEAE | Species *Collybia confluens* | Season Autumn |

TUFTED COLLYBIA

Producing dense tufts of
fruitbodies, this species has
a tall, slender stem clothed in
gray-white felt, and a rounded,
very pale grayish white cap,
smaller than those of most
Collybia species. It has a faint,
pleasantly aromatic smell and
taste, but it is not considered
a worthwhile edible.
• **OCCURRENCE** In deciduous
and coniferous woods, on thick leaf
litter; probably more common on
rich, fertile soil. Widespread in
northern North America.
• **SIMILAR SPECIES** *C. acervata*
also grows in clusters, but
it has reddish coloring,
stems with felt on the
lower half only, and is
always associated with
coniferous trees.

*adnexed
gills*

*dry, smooth,
very pale gray-
white cap*

*flesh is
off-white
to pale
brown*

*dense, gray-
white felt on
entire stem*

*stem is dark
brown on overly
mature specimens*

SECTION

*crowded, narrow,
white to cream gills*

FRUITING In dense tufts,
sometimes in fairy rings.

| Dimensions CAP ⊕ 1–3cm | STEM ↕ 5–9cm ↔ 3–7mm | Spores Pale cream | Edibility |

| Family TRICHOLOMATACEAE | Species *Collybia peronata* | Season Autumn–late autumn |

BITTER WOOLLY-FOOT COLLYBIA

The leather-brown cap of this species is bell-shaped
to almost flat and has radial but irregular, dark brown
streaks. Its main distinguishing features are its stem
and its taste: the pale yellow stem is covered with felty
yellow fibers at the base, becoming downy toward the
top, and the inedible, strongly acrid-tasting flesh is
white to sulfur-yellow, tough, and fibrous. Also useful
in identification are its fairly well-spaced gills.
• **OCCURRENCE** In deciduous and coniferous
woods on leaf litter. Widespread in northern temperate
zones; common in Europe, rare in North America.
• **SIMILAR SPECIES** Both *Collybia
alcalivirens* and *C. fuscopurpurea* have
darker caps and stem felt that is not
yellow. They both
have a mild taste.

*fairly well-
spaced,
narrow,
tough
gills*

*thick, feltlike covering
on lower stem, which
is often curved
and footlike*

*adnexed
or almost
free, tan gills*

*white to
sulfur-
yellow flesh*

FRUITING In troops or small
clusters of fruitbodies.

*dry cap is
leather-brown
with darker
streaks*

SECTION

| Dimensions CAP ⊕ 2.5–6cm | STEM ↕ 4–8cm ↔ 3–5mm | Spores Pale cream | Edibility |

Family TRICHOLOMATACEAE	Species *Marasmius alliaceus*	Season Late summer–autumn

EURO GARLIC MARASMIUS

A pungent smell, reminiscent of rancid garlic, a fairly pale leather-brown cap, and an almost smooth black stem identify this large *Marasmius* species. The cap is convex or umbonate, and its surface may have darker striations, either at the margin or rarely almost to the center. They disappear with age. Despite the very rancid taste, some people use it as a garlic substitute in cooking.
• OCCURRENCE On buried branches or trunks in beech woodland. Widespread in the beech regions of Europe and adjacent parts of Asia.
• SIMILAR SPECIES *M. scorodonius* is smaller and paler but with a similar smell. It often occurs in grassland.

adnexed gills

hollow stem

dark striations in pale leather-brown cap

dry, smooth cap surface

nearly black stem is pale brown at top

SECTION

stem smooth to slightly downy

fairly crowded, off-white to tan gills

fibrillose stem base

FRUITING Solitary or in troops in beech woodland.

DWARF FORM

Dimensions CAP ⊕ 1.5–4cm	STEM ↕ 7–15cm ↔ 3–6mm	Spores Off-white	Edibility 🍴

Family TRICHOLOMATACEAE	Species *Flammulina velutipes*	Season Late autumn–spring

ENOKI COLLYBIA

The orange-brown cap and velvety, dark brown stem make this species easy to identify. It is one of the very few agarics that survive frosts. The gills are adnexed, crowded, and white to pale yellow. The thin, pale yellow flesh has a mild flavor; in Japan, it is cultivated for cooking.
• OCCURRENCE On living but unhealthy trees, especially willow or poplar; on weakened sites, such as where a branch has broken. Rarely found on conifers. Widespread and rather common in northern temperate zones.
• SIMILAR SPECIES *Flammulina fennae* and *F. ononidis* are rarer and have different habitats.

tough, solid stem

velvety brown stem

SYZYGITES MEGALOCARPUS △
A gray-white species, parasitic on a range of agarics, including *Flammulina*. 🍴

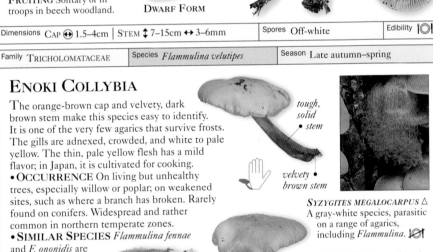

smooth, orange-brown cap surface, greasy when wet

pale yellow cap margin

FRUITING In dense clumps of fruitbodies.

Dimensions CAP ⊕ 1–6cm	STEM ↕ 2–7cm ↔ 0.3–1cm	Spores White	Edibility 🍴

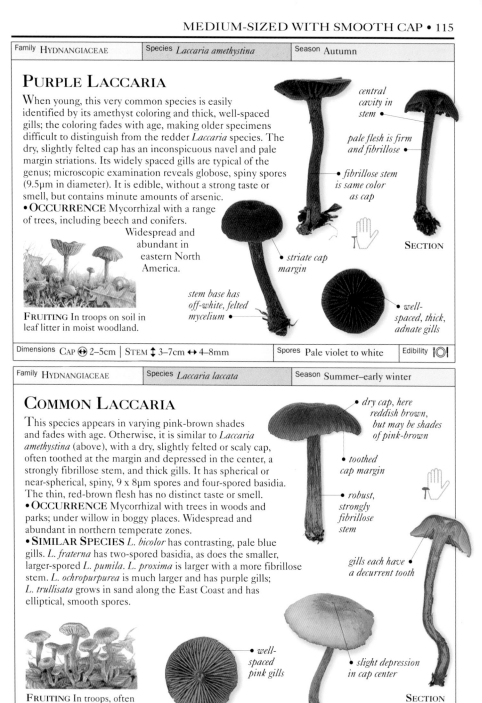

Family HYDNANGIACEAE	Species *Laccaria amethystina*	Season Autumn

PURPLE LACCARIA

When young, this very common species is easily
identified by its amethyst coloring and thick, well-spaced
gills; the coloring fades with age, making older specimens
difficult to distinguish from the redder *Laccaria* species. The
dry, slightly felted cap has an inconspicuous navel and pale
margin striations. Its widely spaced gills are typical of the
genus; microscopic examination reveals globose, spiny spores
(9.5µm in diameter). It is edible, without a strong taste or
smell, but contains minute amounts of arsenic.

• **OCCURRENCE** Mycorrhizal with a range
of trees, including beech and conifers.
Widespread and
abundant in
eastern North
America.

central cavity in stem

pale flesh is firm and fibrillose

fibrillose stem is same color as cap

SECTION

striate cap margin

stem base has off-white, felted mycelium

well-spaced, thick, adnate gills

FRUITING In troops on soil in
leaf litter in moist woodland.

Dimensions CAP ⊕ 2–5cm	STEM ↕ 3–7cm ↔ 4–8mm	Spores Pale violet to white	Edibility

Family HYDNANGIACEAE	Species *Laccaria laccata*	Season Summer–early winter

COMMON LACCARIA

This species appears in varying pink-brown shades
and fades with age. Otherwise, it is similar to *Laccaria
amethystina* (above), with a dry, slightly felted or scaly cap,
often toothed at the margin and depressed in the center, a
strongly fibrillose stem, and thick gills. It has spherical or
near-spherical, spiny, 9 x 8µm spores and four-spored basidia.
The thin, red-brown flesh has no distinct taste or smell.

• **OCCURRENCE** Mycorrhizal with trees in woods and
parks; under willow in boggy places. Widespread and
abundant in northern temperate zones.

• **SIMILAR SPECIES** *L. bicolor* has contrasting, pale blue
gills. *L. fraterna* has two-spored basidia, as does the smaller,
larger-spored *L. pumila*. *L. proxima* is larger with a more fibrillose
stem. *L. ochropurpurea* is much larger and has purple gills;
L. trullisata grows in sand along the East Coast and has
elliptical, smooth spores.

dry cap, here reddish brown, but may be shades of pink-brown

toothed cap margin

robust, strongly fibrillose stem

gills each have a decurrent tooth

well-spaced pink gills

slight depression in cap center

SECTION

FRUITING In troops, often
on damp soil.

Dimensions CAP ⊕ 1–5cm	STEM ↕ 2–6cm ↔ 2–6mm	Spores White	Edibility

Family TRICHOLOMATACEAE	Species *Calocybe carnea*	Season Mid--late autumn

PINK LAWN TRICH

This species is easily identified by its pink cap and stem, contrasting with its crowded, sinuate, notched white gills, although it can be difficult to spot in deep grass. Indistinct in smell and taste, it is considered to be edible but the fruitbodies are so small that it is not really worth the effort.

• OCCURRENCE Grassland, including fertilized agricultural pasture and lawns. Widespread in northern temperate zones; uncommon in North America.

• SIMILAR SPECIES *Calocybe persicolor*, possibly the same species, is said to be duller and have a hairy stem base, often joined in clusters. *C. obscurissima* is even duller and grows on calcareous soil in woods. *Entoloma rosea* is a brighter shade with a pink spore deposit.

smooth, fleshy, pink stem

cap is convex to umbonate

crowded, sinuate, notched white gills

smooth, fleshy, pink cap

△ CALOCYBE IONIDES
Lilac coloring identifies this species, which has an umbonate to depressed, sometimes wavy-margined cap, a club-shaped stem, and cream-white gills.

SECTION

off-white flesh has no smell

FRUITING Singly or in small groups of fruitbodies.

Dimensions CAP ⊕ 1–4cm | STEM ↕ 2–4cm ↔ 3–8mm	Spores Cream-white	Edibility

Family TRICHOLOMATACEAE	Species *Mycena galericulata*	Season Summer–early winter

COMMON TUFTED MYCENA

Two distinguishing features of this common but difficult-to-identify agaric are its unusual toughness compared to other *Mycena* species, and a noticeable tendency for the gills to take on a pale pink hue with age. The cap varies from bell-shaped to convex and may be yellow-brown or gray-brown. The similarly colored stem is hollow but very tough and can be twisted without breaking. The flesh has a yeasty, rancid smell and a similar taste.

• OCCURRENCE In woods on the trunks, stumps, and fallen branches of various types of deciduous trees. Widespread and common in northern temperate zones, extending south. Throughout North America.

dry cap surface, greasy when wet

bell-shaped, umbonate to convex cap

extremely tough stem

tough, adnexed gills, often interveined or forked

SECTION

FRUITING Appears in tufts and troops of fruitbodies.

pale brown cap often has furrows and wrinkles

medium-spaced, white to gray gills age to pale pink

Dimensions CAP ⊕ 1–6cm | STEM ↕ 3–8cm ↔ 2–7mm	Spores Pale cream	Edibility

Family TRICHOLOMATACEAE	Species *Marasmius oreades*	Season Early summer–mid-autumn

FAIRY RING MARASMIUS

Producing characteristic rings in turf, this mushroom has a bell-shaped to convex cap, which becomes flatter with a broad umbo with age; it emerges tan and dries to pale leather-brown from the center. The off-white to pale buff stem is tough and solid. It is pleasant tasting, with a smell reminiscent of bitter almonds, but see SIMILAR SPECIES before eating.
• **OCCURRENCE** In grassland, including lawns. Widespread and common in northern temperate zones.
• **SIMILAR SPECIES**
The poisonous *Clitocybe dealbata* (p.34) is found in the same grassy habitat. It is distinguished by its decurrent gills.

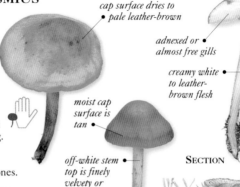

cap surface dries to pale leather-brown

adnexed or almost free gills

creamy white to leather-brown flesh

moist cap surface is tan

SECTION

off-white stem top is finely velvety or powdery

well-spaced, cream to pale leather-brown gills

FRUITING Appears in fairy rings among grasses.

Dimensions CAP ⊕ 1–5cm	STEM ↕ 3–6cm ↔ 3–7mm	Spores Off-white	Edibility

Family TRICHOLOMATACEAE	Species *Oudemansiella radicata*	Season Summer–late autumn

ROOTING COLLYBIA

This species has an umbonate to flattened, greasy, gray- to yellow-brown cap and a twisted, furrowed stem, which is white at the top, brown toward the base. The stem extends 5–15cm into the soil and the buried substrate, with the same amount above ground. This, and some more velvety species, all lacking stem rings, are placed by some in the genus *Xerula*, and by others in *Collybia*.
• **OCCURRENCE** In parks and woods, by trees and stumps. Widespread in northern temperate zones; common in some regions; world distribution unclear.
• **SIMILAR SPECIES** *Oudemansiella pudens* and *O. caussei* have dry caps and strongly velvety stems.

adnate gills, each with a decurrent tooth

greasy, veined cap surface

tough, off-white flesh

pale gray-brown stem, with white upper part

medium-spaced, pale cream gills, often with brown edges

twisted, furrowed stem

SECTION

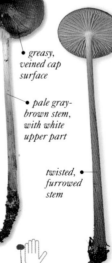

FRUITING Appears singly or in scattered groups.

Dimensions CAP ⊕ 3–10cm	STEM ↕ 5–15cm ↔ 0.5–1cm	Spores Pale cream	Edibility

Family TRICHOLOMATACEAE	Species *Mycena pelianthina*	Season Summer–autumn

DARK GILL-EDGE MYCENA

This somber-looking agaric has a large cap compared to most *Mycena* species. Convex to flat, it is purplish gray when wet, drying to pale gray-lavender. Margin striations are clearer when the cap is wet. The medium-spaced gills are broad and gray-purple with a serrated, almost black edge. The radishlike smell is similar to that of *M. pura* (below). Overall, it is like a *Collybia* (pp.111–113), but microscopic features, such as amyloid spores and large cystidia with colored contents, place it in *Mycena*.
• OCCURRENCE Mostly in rich, alkaline woodland, on thick leaf litter, mainly from beech trees. Widespread but rather local in Europe and adjacent parts of Asia.

cap surface dries from purplish gray to pale
• gray-lavender

hollow stem •
is pale purple
or purple tinged

fragile,
watery
flesh

SECTION

• broad,
narrowly
attached
gills

toothed black
• gill edge

stem thicker
towards base

FRUITING Singly or a few fruitbodies together.

Dimensions CAP ⊕ 3–6cm | STEM ↕ 4–8cm ↔ 4–8mm	Spores White	Edibility ☠

Family TRICHOLOMATACEAE	Species *Mycena pura*	Season Late summer–early winter

POISON RADISH GROUND MYCENA

SECTION

This variable species comes in many different colors, usually with purple tints. Some are considered separate species or varieties; all smell of radishes. A large pink form, *Mycena rosea*, has been implicated in poisonings. The convex to umbonate cap shows a distinct striate margin when wet. The hollow, dry stem may have a yellow hue or can be paler but tinted in the cap color.
• OCCURRENCE In wooded and open habitats on humus-rich soil. Common in northern temperate zones, extending south.
• SIMILAR SPECIES *M. diosma* has a dark cap, which changes color as it dries, smells of cedarwood, and grows on alkaline soils.

adnexed •
to adnate
gills may
be sinuate
and notched

hollow •
stem

stem color •
is usually
similar to the
cap, or paler

fairly
crowded
gills •

pink-colored •
form, also
known as
M. rosea

FRUITING Singly or in small groups on rich soil.

Dimensions CAP ⊕ 2–6cm | STEM ↕ 3–9cm ↔ 0.3–1cm	Spores White	Edibility ☠

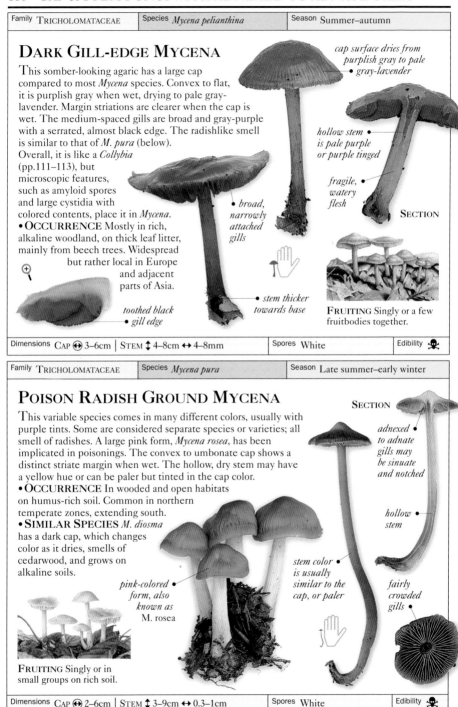

Family TRICHOLOMATACEAE	Species *Mycena crocata*	Season Late summer–autumn

EURO ORANGE-STAINING MYCENA

Conical to convex and more or less umbonate, the cap of this species is brown-gray with a paler margin and striations. Its stem exudes a saffron-orange liquid when cut or broken, leading to its other common name, Orange-milking Mycena. The lower stem is also saffron-orange; the upper part is paler. The well-spaced gills are white, staining yellow.
• **OCCURRENCE** Almost exclusively associated with beech, found mainly on fallen, often half-buried branches or in thick leaf litter. Widespread in beech regions within Europe and locally very common; also found in Japan.
• **SIMILAR SPECIES** A few other *Mycena* species produce colored or white liquid when damaged. *M. haematopus* (p.136) has blood-red juice, as does *M. sanguinolenta*; *M. galopus* (p.137) exudes a white liquid.

gills almost free

liquid mainly stored in stem

immature fruit-bodies

conical to convex cap with an umbo

SECTION

saffron-orange liquid

stiff orange hairs at base

FRUITING A few together or in troops of fruitbodies.

Dimensions CAP ⊕ 1–3cm	STEM ↕ 5–12cm ↔ 1–3mm	Spores Pale cream	Edibility

Family TRICHOLOMATACEAE	Species *Mycena polygramma*	Season Autumn–early winter

GRAY-LINED MYCENA

This fairly large, tough-fleshed *Mycena* species has a silvery stem with distinct grooves along its length. The pale gray to gray-brown cap is umbonate with radiating wrinkles on the dry surface. The off-white flesh is almost odorless. Occasionally forms that are entirely white can be found.
• **OCCURRENCE** In woods, attached to buried deciduous wood and around stumps; also on the base of living trees; occasionally on conifers. Widespread; common in Europe and adjacent Asia; also found in Japan and eastern North America.
• **SIMILAR SPECIES** *M. vitilis* is smaller with an equally tough, smooth, shiny stem. It occurs in the same habitat and is more common. *M. galericulata* (p.116) is even tougher and has a smooth stem.

umbonate cap is pale gray to gray-brown

SECTION

fairly crowded gills

off-white flesh

adnexed, white to pale gray gills can stain pink with age

wrinkles on dry cap surface

grooves along silvery stem

FRUITING Appears singly or in small groups.

Dimensions CAP ⊕ 1–4cm	STEM ↕ 5–12cm ↔ 2–4mm	Spores White	Edibility

WITH CRUMBLY FLESH

T HE SPECIES FEATURED in this sub-section all belong to the genus *Russula*, and all have adnexed to adnate gills and crumbly flesh. The crumbly flesh is created by round tissue cells that are grouped in "nests" in the flesh. Russulas are very similar in appearance to the *Lactarius* (pp.43–55), which also have flesh that is crumbly. However, *Lactarius* species exude a milky liquid when cut and tend to have decurrent gills. Most *Russula* species have brighter-colored fruitbodies than those of the *Lactarius*.

All *Russula* species form mycorrhizal relationships (see pp.18–19) with trees or, in a few cases, shrubs and herbaceous plants. As a rule, mild-tasting russulas are edible, while those that taste hot are considered poisonous.

Family RUSSULACEAE	Species *Russula delica*	Season Summer–autumn

MILK WHITE RUSSULA

This is a large species, with a funnel-shaped cap, stout stem, and firm white flesh. Soil and leaf litter often stick to it, hiding its creamy white coloring. The well-spaced white gills may have a turquoise sheen. This species is known in North America as *Russula brevipes*.
• **OCCURRENCE** Mycorrhizal with coniferous and deciduous trees on well-drained soil. It is widespread and common in many parts of northern temperate zones.
• **SIMILAR SPECIES** *R. brevipes* var. *acrior* has more crowded gills, often with a turquoise zone around the stem top. *Lactarius vellereus* (p.44) is usually larger with a felted cap surface and white milk.

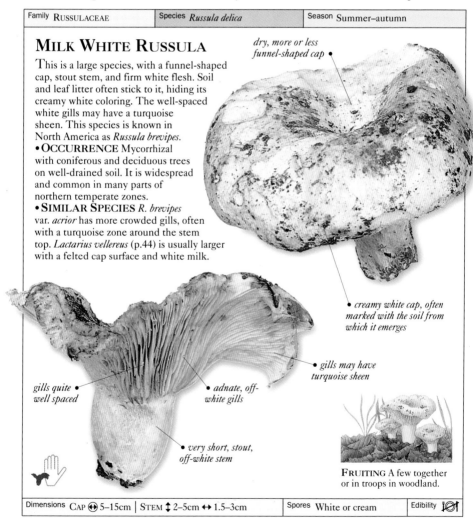

dry, more or less funnel-shaped cap •

• *creamy white cap, often marked with the soil from which it emerges*

• *gills may have turquoise sheen*

gills quite • *well spaced*

• *adnate, off-white gills*

• *very short, stout, off-white stem*

FRUITING A few together or in troops in woodland.

Dimensions CAP ⊕ 5–15cm | STEM ↕ 2–5cm ↔ 1.5–3cm	Spores White or cream	Edibility

Family RUSSULACEAE	Species *Russula foetens*	Season Summer–autumn

FETID RUSSULA

This rancid-smelling species has a fleshy, convex, greasy, orange-brown cap with a grooved margin. Its white stem, stained brown at the base, is short and almost barrel-shaped. The crumbly, very hot-tasting flesh is off-white and may be stained brown.
• **OCCURRENCE** Mycorrhizal with conifers and deciduous trees in woods. Widespread and common in many areas of northern temperate zones.
• **SIMILAR SPECIES** *Russula laurocerasi* smells of marzipan. *R. illota* has a rancid, slightly almondy smell and dark gill edges. The flesh of *R. subfoetens* stains yellow with potassium hydroxide (KOH). *R. foetens* has no reaction.

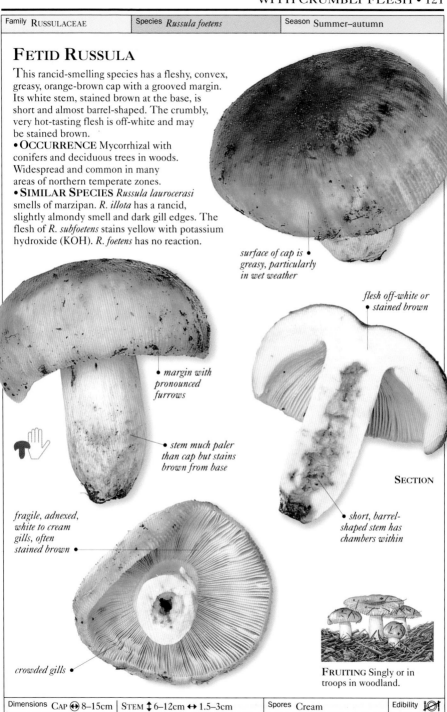

surface of cap is greasy, particularly in wet weather

flesh off-white or stained brown

margin with pronounced furrows

stem much paler than cap but stains brown from base

SECTION

fragile, adnexed, white to cream gills, often stained brown

short, barrel-shaped stem has chambers within

crowded gills

FRUITING Singly or in troops in woodland.

| Dimensions CAP ⊕ 8–15cm | STEM ↕ 6–12cm ↔ 1.5–3cm | Spores Cream | Edibility |

Family RUSSULACEAE	Species *Russula nigricans*	Season Summer–autumn

BLACKENING RUSSULA

This large species has an off-white to sooty brown cap with a depressed center, and a sturdy stem. The crumbly but firm flesh is off-white when cut, slowly turning red and then completely black. It tastes mild to bitter. Unlike most *Russula* species, the gills are of different lengths. Dried-up black fruitbodies persist until the following year.

• OCCURRENCE Mycorrhizal with deciduous trees and conifers, on well-drained soil. Widespread and common in many areas of northern temperate zones.

• SIMILAR SPECIES *R. albonigra* stains black (no red); *R. adusta* stains red then gray and tastes mild. *R. anthracina* and *R. acrifolia* have hot-tasting gills. *R. densifolia* has crowded gills and is smaller.

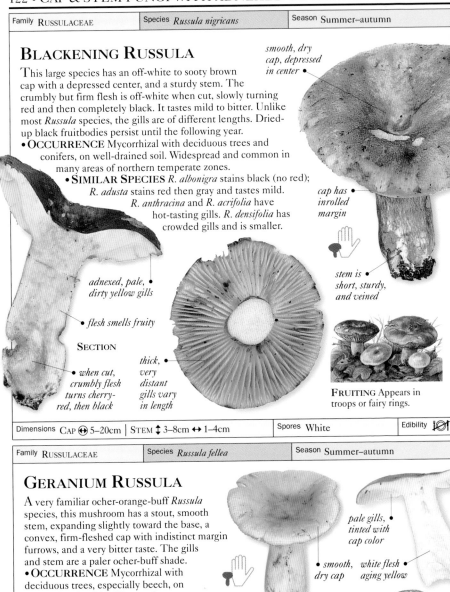

smooth, dry cap, depressed in center

cap has inrolled margin

stem is short, sturdy, and veined

adnexed, pale, dirty yellow gills

flesh smells fruity

SECTION

when cut, crumbly flesh turns cherry-red, then black

thick, very distant gills vary in length

FRUITING Appears in troops or fairy rings.

Dimensions CAP ⊕ 5–20cm | STEM ↕ 3–8cm ↔ 1–4cm	Spores White	Edibility

Family RUSSULACEAE	Species *Russula fellea*	Season Summer–autumn

GERANIUM RUSSULA

A very familiar ocher-orange-buff *Russula* species, this mushroom has a stout, smooth stem, expanding slightly toward the base, a convex, firm-fleshed cap with indistinct margin furrows, and a very bitter taste. The gills and stem are a paler ocher-buff shade.

• OCCURRENCE Mycorrhizal with deciduous trees, especially beech, on well-drained, acid soil in woods. Widespread in Europe; in North America it is represented by its close relative *R. simillima*.

• SIMILAR SPECIES *R. farinipes* has paler gills, stronger marginal grooves, and a powdery stem surface.

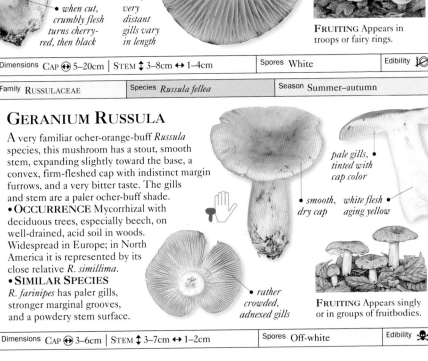

pale gills, tinted with cap color

smooth, dry cap   *white flesh aging yellow*

rather crowded, adnexed gills

FRUITING Appears singly or in groups of fruitbodies.

Dimensions CAP ⊕ 3–6cm | STEM ↕ 3–7cm ↔ 1–2cm	Spores Off-white	Edibility ☠

| Family RUSSULACEAE | Species *Russula claroflava* | Season Summer–autumn |

GRAYING YELLOW RUSSULA

This highly attractive, brightly colored species has a convex to flat, vivid yellow cap and edible, mild-tasting, firm white flesh. The gills are pale yellow and mainly full length (all reaching the stem). Both the flesh and the smooth, cylindrical to barrel-shaped white stem turn gray with age or when bruised.

• **OCCURRENCE** Mycorrhizal with birch in very damp or boggy woodland, where the soil may be so wet that sphagnum moss covers the ground. Widespread and common in northern temperate zones.

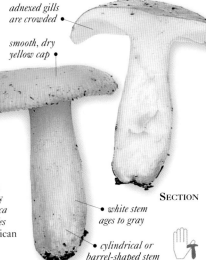

adnexed gills are crowded

smooth, dry yellow cap

SECTION

white stem ages to gray

cylindrical or barrel-shaped stem

• **SIMILAR SPECIES** *Russula claroflava* has a stem that grays strongly on bruising. *R. ochroleuca* (below). *R. ochroleucoides* is a bitter-tasting American equivalent, growing in East Coast oak woods.

FRUITING Appears singly or in troops of fruitbodies.

| Dimensions CAP ⊕ 5–10cm | STEM ↕ 4–10cm ↔ 1–2cm | Spores Ochre | Edibility |

| Family RUSSULACEAE | Species *Russula ochroleuca* | Season Summer–autumn |

YELLOW-OCHER RUSSULA

One of the most common woodland agarics, this species is marked by the matte ocher-yellow coloring of its convex cap and its white gills. The cap sometimes has a green tinge. The barrel-shaped stem is white with a buff base, and the crumbly white flesh has a completely bland taste.

• **OCCURRENCE** Mycorrhizal with both conifers and deciduous trees in well-drained soil in woods. Widespread in northern temperate zones; common in Europe and parts of Asia.

• **SIMILAR SPECIES** *Russula fellea* (p.122) and *R. claroflava* (above).

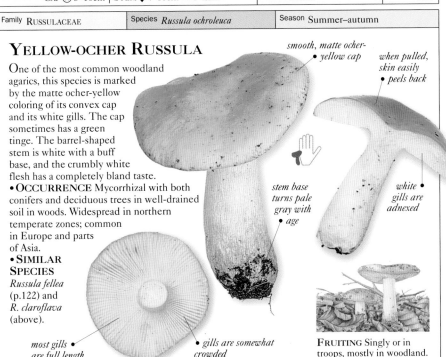

smooth, matte ocher-yellow cap

when pulled, skin easily peels back

stem base turns pale gray with age

white gills are adnexed

most gills are full length

gills are somewhat crowded

FRUITING Singly or in troops, mostly in woodland.

| Dimensions CAP ⊕ 5–12cm | STEM ↕ 3–8cm ↔ 1–2.5cm | Spores White | Edibility |

Family RUSSULACEAE	Species *Russula cyanoxantha*	Season Summer–autumn

VARIABLE RUSSULA

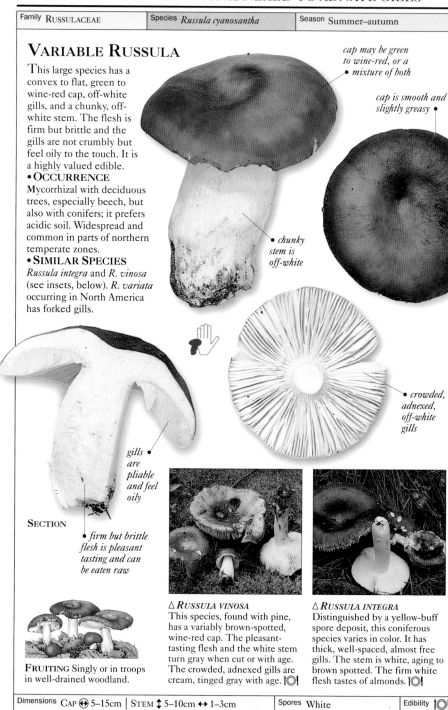

This large species has a convex to flat, green to wine-red cap, off-white gills, and a chunky, off-white stem. The flesh is firm but brittle and the gills are not crumbly but feel oily to the touch. It is a highly valued edible.

• **OCCURRENCE**
Mycorrhizal with deciduous trees, especially beech, but also with conifers; it prefers acidic soil. Widespread and common in parts of northern temperate zones.

• **SIMILAR SPECIES**
Russula integra and *R. vinosa* (see insets, below). *R. variata* occurring in North America has forked gills.

cap may be green to wine-red, or a • mixture of both

cap is smooth and slightly greasy •

• chunky stem is off-white

• crowded, adnexed, off-white gills

gills • are pliable and feel oily

SECTION

• firm but brittle flesh is pleasant tasting and can be eaten raw

FRUITING Singly or in troops in well-drained woodland.

△ *RUSSULA VINOSA*
This species, found with pine, has a variably brown-spotted, wine-red cap. The pleasant-tasting flesh and the white stem turn gray when cut or with age. The crowded, adnexed gills are cream, tinged gray with age. |O|

△ *RUSSULA INTEGRA*
Distinguished by a yellow-buff spore deposit, this coniferous species varies in color. It has thick, well-spaced, almost free gills. The stem is white, aging to brown spotted. The firm white flesh tastes of almonds. |O|

Dimensions CAP ⊕ 5–15cm | STEM ↕ 5–10cm ↔ 1–3cm	Spores White	Edibility |O|

Family RUSSULACEAE	Species *Russula vesca*	Season Summer–autumn

BARE-TOOTHED RUSSULA

This distinctive species owes its
common name to the white gills that
are clearly visible at the cap margin.
The flattened-convex to depressed
cap is pale wine-red, mixed with
brown, and rust-brown spots often
mark the pointed, off-white stem
base. The edible, firm white flesh
has a nutty taste.
• OCCURRENCE Mycorrhizal
with conifers and deciduous trees
in well-drained woods.
Widespread in northern
temperate zones;
common in Europe.

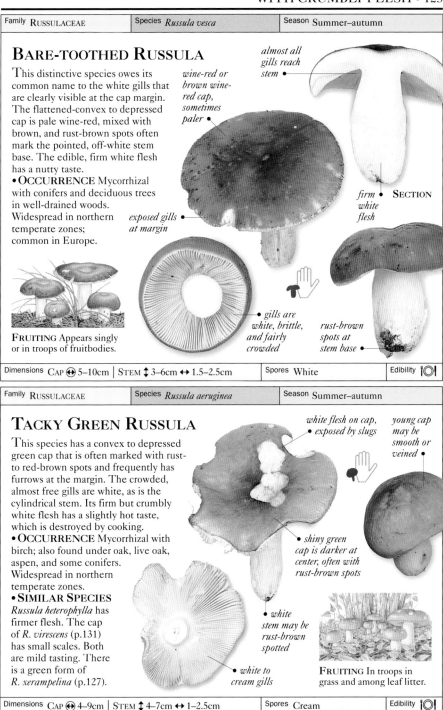

*almost all
gills reach
stem*

*wine-red or
brown wine-
red cap,
sometimes
paler*

firm • SECTION
*white
flesh*

*exposed gills
at margin*

FRUITING Appears singly
or in troops of fruitbodies.

*gills are
white, brittle,
and fairly
crowded*

*rust-brown
spots at
stem base*

Dimensions CAP ⊕ 5–10cm	STEM ↕ 3–6cm ↔ 1.5–2.5cm	Spores White	Edibility

Family RUSSULACEAE	Species *Russula aeruginea*	Season Summer–autumn

TACKY GREEN RUSSULA

This species has a convex to depressed
green cap that is often marked with rust-
to red-brown spots and frequently has
furrows at the margin. The crowded,
almost free gills are white, as is the
cylindrical stem. Its firm but crumbly
white flesh has a slightly hot taste,
which is destroyed by cooking.
• OCCURRENCE Mycorrhizal with
birch; also found under oak, live oak,
aspen, and some conifers.
Widespread in northern
temperate zones.
• SIMILAR SPECIES
Russula heterophylla has
firmer flesh. The cap
of *R. virescens* (p.131)
has small scales. Both
are mild tasting. There
is a green form of
R. xerampelina (p.127).

*white flesh on cap,
exposed by slugs*

*young cap
may be
smooth or
veined*

*shiny green
cap is darker at
center; often with
rust-brown spots*

*white
stem may be
rust-brown
spotted*

*white to
cream gills*

FRUITING In troops in
grass and among leaf litter.

Dimensions CAP ⊕ 4–9cm	STEM ↕ 4–7cm ↔ 1–2.5cm	Spores Cream	Edibility

| Family RUSSULACEAE | Species *Russula puellaris* | Season Summer–autumn |

YELLOW-STAINING RUSSULA

The convex to depressed cap of this fragile species is purplish to reddish brown, possibly even almost black at the center with a paler margin. It takes on ocher-yellow hues with age and when bruised. From the cap margin, the skin can be peeled back almost to the center. It is a mediocre edible, with odorless, thin, mild white flesh.

• **OCCURRENCE** Mycorrhizal with conifers and deciduous trees. Widespread in northern temperate zones in Europe and northern North America.

• **SIMILAR SPECIES** *Russula odorata* has a strong, fruity smell and grows mostly with oak trees. *R. versicolor* has a hot taste and stains only slightly.

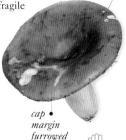

shiny, slightly greasy cap

adnexed to free gills

stem spongy in center, firm at surface

SECTION

cap margin furrowed

white flesh stains orange-yellow

medium-spaced gills

cream to ocher-yellow gills

FRUITING Scattered or in troops in damp woods.

| Dimensions CAP ⊕ 3–6cm | STEM ↕ 3–6cm ↔ 0.7–1.5cm | Spores Dark cream | Edibility |

| Family RUSSULACEAE | Species *Russula rosea* | Season Summer–autumn |

ROSY FIRM RUSSULA

Very hard flesh and a cap of a diluted red color, with very thin, nonpeeling skin, make this russula easy to identify among the many reddish-colored *Russula* species. It has a rather short, cylindrical to club-shaped stem, either white or the color of the convex to flat cap. Its taste has been compared to the wood of a pencil. There is disagreement over its name and many experts prefer to call it *R. lepida*.

• **OCCURRENCE** Often mycorrhizal with beech, it is found on well-drained soil in deciduous woods. Widespread and common in European beech woods; reported in northeastern North America.

• **SIMILAR SPECIES** *R. velutipes* has peelable cap skin and more fragile flesh.

dry cap is diluted red and matte with non-peeling skin

stem flesh is hard but crumbly

nearly free, pale cream gills may have pinkish edges

FRUITING Singly or in troops on woodland soil.

medium-spaced gills are brittle

stem either off-white or tinted with cap color

| Dimensions CAP ⊕ 4–12cm | STEM ↕ 3–8cm ↔ 1–3cm | Spores Pale cream | Edibility |

Family RUSSULACEAE	Species *Russula turci*	Season Summer–autumn

IODINE RUSSULA

This species has a cap with a depressed center and a smooth margin, which may have a fine dustlike coating. It is colored in shades of wine-red, sometimes mixed with green, black, or orange. A distinct smell of iodine, especially at the base of the club-shaped stem, along with a pale ocher spore deposit, helps to identify it. The crumbly white flesh has a mild taste.

• OCCURRENCE Mycorrhizal with pine trees (mainly two-needled species) and possibly also with spruce. Widespread in Europe and also across northern North America.

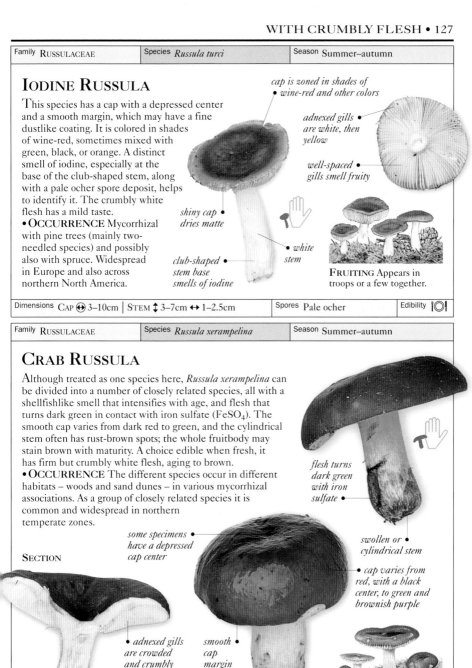

cap is zoned in shades of wine-red and other colors

adnexed gills are white, then yellow

well-spaced gills smell fruity

shiny cap dries matte

white stem

club-shaped stem base smells of iodine

FRUITING Appears in troops or a few together.

Dimensions CAP ⊕ 3–10cm	STEM ↕ 3–7cm ↔ 1–2.5cm	Spores Pale ocher	Edibility 🍽

Family RUSSULACEAE	Species *Russula xerampelina*	Season Summer–autumn

CRAB RUSSULA

Although treated as one species here, *Russula xerampelina* can be divided into a number of closely related species, all with a shellfishlike smell that intensifies with age, and flesh that turns dark green in contact with iron sulfate ($FeSO_4$). The smooth cap varies from dark red to green, and the cylindrical stem often has rust-brown spots; the whole fruitbody may stain brown with maturity. A choice edible when fresh, it has firm but crumbly white flesh, aging to brown.

• OCCURRENCE The different species occur in different habitats – woods and sand dunes – in various mycorrhizal associations. As a group of closely related species it is common and widespread in northern temperate zones.

flesh turns dark green with iron sulfate

swollen or cylindrical stem

cap varies from red, with a black center, to green and brownish purple

SECTION

some specimens have a depressed cap center

smooth cap margin

adnexed gills are crowded and crumbly

white flesh, staining brown with age

white, pink, or red stem

FRUITING In troops under willow or pine trees.

Dimensions CAP ⊕ 6–15cm	STEM ↕ 4–8cm ↔ 1.5–3cm	Spores Ocher	Edibility 🍽

Family RUSSULACEAE	Species *Russula paludosa*	Season Summer–autumn

TALL BOG RUSSULA

Taller than most, this large, attractive *Russula* species has a convex to depressed, orange-red cap, with yellow discoloration in the center and a slightly sticky surface when damp. The crowded, adnexed gills are off-white. Both the gill edges and the cap margin are often red. The cylindrical to narrowly club-shaped stem is white, flushed pink, and turns slightly gray with age. It is good to eat, with firm, crumbly, mild-tasting flesh, but see SIMILAR SPECIES.

• **OCCURRENCE** Mycorrhizal with conifers, especially pine. Widespread and locally common in northern temperate zones.

• **SIMILAR SPECIES** The poisonous and hot-tasting *R. emetica* (below) has no yellow coloring on the cap.

cap surface is slightly sticky when wet

crowded, off-white gills

cap discolors to yellow in center

cap margin may be red

white stem is flushed pink, gray with age

FRUITING Appears in troops or scattered under conifers often in boggy areas.

Dimensions CAP ⊕ 8–16cm │ STEM ↕ 10–15cm ↔ 1–3cm	Spores Pale ocher	Edibility ⏺

Family RUSSULACEAE	Species *Russula emetica*	Season Summer–autumn

EMETIC RUSSULA

This species has a convex to slightly depressed, scarlet-red cap, the surface of which is smooth and often shiny, becoming sticky when wet. Its white stem is club-shaped with a scurfy skin. The crumbly, odorless white flesh has a very hot taste, which soon alerts an unwary eater, but in any case it is not highly poisonous.

• **OCCURRENCE** Mycorrhizal, mainly with coniferous trees in boggy areas. Widespread and common in northern temperate zones.

• **SIMILAR SPECIES** *Russula silvicola* is the common dry woodland species across North America. *R. fageticola* usually grows under beech and also tastes hot. *Amanita muscaria* (p.146) has veil patches on the cap, a stem ring, and a bulb.

convex to slightly depressed, smooth and often shiny, scarlet-red cap

slightly scurfy, club-shaped stem

faintly furrowed margin

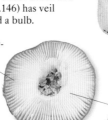

medium-spaced gills

adnexed to free, white to pale cream gills

FRUITING In troops or singly in damp sites under conifers.

Dimensions CAP ⊕ 3–8cm │ STEM ↕ 5–8cm ↔ 1–2cm	Spores White	Edibility

| Family RUSSULACEAE | Species *Russula mairei* | Season Summer–autumn |

EURO EMETIC RUSSULA

The smooth, matte, strongly scarlet-red cap of this species is convex to flat and sticky when wet. The club-shaped, off-white stem has a smooth surface. Its crumbly poisonous flesh is firm and white and smells slightly sweet.
• OCCURRENCE Mycorrhizal with beech trees in woods. Widespread and common in the beechwood regions of Europe and adjacent parts of Asia.
• SIMILAR SPECIES *Russula emetica* (p.128). *R. velenovskyi*, which is edible, is smaller, and typically occurs near birch.

• *convex cap of vivid scarlet-red*

smooth, matte cap surface, damaged by slugs •

slightly club-shaped stem •

adnexed, brittle gills •

smooth, off-white stem •

• *medium-spaced, often glaucous blue-tinged, white gills*

FRUITING In troops or singly in well-drained beech woods.

| Dimensions CAP ⊕ 3–7cm │ STEM ↕ 3–5cm ↔ 0.7–2cm | Spores White | Edibility ☠ |

| Family RUSSULACEAE | Species *Russula fragilis* | Season Summer–autumn |

FRAGILE RUSSULA

A small species, the Fragile Russula is best identified with a hand lens, which will reveal the serrated edges of its white to cream gills. The convex to depressed cap is a mixture of reds and purples, with a touch of olive-green; the colors are darkest in the center. The slightly club-shaped stem is white. The crumbly white flesh tastes very hot and is poisonous.
• OCCURRENCE Mycorrhizal with a variety of trees, often birch and oak, in woods. Widespread and locally common in northern temperate zones.

• *gill edges are serrated*

• *cap purple, purplish red, or with olive-green tint*

depressed dark cap center •

medium-spaced, white to cream gills •

adnexed gills •

SECTION

cap margin slightly furrowed •

slightly club-shaped white stem •

FRUITING In troops or small groups, rarely singly.

| Dimensions CAP ⊕ 2–5cm │ STEM ↕ 3–7cm ↔ 0.5–2cm | Spores White | Edibility ☠ |

Family RUSSULACEAE	Species *Russula sanguinea*	Season Summer–autumn

BLOOD-RED RUSSULA

Known as *Russula rosacea* in North America, this slightly poisonous species has a convex to depressed blood-red cap and a red-streaked stem that turns grayish pink with age. It has crumbly white flesh and can be identified by its moderately hot taste and the pale ocher color of its spore deposit.

• OCCURRENCE Mycorrhizal with conifers, mostly pine. Widespread in northern temperate zones.

• SIMILAR SPECIES *Russula helodes* has a lighter stem that turns a more distinct gray with age; often found in sphagnum moss.

gills may be slightly decurrent •

cap with thin, blood-red skin •

cylindrical • to tapering stem

SECTION

• crumbly white flesh

crowded • gills

stem is • streaked blood-red, and ages to grayish pink

fragile, cream to ocher gills

FRUITING Appears singly or in troops on acid soil.

Dimensions CAP ⊕ 5–10cm | STEM ↕ 4–7cm ↔ 1–2cm	Spores Pale ocher	Edibility ☠

Family RUSSULACEAE	Species *Russula atropurpurea*	Season Summer–autumn

SPRING RUSSULA

This rather fleshy species has a convex cap, the usually depressed center of which is almost black; the rest of the cap surface is purple or violet, often spotted yellow. The cap color contrasts strongly with the white to cream stem and gills. The stem is fairly short and club-shaped, and the gills are crowded and adnexed. The white to gray flesh is slightly hot tasting and inedible.

• OCCURRENCE Mycorrhizal with oak trees, rarely found with other trees. Widespread in northern temperate zones.

• SIMILAR SPECIES *Russula brunneoviolacea* has a darker spore deposit, as does *R. romellii*.

center of cap is almost black •

purple or violet cap may have yellow spots •

short, white to cream stem •

adnexed gills are white to cream and crowded •

FRUITING In troops beneath oak trees, mostly on acidic soil, in woodland sites.

Dimensions CAP ⊕ 4–10cm | STEM ↕ 3–6cm ↔ 1–2.5cm	Spores White	Edibility

Family RUSSULACEAE	Species *Russula sardonia*	Season Summer–autumn

PUNGENT RUSSULA

An attractive, comparatively large species with a convex, shiny dark purple cap and contrasting lemon-yellow gills; its purple to wine-red stem is club-shaped. It actually has a slightly fruity smell and a hot taste. The gills and white flesh turn pink when they come in contact with ammonia vapor.

• **OCCURRENCE** Mycorrhizal strictly with pine trees. Widespread and common in regions of northern temperate zones; western US.

• **SIMILAR SPECIES** *Russula queletii* is smaller, with paler gills, a paler spore deposit, and tastes just as hot. It does not react to ammonia.

dark purple to rich wine-red cap

smooth, shiny, convex cap

adnexed to slightly decurrent gills

crowded, lemon-yellow to ocher gills

purple to wine-red stem with hint of gray

FRUITING In troops under pine trees.

Dimensions CAP ⊕ 4–10cm | STEM ↕ 4–10cm ↔ 1–2.5cm	Spores Pale ocher	Edibility ☠

Family RUSSULACEAE	Species *Russula virescens*	Season Summer–autumn

GREEN QUILT RUSSULA

This firm-fleshed species is best identified by the velvety, yellow- to blue-green cap surface, which soon cracks, creating a scaly appearance. The stem is white but the base develops a brown-scaly surface. The brittle white gills are fairly crowded and adnexed. This mushroom turns orange-pink in contact with iron sulphate (FeSO₄).

• **OCCURRENCE** Mycorrhizal with deciduous trees, such as beech. Widespread and locally common in northern temperate zones.

• **SIMILAR SPECIES** *Russula crustosa* has orange tones in its cap and has an orange-yellow spore print.

convex to flat cap feels velvety

cap surface cracks, creating scales

blue-green to yellow or cream cap

white stem with brown-scaly base

FRUITING Appears singly or in small groups of fruitbodies on well-drained soil.

Dimensions CAP ⊕ 4–10cm | STEM ↕ 4–8cm ↔ 1–3cm	Spores White	Edibility

VERY SMALL WITH SMOOTH CAP

T HERE ARE MANY small agarics with smooth caps, and they belong to an extremely wide range of genera and families, although, in this book, it is the small, gilled, white-spored members of the Tricholomataceae that predominate. Species included here may have a fine bloom on the cap but never have distinct hairs, coarse fibers, or scales (see pp.142–144).

Family TRICHOLOMATACEAE	Species *Lyophyllum palustre*	Season Summer–autumn

BOG LYOPHYLLUM

On a thin, pale gray-brown stem, the grayish brown cap of this species is convex, expanding to flat or slightly depressed. The cap surface is striated from the margin to its center, and it has inedible, thin flesh, which smells faintly of yeast. The white to pale gray gills are adnexed and medium spaced.
• **OCCURRENCE** Found only in boggy locations on sphagnum moss, which it kills. Widespread throughout northern temperate zones; in eastern North American bogs.
• **SIMILAR SPECIES** Other species found with sphagnum moss, such as *Galerina paludosa*, *G. tibiicystis*, *Omphalina sphagnicola*, and *O. philonotis*, usually have brown spores or decurrent gills.

cap is convex to flat or depressed • *long, rooting stem is gray-brown •* *striations from margin to cap • center*

FRUITING Appears in troops or fairy rings on sphagnum moss in boggy areas.

Dimensions CAP ⊕ 1–3cm	STEM ↕ 4–8cm ↔ 1–3mm	Spores White	Edibility 🖐⊘

Family TRICHOLOMATACEAE	Species *Baeospora myosura*	Season Autumn–late autumn

CROWDED-GILL CONE COLLYBIA

This pale brown member of the small genus *Baeospora* has a flat to slightly umbonate, dry cap and a powder-covered stem. It has a musty smell and indistinct taste. The gills are almost free.
• **OCCURRENCE** In parks and woods on cones and cone scales from various conifers, including spruce and pine. Widespread and common in northern temperate zones.
• **SIMILAR SPECIES** *B. myriadophylla* is also pale brown but has brighter, more or less lilac gills. It grows mainly on fallen trunks of conifers and is rare or absent in most regions. Other mushrooms found on conifer cones include *Strobilurus esculentus* (p.133) and *Mycena seyneii*, which has a pale wine-pink cap and dark red-brown gill edges.

crowded, fairly narrow, • pale gray gills

adnexed • or free gills

dry, pale brown • cap surface SECTION

FRUITING A few on a cone or singly on detached scales.

Dimensions CAP ⊕ 0.5–2cm	STEM ↕ 1–4cm ↔ 1–2mm	Spores White	Edibility 🖐⊘

Family TRICHOLOMATACEAE	Species *Strobilurus esculentus*	Season Late autumn–spring

DISTANT-GILL CONE COLLYBIA

This small agaric has a convex brown cap with a thin margin and a smooth, orange-yellow stem, white near the top. The tough white flesh smells pleasant. It is edible but not worthwhile because it is so small.
• OCCURRENCE Only on fallen spruce cones; on cones that are above ground in damp areas. Widespread and common in European and Asian spruce regions; not reported in North America.
• SIMILAR SPECIES *Strobilurus stephanocystis* and *S. tenacellus* favor pine cones. Small *Collybia* species (pp.67, 111–113), differ in various microcscopic features.

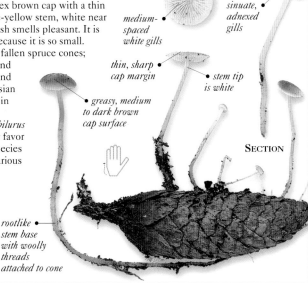

medium-
spaced
white gills •

thin, sharp •
cap margin

sinuate, •
adnexed
gills

• stem tip
is white

• greasy, medium
to dark brown
cap surface

SECTION

FRUITING In small groups in spruce forests.

rootlike •
stem base
with woolly
threads
attached to cone

Dimensions CAP ⊕ 0.5–3cm | STEM ↕ 2–5cm ↔ 1–2.5mm	Spores Pale cream	Edibility

Family TRICHOLOMATACEAE	Species *Mycena inclinata*	Season Summer–early winter

CLUSTERED OAK MYCENA

The bell-shaped cap of this species has a toothed margin and radial striations; the tough stem has a white powdery covering and an orange-brown base. Identification is helped by the characteristic spicy to rancid smell.
• OCCURRENCE Prefers mature trees in ancient forests. Mostly found on stumps or dead parts of standing oak trees; sometimes on such deciduous trees as sweet chestnut. Widespread and common in Europe and North America.
• SIMILAR SPECIES *Mycena maculata* has an earthy smell, a smooth cap margin, and a purplish brown stem. It is rarer but also tends to be overlooked.

reddish stains •
on lead-gray to
whitish
gray
cap

tough
stem with
powdery
surface •

SECTION

dark
orange-
brown base •

adnexed •
gills

crowded,
white to
pink gills •

• paler stem
of young
specimen

FRUITING Appears in clusters of fruitbodies on wood.

Dimensions CAP ⊕ 1–4cm | STEM ↕ 6–12cm ↔ 2–3mm	Spores Pale cream	Edibility

Family TRICHOLOMATACEAE	Species *Mycena arcangeliana*	Season Autumn–early winter

LATE-SEASON MYCENA

This species is not easy to identify in the field, although the young fruitbodies often have a lilac stem. The cap can be any shape from convex to bell-like, in various shades of dull gray. If put inside an airtight can, a strong, antiseptic, iodine-like smell will become noticeable in a few minutes.

• **OCCURRENCE** In gardens, cemeteries, parks, and rich woods, on mossy bark at the base of living trees or bushes, or on woody debris, such as fallen branches. Widespread and common in Europe; rare but widespread in North America.

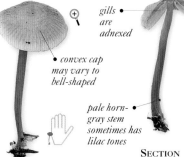

gills • are adnexed

• *convex cap may vary to bell-shaped*

pale horn-gray stem sometimes has lilac tones

SECTION

stem has smooth • surface

dry gray cap • surface may have faint pink or olive hues

FRUITING Often in troops on varied woody debris.

fairly crowded, • white to pink gills

Dimensions CAP ⊕ 1–2.5cm | STEM ↕ 3–7cm ↔ 2–3mm	Spores White	Edibility

Family TRICHOLOMATACEAE	Species *Mycena olivaceomarginata*	Season Autumn

EURO FIELD MYCENA

Occurring in a wide range of cap colors from gray-brown to yellow or shades of pink, this mushroom is most easily identified by using a hand lens. This reveals a distinctive, olive-brown edge to the adnate gills. It has a fairly fragile stem, thin flesh, and, like many *Mycena* species, smells weakly of radishes; some forms smell faintly of chlorine.

• **OCCURRENCE** On mossy turf and in cut or grazed grassland, including open parks and coastal areas. Widespread and common in Europe; not reported in North America.

• **SIMILAR SPECIES** Other *Mycena* species have colored gill edges: red – *M. rubromarginata*, found on wood, and *M. seyneii*, found on cones; yellow – *M. citrinomarginata* and *M. flavescens*, occuring in grass or woodland litter.

• *convex to conical cap*

gills are sinuate, adnate •

fairly fragile, hollow stem •

stem gray-brown or in paler tones of cap color

radial striations on cap •

brown or gray cap, sometimes with yellow or pink tints •

SECTION

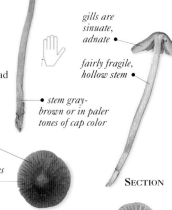

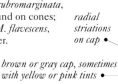

FRUITING Singly or in troops in short grass.

• *fine olive-brown gill edge*

medium-spaced, • pale gray to gray-brown gills

Dimensions CAP ⊕ 0.7–1.5cm | STEM ↕ 3–6cm ↔ 1–2mm	Spores White	Edibility

Family TRICHOLOMATACEAE	Species *Mycena epipterygia*	Season Summer–early winter

YELLOW-STALKED MYCENA

One of the comparatively few slimy *Mycena* species, *M. epipterygia* is identified by its vivid yellow stem, often tinged rusty brown, but otherwise quite variable in size, shape, and coloring. The smell is typically somewhat yeasty and rancid.
• **OCCURRENCE** On plant litter, mostly in coniferous woods; also in more open habitats on acidic soil with brambles and bracken. Widespread and common in northern temperate zones.
• **SIMILAR SPECIES** Other slimy *Mycena* species include *M. rorida*, the most slimy, which has a thick, slimy stem covering, thicker than the stem itself, and the slightly slimy-stemmed *M. belliae*, which grows only on reeds and has strongly decurrent gills.

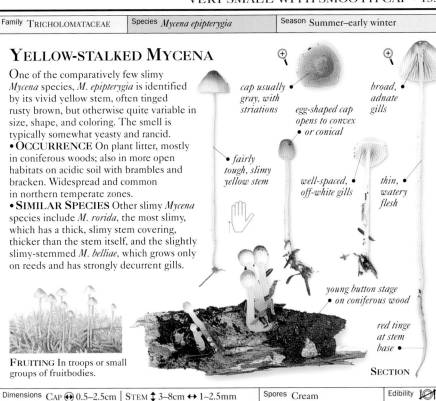

cap usually gray, with striations •

egg-shaped cap opens to convex • or conical

broad, • adnate gills

• *fairly tough, slimy yellow stem*

well-spaced, off-white gills

thin, • watery flesh

young button stage • on coniferous wood

red tinge at stem base •

SECTION

FRUITING In troops or small groups of fruitbodies.

Dimensions CAP ⊕ 0.5–2.5cm	STEM ↕ 3–8cm ↔ 1–2.5mm	Spores Cream	Edibility

Family TRICHOLOMATACEAE	Species *Mycena leptocephala*	Season Summer–winter

CHLORINE LAWN MYCENA

The bell-shaped to conical, pale gray to lead-gray cap of this species is distinctly striate when moist. The stem is rather fragile, as is the watery flesh. This is by far the most common of a group of *Mycena* species that smell similar to bleach or chlorinated water.
• **OCCURRENCE** On mossy lawns and among tall grasses, woodland litter, or brambles. Widespread and common throughout northern temperate zones.
• **SIMILAR SPECIES** *M. abramsii* is larger with a less greasy cap. In North America, *M. alcalina* is a complex of species growing on decaying conifer wood. *M. capillaripes* has red gill lining (seen when viewed under a hand lens) and grows on conifer debris. All smell of chlorine.

striations on pale gray to lead-gray • cap surface

• *stem top has powdery covering*

SECTION

• *smooth, pale horn-gray stem*

adnexed • gills

fragile, watery • flesh smells like chlorinated water

• *medium-spaced, pale gray gills*

FRUITING Singly or often in troops on mossy lawns.

Dimensions CAP ⊕ 0.6–1.5cm	STEM ↕ 3–7cm ↔ 1–2mm	Spores White	Edibility

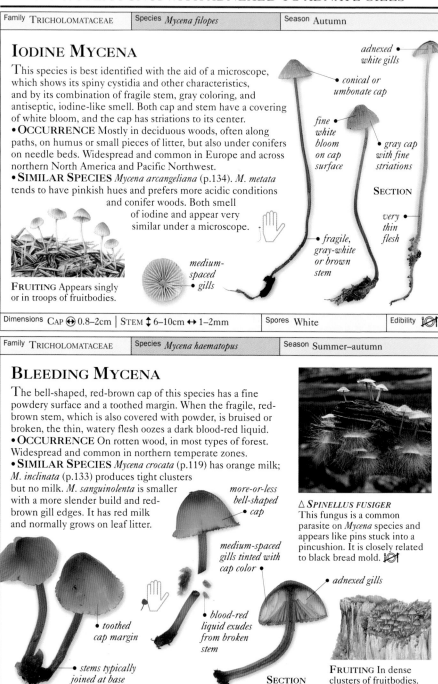

| Family TRICHOLOMATACEAE | Species *Mycena filopes* | Season Autumn |

IODINE MYCENA

This species is best identified with the aid of a microscope, which shows its spiny cystidia and other characteristics, and by its combination of fragile stem, gray coloring, and antiseptic, iodine-like smell. Both cap and stem have a covering of white bloom, and the cap has striations to its center.
• **OCCURRENCE** Mostly in deciduous woods, often along paths, on humus or small pieces of litter, but also under conifers on needle beds. Widespread and common in Europe and across northern North America and Pacific Northwest.
• **SIMILAR SPECIES** *Mycena arcangeliana* (p.134). *M. metata* tends to have pinkish hues and prefers more acidic conditions and conifer woods. Both smell of iodine and appear very similar under a microscope.

adnexed • white gills

• conical or umbonate cap

fine • white bloom on cap surface

• gray cap with fine striations

SECTION

very • thin flesh

• fragile, gray-white or brown stem

medium-spaced • gills

FRUITING Appears singly or in troops of fruitbodies.

| Dimensions CAP ⊕ 0.8–2cm | STEM ↕ 6–10cm ↔ 1–2mm | Spores White | Edibility |

| Family TRICHOLOMATACEAE | Species *Mycena haematopus* | Season Summer–autumn |

BLEEDING MYCENA

The bell-shaped, red-brown cap of this species has a fine powdery surface and a toothed margin. When the fragile, red-brown stem, which is also covered with powder, is bruised or broken, the thin, watery flesh oozes a dark blood-red liquid.
• **OCCURRENCE** On rotten wood, in most types of forest. Widespread and common in northern temperate zones.
• **SIMILAR SPECIES** *Mycena crocata* (p.119) has orange milk; *M. inclinata* (p.133) produces tight clusters but no milk. *M. sanguinolenta* is smaller with a more slender build and red-brown gill edges. It has red milk and normally grows on leaf litter.

more-or-less bell-shaped • cap

medium-spaced gills tinted with cap color •

△ **SPINELLUS FUSIGER**
This fungus is a common parasite on *Mycena* species and appears like pins stuck into a pincushion. It is closely related to black bread mold.

• adnexed gills

• toothed cap margin

• blood-red liquid exudes from broken stem

• stems typically joined at base

SECTION

FRUITING In dense clusters of fruitbodies.

| Dimensions CAP ⊕ 0.5–3cm | STEM ↕ 3–7cm ↔ 2–4mm | Spores Whitish cream | Edibility |

Family TRICHOLOMATACEAE	Species *Mycena galopus*	Season Late summer–winter

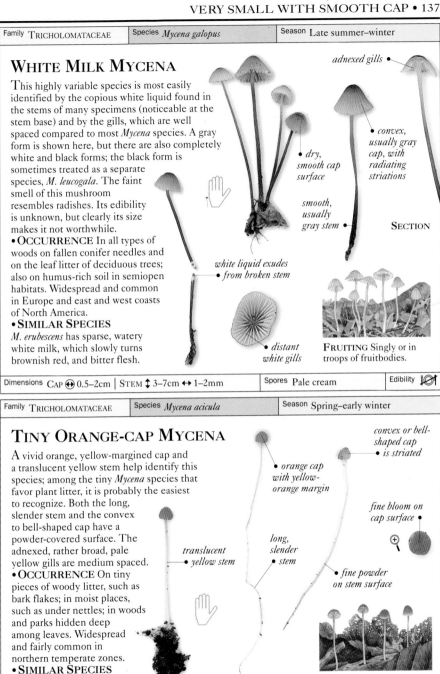

WHITE MILK MYCENA

This highly variable species is most easily identified by the copious white liquid found in the stems of many specimens (noticeable at the stem base) and by the gills, which are well spaced compared to most *Mycena* species. A gray form is shown here, but there are also completely white and black forms; the black form is sometimes treated as a separate species, *M. leucogala*. The faint smell of this mushroom resembles radishes. Its edibility is unknown, but clearly its size makes it not worthwhile.

• **OCCURRENCE** In all types of woods on fallen conifer needles and on the leaf litter of deciduous trees; also on humus-rich soil in semiopen habitats. Widespread and common in Europe and east and west coasts of North America.

• **SIMILAR SPECIES** *M. erubescens* has sparse, watery white milk, which slowly turns brownish red, and bitter flesh.

adnexed gills

convex, usually gray cap, with radiating striations

dry, smooth cap surface

smooth, usually gray stem

SECTION

white liquid exudes from broken stem

distant white gills

FRUITING Singly or in troops of fruitbodies.

| Dimensions CAP ⊕ 0.5–2cm | STEM ↕ 3–7cm ↔ 1–2mm | Spores Pale cream | Edibility |

Family TRICHOLOMATACEAE	Species *Mycena acicula*	Season Spring–early winter

TINY ORANGE-CAP MYCENA

A vivid orange, yellow-margined cap and a translucent yellow stem help identify this species; among the tiny *Mycena* species that favor plant litter, it is probably the easiest to recognize. Both the long, slender stem and the convex to bell-shaped cap have a powder-covered surface. The adnexed, rather broad, pale yellow gills are medium spaced.

• **OCCURRENCE** On tiny pieces of woody litter, such as bark flakes; in moist places, such as under nettles; in woods and parks hidden deep among leaves. Widespread and fairly common in northern temperate zones.

• **SIMILAR SPECIES** *Rickenella fibula* (p.36) has very arched, decurrent gills.

convex or bell-shaped cap is striated

orange cap with yellow-orange margin

fine bloom on cap surface

translucent yellow stem

long, slender stem

fine powder on stem surface

FRUITING Singly or in small groups; well hidden.

| Dimensions CAP ⊕ 0.3–1cm | STEM ↕ 2–6cm ↔ 0.5–1mm | Spores Off-white | Edibility |

Family TRICHOLOMATACEAE	Species *Mycena flavoalba*	Season Autumn

YELLOW-WHITE MYCENA

A characteristic of this species is the diluted yellow of its convex or conical cap. It may also have a dark "eye-spot" and faint striations; the gills are white. The stem is translucent yellow-white. The thin white flesh smells and tastes of radishes.
• **OCCURRENCE** In mossy grassland; on litter in coniferous woods. Widespread and common in Europe, eastern North America, the Rockies, and Pacific Northwest.
• **SIMILAR SPECIES** It is easily mistaken for a variety of other cream-colored species, such as those that belong to the genus *Hemimycena*.

• *conical to convex cap*

• *translucent, yellow-white stem*

△ *MYCENA ADONIS*
This is a beautiful species, which fruits in modest numbers. It has a striking, coral-red cap, which fades with age, and a translucent white stem.

• *dark "eye-spot" in cap center*

adnexed, well-spaced gills, each with a decurrent tooth •

• *thin, serrated cap margin*

• *faint striations on cap surface*

FRUITING In huge troops, often of over a hundred.

Dimensions CAP ⊕ 0.5–2cm	STEM ↕ 3–5cm ↔ 1–2mm	Spores Off-white	Edibility

Family TRICHOLOMATACEAE	Species *Marasmius androsaceus*	Season Summer–late autumn

HORSEHAIR MARASMIUS

This species has a very thin, extremely tough, shiny stem and a convex, flat-topped, dark-centered, pale brown cap with radial furrows, striations, and often wrinkles. Its gills are attached directly to the stem, instead of to a little wheel around the stem like many *Marasmius* species. It produces tough, horsehairlike threads of densely interwoven hyphae to colonize a new substrate, enabling it to grow in inhospitable habitats. It has a faint smell and a mild taste and is not worth eating.
• **OCCURRENCE** In pine woods, on pine needles and other small pieces of tree litter; also among sand dunes near pine stands. Widespread and common in northern temperate zones.
• **SIMILAR SPECIES** *Micromphale perforans* has a finely felted stem and smells of rotten cabbage.

smooth, shiny • *stem*

horsehairlike mycelial • *threads*

gills attached to stem •

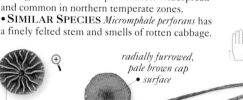

radially furrowed, pale brown cap • *surface*

• *very narrow, well-spaced gills*

FRUITING In troops in a wide variety of sites.

Dimensions CAP ⊕ 0.3–1cm	STEM ↕ 2.5–5cm ↔ 0.3–0.5mm	Spores White	Edibility

Family TRICHOLOMATACEAE	Species *Micromphale foetidum*	Season Autumn–late autumn

FETID MARASMIUS

Occasionally, this fairly small species can be detected by its strong smell alone, which is similar to that of rotten cabbage. It has a convex, smooth, orange-brown cap, darker at the center, with striations and furrows and a thin, sharp, upturned margin. The hollow stem is velvety black and widens at the top.
• **OCCURRENCE** Only on fallen branches in deciduous woods, preferring areas of rich alkaline soil. Widespread but local in northern temperate zones.
• **SIMILAR SPECIES** *Micromphale brassicolens* grows on beech twigs and leaves. It has more crowded, paler gills. *M. perforans* is smaller and occurs on pine needles. Both smell rotten.

well-spaced, often forked gills, connected by veins

adnate to decurrent gills

slightly gelatinous, reddish brown flesh

SECTION

upturned, thin cap margin

furrowed cap with dark striations when moist

hollow, velvety black stem

orange-brown cap dries to leather-brown

center of cap is darker

FRUITING Appears in dense groups of fruitbodies.

Dimensions CAP ⊕ 0.5–3cm │ STEM ↕ 1–4cm ↔ 2–4mm	Spores Off-white	Edibility

Family TRICHOLOMATACEAE	Species *Marasmiellus ramealis*	Season Summer–autumn

TWIG MARASMIUS

This tiny *Marasmiellus* species has a cream to pale leather-brown cap that is convex, aging flat, and finely wrinkled and furrowed. The short, curved, pale tan stem is clothed in pale scales at its base. Similar in color to the stem, the flesh is thin, tough, and fibrous. The broad gills are well spaced; the smooth spores, 9 x 3µm, are spindle-shaped to ellipsoid.
• **OCCURRENCE** In damp woods, growing on dead sticks and twigs or *Rubus* (raspberry and blackberry) canes. It will also tolerate fairly dry conditions. Widespread and common in Europe and North America.
• **SIMILAR SPECIES** *M. candidus* has a whiter cap and a black stem base. *M. vaillantii* is best distinguished by microscopic examination of the cystidia and spores.

finely wrinkled and furrowed cap surface

small pale scales at base of curved stem

cream to pale leather-brown cap

adnate, off-white to pinkish cream gills

pale tan stem becomes reddish tan toward base

broad, well-spaced gills

FRUITING Appears in crowds of fruitbodies.

SECTION

Dimensions CAP ⊕ 0.3–1.5cm │ STEM ↕ 0.5–2cm ↔ 0.5–1.5mm	Spores White	Edibility

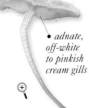

Family CORTINARIACEAE	Species *Galerina calyptrata*	Season Summer–autumn

TINY BOG GALERINA

This is a small, slender, honey-brown agaric with a convex, striate cap that dries to paler cream-brown. It has thin, pale brown flesh and gills, and usually smells of yeast. The stem is long, thin, and smooth. Microscopic examination is needed to distinguish it from similar species; its spores are warty and broadly spindle-shaped with a loosening outer wall.

• **OCCURRENCE** On lawns or in damp woods. Widespread, but not reported in North America.

• **SIMILAR SPECIES** *Galerina hypnorum* is differentiated by its spores – the outer wall does not loosen. *G. sphagnorum* grows only in sphagnum moss and has a ring zone on the stem. There are many other *Galerina* species, mostly associated with various mosses or rotten wood.

• cap is honey-brown, drying paler

extremely long, thin stem •

translucent, yellow-brown stem •

SECTION

very thin, pale brown flesh •

tiny, convex cap with distinct striations •

widely spaced, adnate, pale brown gills •

base of stem rooting in moss •

FRUITING Singly or in small groups on mossy ground.

Dimensions CAP ⊕ 0.3–0.8cm | STEM ↕ 3–5cm ↔ 1–2mm	Spores Ocher-brown	Edibility

Family BOLBITIACEAE	Species *Conocybe lactea*	Season Summer–autumn

WHITE LAWN CONOCYBE

Its elongated cap and ivory coloring enables *Conocybe lactea* to be identified without the aid of a microscope, unlike most *Conocybe* species. The cap is faintly striate and becomes wrinkled with age; the gills are crowded and pale to rust-brown. The surface of the stem is covered in powder and faintly lined. The flesh is thin and fragile.

• **OCCURRENCE** In grass on fertile soil. Disappears by mid-day. Widespread in northern North America, Gulf Coast, California.

• **SIMILAR SPECIES** *C. huijsmanii* has an almost rounded to convex cap. *Bolbitius lacteus* has a more viscid cap and smaller spores, 9.5 x 5.5µm: those of *C. lactea* are 12.5 x 8µm. *Galerina* species (pp.91, 140) typically have gills that are more distant and usually adnate.

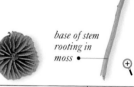

• smooth cap surface develops slight wrinkles with age

• elongated, ivory-white cap

• when moist, cap margin has fine striations

gills are • adnexed at first, becoming free

faint lines • on stem surface

SECTION

hollow, very • slender stem

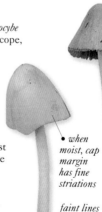

FRUITING In troops or a few fruitbodies together.

Dimensions CAP ⊕ 1–1.5cm | STEM ↕ 5–11cm ↔ 1–3cm	Spores Orange-brown	Edibility

Family STROPHARIACEAE	Species *Psilocybe semilanceata*	Season Summer–autumn

LIBERTY CAP PSILOCYBE

This well-known hallucinogenic agaric has an elegant, conical cap with a distinct pimple on the top; striate and olive-gray in young specimens, it quickly dries to cream without striations. The slender stem is colored like the cap but may have a blue base. The flesh is cream or pale in color and has a musty smell. The symptoms from ingesting this species range from hilarity to incoordination to disorientation, lasting up to four hours.
• **OCCURRENCE** In fertilized grassland, either on heavily grazed or mown areas or hidden deep among clumps of grass.
• **SIMILAR SPECIES** *Psilocybe fimetaria* has a white veil at the margin. It grows in horse manure.

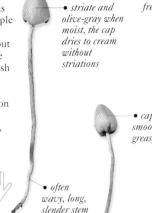

striate and olive-gray when moist, the cap dries to cream without striations

medium-spaced, adnexed to nearly free gills

pale olive-gray gills, purplish black when mature

cap surface smooth, often greasy and sticky

SECTION

often wavy, long, slender stem

stem usually same color as cap

stem base is occasionally blue

FRUITING Singly or in large troops of fruitbodies.

Dimensions CAP ⊕ 0.5–2cm	STEM ↕ 4–10cm ↔ 2–3mm	Spores Purplish black	Edibility ☠

Family COPRINACEAE	Species *Panaeolina foenisecii*	Season Late spring–autumn

LAWN MOWER'S MUSHROOM

This very common grassland species has a hemispherical to flat, smooth, red-brown cap, and a similarly colored stem with a pale surface bloom. As the cap dries, its colors become zoned, and its surface may break into minute, flattened scales. It has well-spaced, free gills. This species is also placed in the genera *Panaeolus* and *Psathyrella*, but its spores are dark brown; a microscope reveals warty spores, each with a pore. Its flesh has a pleasant, spicy smell but is poisonous.
• **OCCURRENCE** In damp grass. Extremely common in Europe and North America.
• **SIMILAR SPECIES** *P. ater* has black gills and smooth spores.

red-brown cap dries to pale brown

cap surface may break into minute scales

red-brown stem with surface bloom

FRUITING In troops in soil, particularly nutrient-rich soil, in a variety of grassland, including lawns.

Dimensions CAP ⊕ 1–3cm	STEM ↕ 4–6cm ↔ 2–3mm	Spores Dark brown	Edibility ☠

VERY SMALL, CAP NOT SMOOTH

AGARICS IN THIS SUBSECTION, as in the last (pp.132–141), have very small fruitbodies, but are characterized by their very varied, never smooth, cap surfaces. They too are represented in many different families and genera. Their cap surfaces may be fibrous or scaly, or they can be covered with loose grains, as in *Coprinus disseminatus* (p.143), which also has fine hairs.

Family TRICHOLOMATACEAE	Species *Crinipellis stipitaria*	Season Summer–autumn

SCALY ZONED COLLYBIA

The stem of this tough species has a dense covering of stiff, gray to brown hairs. The convex to umbonate, sometimes depressed cap has silky, pale brown hairs, arranged in concentric zones, and has radial streaks. The flesh is off-white and tough; neither the smell nor the taste is noteworthy.

• **OCCURRENCE** In dry grassy areas and on sand dunes. Widespread and locally common in northern temperate zones; widely distributed in northeastern and northcentral US.

• **SIMILAR SPECIES** There are only a few *Crinipellis* species in temperate zones. One tropical species (*C. perniciosa*) causes severe damage to cacao trees.

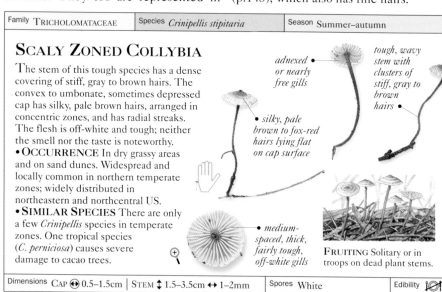

adnexed or nearly free gills

tough, wavy stem with clusters of stiff, gray to brown hairs

silky, pale brown to fox-red hairs lying flat on cap surface

medium-spaced, thick, fairly tough, off-white gills

FRUITING Solitary or in troops on dead plant stems.

| Dimensions CAP ⊕ 0.5–1.5cm \| STEM ↕ 1.5–3.5cm ↔ 1–2mm | Spores White | Edibility |

Family TRICHOLOMATACEAE	Species *Asterophora parasitica*	Season Autumn

RUSSULA PARASITE

This species has a silky-fibrillose gray cap and stem and well-developed, thick, widely spaced gills with decurrent teeth. It is not considered a worthwhile edible.

• **OCCURRENCE** On rotten fruitbodies of *Russula* and *Lactarius*, typically *R. nigricans* group (p.122), in wooded sites. Widespread in northern temperate zones; rare.

• **SIMILAR SPECIES** Other mushrooms that grow on rotting agarics include *Asterophora lycoperdoides*, which looks similar to a small puffball; *Volvariella surrecta*, on *Clitocybe nebularis* (p.40); and a few small *Collybia* species.

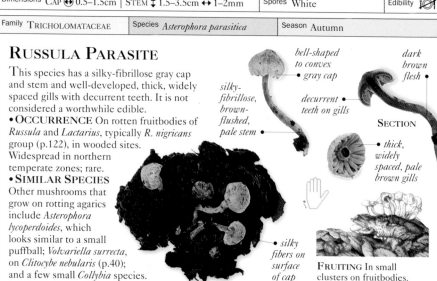

bell-shaped to convex gray cap

dark brown flesh

silky-fibrillose, brown-flushed, pale stem

decurrent teeth on gills

SECTION

thick, widely spaced, pale brown gills

silky fibers on surface of cap

FRUITING In small clusters on fruitbodies.

| Dimensions CAP ⊕ 0.5–1.5cm \| STEM ↕ 1–3cm ↔ 2–4mm | Spores White | Edibility |

| Family COPRINACEAE | Species *Coprinus disseminatus* | Season Spring–early autumn |

MASSED LESSER INKY CAP

Cream-white when young, the pleated (parachute-like) cap of this species ages gray, but, unlike many *Coprinus* species, produces only a little ink. Fine hairs and grains on the surface are visible through a hand lens. The delicate stem is white, as is the very thin flesh.
• **OCCURRENCE** On and around stumps and dying deciduous trees. Widespread and common in northern temperate zones.
• **SIMILAR SPECIES** *Psathyrella pygmaea* is similar in appearance and habitat, but its cap surface has neither hairs nor grains and is less pleated.

medium- to closely spaced gills

pleats clearly visible on young cap

cap color is darker in center

fine hairs and grains on cap surface

free gills are white to gray-black

SECTION

thin white flesh

broadly egg-shaped cap with pleated surface

FRUITING Appears in huge troops near deciduous stumps.

delicate, off-white stem

huge troops appear on stumps or by dying trees

| Dimensions CAP ⊕ 0.5–1.5cm | STEM ↕ 1–4cm ↔ 1–2mm | Spores Black | Edibility |

| Family HYGROPHORACEAE | Species *Hygrocybe miniata* | Season Summer–autumn |

FINE-SCALY RED WAX CAP

This mushroom is one of several small *Hygrocybe* species with dry caps densely covered in small scales. They are difficult to tell apart without examining the spores under a microscope: those of this Wax Cap are mostly pear-shaped. The fruitbodies are bright scarlet with a convex, scaly cap and a smooth, shiny stem. The gills are adnate, and the red-orange flesh has an unremarkable smell and taste.
• **OCCURRENCE** In open deciduous or mixed woods, on unimproved grassland. Widespread in northern temperate zones and widely distributed throughout North America.
• **SIMILAR SPECIES** The early fruiting *H. helobia* prefers less acidic conditions, smells of garlic, and has spores of a more regular ellipsoid shape. *H. calciphila* also has more regular-shaped spores and tends to occur on alkaline soil.

bright scarlet cap with scurfy surface

smooth, shiny, bright scarlet stem

adnate gills are yellow to pale red

FRUITING In troops, mostly on slightly acidic soil, in undisturbed grassland.

| Dimensions CAP ⊕ 1–3cm | STEM ↕ 1–6cm ↔ 2–8mm | Spores White | Edibility |

| Family ENTOLOMATACEAE | Species *Entoloma serrulatum* | Season Late summer–autumn |

SAW-GILLED BLUE-CAP ENTOLOMA

The convex, dark blue-black cap surface of this mushroom is dry to the touch with tiny, erect scales and a central, navel-like depression. The stem is a similar color to the cap. The adnexed, pale blue gills have a serrated, blue-black edge.
• **OCCURRENCE** In grassland, among sparse roadside vegetation, or in open woods. Widespread in Europe and North America.
• **SIMILAR SPECIES** Similar, more-or-less blue *Entoloma* species with colored gill edges include *E. caesiocinctum*, with a browner cap; *E. chalybaeum*, with brown-edged, blue gills that are less serrated; and *E. querquedula*, which has an olive-tinged cap.

central depression on dry,
• blue-black cap surface

• cap surface has tiny, erect scales

thin, bluish white flesh has faint aroma •

FRUITING In small groups on most types of soil.

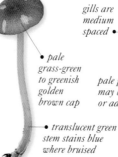

medium-spaced gills are adnexed •

gill edge is • serrated and blue-black

pale blue gills turn • pinkish blue with age

SECTION

| Dimensions CAP ⊕ 1–2.5cm | STEM ↕ 2–6cm ↔ 2–4mm | Spores Pale pink | Edibility ☠ |

| Family ENTOLOMATACEAE | Species *Entoloma incanum* | Season Summer–early autumn |

GREENISH ENTOLOMA

The overall color of this species is green or green-brown, but the flesh discolors to sky-blue when bruised and smells strongly of mice. The cap is convex, with a slightly depressed center, and the slender stem is hollow. It is probably poisonous. Although perhaps the most striking of the smaller *Entoloma* species, its coloring camouflages it well in its grassy habitat.
• **OCCURRENCE** On soil in calcareous grassland or along paths in forests. Widespread but uncommon in Europe and North America.

gills are medium spaced •

• pale grass-green to greenish golden brown cap

pale pink gills • may be adnate or adnexed

• translucent green stem stains blue where bruised

hollow • stem

FRUITING Appears singly or in troops of fruitbodies among herbaceous plants.

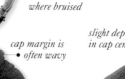

cap margin is • often wavy

• striations at cap margin

slight depression in cap center •

SECTION

stem base is white and stains blue •

| Dimensions CAP ⊕ 1–3cm | STEM ↕ 2–6cm ↔ 2–4mm | Spores Pale pink | Edibility ☠ |

CAP & STEM FUNGI WITH FREE GILLS

This section features the few families of agarics – Amanitaceae, Agaricaceae, and Pluteaceae – in which the species have "free" gills, meaning those that are not attached to the stem. Often the stem can be twisted from the cap flesh without damage to the gills.

• *free gills not attached to stem*

WITH VOLVA AND/OR VEIL SCALES ON CAP

THIS GROUP OF AGARICS consists of species from the genera *Amanita* and *Volvariella*. They are comparatively large and fleshy, and distinct remains of the universal veil persist as a saclike structure at the stem base (volva) and/or as loose scales on the cap. Some also have a ring around the stem.

Family AMANITACEAE	Species *Amanita caesarea*	Season Summer–autumn

CAESAR'S AMANITA

A legend in warm regions, this mushroom has a convex to flat, golden orange cap and an orange stem with a prominent, loose white volva (up to 5cm wide), at the base. The soft gills are crowded and cream to golden yellow. This is a choice edible, but unless it is positively identified by an expert, it should not be eaten (see SIMILAR SPECIES).
• **OCCURRENCE** Mycorrhizal with oak. A complex of similar species occurs in eastern and southwestern North America.
• **SIMILAR SPECIES** *Amanita muscaria* (p.146) has a yellow-orange form.

FRUITING Singly or in troops on sandy soil.

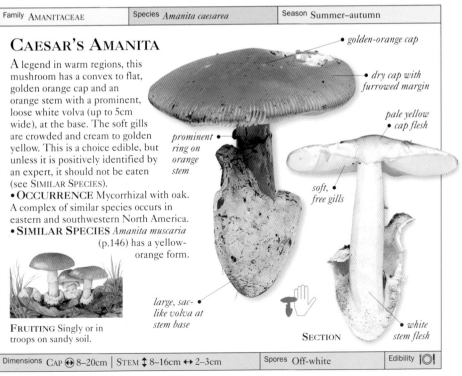

• *golden-orange cap*

• *dry cap with furrowed margin*

pale yellow • cap flesh

prominent • ring on orange stem

soft, • free gills

large, sac-like volva at stem base

SECTION

• *white stem flesh*

| Dimensions CAP ⊕ 8–20cm | STEM ↕ 8–16cm ↔ 2–3cm | Spores Off-white | Edibility |

| Family AMANITACEAE | Species *Amanita muscaria* | Season Summer–autumn |

FLY AMANITA

This is the classic fairy-tale toadstool. It has a convex to flattened cap with a smooth or faintly grooved margin and white veil scales on the surface. It occurs in several color forms, including yellow-orange and orange (eastern North America); the brilliant red version (Alaska) is the most familiar. The swollen stem base lacks the loose volva found in other *Amanita* species, such as *A. virosa* (p.150). Although used in minute amounts by native people in Siberia for shamanic purposes, this mushroom is poisonous if eaten in larger quantities.

• **OCCURRENCE** Mycorrhizal, mostly with birch or spruce, usually on acidic soil.

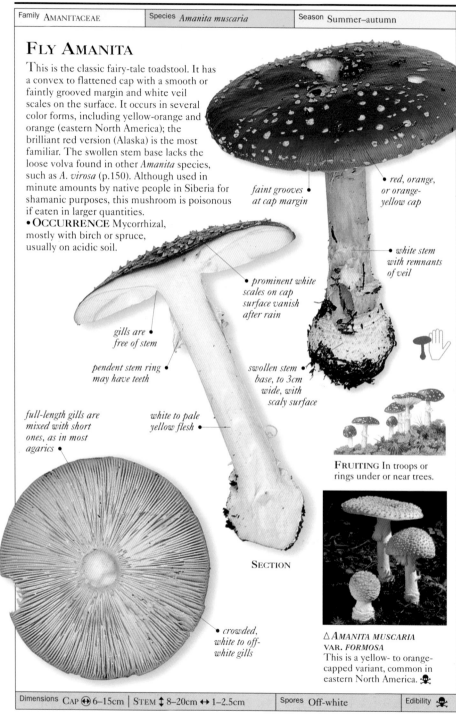

• *faint grooves at cap margin*

• *red, orange, or orange-yellow cap*

• *white stem with remnants of veil*

• *prominent white scales on cap surface vanish after rain*

gills are free of stem •

pendent stem ring may have teeth •

• *swollen stem base, to 3cm wide, with scaly surface*

full-length gills are mixed with short ones, as in most agarics •

white to pale yellow flesh •

SECTION

• *crowded, white to off-white gills*

FRUITING In troops or rings under or near trees.

△ *AMANITA MUSCARIA* VAR. *FORMOSA*
This is a yellow- to orange-capped variant, common in eastern North America. ☠

| Dimensions CAP ⊕ 6–15cm | STEM ↕ 8–20cm ↔ 1–2.5cm | Spores Off-white | Edibility ☠ |

| Family AMANITACEAE | Species *Amanita rubescens* | Season Summer–autumn |

BLUSHING AMANITA

The convex cap of this species is pinkish brown with gray to pink veil patches. The downy, gray, white, or pink stem bears a prominent pendent ring with furrows on its upper surface; the base is swollen and girdled. Small insects lay eggs in the fruitbodies, and the damaged flesh becomes pink tinged – often the best clue to its identity. It is difficult to recognize so should be picked for eating only by experienced foragers.
• **OCCURRENCE** Mycorrhizal with trees, such as beech, and conifers. Widespread and common in northern temperate zones.

gray to pink veil patches on cap surface

convex cap is pinkish brown

SECTION

pendent ring, with furrows on upper surface

swollen stem base, to 4cm wide, is girdled with veil remains

downy stem is gray, white, or pink

pink tinges appear on damaged areas

soft white flesh slowly stains pink

△ *HYPOMYCES HYALINUS*
A white flask fungus, parasitic on *Amanita rubescens* in eastern North America. It can also occur on *A. virosa* (p.150). ☣

gills are free of stem

crowded, soft, white to off-white gills

FRUITING Singly or in groups, often on acidic soil.

| Dimensions CAP ⊕ 6–18cm | STEM ↕ 6–15cm ↔ 1.5–4cm | Spores White | Edibility 🍽 |

Family AMANITACEAE	Species *Amanita spissa*	Season Summer–autumn

STOUT-STALKED AMANITA

This species has a convex, usually dark brown cap with a smooth margin and gray veil patches. The ring on its club-shaped stem has grooves on the upper surface. It smells faintly of canola oil. Although this mushroom is edible after cooking, it is not recommended; see SIMILAR SPECIES. *A. excelsa*, considered by some to be a separate species, is paler with a rooting stem and no smell.

• **OCCURRENCE** Typically with beech or spruce in woods. Widespread in northern temperate Europe, Asia, and eastern North America.

• **SIMILAR SPECIES** Poisonous *A. pantherina* (p.149). *A. rubescens* (p.147) has pink tinges.

dark brown cap with pale gray veil patches •

free gills are white, crowded, and soft •

smooth or • slightly striate cap margin

clearly • defined grooves on pendent stem ring

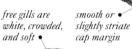

FRUITING Appears singly or a few together.

club-shaped stem • base with brown to gray-brown veil girdles

Dimensions CAP ⊕ 7–15cm │ STEM ↕ 8–14cm ↔ 2–4cm	Spores White	Edibility 🍴⊘

Family AMANITACEAE	Species *Amanita smithiana*	Season Autumn

TOXIC LEPIDELLA AMANITA

This species has a convex to flat white cap with conical veil patches. The veil is also visible in shreds around the smooth cap margin. The scaly white stem has a ragged ring and gets larger toward the rooting base, where the basal bulb may be up to 5cm wide. The thick, white, faintly pungent flesh can cause kidney failure or liver disease.

• **OCCURRENCE** Mycorrhizal with conifers. Widespread and common in the Pacific Northwest.

• **SIMILAR SPECIES** *Tricholoma magnivelare* (p.81) has a spicy smell and a rooting stem. *Amanita virosa* complex (p.150), with a smooth cap and saclike volva, is easily distinguished.

veil shreds at smooth cap margin •

crowded, free white or cream gills •

scaly white • stem with ragged ring

FRUITING Singly or in scattered groups under conifers in woods.

Dimensions CAP ⊕ 5–12.5cm │ STEM ↕ 10–20cm ↔ 1–3cm	Spores White	Edibility ☠

Family AMANITACEAE	Species *Amanita pantherina*	Season Summer–autumn

PANTHER AMANITA

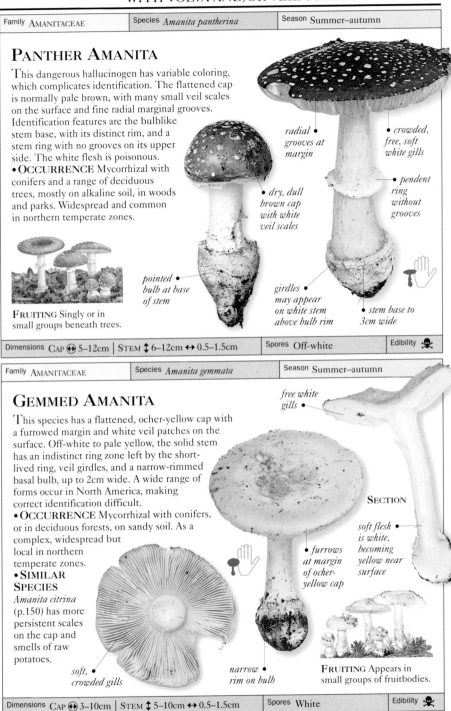

This dangerous hallucinogen has variable coloring, which complicates identification. The flattened cap is normally pale brown, with many small veil scales on the surface and fine radial marginal grooves. Identification features are the bulblike stem base, with its distinct rim, and a stem ring with no grooves on its upper side. The white flesh is poisonous.

• OCCURRENCE Mycorrhizal with conifers and a range of deciduous trees, mostly on alkaline soil, in woods and parks. Widespread and common in northern temperate zones.

radial • grooves at margin

• crowded, free, soft white gills

• dry, dull brown cap with white veil scales

• pendent ring without grooves

pointed • bulb at base of stem

girdles • may appear on white stem above bulb rim

• stem base to 3cm wide

FRUITING Singly or in small groups beneath trees.

Dimensions CAP ⊕ 5–12cm	STEM ↕ 6–12cm ↔ 0.5–1.5cm	Spores Off-white	Edibility ☠

Family AMANITACEAE	Species *Amanita gemmata*	Season Summer–autumn

GEMMED AMANITA

free white gills •

This species has a flattened, ocher-yellow cap with a furrowed margin and white veil patches on the surface. Off-white to pale yellow, the solid stem has an indistinct ring zone left by the short-lived ring, veil girdles, and a narrow-rimmed basal bulb, up to 2cm wide. A wide range of forms occur in North America, making correct identification difficult.

• OCCURRENCE Mycorrhizal with conifers, or in deciduous forests, on sandy soil. As a complex, widespread but local in northern temperate zones.

SECTION

soft flesh • is white, becoming yellow near surface

• SIMILAR SPECIES *Amanita citrina* (p.150) has more persistent scales on the cap and smells of raw potatoes.

• furrows at margin of ocher-yellow cap

soft, • crowded gills

narrow • rim on bulb

FRUITING Appears in small groups of fruitbodies.

Dimensions CAP ⊕ 3–10cm	STEM ↕ 5–10cm ↔ 0.5–1.5cm	Spores White	Edibility ☠

| Family AMANITACEAE | Species *Amanita virosa* | Season Summer–autumn |

DESTROYING ANGEL

The saclike volva of this species is normally buried in the soil, so specimens should be dug up carefully for correct identification. The shiny, white to ivory cap usually lacks veil patches and is bell-shaped or conical. Unlike many *Amanita* species, the stem ring is indistinct and the stem tends to have girdles of fine fibers. It is deadly poisonous; anyone picking edible mushrooms should make sure they are familiar with this species.

• **OCCURRENCE** Mycorrhizal with spruce in northern Europe but with oak in eastern and western North America. Widespread in northern temperate zones.

• **SIMILAR SPECIES** *A. bisporigera* is a smaller, more slender, two-spored, but equally deadly mushroom of eastern oak woods. Also in this complex is *A. ocrata*, common in West Coast oak woods.

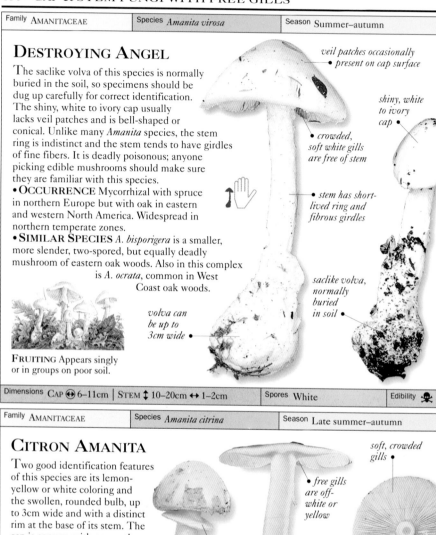

veil patches occasionally • present on cap surface

shiny, white to ivory cap

• crowded, soft white gills are free of stem

• stem has short-lived ring and fibrous girdles

saclike volva, normally buried in soil

volva can be up to 3cm wide •

FRUITING Appears singly or in groups on poor soil.

| Dimensions CAP ⊕ 6–11cm | STEM ↕ 10–20cm ↔ 1–2cm | Spores White | Edibility ☠ |

| Family AMANITACEAE | Species *Amanita citrina* | Season Late summer–autumn |

CITRON AMANITA

Two good identification features of this species are its lemon-yellow or white coloring and the swollen, rounded bulb, up to 3cm wide and with a distinct rim at the base of its stem. The cap is convex, with a smooth margin and often veil remnants; the stem bears a large pendent ring toward its top. The white flesh has a distinctive and strong smell of raw potatoes.

• **OCCURRENCE** Mycorrhizal with conifers and deciduous trees, mostly on acidic soil. Widespread and common in northern temperate zones.

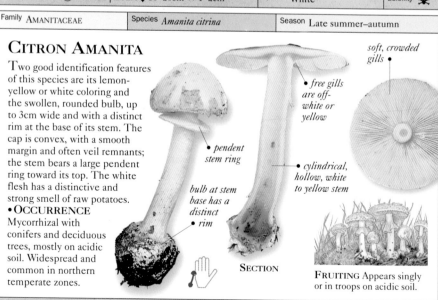

soft, crowded gills •

• free gills are off-white or yellow

• cylindrical, hollow, white to yellow stem

• pendent stem ring

bulb at stem base has a distinct • rim

SECTION

FRUITING Appears singly or in troops on acidic soil.

| Dimensions CAP ⊕ 5–10cm | STEM ↕ 6–13cm ↔ 0.8–1.5cm | Spores Off-white | Edibility 🍴 |

| Family AMANITACEAE | Species *Amanita phalloides* | Season Late summer–autumn |

DEATH CAP AMANITA

This species has a convex to flattened, green to gray cap with a smooth margin but a fibrous surface. The stem may be similarly colored or off-white with a prominent white volva, 3–5cm wide. Young specimens are relatively easy to identify by their green tinges, free gills, and prominent white volvas. There is usually a stem ring, but it may be absent. Older specimens may have gray caps (see SIMILAR SPECIES). This is a deadly poisonous mushroom.

• OCCURRENCE Mycorrhizal with American oaks, pines, and Norway spruce, on rich soil. Widespread and common in parts of Europe and northern North America.

• SIMILAR SPECIES Some *Volvariella* species (pp.154–55) look similar to older specimens of *Amanita phalloides*. They are distinguished by a pale pink spore deposit and lack of a stem ring. *A. virosa* (p.150) is completely white.

FRUITING Singly or in troops of fruitbodies.

• *surface of gray or green cap is fibrous*

• *smooth cap margin*

SECTION

soft, free white gills

pendent ring on stem

prominent white volva, half buried in soil

immature, green-capped fruitbody

| Dimensions CAP ⊕ 8–15cm | STEM ↕ 8–16cm ↔ 1–2.5cm | Spores Off-white | Edibility ☠ |

| Family AMANITACEAE | Species *Amanita porphyria* | Season Summer–autumn |

PURPLE-BROWN AMANITA

Named after the color of its convex to umbonate cap, which is porphyrous (purplish brown), the Purple-brown Amanita has a pendent gray ring around its stem, which is bulbous at the base, with an off-white or pale gray volva, to 2.5cm wide. It smells like raw, peeled potatoes and is slightly poisonous. It could easily be confused with its deadly relatives so should be avoided.

• OCCURRENCE Mycorrhizal with conifers on acidic soil. Widespread in northern temperate Europe, Asia, and northern North America.

• SIMILAR SPECIES *A. citrina* (p.150) has a similar smell, but its habitat and coloring are different. *A. spissa* (p.148) has similar coloring but lacks the smell.

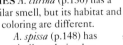

FRUITING Appears singly or in small groups.

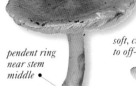

• *gray-brown to purple-gray cap surface has few or no veil patches*

soft, crowded, free white to off-white gills •

pendent ring near stem middle •

SECTION

white or pale yellow stem is smooth

soft white to yellow flesh smells of raw potato •

bulb at stem base is pale gray or off-white •

| Dimensions CAP ⊕ 5–9cm | STEM ↕ 8–13cm ↔ 1–2cm | Spores White | Edibility ⊘ |

Family AMANITACEAE	Species *Amanita fulva*	Season Summer–autumn

TAWNY GRISETTE

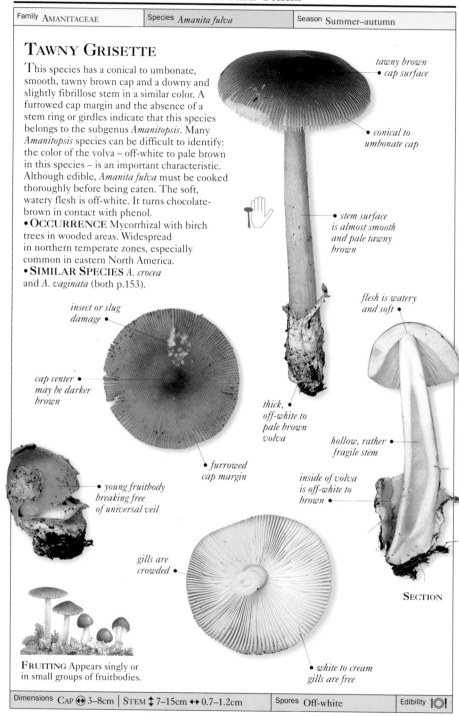

This species has a conical to umbonate, smooth, tawny brown cap and a downy and slightly fibrillose stem in a similar color. A furrowed cap margin and the absence of a stem ring or girdles indicate that this species belongs to the subgenus *Amanitopsis*. Many *Amanitopsis* species can be difficult to identify: the color of the volva – off-white to pale brown in this species – is an important characteristic. Although edible, *Amanita fulva* must be cooked thoroughly before being eaten. The soft, watery flesh is off-white. It turns chocolate-brown in contact with phenol.

• **OCCURRENCE** Mycorrhizal with birch trees in wooded areas. Widespread in northern temperate zones, especially common in eastern North America.

• **SIMILAR SPECIES** *A. crocea* and *A. vaginata* (both p.153).

tawny brown cap surface

conical to umbonate cap

stem surface is almost smooth and pale tawny brown

flesh is watery and soft

insect or slug damage

cap center may be darker brown

thick, off-white to pale brown volva

hollow, rather fragile stem

young fruitbody breaking free of universal veil

furrowed cap margin

inside of volva is off-white to brown

SECTION

gills are crowded

FRUITING Appears singly or in small groups of fruitbodies.

white to cream gills are free

Dimensions CAP ⊕ 3–8cm	STEM ↕ 7–15cm ↔ 0.7–1.2cm	Spores Off-white	Edibility

Family AMANITACEAE	Species *Amanita crocea*	Season Early summer–autumn

ORANGE GRISETTE

This striking species has a convex to umbonate, shiny orange cap, which is smooth with a furrowed margin. The stem, which is without a ring, has thin orange girdles and a prominent, thick white volva. Like *Amanita fulva* (p.152), it belongs to the subgenus *Amanitopsis*. Although both species are often found near birch, *A. crocea* prefers much richer soil. It is edible, with soft, off-white flesh, but must be thoroughly cooked before eating. If harvested for eating, the fruitbodies should be used as soon as possible since they do not keep well.
• **OCCURRENCE** Mycorrhizal with birch trees, and possibly also spruce, beech, and oak, on fairly rich soil in lowland areas and at higher altitudes, near the tree line. Widespread in Europe and North America.
• **SIMILAR SPECIES**
A. fulva (p.152) has off-white flesh turning chocolate-brown in contact with phenol, whereas the flesh of *A. crocea* turns dark wine-red. *A. vaginata* (inset, below).

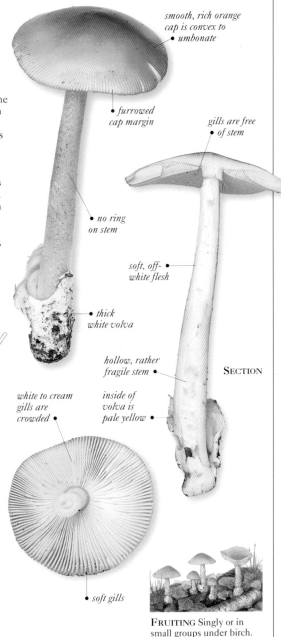

smooth, rich orange cap is convex to • umbonate

• furrowed cap margin

gills are free • of stem

• no ring on stem

soft, off- white flesh

• thick white volva

hollow, rather fragile stem •

SECTION

inside of volva is pale yellow •

white to cream gills are crowded •

• soft gills

△ *AMANITA VAGINATA*
This gray to near white species has a convex to umbonate cap, furrowed at the margin. The stem has a mealy surface and a prominent volva. It occurs mainly under deciduous trees on rich soil. Beware of the deadly look-alike *Amanita virosa* (p.150).

FRUITING Singly or in small groups under birch.

Dimensions CAP ⊕ 6–12cm | STEM ↕ 10–20cm ↔ 1–2cm	Spores Off-white	Edibility

Family PLUTEACEAE	Species *Volvariella bombycina*	Season Summer–autumn

TREE VOLVARIELLA

An easy species to identify, but not so easy to find; it is rare and may be high up in trees. It has a very large, conical to umbonate, white to pale yellow cap, covered in silky fibers, and a pronounced volva at the base of the white to yellowish cream stem. It has a pleasant smell and is edible, but because of its saclike volva it must be identified accurately.

• **OCCURRENCE**
On standing dead trees, on stored wood, or in buildings. Widespread in northern temperate zones, but mostly local; also farther south.

• **SIMILAR SPECIES** The Deadly Amanitas also have a saclike volva but grow on the ground.

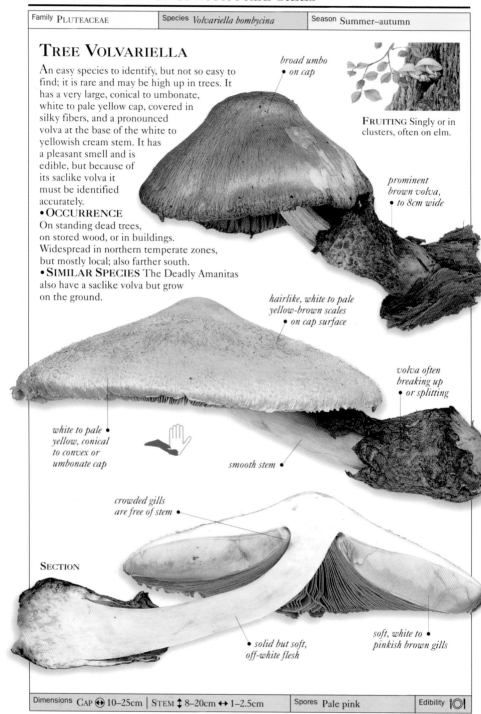

broad umbo on cap

FRUITING Singly or in clusters, often on elm.

prominent brown volva, to 8cm wide

hairlike, white to pale yellow-brown scales on cap surface

volva often breaking up or splitting

white to pale yellow, conical to convex or umbonate cap

smooth stem

crowded gills are free of stem

SECTION

solid but soft, off-white flesh

soft, white to pinkish brown gills

Dimensions CAP ⊕ 10–25cm	STEM ↕ 8–20cm ↔ 1–2.5cm	Spores Pale pink	Edibility

Family PLUTEACEAE	Species *Volvariella gloiocephala*	Season Summer–autumn

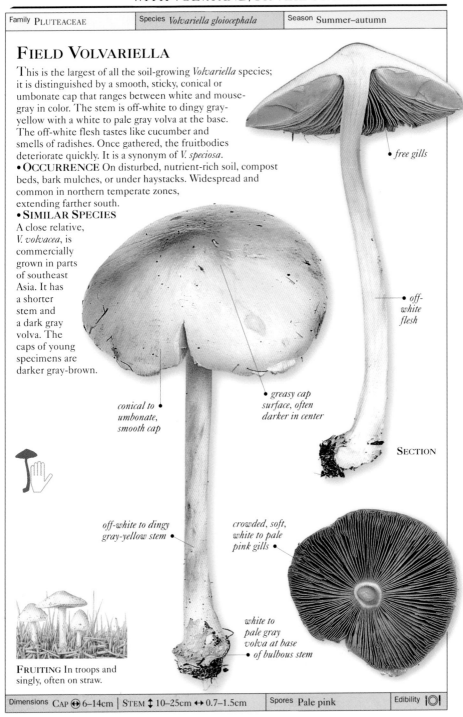

FIELD VOLVARIELLA

This is the largest of all the soil-growing *Volvariella* species; it is distinguished by a smooth, sticky, conical or umbonate cap that ranges between white and mouse-gray in color. The stem is off-white to dingy gray-yellow with a white to pale gray volva at the base. The off-white flesh tastes like cucumber and smells of radishes. Once gathered, the fruitbodies deteriorate quickly. It is a synonym of *V. speciosa*.

• **OCCURRENCE** On disturbed, nutrient-rich soil, compost beds, bark mulches, or under haystacks. Widespread and common in northern temperate zones, extending farther south.

• **SIMILAR SPECIES** A close relative, *V. volvacea*, is commercially grown in parts of southeast Asia. It has a shorter stem and a dark gray volva. The caps of young specimens are darker gray-brown.

free gills •

• off-white flesh

conical to umbonate, smooth cap

• greasy cap surface, often darker in center

SECTION

off-white to dingy gray-yellow stem •

crowded, soft, white to pale pink gills •

white to pale gray volva at base • of bulbous stem

FRUITING In troops and singly, often on straw.

| Dimensions CAP ⊕ 6–14cm | STEM ↕ 10–25cm ↔ 0.7–1.5cm | Spores Pale pink | Edibility |◯| |

WITH STEM RING OR RING ZONE

THE SPECIES in this subsection have free gills (see p.145) and the remains of the partial veil clearly visible on the stem, as either a ring or a ring zone. The ring varies from large to small and may be persistent or short-lived. Where there is no ring, the area where it would be – the ring zone – is marked by threads or darker marking. Most species featured have white or dark brown to black spore deposits and belong to the family Agaricaceae.

Family AGARICACEAE	Species *Agaricus sylvicola*	Season Summer–autumn

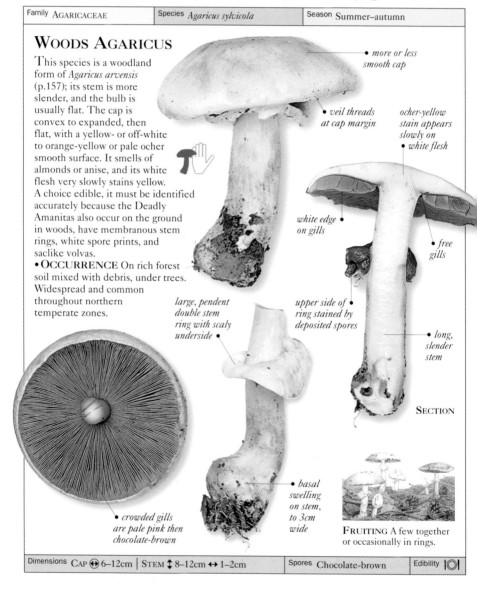

WOODS AGARICUS

This species is a woodland form of *Agaricus arvensis* (p.157); its stem is more slender, and the bulb is usually flat. The cap is convex to expanded, then flat, with a yellow- or off-white to orange-yellow or pale ocher smooth surface. It smells of almonds or anise, and its white flesh very slowly stains yellow. A choice edible, it must be identified accurately because the Deadly Amanitas also occur on the ground in woods, have membranous stem rings, white spore prints, and saclike volvas.

• **OCCURRENCE** On rich forest soil mixed with debris, under trees. Widespread and common throughout northern temperate zones.

• *more or less smooth cap*

• *veil threads at cap margin*

ocher-yellow stain appears slowly on • *white flesh*

white edge • *on gills*

• *free gills*

large, pendent double stem ring with scaly underside •

upper side of • *ring stained by deposited spores*

• *long, slender stem*

SECTION

• *crowded gills are pale pink then chocolate-brown*

• *basal swelling on stem, to 3cm wide*

FRUITING A few together or occasionally in rings.

Dimensions CAP ⊕ 6–12cm	STEM ↕ 8–12cm ↔ 1–2cm	Spores Chocolate-brown	Edibility 🍴

Family AGARICACEAE	Species *Agaricus arvensis*	Season Summer–autumn

HORSE AGARICUS

This species has a rounded to convex cap with a smooth, yellow- to off-white surface that very slowly stains orange-yellow to ocher, particularly where bruised. The yellowish stem, which thickens toward the base, has a pendent ring with a wheel-like pattern on its underside. The thick, firm white flesh also stains very slowly. It smells strongly of almonds and is edible but contains high levels of cadmium.

• **OCCURRENCE** Often found in horse-grazed pasture and on lawns and in parks, near spruce. Widespread and common in northern temperate zones; throughout western North America.

• **SIMILAR SPECIES** There are several similar species. *Agaricus augustus* (p.158). *A. macrosporus* is very fleshy, with scaly stem girdles. *A. sylvicola* (p.156) is a woodland form. *A. xanthoderma* (p.159).

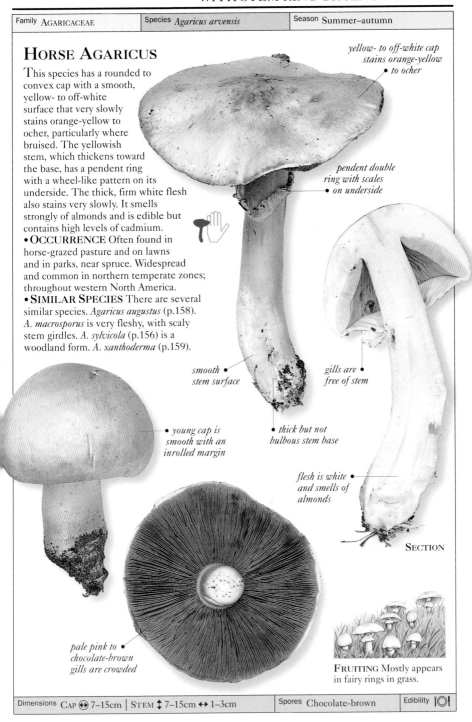

yellow- to off-white cap stains orange-yellow to ocher

pendent double ring with scales on underside

smooth stem surface

gills are free of stem

young cap is smooth with an inrolled margin

thick but not bulbous stem base

flesh is white and smells of almonds

SECTION

pale pink to chocolate-brown gills are crowded

FRUITING Mostly appears in fairy rings in grass.

Dimensions CAP ⊕ 7–15cm	STEM ↕ 7–15cm ↔ 1–3cm	Spores Chocolate-brown	Edibility

Family AGARICACEAE	Species *Agaricus augustus*	Season Autumn

PRINCE AGARICUS

Orange-brown scales on the surface of both cap and stem, together with yellow-staining flesh that smells of almonds, identify this species. The scales are in a concentric pattern on the convex to expanded cap, and the stem has a large, pendent ring. With its firm, abundant flesh, it makes a choice edible, but should only be eaten in moderation because, like some other edible *Agaricus* species, it concentrates heavy metals like cadmium.
• OCCURRENCE In all types of woods and parks, on rich soil, and on garden compost. Widely distributed in North America.

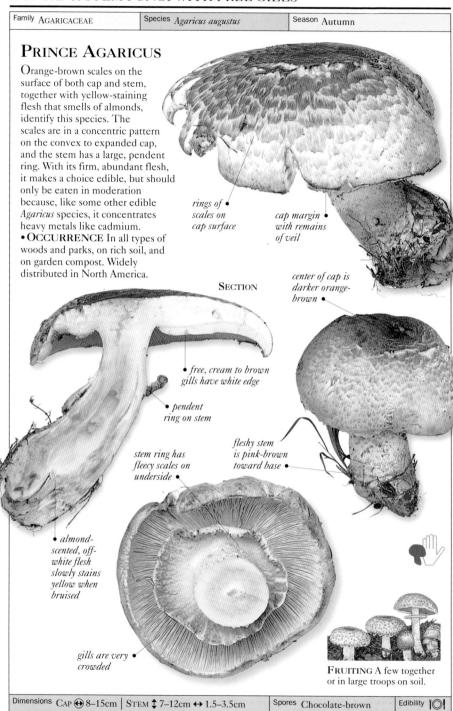

rings of •
scales on
cap surface

cap margin •
with remains
of veil

center of cap is
darker orange-
brown •

SECTION

• free, cream to brown
gills have white edge

• pendent
ring on stem

stem ring has
fleecy scales on
underside •

fleshy stem
is pink-brown
toward base •

• almond-
scented, off-
white flesh
slowly stains
yellow when
bruised

gills are very •
crowded

FRUITING A few together
or in large troops on soil.

Dimensions CAP ⊕ 8–15cm | STEM ↕ 7–12cm ↔ 1.5–3.5cm	Spores Chocolate-brown	Edibility 🍽️

Family AGARICACEAE	Species *Agaricus xanthoderma*	Season Summer–autumn

TOXIC YELLOWING AGARICUS

Despite having a yellow-staining surface and flesh, this poisonous mushroom appears whiter, almost chalk-white in comparison with the other, slower-staining *Agaricus* species. Its most obvious characteristics are its stem base, which is very bright yellow at the tip when cut lengthwise, and its smell, which is very similar to that of ink.

• **OCCURRENCE** On bare soil or in grass in parks, cemeteries, and similar places. Widespread throughout northern temperate zones and elsewhere.

• **SIMILAR SPECIES** *A. arvensis* (p.157) and *A. sylvicola* (p.156) have a distinctive almond smell. Both are slower to stain yellow and are edible. *A. praeclaresquamosus* (p.160) is darker in color and poisonous.

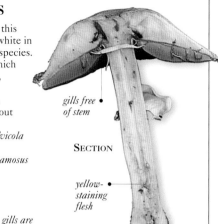

gills free • of stem

SECTION

yellow- • staining flesh

smooth cap is chalk-white or pale gray toward center •

cap often "squared-off" with near-vertical sides • and flat top

gills are crowded •

• flesh at stem base turns very bright yellow

• pendent double stem ring with scales on underside

• pink-gray to chocolate-brown gills

FRUITING Often in large troops or fairy rings.

△ *AGARICUS CALIFORNICUS*
This species from California has a convex white to pale brown cap with a scaly surface, a pendent ring on the white stem, and white gills that turn bright pink then dark brown. Most parts stain yellow. ☠

△ *AGARICUS HONDENSIS*
This is a foul-smelling woodland species from the Pacific coast of North America. Its cap is white to pinkish gray, aging darker, and there is a flaring to pendent stem ring. The gills are grayish pink. ☠

Dimensions CAP ⊕ 5–13cm	STEM ↕ 5–10cm ↔ 1–2cm	Spores Chocolate-brown	Edibility ☠

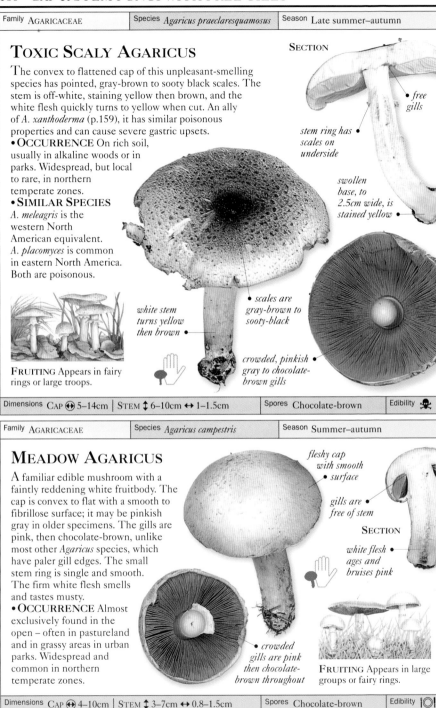

| Family AGARICACEAE | Species *Agaricus praeclaresquamosus* | Season Late summer–autumn |

TOXIC SCALY AGARICUS

The convex to flattened cap of this unpleasant-smelling species has pointed, gray-brown to sooty black scales. The stem is off-white, staining yellow then brown, and the white flesh quickly turns to yellow when cut. An ally of *A. xanthoderma* (p.159), it has similar poisonous properties and can cause severe gastric upsets.

• **OCCURRENCE** On rich soil, usually in alkaline woods or in parks. Widespread, but local to rare, in northern temperate zones.

• **SIMILAR SPECIES** *A. meleagris* is the western North American equivalent. *A. placomyces* is common in eastern North America. Both are poisonous.

FRUITING Appears in fairy rings or large troops.

SECTION

• *free gills*

stem ring has scales on underside

swollen base, to 2.5cm wide, is stained yellow •

white stem turns yellow then brown •

• *scales are gray-brown to sooty-black*

• *crowded, pinkish gray to chocolate-brown gills*

| Dimensions CAP ⊕ 5–14cm | STEM ↕ 6–10cm ↔ 1–1.5cm | Spores Chocolate-brown | Edibility ☠ |

| Family AGARICACEAE | Species *Agaricus campestris* | Season Summer–autumn |

MEADOW AGARICUS

A familiar edible mushroom with a faintly reddening white fruitbody. The cap is convex to flat with a smooth to fibrillose surface; it may be pinkish gray in older specimens. The gills are pink, then chocolate-brown, unlike most other *Agaricus* species, which have paler gill edges. The small stem ring is single and smooth. The firm white flesh smells and tastes musty.

• **OCCURRENCE** Almost exclusively found in the open – often in pastureland and in grassy areas in urban parks. Widespread and common in northern temperate zones.

fleshy cap with smooth surface •

gills are free of stem •

SECTION

white flesh ages and bruises pink •

• *crowded gills are pink then chocolate-brown throughout*

FRUITING Appears in large groups or fairy rings.

| Dimensions CAP ⊕ 4–10cm | STEM ↕ 3–7cm ↔ 0.8–1.5cm | Spores Chocolate-brown | Edibility ¡◎! |

Family AGARICACEAE	Species *Agaricus bitorquis*	Season Summer–autumn

SPRING AGARICUS

This species has several distinguishing features: a prominent double stem ring, which is sheathed and upturned; its acidic-smelling, firm flesh slowly turns pink; it has a squared cap with an inrolled margin. Although it is edible, it is safer collected in parks than along roadsides.

• **OCCURRENCE** Mostly found in urban areas, in hard or packed soil, or in schoolyards. Widespread and common in Europe and North America.

• **SIMILAR SPECIES** *Stropharia rugoso-annulata* (p.89) has gills that are attached to the stem and a purple-black spore print;

cap has distinct shoulders •

smooth cap is white to off-white •

stem ring is double and • upturned

cap surface is often soiled •

free gills are • pink then chocolate-brown

FRUITING A few together. They can be found emerging from hard soil or tarmac.

Dimensions CAP ⊕ 5–12cm | STEM ↕ 4–8cm ↔ 1–3.5cm	Spores Chocolate-brown	Edibility ¡⊙!

Family AGARICACEAE	Species *Agaricus bisporus*	Season Late summer–autumn

CULTIVATED AGARICUS

SECTION

This species is perhaps the best known of all edible mushrooms. It is cultivated on a large scale; only species like *Volvariella volvacea* (Paddy Straw Mushroom), *Pleurotus ostreatus* (Common Oyster Mushroom, p.178), and *Lentinula edodes* (Shiitake) compete in commercial importance. Its convex cap varies from white to dark brown, and its stem has an upturned ring. Its flesh stains very slightly red.

• **OCCURRENCE** By roadsides, in cemeteries, and other sites with rich, disturbed soil. Widespread throughout northern temperate zones.

crowded gills are free •

• stem ring turns upward when young

convex to flat • cap with smooth, dry surface

• white to dark brown cap

veil remains at margin •

FRUITING Appears in troops and fairy rings.

faint carrot- • red stain on stem from handling or bruising

gills are chocolate- • brown when mature

Dimensions CAP ⊕ 5–10cm | STEM ↕ 3–6cm ↔ 1–2cm	Spores Chocolate-brown	Edibility ¡⊙!

Family AGARICACEAE	Species *Agaricus bernardii*	Season Summer–autumn

SALT-LOVING AGARICUS

This very fleshy mushroom tolerates soil that is rich in salt. It has a flattened or convex, white to gray-white cap, the surface of which often cracks into a scaly pattern. The thickset stem has a sheathing ring with a narrow, upturned rim. The Salt-loving Agaricus has firm, white, foul-smelling flesh that slowly turns pink with age. It is edible but is not worth eating.

• **OCCURRENCE** In the salt-spray zones of coastal areas or along roads that are salted during the winter. Widespread on east and west coasts of North America and in Europe.

• **SIMILAR SPECIES** *Agaricus bitorquis* (p.161) is found in similar sites.

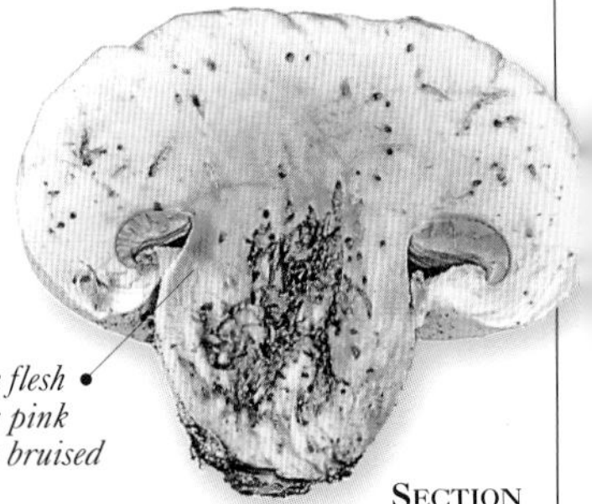

white flesh • turns pink when bruised

SECTION

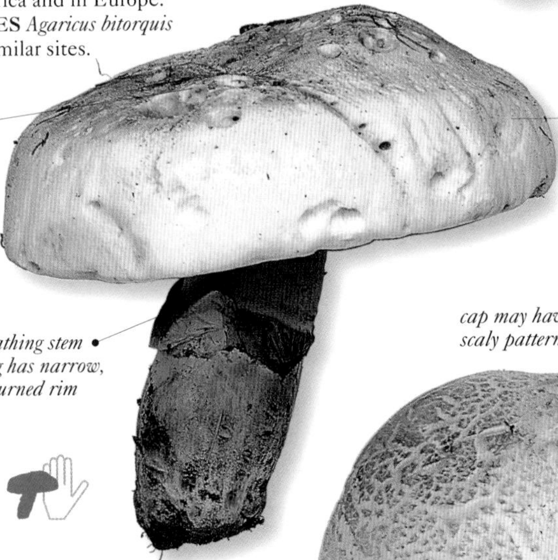

convex or flattened • cap with dry surface

• extremely fleshy, white to gray-white cap

sheathing stem • ring has narrow, upturned rim

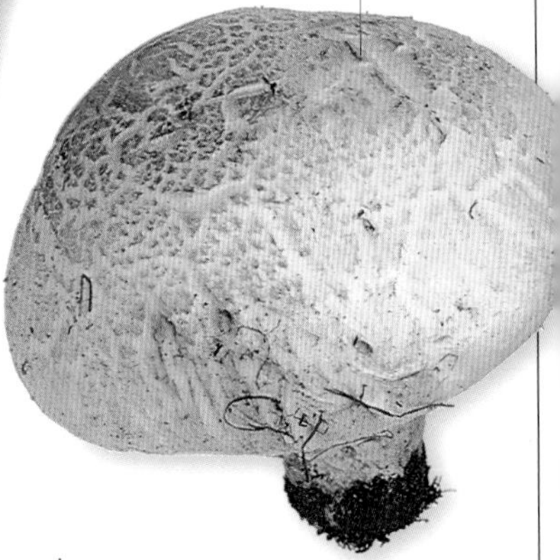

cap may have scaly pattern •

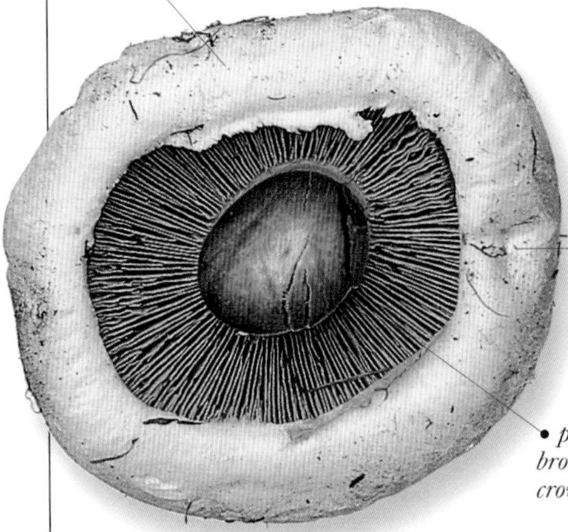

smooth cap margin •

• cap margin is inrolled

• pink to chocolate-brown gills are crowded and free

FRUITING Appears in troops of fruitbodies.

Dimensions CAP ⊕ 7–15cm	STEM ↕ 5–10cm ↔ 2–4cm	Spores Chocolate-brown	Edibility

| Family AGARICACEAE | Species *Agaricus sylvaticus* | Season Summer–autumn |

RED-STAINING AGARICUS

The convex to umbonate cap of this species is covered with fine brown fibers. The stem, with its pendent ring, may have a fibrous-scaly surface. Also known as the Pinewood Mushroom, Wood Mushroom, and Scaly Wood Mushroom, this choice edible has pleasant-smelling, off-white flesh that stains deep red, mostly after bruising, although the color reaction is less marked than in some of its relatives.

• **OCCURRENCE** On conifer debris in forests, parks, and damp woods. Widespread in northern temperate zones.

• **SIMILAR SPECIES** *Agaricus langei*, also a good edible, is more fleshy and stains a deeper red. *A. phaeolepidotus* stains yellow and is poisonous.

SECTION

gills are crowded and free

pendent ring on brown stem

convex to umbonate cap with radiating scales on surface

fibrous scales may be present on stem surface

base up to 2.5cm wide

dark brown cap center

pale gray gills are rose-pink then chocolate-brown

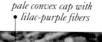

FRUITING Appears in troops or fairy rings.

| Dimensions CAP ⊕ 5–10cm | STEM ↕ 5–10cm ↔ 0.5–1.5cm | Spores Chocolate-brown | Edibility |

| Family AGARICACEAE | Species *Agaricus porphyrizon* | Season Throughout autumn |

PURPLISH YELLOW AGARICUS

This species is an unusually sturdy, fleshy member of a group of mostly small *Agaricus* species, called section *Minores*, that all have an almond smell, yellow-staining flesh, and, often, purple cap colors. The cap is convex, with a covering of fine, purple-lilac fibers on a paler background, and the stem is white with a bulbous yellow to orange base and a fragile, narrow stem ring. The gills are gray-pink to purple-black. It has edible white flesh that slowly stains yellow.

• **OCCURRENCE** On soil and leaf litter in deciduous woods, but also on conifer debris and in gardens. Widespread but local in Europe; not reported in North America.

pale convex cap with lilac-purple fibers

gray-pink, free gills

FRUITING Appears singly or a few fruitbodies together on rich soil among leaf litter.

| Dimensions CAP ⊕ 5–8cm | STEM ↕ 4–6cm ↔ 0.7–1cm | Spores Chocolate-brown | Edibility |

| Family AGARICACEAE | Species *Leucoagaricus leucothites* | Season Late summer–autumn |

SMOOTH LEPIOTA

The convex cap of this white species has a smooth, dry surface. The stem has a thin ring, which may be loose, and a club-shaped base. The white flesh smells pleasant but is poisonous. Subtle color differences have led some experts to divide *Leucoagaricus leucothites* into a small group of separate species. This complex is known in the US as *L. naucinoides*.
• **OCCURRENCE** In grass along roadsides and in parks, gardens, and sand dunes. Widespread in Europe and North America.
• **SIMILAR SPECIES** Several *Agaricus* species are similar, but their spore deposits and mature gills are chocolate-brown.

silky smooth or • splitting cap skin

cap flesh is firm and white •

delicate • stem ring is movable

gills are • free

white coloring throughout •

• club-shaped stem base

crowded gills •

FRUITING In small groups or fairy rings, mostly in grass.

• gills are off-white or with pink tinge

SECTION

| Dimensions CAP ⊕ 5–8cm | STEM ↕ 4–8cm ↔ 0.8–2cm | Spores White | Edibility ☠ |

| Family AMANITACEAE | Species *Limacella guttata* | Season Late summer–autumn |

SLIME-VEIL FALSE LEPIOTA

The slightly greasy, convex cap of this species is creamy ocher to very pale red-brown. The stem is dry with a prominent ring that exudes a clear liquid, which dries as olive-brown spots. There is no volva at the stem base. The white gills are free and crowded. This white-fleshed, yeasty-smelling mushroom is edible but not recommended.
• **OCCURRENCE** Found in deciduous or coniferous forests, on rich soil among thick leaf litter. Widespread but local in Europe; in the Midwest and Rockies in North America.
• **SIMILAR SPECIES** *Limacella glioderma* is extremely slimy with an orange-brown cap. Some *Amanita* and *Lepiota* species are superficially similar, but neither genus has species with a slimy outer veil.

cap is creamy ocher, darker with age •

pale red-brown center of convex, greasy cap •

crowded gills are white • and free

pendent stem ring is very prominent •

FRUITING Appears in troops of fruitbodies or singly in rich soil and litter in woodland areas.

| Dimensions CAP ⊕ 7–15cm | STEM ↕ 8–14cm ↔ 1–2.5cm | Spores White | Edibility |

Family AGARICACEAE	Species *Macrolepiota procera*	Season Summer–autumn

PARASOL LEPIOTA

This spectacular large mushroom is distinguished by a beautiful snakeskin pattern on its stem, which also has a large, movable ring. The cap is umbrella-shaped to flat with a raised, dark gray-brown center, and with a concentric pattern of attached scales. The pale flesh does not stain when bruised. Some consider this to be one of the best edible mushrooms.

• **OCCURRENCE** In dunes, dry grassland, and small grassy areas in woods and parks. Widespread and fairly common in Europe and North America.

• **SIMILAR SPECIES** The poisonous *Chlorophyllum molybdites* (p.166) has a stouter stalk and a green spore print. *M. rhacodes* (p.166).

cap center is dark gray-brown

concentric brown scales on cap surface

very tall stem with delicate snakeskin pattern

stem ring is large and movable

cap emerges egg-shaped, becoming umbrella-shaped or flat with a raised center

crowded, free, white to cream gills

slightly bulbous stem base

stem may be 4cm wide at base

FRUITING In scattered troops on sandy grass or soil.

Dimensions CAP ⊕ 10–30cm | STEM ↕ 15–30cm ↔ 0.8–2cm	Spores White or pale pink	Edibility ⊙

| Family AGARICACEAE | Species *Macrolepiota rhacodes* | Season Summer–autumn |

SHAGGY PARASOL LEPIOTA

This shaggy species has concentric, pale brown scales covering the surface of the convex cap, which flattens with age; very young specimens resemble flower bulbs. The stem has a prominent double ring. Its white flesh turns bright carrot-red when bruised. Although edible, some varieties cause stomach upsets, so only small quantities should be eaten (see also SIMILAR SPECIES).

•**OCCURRENCE** On rich soil in parks and gardens; also under conifers. Widespread and common throughout Europe and North America.

•**SIMILAR SPECIES** *Macrolepiota permixta* and *M. procera* (p.165) are larger, with snakeskin-patterned stems. *Chlorophyllum molybdites* (inset, below) is poisonous and has a green spore deposit.

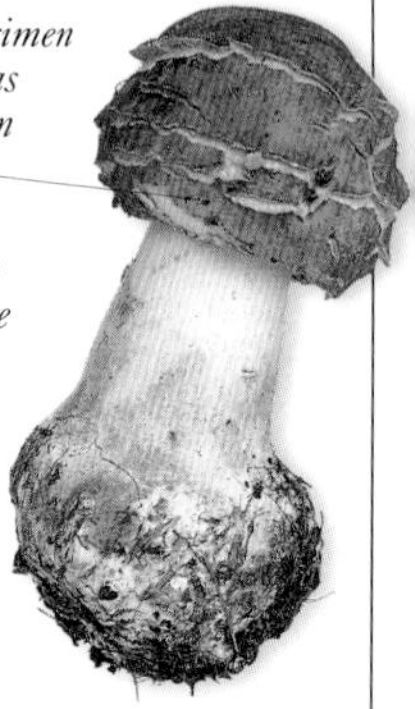

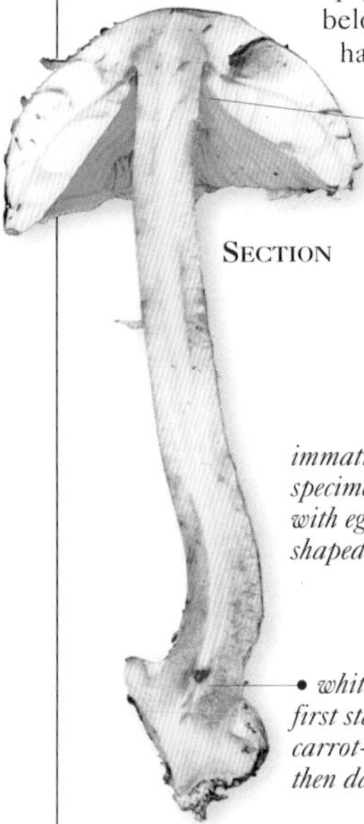

young specimen already has pale brown scales •

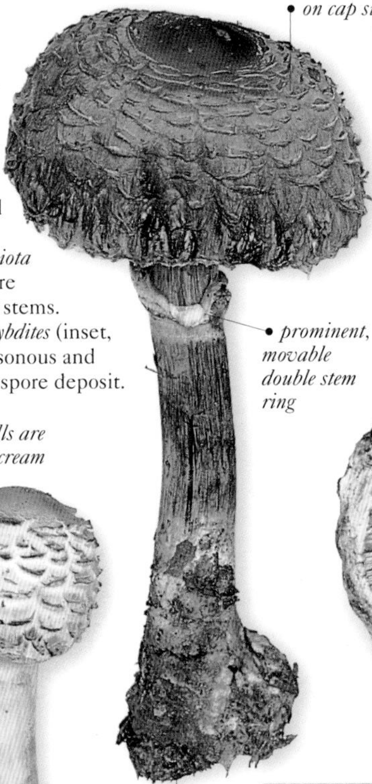

concentric scales • on cap surface

• prominent, movable double stem ring

gills are crowded •

• free gills are white to cream

SECTION

immature • specimen with egg-shaped cap

• white flesh first stains carrot-red then dark red

basal • bulb to 4cm wide

• smooth to fibrillose stem

• cap margin is shaggy

△ *CHLOROPHYLLUM MOLYBDITES*
Also known as *Macrolepiota molybdites*, this scaly-capped species is pale brown, bruising red-brown, with a double stem ring. As they mature, the white gills become olive-green. ☠

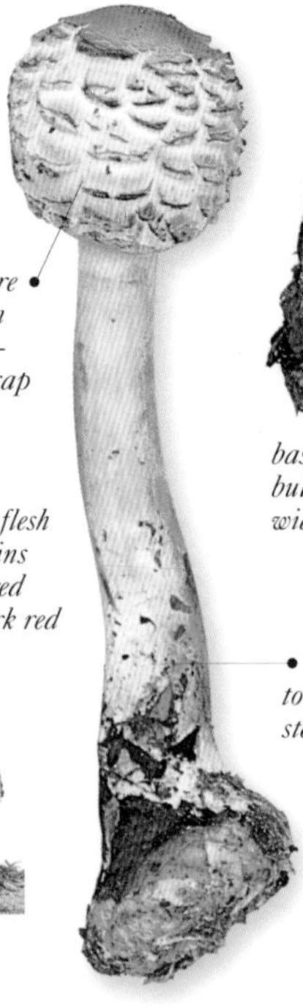

FRUITING Appears in troops or fairy rings.

| Dimensions CAP ⊕ 5–15cm \| STEM ↕ 10–15cm ↔ 1–2cm | Spores White | Edibility 🍴 |

Family AGARICACEAE	Species *Lepiota aspera*	Season Late summer–autumn

SHARP-SCALED LEPIOTA

This large species has a convex, off-white cap, covered with conical or pyramidal brown scales that wear away with age. The stem is brown with a large, pendent, dark-rimmed ring and a swollen base; its surface is scaly or fibrous below the ring. It has an unpleasant smell and may be poisonous.
• **OCCURRENCE** In woods along roadsides in rich, alkaline soil. Widespread in northern temperate zones.
• **SIMILAR SPECIES** *Lepiota hystrix* exudes brown liquid from its very dark scales. *L. perplexum* tends to be smaller with less crowded gills. *Macrolepiota procera* (p.165) has a movable stem ring and a faint, pleasant smell.

• brown scales on off-white cap

• stem below ring is brown and scaly or fibrous

free, • white to pale cream, very crowded gills

• large, pendent stem ring

• swollen base of stem, to 2cm wide

SECTION

FRUITING Appears singly or in small groups.

Dimensions CAP ⊕ 5–15cm	STEM ↕ 5–12cm ↔ 0.5–1.5cm	Spores White	Edibility ☠

Family AGARICACEAE	Species *Lepiota oreadiformis*	Season Autumn

EURO GRASS LEPIOTA

A conical cap and crowded, thin, free white gills make this species typical of the genus; however, unlike most *Lepiota* species, the stem ring is hardly visible. The overall coloring of the fruitbody is off-white to cream, with the cap having a browner center. The stem is girdled with the remains of the veil, and the cap margin also bears veil remnants. Some mycologists separate *L. oreadiformis* into three or more distinct species.
• **OCCURRENCE** In dry open grassland, often in coastal sites and on sand dunes. Widespread throughout Europe; not reported in North America.
• **SIMILAR SPECIES** *Marasmius oreades* (p.117) is superficially similar but has adnexed gills, tough flesh, and no sign of any veil remnants.

stem ring is hardly visible, if seen at all •

free, crowded gills are pale • cream

cap is off-white to cream with a darker center •

FRUITING In troops of fruitbodies among lichens and short grass in open grassland and coastal sites.

Dimensions CAP ⊕ 2–6cm	STEM ↕ 3–5cm ↔ 0.8–1.2cm	Spores White	Edibility 🍴

| Family AGARICACEAE | Species *Lepiota ignivolvata* | Season Throughout autumn |

EURO ORANGE LEPIOTA

This fairly fleshy *Lepiota* species is best identified by its orange-margined ring, situated low on the club-shaped white stem. The convex cap has concentric, fine, orange-brown scales and a raised ocher-brown center. Its off-white flesh has an unpleasant chemical smell, reminiscent of *L. cristata* (p.169) and similar to the odor when metal is cut.

• OCCURRENCE Under conifers and deciduous trees on calcareous soil. Widespread across Europe; not reported in North America.

• SIMILAR SPECIES *L. ventriosospora* lacks the orange on the veil and the stem base.

orange-brown cap surface breaks into delicate scales

soft, free gills

crowded, white to cream gills

stem has one or more orange rings or veil girdles

stem base is often swollen and becomes orange-tinged with age

off-white flesh throughout

SECTION

FRUITING Appears in troops or singly in leaf litter.

| Dimensions CAP ⊕ 4–11cm | STEM ↕ 5–15cm ↔ 0.5–2cm | Spores White | Edibility ☠ |

| Family AGARICACEAE | Species *Lepiota clypeolaria* | Season Throughout autumn |

SHAGGY-STALKED LEPIOTA

This fairly large but not very fleshy species is mainly white to cream, although the bell-shaped to flat cap may have brown-tinged scales; the specimen shown is a brown example. The cap margin and the stem bear clear remnants of the pure white veil, making young specimens appear shaggy. The faint-smelling flesh is white to pale brown. The spores are spindle-shaped.

• OCCURRENCE In deciduous or coniferous forests on fertile soil among leaf litter or on needle beds. Widespread and common in northern temperate zones.

• SIMILAR SPECIES *Lepiota alba* grows in open habitats and has a smoother stem. *L. ventriosospora* has yellow or yellow-brown tinges to the stem veil and cap.

cap surface with pale ocher-brown scales

free gills

SECTION

cottonlike remnants of white veil

veil girdles on stem

thin, white to pale brown flesh

club-shaped stem base

white to cream gills are crowded

FRUITING Appears singly or in small groups.

| Dimensions CAP ⊕ 3–7cm | STEM ↕ 5–12cm ↔ 0.5–1cm | Spores White | Edibility ☠ |

Family AGARICACEAE	Species *Lepiota cristata*	Season Summer–autumn

BURNT-RUBBER LEPIOTA

This is the most common of the smaller *Lepiota* species. Its best identification characteristics are its pale colors, the concentric pattern of flat, orange-brown scales on the convex cap, and an unpleasant chemical smell. The stem ring is short lived but can be seen as an upturned cuff on younger specimens.

• **OCCURRENCE** In lawns, among mosses, or near nettles, at the edges of paths and roads, on fairly rich soil. Widespread and common in northern temperate zones.

• **SIMILAR SPECIES** The very poisonous *L. lilacea* is much rarer, with a similar shape but with purple to purple-brown colors.

orange-brown scales on pale cap surface

white where cap skin splits

short-lived ring on off-white stem

stem is smooth below ring

center is always darker red-brown than rest of cap

crowded, free white gills

FRUITING In small groups or troops on bare soil.

Dimensions CAP ⊕ 1–4cm	STEM ↕ 2.5–5cm ↔ 2–4mm	Spores White	Edibility ☠

Family AGARICACEAE	Species *Lepiota castanea*	Season Throughout autumn

DEADLY LEPIOTA COMPLEX

This small and dark species has dark brown scales on both the convex to flat cap and the stem. It also has a strong, fairly unpleasant smell. The stem ring is short lived. Microscopic features are important when identifying small *Lepiota* species; the genus has three different spore shapes: projectile, egg, or spindle. Those of *L. castanea* are projectile-shaped.

• **OCCURRENCE** On disturbed rich soil, often along woodland ditches and paths. Widespread, mostly in the south of northern temperate zones.

• **SIMILAR SPECIES** *L. fulvella* is paler orange-brown and bigger; *L. pseudohelveola* has a more prominent stem ring and a fainter smell. Because some are deadly and many are poisonous, no small *Lepiota* species should be eaten.

△ *LEPIOTA BRUNNEOINCARNATA* The convex cap of this sturdy species has concentric, dark pink-brown scales on the surface. The pink-tinged stem has dark scales below the indistinct ring zone. ☠

pale or ocher flesh

SECTION

dark brown scales on cap surface

stem ring soon disappears

dark brown scales on stem

free white gills are crowded

FRUITING Mostly a few fruitbodies together.

Dimensions CAP ⊕ 2–4cm	STEM ↕ 2–5cm ↔ 2–4mm	Spores White	Edibility ☠

Family AGARICACEAE	Species *Leucocoprinus badhamii*	Season Late summer–late autumn

EURO RED-STAINING LEPIOTA

Initially almost white, with a pattern of delicate, pale brown scales on the flattened cap, any part of this agaric turns saffron-red or deep blood-red when handled, finally becoming nearly black. It belongs to a group of rare, red-staining species that are considered to be toxic. Prominent on the velvety stem, the ring is fragile and turns upward. The edible, red-staining *L. americana* occurs in sawdust and plant debris.

• **OCCURRENCE** Found growing on calcareous or nutrient-rich soil, among leaf and garden litter, or on needle beds; particularly under yew trees but also under deciduous trees. Widespread in the warmer parts of Europe; not known in North America.

white to cream gills are crowded and free •

• flat cap

• white flesh stains blood-red

SECTION

brown scales in • concentric circles on cap surface

• prominent, upturned stem ring

• club-shaped stem base

surface of stem stained after handling •

FRUITING Singly or in small groups on rich soil.

Dimensions CAP ⊕ 3–8cm	STEM ↕ 3–7cm ↔ 4–8mm	Spores White	Edibility ☠

Family AGARICACEAE	Species *Leucocoprinus luteus*	Season All year

FLOWERPOT LEPIOTA

This species has distinctive yellow coloring. The surface of the bell-shaped cap has fine, golden yellow to orange-yellow or yellow-brown scales on a sulfur-yellow ground. The stem is a similar color with a short-lived ring and becomes club-shaped toward the base, which is up to 6mm wide. The gills are also yellow and are crowded and free. Inedible, possibly poisonous, it has thin yellow flesh. The fruitbodies are short lived, almost like those of the Inky Caps (*Coprinus*, pp.174–76); the genus name means White Inky Cap, a reference to the white spore deposit.

• **OCCURRENCE** In flowerpots and greenhouses in northern temperate zones, or in the wild in warm subtropical or tropical climates; widespread.

fine golden yellow scales on bell-shaped cap •

yellow stem ring is mostly short lived •

club-shaped • stem base is yellow and powdery

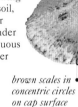

FRUITING Often found growing in tufts on soil that is rich in compost.

Dimensions CAP ⊕ 1–5cm	STEM ↕ 4–10cm ↔ 2–4mm	Spores White	Edibility 🖐

WITHOUT VEIL

THIS SUBSECTION FEATURES one genus, *Pluteus*. It is the only genus to combine gills that are free of the stem with a complete lack of a universal veil. All the species in the genus produce pink spore deposits and have very crowded gills. The majority of species grow on decayed wood, either in the form of fallen trunks or on beds of wood chips or sawdust.

The genus *Volvariella* is a close relative of *Pluteus*, but *Volvariella* species, such as *V. bombycina* (p.154), have a universal veil that covers the immature fruitbody; the veil splits to reveal a volva at the base.

Family PLUTEACEAE	Species *Pluteus cervinus*	Season Late spring–late autumn

FAWN PLUTEUS

Typically, this highly variable species has a dark brown cap and a white stem, with dark fibers that are particularly pronounced at the club-shaped base. The cap may be convex to umbonate or flat; its surface is felted at the center and greasy when wet. It is edible but has an indistinct taste.
• **OCCURRENCE** On decaying deciduous trees in woods, parks, and gardens; it reaches its most impressive dimensions when growing on sawdust or wood chips. Widespread in northern temperate zones and extending south.
• **SIMILAR SPECIES** *Entoloma* species, many of which are poisonous, have a similar spore print color, attached gills, and occur on the ground or near very rotten wood.

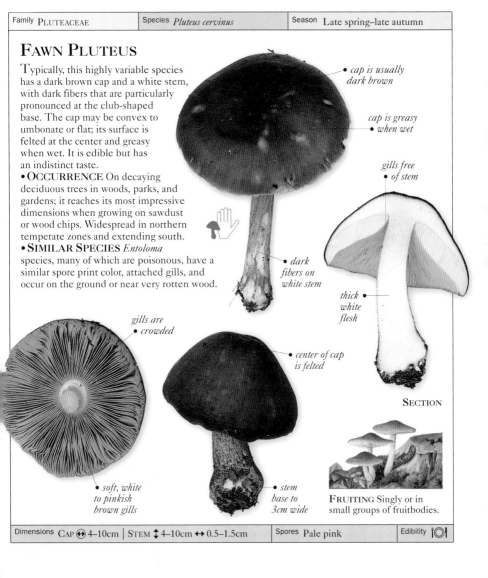

• *cap is usually dark brown*

cap is greasy when wet •

gills free • *of stem*

• *dark fibers on white stem*

thick • *white flesh*

gills are • *crowded*

• *center of cap is felted*

SECTION

• *soft, white to pinkish brown gills*

• *stem base to 3cm wide*

FRUITING Singly or in small groups of fruitbodies.

Dimensions CAP ⊕ 4–10cm | STEM ↕ 4–10cm ↔ 0.5–1.5cm	Spores Pale pink	Edibility ⫯◎⫯

Family PLUTEACEAE	Species *Pluteus umbrosus*	Season Summer–autumn

VELVETY PLUTEUS

Velvety, dark brown cap and stem surfaces and dark gill edges make this *Pluteus* species easy to identify. Its cap is umbonate with a radiating vein pattern on the surface, while the pale stem is heavily dotted with brown scales. The flesh is white to pale brown and smells acidic.

• **OCCURRENCE** Often on large-diameter, naturally decaying deciduous trunks alongside other *Pluteus* species. Widespread in northern temperate zones; mostly uncommon.

• **SIMILAR SPECIES** *P. cervinus* (p.171) is darker, with no vein patterning on the cap. *P. atromarginatus* is similar but grows on conifer wood and has different microscopic characters.

fringed cap margin

umbo in cap center

radiating vein pattern on cap surface

heavy brown dotting on pale stem

grows on well-rotted deciduous trees

paler cap flesh may be visible in places

gills are pale pink-brown

gill edges are downy and brown

SECTION

cap surface is velvety dark brown

gills are free of stem

white to pale brown flesh in stem

FRUITING Appears singly or in small groups.

crowded, soft gills

Dimensions CAP ⊕ 4–11cm | STEM ↕ 5–8cm ↔ 0.4–2cm	Spores Pale pink	Edibility

Family PLUTEACEAE	Species *Pluteus aurantiorugosus*	Season Summer–autumn

FLAME PLUTEUS

This species has a vivid, flame-red cap that varies from convex to nearly flat; the color makes it easy to distinguish from its relatives. The cap surface consists of round cells, making it very delicate, in contrast to the fiber-covered *Pluteus cervinus* (p.171). The pale, more or less yellow stem curves, allowing the fruitbody to fit inside the cracks and hollows of decaying wood. It has no distinctive smell or taste.

• OCCURRENCE On fallen trunks or logs, or on pollarded trees such as poplar, ash, and elm. Widespread but uncommon in northern temperate zones.

• SIMILAR SPECIES *P. admirabilis*, a North American species, is more golden.

vivid, orange-red cap fades to yellow-orange

curved stem

convex to conical, umbonate, or almost flat cap

watery, off-white flesh

gills free of stem

SECTION

finely velvety cap surface is thin and very delicate

crowded, soft, pale pink gills

FRUITING Singly or in small groups on decaying wood.

Dimensions CAP ⊕ 2–5cm │ STEM ↕ 3–8cm ↔ 3–6mm	Spores Pale pink	Edibility

Family PLUTEACEAE	Species *Pluteus chrysophaeus*	Season Summer–autumn

GOLDEN PLUTEUS

There are many forms of this conspicuous species, thought by some experts to be separate species. Although all have yellow caps and pale yellow stems, the color distribution and intensity vary. The cap is convex to umbonate with a smooth surface, the margins showing striations when wet. The stem is paler than the cap, and the off-white to yellow flesh is odorless and tasteless.

• OCCURRENCE On well-rotted deciduous stumps and fallen, moss-covered trunks. Widespread in Europe and eastern North America.

• SIMILAR SPECIES *P. xanthophaeus* has green tones, whereas *P. chrysophaeus* tends toward reddish. *P. romellii* has a darker cap and yellow coloring at the stem base.

free gills

SECTION

convex to umbonate cap

cap is mainly yellow

pale yellow stem has translucent quality

smooth cap has striations at margin

soft, crowded, pink-toned gills

FRUITING Singly or in small groups on rotten wood.

Dimensions CAP ⊕ 1–6cm │ STEM ↕ 3–8cm ↔ 3–8mm	Spores Pale pink	Edibility

INKY WITH AGE

THIS SUBSECTION consists solely of a selection of members of the large genus *Coprinus*, the Inky Caps. Most species of *Coprinus* have gills that dissolve (deliquesce) from the margin inward into an inklike liquid, colored black by mature spores. Other spores are shot into the air, just before the dissolving process reaches the point on the gills where the spores are produced. The gills are usually much more crowded than in most agarics.

Coprinus species are often tiny with thin flesh, and many grow on the dung of herbivorous animals such as deer, cows, horses, and rabbits.

Family COPRINACEAE	Species *Coprinus comatus*	Season Autumn

SHAGGY-MANE INKY CAP

The cap of this species is either an elongated egg shape or broadly conical. It is 5–20cm high and has a shaggy or scaly surface that is off-white to pink tinged, soon becoming black from the margin. The stem has a distinctive ring that stains black by falling spores. This species deliquesces quickly and is more fleshy than most members of the genus. The young fruitbodies are popular edibles because of their fleshy texture and mild, pleasant flavor. Specimens for eating should be collected early in the day and cooked soon after.
• OCCURRENCE In lawns and along roads and forest paths, on disturbed soil. Widespread and common in northern temperate zones.

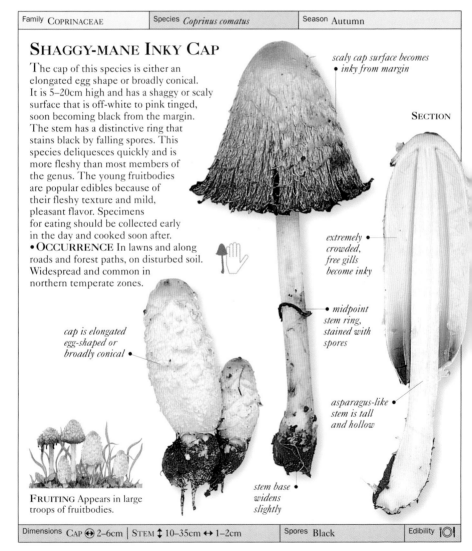

scaly cap surface becomes • inky from margin

SECTION

extremely • crowded, free gills become inky

• midpoint stem ring, stained with spores

cap is elongated egg-shaped or broadly conical •

asparagus-like • stem is tall and hollow

FRUITING Appears in large troops of fruitbodies.

stem base • widens slightly

Dimensions CAP ⊕ 2–6cm | STEM ↕ 10–35cm ↔ 1–2cm	Spores Black	Edibility

| Family COPRINACEAE | Species *Coprinus atramentarius* | Season Spring–autumn |

ALCOHOL INKY CAP

The cap of this fleshy species is egg-shaped, expanding to become slightly umbonate with age. Gray to gray-brown, it deliquesces slowly from the margin. It causes palpitations and nausea if eaten with alcohol; avoid drinking alcohol for several days after eating this mushroom. A more red-brown, scaly form is sometimes called *Coprinus romagnesianus*.

• **OCCURRENCE** In woods, parks, and gardens, at soil level but always associated with decaying deciduous stumps or dying trees. Often found growing on the base of unhealthy city trees. Widespread and common in northern temperate zones.

• **SIMILAR SPECIES** *Coprinus insignis* has warty spores; *C. micaeus* is smaller and more fragile. It has a brownish cap with glistening granules (when young).

free gills are extremely • crowded

• gills edged with white

SECTION

gray to • gray-brown cap without obvious veil remains

FRUITING In dense clusters of fruitbodies.

fine, reddish brown fibrils at stem base •

| Dimensions CAP ⊕ 3–7cm | STEM ↕ 5–12cm ↔ 0.8–1.5cm | Spores Black | Edibility ☠ |

| Family COPRINACEAE | Species *Coprinus picaceus* | Season Autumn |

MAGPIE INKY CAP

This unmistakable mushroom has a black and white pattern on the cylindrical or bell-shaped cap, caused by the veil breaking up into scales as the cap expands. The cap is 5–10cm high; the stem is tall and white, with a fine fleecy covering. It has an unpleasant, fetid smell and is not recommended as an edible.

• **OCCURRENCE** In deciduous woods; occasionally occurs in great numbers where wood chips have been used as a mulch. Widespread in beech regions of Europe; reported in California.

cap quickly becomes inky •

very crowded gills are white or pinkish beige • when immature

• white veil remains pattern cap surface

• hollow stem

young • fruitbody

• tall white stem

FRUITING Appears singly or in small clusters.

SECTION

| Dimensions CAP ⊕ 2–6cm | STEM ↕ 8–30cm ↔ 0.6–2cm | Spores Black | Edibility |

Family COPRINACEAE	Species *Coprinus micaceus*	Season Late spring–early winter

MICA INKY CAP

Grainy veil remnants create a sheen on the surface of the egg-shaped to slightly expanded, pleated, tawny brown cap of this species, which has a splitting or lobed margin. The stem is white, thin, and fragile; the flesh is pale. The mycelium produces many fruitings in one season.

• **OCCURRENCE**
Abundant both in urban areas and in the heart of wood, on and around old stumps and unhealthy trees. Widespread and common in northern temperate zones.

• **SIMILAR SPECIES** Some close relatives produce a thick, orange-yellow mat (ozonium) on the substrate. One of these, *Coprinus domesticus*, is often found in damp cellars. Along with others, it is also found behind loose bathroom tiles and in other damp sites. *C. radicans* is another, like *C. domesticus*, that produces ozonium. *C. micaceus* is most common near the base of elm stumps.

pleated cap is shiny from grainy veil remains •

cap is 1–3.5cm high •

white to brown gills shrivel and become inky with age •

SECTION

off-white • stems are hollow and fragile

FRUITING In dense clusters of fruitbodies.

Dimensions CAP ⊕ 2–4cm	STEM ↕ 4–10cm ↔ 2–5mm	Spores Black	Edibility

Family COPRINACEAE	Species *Coprinus niveus*	Season Summer–autumn

SNOW-WHITE INKY CAP

Best identified by its snow-white coloring and the loose, mealy remnants of the veil over its cap surface, this species is quite small, although not the tiniest of the *Coprinus*. The conical to bell-shaped cap has an upturned margin, the crowded gills are gray when young, black when mature, and the stem has a slightly swollen base. The inedible flesh is very thin and pale.

• **OCCURRENCE** Nearly always found on fairly fresh horse manure in wet grass. Widespread and common in Europe and North America.

• **SIMILAR SPECIES** *C. cortinatus* grows on soil. *C. cothurnatus* often has brown scales at the cap center. Tiny *C. friesii* is found growing on rotten grass. *C. stercoreus* has a slight, fetid smell.

fine mealy covering on cap • may wash off in rain

• rolled back cap margin

cap is egg-shaped when young •

free gills • are black and inky when mature

mealy white • stem

FRUITING Appears in groups of a few fruitbodies.

Dimensions CAP ⊕ 1–3cm	STEM ↕ 5–8cm ↔ 1–3mm	Spores Black	Edibility

WITH GILLS JOINED TO A COLLAR

THIS SUBSECTION FEATURES species from a group of agarics that have gills attached to a "wheel" (collarium), rather than being free or joining the stem. The arrangement resembles the spokes of a bicycle wheel. Most species in the group are in the genus *Marasmius* and occur in the tropics.

Family TRICHOLOMATACEAE	Species *Marasmius rotula*	Season Midsummer–autumn

PINWHEEL MARASMIUS

The gills of this species are attached to a little "wheel," or collar, rather than the stem top. The convex ivory cap has a darker, navel-like center, deep, radial grooves, and thin, tough, off-white flesh. This mushroom can revive after being totally desiccated.

• **OCCURRENCE** On twigs and branches in deciduous and coniferous woods. Widespread and common in northern temperate zones.

• **SIMILAR SPECIES** Many other *Marasmius* species also have a "wheel"; most occur in tropical rainforests, but a few tiny species can also be found in temperate zones: brick-red *M. curreyi* grows in grass; pale brown *M. bulliardii* occurs in swarms on leaf litter in damp woods; pale *M. limosus* grows on reeds. *Marasmiellus ramealis* (p.139), found in similar sites, lacks the gill "wheel" and the cap grooves.

radial grooves on cap surface

ivory gills attached to "wheel"

distinct dark navel in ivory cap center

upper stem is off-white

very tough black stem

FRUITING Appears in troops of fruitbodies.

Dimensions CAP ⊕ 0.5–2cm | STEM ↕ 2–4cm ↔ 1mm	Spores Off-white	Edibility

Family COPRINACEAE	Species *Coprinus plicatilis*	Season Early summer–autumn

UMBRELLA INKY CAP

When fully expanded, the cap of this small *Coprinus* species has a pleated surface, resembling a Japanese umbrella. The cap is smooth, without hairs or veil remnants. The gills are joined to a collar, are more distant, and become less inky than in most *Coprinus* species (pp.174–76).

• **OCCURRENCE** In lawns, appearing after rainfall. Widespread and common in northern temperate zones.

• **SIMILAR SPECIES** *C. auricomus* tends to be a bit bigger and has a browner cap. A microscope reveals thick-walled brown hairs, confirming its identity. Other similar species include *C. kuehneri*, *C. leiocephalus*, and *C. nudiceps*. They can be distinguished only by carefully measuring the spores.

very thin stem is delicate and smooth

conical to flat cap is smooth and pleated

rather distant gills are joined to a collar

FRUITING Singly or in small groups. Appears overnight and withers by noon.

Dimensions CAP ⊕ 0.8–2cm | STEM ↕ 4–8cm ↔ 1–2mm	Spores Black	Edibility

CAP FUNGI WITH STEM OFF-CENTER OR ABSENT

Among the gilled fungi are some species with a stem that is not centrally placed under the cap. It may be attached to the side of the cap and, in some species, can be very small. Other gilled species lack a stem altogether. Most of these fungi are known as oyster mushrooms, but not all are related to each other.

• stem off-center

stem absent •

Family POLYPORACEAE	Species *Pleurotus ostreatus*	Season Autumn–winter

COMMON OYSTER MUSHROOM

smooth cap surface •

The cap of this species is more or less oyster-shaped; in Europe, the coloring ranges from cream to almost black; in North America, from cream to gray-brown. The white stem is positioned at the cap margin or may be absent. The white flesh has a pleasant taste, and its firm texture makes it a popular edible. The complex is now commercially cultivated. This species prefers cold weather and appears later in the season than some similar species (see below).

• **OCCURRENCE** On a wide range of dead or dying deciduous trees; more rarely on conifers. Widespread in northern temperate zones.

• **SIMILAR SPECIES** *Pleurotus dryinus* has a veil on the stem when young. *P. pulmonarius* is cream to pale brown; it appears earlier in the season.

• dark gray-blue to brown cap

• more or less oyster-shaped cap

stem at cap margin or • absent

crowded, decurrent, soft, • cream gills

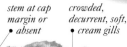

FRUITING In tiers and rows on deciduous trees.

△ *LENTINELLUS URSINUS*
Although edible, this species has a bitter taste. The cap is densely hairy and pale brown, and the gills have toothed edges. |O|

Dimensions CAP ⊕ 6–20cm | STEM ↕ 0–5cm ↔ 1–2cm	Spores Pale gray-lilac	Edibility |O|

Family POLYPORACEAE	Species *Pleurotus cornucopiae*	Season Spring–autumn

EURO TRUMPET OYSTER

This species has a distinctive trumpet-shaped, pale leather-brown cap and a fairly central stem with decurrent gills that join together to form a net. The white flesh has a pleasant taste and smells floury.

• **OCCURRENCE** Forms a white rot on deciduous trees, often elm; it has increased where Dutch elm disease has left abundant substrate. Widespread but mainly in southern Europe; not reported in North America.

• **SIMILAR SPECIES** *Pleurotus citrinopileatus* occurs in east Asia and is yellow. *P. pulmonarius* has simple gills and less of a stem.

smooth cap surface •

trumpet- • shaped cap

off-white stem is • tinged with cap color

clustered • fruitbodies are typical

• network of decurrent gills

△ *PLEUROTUS ERYNGII*
This European choice edible occurs on umbellifer roots. The pale cap has a suedelike surface and an inrolled margin. The stem is off-center or absent. |◎|

FRUITING Appears in clustered groups or singly.

Dimensions CAP ⊕ 4–12cm	STEM ↕ 1–5cm ↔ 0.5–2.5cm	Spores Pale lilac	Edibility |◎|

Family AURISCALPIACEAE	Species *Lentinellus cochleatus*	Season Late summer–autumn

COCKLESHELL LENTINELLUS

This species has a more or less cockleshell-shaped, smooth, red-brown cap with an inrolled margin. The stem is attached to one side. The pale white-brown gills are decurrent and, like all *Lentinellus* species, have toothed edges. Some smell of anise; others are odorless.

• **OCCURRENCE** Rotting deciduous stumps. Widespread in northern temperate zones; locally common.

• **SIMILAR SPECIES** *Clitocybe* species have central stems; *Pleurotus* species have gills with smooth edges.

inrolled • cap margin

smooth, • red-brown cap surface

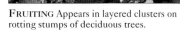

FRUITING Appears in layered clusters on rotting stumps of deciduous trees.

Dimensions CAP ⊕ 2–6cm	STEM ↕ 2–5cm ↔ 0.8–1.5cm	Spores White	Edibility |◎|

Family TRICHOLOMATACEAE	Species *Pleurocybella porrigens*	Season Autumn

ANGEL'S WINGS OYSTER

This small edible species is easily noticed from a distance because its light coloring contrasts strongly with the dark wood substrate. It has a clean, fan-shaped, stemless fruitbody with a distinct incurved margin and crowded gills. It is white, becoming tinted with yellow as it ages. The thin white flesh smells and tastes pleasant.

• **OCCURRENCE** On the decaying trunks and stumps of coniferous wood, such as spruce and fir. Widespread and locally common in northern temperate zones.

• **SIMILAR SPECIES** *Panellus mitis* is much smaller and grows on the twigs and branches of conifers.

fruitbody is like an oyster mushroom •

color of • *fruitbody is overall white*

fan-shaped cap has a smooth, dry surface •

cap margin is distinctly incurved •

gills are white and • *crowded*

FRUITING Appears in large clusters on decaying conifers in open or dense woodlands.

Dimensions FRUITBODY ↕ 2–10cm ↔ 2–7cm	Spores White	Edibility

Family TRICHOLOMATACEAE	Species *Panellus serotinus*	Season Late autumn

FALL OYSTER MUSHROOM

Shaped like an oyster mushroom (*Pleurotus*, pp.178–79), the Fall Oyster Mushroom is easy to identify. It has olive and yellow coloring, a velvety cap surface, and a short, indistinct stem. Not worthwhile as an edible, it has more or less gelatinous white flesh, which tastes mild to slightly bitter and smells faintly mushroomy. Some mycologists prefer to classify *Panellus serotinus* in the genus *Sarcomyxa*.

• **OCCURRENCE** Often found fruiting near water on dead or living tree trunks and fallen branches, rarely on conifers. Widespread throughout northern temperate zones.

• **SIMILAR SPECIES** The stemless, ocher-gilled *Phyllotopsis nidulans* is similar to old or atypical specimens but has an ocher-pink spore deposit.

• *stem on immature specimen*

• *immature gills*

oyster-shaped, • *velvety cap*

short, ocher-yellow stem • *with dark, dotlike scales*

• *gills are slightly decurrent*

crowded • *cream gills*

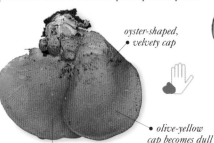

• *olive-yellow cap becomes dull brown with age*

• *cap surface greasy in wet weather*

FRUITING In often dense rows of fruitbodies.

Dimensions CAP ⊕ 3–10cm	STEM ↕ 0.8–1.5cm ↔ 0.5–1cm	Spores White	Edibility

Family TRICHOLOMATACEAE	Species *Panellus stypticus*	Season Autumn–winter

LUMINESCENT PANELLUS

This inedible small, oyster-shaped, pale leather-brown species has tough fruitbodies that usually survive until spring. It has a mealy cap surface and a very short stem. The off-white to pale yellow flesh has an aromatic, fruity smell but tastes bitter and astringent. American specimens have luminescent gills, but European ones do not.

• **OCCURRENCE** In woods on stumps of deciduous trees such as beech and oak. Widespread in northern temperate zones; common in eastern North America.

• **SIMILAR SPECIES** *Panellus mitis* is whiter, smaller, and has a mild taste. It occurs very late in the season on conifers.

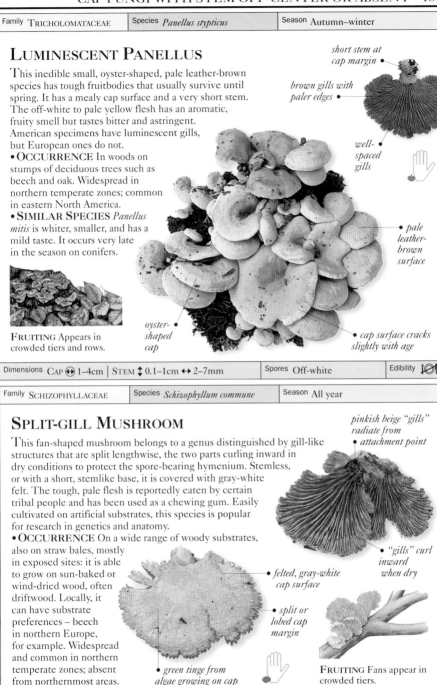

short stem at cap margin

brown gills with paler edges

well-spaced gills

pale leather-brown surface

cap surface cracks slightly with age

oyster-shaped cap

FRUITING Appears in crowded tiers and rows.

Dimensions CAP ⊕ 1–4cm | STEM ↕ 0.1–1cm ↔ 2–7mm	Spores Off-white	Edibility

Family SCHIZOPHYLLACEAE	Species *Schizophyllum commune*	Season All year

SPLIT-GILL MUSHROOM

This fan-shaped mushroom belongs to a genus distinguished by gill-like structures that are split lengthwise, the two parts curling inward in dry conditions to protect the spore-bearing hymenium. Stemless, or with a short, stemlike base, it is covered with gray-white felt. The tough, pale flesh is reportedly eaten by certain tribal people and has been used as a chewing gum. Easily cultivated on artificial substrates, this species is popular for research in genetics and anatomy.

• **OCCURRENCE** On a wide range of woody substrates, also on straw bales, mostly in exposed sites: it is able to grow on sun-baked or wind-dried wood, often driftwood. Locally, it can have substrate preferences – beech in northern Europe, for example. Widespread and common in northern temperate zones; absent from northernmost areas.

pinkish beige "gills" radiate from attachment point

"gills" curl inward when dry

felted, gray-white cap surface

split or lobed cap margin

green tinge from algae growing on cap

FRUITING Fans appear in crowded tiers.

Dimensions FRUITBODY ⊕ 1–5cm	Spores White	Edibility

Family PAXILLACEAE	Species *Paxillus atrotomentosus*	Season Summer–autumn

VELVET PAX

This fleshy, velvet-covered species has a dark brown cap with a depressed center and an inrolled margin. Its thick stem is usually attached to the side of the cap. The soft, cream to brown gills are crowded, and the pale flesh is bitter and odorless.

• **OCCURRENCE** Mycorrhizal; in woods and tree stands, on and around conifer stumps. Widespread and common in many northern temperate regions; common in eastern North America.

• **SIMILAR SPECIES** *P. panuoides* is thinner and paler, has no real stem, and occurs on conifer wood. It may belong to the genus *Tapinella*.

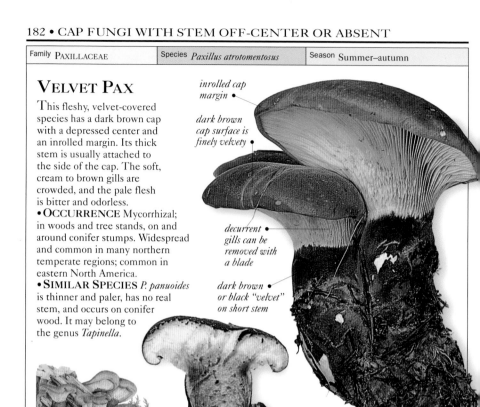

inrolled cap margin

dark brown cap surface is finely velvety

decurrent gills can be removed with a blade

dark brown or black "velvet" on short stem

cream, ocher, or buff flesh

FRUITING Singly or a few together around stumps.

SECTION

Dimensions CAP ⊕ 10–25cm	STEM ↕ 5–10cm ↔ 2–5cm	Spores Yellowish brown	Edibility

Family PAXILLACEAE	Species *Paxillus corrugatus*	Season Summer–autumn

CRINKLE-GILLED PAX

Distinctly furrowed and ridged gills are the most easily recognized features of this stemless, shelf-forming, yellowish brown to olive-orange species. It has an oyster-shaped cap and widely spaced, yellow to orange gills. Not mycorrhizal like *P. involutus* (p.35), this species may be closely related to the genus *Pseudomerullius*.

• **OCCURRENCE** Found growing on dead conifers and deciduous trees. Widespread and common in eastern North America; absent from Europe.

• **SIMILAR SPECIES** *Paxillus panuoides*, a species found in Europe, Asia, and Japan, is similar but with mostly even gills.

oyster-shaped, brownish yellow cap

corrugated or wrinkled gills

gills are yellow to orange

FRUITING Large, shelved clusters on trees in woodland and parks.

Dimensions FRUITBODY ⊕ 5–10cm	Spores Olive-buff	Edibility

| Family CREPIDOTACEAE | Species *Crepidotus mollis* | Season Autumn |

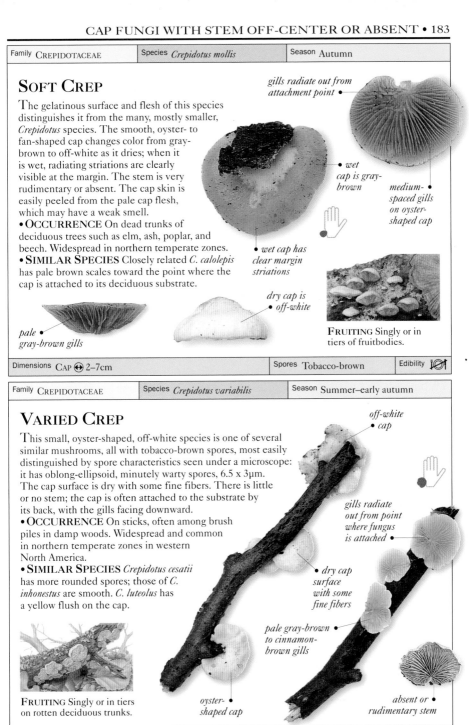

SOFT CREP

gills radiate out from attachment point •

The gelatinous surface and flesh of this species distinguishes it from the many, mostly smaller, *Crepidotus* species. The smooth, oyster- to fan-shaped cap changes color from gray-brown to off-white as it dries; when it is wet, radiating striations are clearly visible at the margin. The stem is very rudimentary or absent. The cap skin is easily peeled from the pale cap flesh, which may have a weak smell.
• **OCCURRENCE** On dead trunks of deciduous trees such as elm, ash, poplar, and beech. Widespread in northern temperate zones.
• **SIMILAR SPECIES** Closely related *C. calolepis* has pale brown scales toward the point where the cap is attached to its deciduous substrate.

• wet cap is gray-brown

medium-spaced gills on oyster-shaped cap

• wet cap has clear margin striations

dry cap is • off-white

pale • gray-brown gills

FRUITING Singly or in tiers of fruitbodies.

| Dimensions CAP ⊕ 2–7cm | Spores Tobacco-brown | Edibility |

| Family CREPIDOTACEAE | Species *Crepidotus variabilis* | Season Summer–early autumn |

VARIED CREP

off-white • cap

This small, oyster-shaped, off-white species is one of several similar mushrooms, all with tobacco-brown spores, most easily distinguished by spore characteristics seen under a microscope: it has oblong-ellipsoid, minutely warty spores, 6.5 x 3µm. The cap surface is dry with some fine fibers. There is little or no stem; the cap is often attached to the substrate by its back, with the gills facing downward.
• **OCCURRENCE** On sticks, often among brush piles in damp woods. Widespread and common in northern temperate zones in western North America.
• **SIMILAR SPECIES** *Crepidotus cesatii* has more rounded spores; those of *C. inhonestus* are smooth. *C. luteolus* has a yellow flush on the cap.

gills radiate out from point where fungus is attached •

• dry cap surface with some fine fibers

pale gray-brown • to cinnamon-brown gills

FRUITING Singly or in tiers on rotten deciduous trunks.

oyster- • shaped cap

absent or • rudimentary stem

| Dimensions CAP ⊕ 0.5–3cm | Spores Tobacco-brown | Edibility |

CAP & STEM FUNGI WITH PORES

This section consists of fungi that produce spores in crowded tubes. The spores are released through pores on the fruitbody underside. Some of these fungi look similar to agarics (see p.10). Boletes have soft flesh (see below). Polypores have tough flesh (see p.202). For bracketlike fungi with pores see p.211.

• pores on underside

WITH SOFT FLESH

THE MUSHROOMS in this subsection are known as boletes. They all have fairly short-lived fruitbodies, characterized by their soft, firm flesh, combined with pores on the underside of the cap. The fruitbodies of many of the species that belong here are attractive as food to a wide range of animals, including humans.

All of the boletes form mutually beneficial (mycorrhizal) associations with trees (see pp.18–19).

Family BOLETACEAE	Species *Porphyrellus porphyrosporus*	Season Summer–autumn

BLUEING CHOCOLATE BOLETE

This dark bolete is well camouflaged in its litter-rich habitat. Its convex cap is sepia colored with a velvety-textured surface, which may crack into scales; the stem is the same color with a velvety to smooth surface. The adnate or notched tubes, 1–2cm long, have wine-buff pores that become blue-green or black when bruised or otherwise damaged. The pale-colored flesh smells and tastes unpleasant; on cutting, it turns blue, green, black, or sometimes red. It has been reported as poisonous.

• **OCCURRENCE** Mycorrhizal with deciduous trees, such as beech, and conifers. As a complex, widespread and common to locally absent in northern temperate zones.

pores are wine-buff, bruising blue-green or black •

cap surface may crack into scales

velvety surface on convex cap •

pale flesh turns blue, green, or black •

stem is • velvety to smooth, and sepia colored

FRUITING Appears singly or in troops of fruitbodies, often in deep litter in woodland areas.

Dimensions CAP ⊕ 5–15cm | STEM ↕ 5–12cm ↔ 1–3cm	Spores Purple-brown	Edibility

| Family BOLETACEAE | Species *Strobilomyces floccopus* | Season Summer–autumn |

OLD MAN OF THE WOODS

The convex cap of this unusual bolete has a scaly, gray-black and white surface resembling a pine cone. It has a tough, fibrous, scaly, gray-black stem and tough flesh that stains pink then black when cut. The pores are rounded to angular. Also known as *S. strobilaceus* and placed by some in its own family.

• OCCURRENCE Grows with both conifers and deciduous trees, mostly on fertile soil. Widespread but rather local in northern temperate zones.

• SIMILAR SPECIES *S. confusus* has erect scales on its cap.

convex, gray-black cap

cap surface is broken into scales

adnate to near decurrent tubes are 1–1.5cm long

pores are white then gray to grayish olive-brown

white to gray flesh turns pink then black

FRUITING Often appears singly or in small groups.

gray-black stem is tough, fibrous, and scaly

stem base often roots

SECTION

| Dimensions CAP ⊕ 5–10cm \| STEM ↕ 8–16cm ↔ 1–2cm | Spores Purplish black | Edibility |

| Family BOLETACEAE | Species *Chalciporus piperatus* | Season Summer–autumn |

PEPPERY BOLETE

SECTION

A very small bolete that is cinnamon-brown throughout, except for the chrome-yellow stem flesh; it does not stain blue on bruising. The slightly greasy cap is convex in shape, and the stem is slender; the tubes are 0.3–1cm long. The flesh has an intensely hot and peppery flavor, making this species inedible, although it has been used as a spice.

• OCCURRENCE Mycorrhizal with trees. Widespread throughout northern temperate zones.

• SIMILAR SPECIES *Chalciporus piperatoides* is similar but can be distinguished by the blue bruising of its cap, tubes, and pores. *C. amarellus* has pinker coloring and a less peppery taste.

tubes are adnate to decurrent

slender, cinnamon-brown stem

chrome-yellow flesh is fairly soft

FRUITING Mostly a few together or singly.

angular, cinnamon-to rust-brown pores

base of stem is tapering

| Dimensions CAP ⊕ 3–5cm \| STEM ↕ 4–6cm ↔ 0.3–1cm | Spores Rusty brown | Edibility |

Family BOLETACEAE	Species *Tylopilus felleus*	Season Summer–autumn

BITTER BOLETE

Slightly to distinctly pink pores on the underside of the bun-shaped brown cap and a dark net on the thick stem are characteristic of this bolete. It has soft, white to cream flesh with an unpleasant smell and a taste that is too bitter to make it edible (see also SIMILAR SPECIES).

• **OCCURRENCE**
Mycorrhizal with conifers and deciduous trees on acidic soil. Widespread and common in eastern North America.

• **SIMILAR SPECIES** When young this is easily mistaken for the King Bolete, *Boletus edulis* (p.187) except that it is very bitter and has a dark stem net.

immature pores are off-white •

brown cap feels • like suede

notched tube layer, 1–2.5cm long, • has fine pores

stem is thick with • a prominent coarse, dark net

pores • mature to deep pink

FRUITING Singly or in troops on well-drained, acidic soil.

Dimensions CAP ⊕ 6–15cm │ STEM ↕ 5–12cm ↔ 2.5–5cm	Spores Dingy pink	Edibility

Family BOLETACEAE	Species *Boletus barrowsii*	Season Summer

BARROW'S BOLETE

This species has a convex to flat, white to gray or tan cap with pores that are white when young, aging to yellowish green. The tube layer, 2–3cm deep, is adnate to slightly depressed around the club-shaped stem, which is white with a distinctive off-white net pattern. The white flesh is thick and tastes sweet.

• **OCCURRENCE**
Mycorrhizal with both conifers and deciduous trees. Widespread and common in North America; not found in Europe.

• **SIMILAR SPECIES** *Boletus edulis* (p.187) and closely related boletes have the white net patterning but darker caps.

white pores age yellowish • green

cap is dry and white to gray or tan •

convex cap becomes flat • with age

distinctive net pattern on upper stem •

FRUITING Appears in large groups of fruitbodies, or scattered under conifers and deciduous trees.

Dimensions CAP ⊕ 7.5–25cm │ STEM ↕ 10–25cm ↔ 2–4cm	Spores Olive-brown	Edibility

Family BOLETACEAE	Species *Boletus edulis*	Season Summer–autumn

KING BOLETE

Widely known as cepe, porcini, steinpilz, and belyigrib, this bolete has a white net pattern on the upper stem and pale yellow to olive-brown pores. It has a bun-shaped, pale or dark brown cap, and a barrel-shaped stem. Its white, nonstaining flesh is pleasant-smelling and tastes mild and nutty.

• **OCCURRENCE** Mycorrhizal with trees in moss-rich woods. As a complex, widespread in northern temperate zones.

• **SIMILAR SPECIES** *Boletus variipes* has a dry, tan cap and grows with oak; *Tylopilus felleus* (p.186) is similar when young but tastes bitter.

smooth, slightly greasy cap surface

bun-shaped brown cap

skin slightly over-hanging cap margin

white net of veins on upper stem

fine, rounded, white to yellow pores

notched tubes

tubes, 1–4cm long, mature olive-brown and are easily loosened

white flesh may have maggot holes or yellow staining from the parasite Sepedonium chrysospermum *(inset, right)*

SECTION

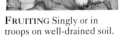

FRUITING Singly or in troops on well-drained soil.

△ **BOLETUS PINOPHILUS**
This rich brown species is found under pine. It has a pale stem net. The cap surface is slightly sticky; it dries felty or granular, often with distinct wrinkles. ¡○!

△ **SEPEDONIUM CHRYSOSPERMUM**
A parasite of boletes, this species appears first as a white mold, becoming powdery golden yellow due to the asexual spores. ¡○!

Dimensions CAP ⊕ 10–25cm | STEM ↕ 10–20cm ↔ 3–10cm	Spores Olive-brown	Edibility ¡○!

Family BOLETACEAE	Species *Boletus appendiculatus*	Season Summer–autumn

SPINDLE-STEMMED BOLETE

The tubes of this species are vivid lemon-yellow, aging to brownish yellow and staining blue; the stem net pattern is similar in color. The tapering stem is often rooting. A choice edible, it has firm, pale yellow to rusty flesh, which stains slightly blue, and a faint, pleasant smell.

• **OCCURRENCE** Mycorrhizal with oak trees in woods. Widespread in southern Europe; reported in California.

• **SIMILAR SPECIES** The cap of *Boletus radicans* is paler with a stouter stem.

firm flesh is pale yellow and stains slightly blue •

notched tubes are • 1–2.5cm long with fine, rounded pores

stem • apex can be wide

SECTION

fine felted, golden • reddish brown skin on bun-shaped cap

stem tapers sharply toward base •

• lemon- to brownish yellow pores stain blue

• lemon-yellow net pattern

FRUITING Appears singly or a few together.

| Dimensions CAP ⊕ 8–20cm | STEM ↕ 7–15cm ↔ 2.5–6cm | Spores Olive-brown | Edibility |

Family BOLETACEAE	Species *Boletus badius*	Season Late autumn

BAY BOLETE

The bun-shaped cap of this species is smooth, rather greasy, and dark chestnut-brown with white to yellow-olive pores, which stain blue. The cylindrical stem is brown without a net pattern. It is easiest to find in late autumn when other boletes are less common. Staining on the white flesh disappears with cooking.

• **OCCURRENCE** Mycorrhizal with pine; also found with deciduous trees. As a complex, widespread and common in eastern North America.

• **SIMILAR SPECIES** *Boletus edulis* (p.187) has a barrel-shaped stem with net patterning.

sinuate tubes, 0.6–1.5cm long •

fine, rounded • pores are white to yellow-olive, as are tubes

• bun-shaped, dark chestnut-brown cap

• smooth, rather greasy cap

SECTION

brown stem is • paler than cap and finely streaked

• blue staining appears on bruised pores

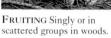

FRUITING Singly or in scattered groups in woods.

| Dimensions CAP ⊕ 4–15cm | STEM ↕ 4–12cm ↔ 1–4cm | Spores Olive-brown | Edibility |

Family BOLETACEAE	Species *Boletus reticulatus*	Season Summer–autumn

SUMMER BOLETE

The bun-shaped cap of this species has a dry, matte skin that tends to crack; it is warm orange-brown. A white to brown net pattern covers the barrel-shaped, pale brown stem. It has firm, nutty-flavored white flesh, which does not stain when cut.

• **OCCURRENCE** Mycorrhizal with deciduous trees like beech and oak; with *Boletus luridiformis* (below) in some areas. Widespread in northern temperate zones; absent in North America.

• **SIMILAR SPECIES** *B. edulis* (p.187) has a darker cap and a less extensive, paler stem net.

sinuate, notched tubes, 1–1.5cm long •

tubes are white • then green-yellow to olive-brown

fine cracks may • cover surface of dry, matte cap

white to brown • net over surface of pale brown stem

• cap skin tends to overhang at margin

SECTION

△ **BOLETUS AEREUS**
A late-fruiting, brown species, reported in California, this has a velvety cap and a pale stem net. The flesh stays white. 🍴

FRUITING In troops or a few together in woodland.

Dimensions CAP ⊕ 7–15cm	STEM ↕ 6–15cm ↔ 2–5cm	Spores Olive-brown	Edibility 🍴

Family BOLETACEAE	Species *Boletus luridiformis*	Season Summer–autumn

DOTTED-STEM BOLETE

Belonging to the group of boletes whose flesh turns blue when cut, this choice edible has a bun-shaped, dark brown cap with deep blood-red pores and yellow tubes. The yellow stem is densely covered with red dots and has no net pattern.

• **OCCURRENCE** Mycorrhizal with trees, in well-drained, mostly acidic and moss-rich, woodland soil. Widespread and common in Europe; not reported from North America.

• **SIMILAR SPECIES** *Boletus erythropus* and *B. subvelutipes* are two nearly indistinguishable species reported from North America. *B. luridus* (p.190) has a stem net.

notched yellow tubes, 1–3cm long, stain blue-black •

SECTION

• cap is velvety to smooth

• dark rich brown cap

blood- • red pores

yellow • flesh stains blue-black

• club-shaped stem

FRUITING Singly or a few fruitbodies together.

Dimensions CAP ⊕ 5–20cm	STEM ↕ 5–15cm ↔ 2–6cm	Spores Brown to olive-brown	Edibility 🍴

Family BOLETACEAE	Species *Boletus calopus*	Season Summer–autumn

SCARLET-STEMMED BOLETE

The skin on the bun-shaped cap of this bolete overhangs the margin and is felted, somewhat veined, and smoky gray or gray-brown. The cylindrical, barrel-shaped, or tapered stem is red at the base, yellow toward the top. It has a pale yellow net pattern, which is pale yellow above, darker and redder toward the base. The inedible, and possibly slightly poisonous flesh tastes bitter and is pale yellow, staining pale blue.

• **OCCURRENCE** Mycorrhizal with trees on acidic, sandy soil. Widespread but mostly local in northern temperate zones; not reported from North America.

• **SIMILAR SPECIES** Two similar bitter boletes, which can be found under conifers in western North America, both with blue-staining yellow pores, are *B. frustosus* and *B. conferarum*.

felted, somewhat veined cap skin

smoky gray or gray-brown cap sometimes olive flushed

cylindrical, tapering, to barrel-shaped stem

cap skin overhangs at cap margin

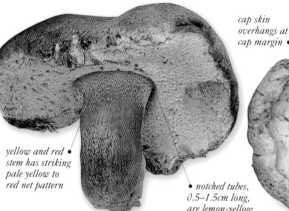

yellow and red stem has striking pale yellow to red net pattern

notched tubes, 0.5–1.5cm long, are lemon-yellow

lemon-yellow pores stain pale blue

△ **BOLETUS LURIDUS**
This species has a prominent, orange-red stem net and lemon-yellow flesh that turns blue-black, as do the orange pores. There is a red line above the tube layer.

△ **BOLETUS BICOLOR**
A common summer species in eastern North America, this bolete has a bright rose-red cap and stem, and yellow pores. Its thick yellow flesh slowly bruises to blue.

FRUITING Appears singly or in troops under trees.

Dimensions CAP ⊕ 6–14cm	STEM ↕ 6–10cm ↔ 3–5cm	Spores Olive-brown	Edibility

Family BOLETACEAE	Species *Boletus satanas*	Season Summer–early autumn

SATAN'S BOLETE

yellow to red stem with net pattern •
smooth cap is pale, almost white •

A fleshy species with a bun-shaped, smooth, pale, almost white cap, Satan's Bolete is best identified by its orange to blood-red pores and the prominent yellow to blood-red net pattern on its fat, yellow to red stem. The yellow to white flesh stains slightly blue, as do the pores. The notched tubes, 1–3cm long, are yellowish green. Mature fruitbodies smell unpleasant and taste mild but are poisonous, causing gastrointestinal problems.

• OCCURRENCE Mycorrhizal with deciduous trees. Widespread in southern Europe; reported in California.

FRUITING Singly, a few together, or in troops with trees such as beech and oak.

Dimensions CAP ⊕ 10–25cm | STEM ↕ 5–15cm ↔ 4–12cm	Spores Olive-brown	Edibility ☠

Family BOLETACEAE	Species *Boletus pulcherrimus*	Season Late summer–autumn

PRETTY POISON BOLETE

stem is swollen and reddish brown •
bun-shaped cap with felty covering •

This brightly colored species is easily recognizable by its blood-red pores that turn blue-black when they are bruised; its bun-shaped, felted, reddish to olive-brown cap; its firm yellow flesh, which turns blue on cutting; and its swollen, but not abruptly bulbous, reddish brown stem that has a dark red net pattern covering the upper part. The notched tubes are 0.5–1.5cm long and yellow-green.

• OCCURRENCE Mycorrhizal with tanbark oak, Douglas fir, and giant fir in mixed forests and woodland. Widespread on the west coast of North America and New Mexico. Not found in Europe.

FRUITING Appears singly or in troops in forests that consist of a mixture of trees.

Dimensions CAP ⊕ 7.5–25cm | STEM ↕ 7.5–15cm ↔ to 10cm	Spores Brown	Edibility ☠

Family BOLETACEAE	Species *Boletus legaliae*	Season Summer–early autumn

LE GAL'S BOLETE

pink-orange stem is swollen, with a net •
smooth, bun-shaped cap is pink-orange •

This species belongs to a group of red-colored, net-stemmed boletes. It has a smooth, pink-orange cap and a similarly colored stem with red netting at the top. The pores are red, and the notched tubes are 1–2cm long. The off-white to pale yellow flesh bruises light blue; the stem base stains pale pink. It has a mild taste and smell but is poisonous.

• OCCURRENCE Mycorrhizal with deciduous trees, preferring calcareous soil. Widespread throughout much of southern Europe; not reported in North America.

• SIMILAR SPECIES The cap of *Boletus rhodoxanthus* is purple-orange.

FRUITING Appears singly or a few fruitbodies together on alkaline soil.

Dimensions CAP ⊕ 5–15cm | STEM ↕ 8–16cm ↔ 2.5–5cm	Spores Olive-brown	Edibility ☠

Family BOLETACEAE	Species *Boletus pulverulentus*	Season Summer–autumn

MIDNIGHT BLUE BOLETE

When bruised, all parts of this distinctive bolete almost immediately turn dark blue. It has a convex, brown to red-brown cap with pointed, dull yellow pores on the underside. The red-dotted, yellow stem is comparatively thin. The slightly notched to slightly decurrent tubes are 0.5–1.5cm long and pale yellow to olive-yellow; the firm flesh is yellow. It has a mild taste but does not rate as a choice edible.
• **OCCURRENCE** Mycorrhizal with deciduous trees, often oak, on fertile soil. Widespread in northern temperate zones.
• **SIMILAR SPECIES** *Boletus luridiformis* (p.189) has a similar, but typically thicker, stem and has red pores. Its flesh turns blue when cut.

cap is brown to red-brown and convex •

pale yellow pores stain black •

yellow stem has red surface • *dotting*

FRUITING Appears singly or a few fruitbodies together; rarely, it may occur in troops.

Dimensions CAP ⊕ 4–10cm	STEM ↕ 4–10cm ↔ 1–3cm	Spores Olive-brown	Edibility |O|

Family BOLETACEAE	Species *Boletus chrysenteron*	Season Summer–autumn

RED-CRACKING BOLETE

One of the smaller, less fleshy boletes, this species has a convex, red-brown cap, with skin that tends to crack, revealing a red layer. The thin, cylindrical, yellow to red stem is streaked but lacks distinct patterning. The angular, yellow to olive pores bruise faintly blue; the pale flesh hardly blues at all. It is edible but bland.
• **OCCURRENCE** Mycorrhizal with deciduous trees, often beech, on well-drained, humus-rich soil formed under acidic conditions. Widespread and common in parts of northern temperate zones; under conifers in California.
• **SIMILAR SPECIES** *B. truncatus* has an abruptly tapering stem and truncated spores.

cap surface cracked, showing red • *underlayer*

△ **BOLETUS POROSPORUS**
This bolete has a white-cracked brown cap and lemon-yellow flesh, pores, and tubes that stain blue. It is best identified by its truncated, spindle-shaped spores, 13 x 5µm |Ø|

• *convex cap is red-brown, often with red edge*

• *stem is streaked in yellow and red*

slightly • *notched to decurrent tubes, to 1cm long*

FRUITING Often in large troops but also singly.

• *yellow to olive pores stain slightly blue*

• *pale yellow young pores*

SECTION

Dimensions CAP ⊕ 3–10cm	STEM ↕ 3–10cm ↔ 0.5–2cm	Spores Olive-brown	Edibility |O|

| Family BOLETACEAE | Species *Boletus rubellus* | Season Summer–autumn |

RED-CAPPED BOLETE

A small species with a deep red cap and stem. The cap is convex; the stem may have a thickened, pointed base. The yellow-olive pores stain blue when bruised; the yellow tubes are 0.5–1cm long. It has slowly blue-staining, pale yellow flesh. It is often placed in the genus *Xerocomus* with similar colored species as *Boletus chrysenteron* (p.192).

• OCCURRENCE Mycorrhizal with deciduous trees in grass, open woods, and parks. Widespread but local in northern temperate zones.

• SIMILAR SPECIES Although eaten in Europe, it is not a safe edible in North America.

yellow tubes are notched to decurrent •

smooth, convex cap is dark red, becoming • browner with age

SECTION

• angular, yellow-olive pores stain blue

pale • yellow flesh

• stem is paler red than cap

stem base may be thickened and • pointed

FRUITING Mostly in troops of fruitbodies.

| Dimensions CAP ⊕ 3–6cm | STEM ↕ 3–8cm ↔ 0.5–1cm | Spores Olive-brown | Edibility ¡⊘¡ |

| Family BOLETACEAE | Species *Boletus subtomentosus* | Season Summer–autumn |

YELLOW-CRACKING BOLETE

Despite its common name, the surface of the golden brown cap of this species rarely cracks or does so only with age. The stem is also golden brown, and the angular pores and the tubes, 0.5–1.5cm long, are yellow. The pores stain slightly blue when they are bruised. Although edible, the soft, pale yellow flesh tastes bland.

• OCCURRENCE Mycorrhizal with both deciduous trees and conifers. Widespread and fairly common in northern temperate zones, extending into subarctic and alpine regions.

• SIMILAR SPECIES *B. chrysenteron* has a reddish brown cap that cracks to reveal a red underlayer. *B. pruinatus* is smaller.

• felty surface of bun-shaped cap

golden brown to olive-brown • cap

yellow tube layer is notched •

faint streaks on pointed stem •

large, yellow to olive pores bruise slighlty blue •

pale yellow flesh stains slightly blue

FRUITING Singly or a few fruitbodies together.

golden brown • or pale yellow stem

SECTION

| Dimensions CAP ⊕ 6–10cm | STEM ↕ 6–10cm ↔ 1–2.5cm | Spores Olive-brown | Edibility ¡⊘¡ |

Family BOLETACEAE	Species *Boletus parasiticus*	Season Summer–autumn

EARTH-BALL BOLETE

An unusual habitat helps to distinguish this small bolete (see OCCURRENCE). Fairly uniformly ocher-brown all over, with no blue-staining reaction, it has a convex cap and a thin stem. The yellow to ocher tubes are 3–7mm long and decurrent. The flesh is pale yellow. Its is not recommended as an edible because its host is toxic.

• **OCCURRENCE** Mycorrhizal with deciduous trees, it grows on the fruitbodies of the fungus *Scleroderma citrinum* (p.256), to which it does little or no damage. Widespread in Europe and reported in eastern North America.

convex, ocher-brown cap

surface of cap is slightly velvety and a little greasy

coarse pores are lemon-yellow to rust-brown

grows on the fruitbodies of Scleroderma citrinum

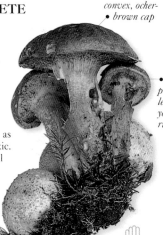

FRUITING In clusters on *Scleroderma citrinum.*

Dimensions CAP ⊕ 2–7cm	STEM ↕ 3–6cm ↔ 0.8–1.5cm	Spores Olive-brown	Edibility

Family BOLETACEAE	Species *Gyroporus castaneus*	Season Summer–autumn

CHESTNUT BOLETE

As with all *Gyroporus* species, the Chestnut Bolete has pale spores; a fragile, chambered stem; and off-white to pale brown tubes, 3–6mm long, which are almost free. The convex to flat cap and smooth stem are a distinctive rich orange-brown. Its flesh, which does not stain when cut, tastes pleasantly nutty.

• **OCCURRENCE** Mycorrhizal with deciduous trees, especially oak, but also with pine. Often found on sandy soil. Widespread and locally quite common in northern temperate zones.

• **SIMILAR SPECIES** There is an apparently poisonous species in coastal Portugal.

pores are off-white to pale brown

smooth, pale orange-brown stem

brittle, off-white flesh does not stain

velvety cap surface

rich orange-brown cap is convex to flat

FRUITING Singly or a few under deciduous trees.

SECTION

Dimensions CAP ⊕ 3–8cm	STEM ↕ 4–7cm ↔ 1–3cm	Spores Pale yellow	Edibility

Family BOLETACEAE	Species *Gyroporus cyanescens*	Season Summer–autumn

BLUEING CHAMBERED BOLETE

SECTION

The most distinctive feature of this species is revealed when it is cut or its tube layer is scratched – the off-white flesh and tubes turn greenish blue to indigo; other blue-staining boletes (mainly *Boletus* species) typically turn darker blue or even blue-black. Otherwise, it has the characteristic fragile flesh, almost free tubes, 5–10mm long, and chambered stem of the genus. It has small, rounded pores and a bulbous stem base that tapers abruptly to a point. A choice edible, it has a pleasantly nutty flavor.

• blue-staining, off-white flesh and tubes

• **OCCURRENCE**
Mycorrhizal with conifers and deciduous trees in woods. Widespread and locally common but rare in most northern temperate zones.

• *convex or flat cap has finely felted, matte surface*

• *stem is pale yellow-ocher*

FRUITING Singly or a few together on sandy soil.

abrupt point on bulbous stem •

white to • straw-yellow pores turn blue if scratched

Dimensions CAP ⊕ 5–8cm | STEM ↕ 6–10cm ↔ 2–3cm	Spores Pale yellow	Edibility

Family BOLETACEAE	Species *Leccinum crocipodium*	Season Summer–autumn

YELLOW-PORED SCABER-STALK

yellow-brown cap, sometimes with • scales

notched, lemon-yellow tubes, 1.5–2.5cm long •

The yellow coloring of this fungus is unusual among species in the *Leccinum* genus, as is the cracking cap skin. The pores are ocher-yellow, staining lilac-brown, and the stem is yellow with ocher-yellow spotting, becoming net-like and brown toward the base; the bun-shaped cap is yellow-brown with a slightly velvety surface. The pale yellow flesh stains wine-red to violet-black. All species of *Leccinum* should be cooked thoroughly before eating.

• **OCCURRENCE**
Mycorrhizal with oak trees in warmer parts of eastern North America.

firm, pale • yellow flesh stains wine-red to violet-black

FRUITING Singly or a few together; prefers fertile soil.

club-shaped • stem

SECTION

Dimensions CAP ⊕ 4–10cm | STEM ↕ 5–12cm ↔ 1–3cm	Spores Olive-ocher	Edibility

Family BOLETACEAE	Species *Leccinum scabrum*	Season Summer–autumn

BROWN SCABER-STALK BOLETE

A brown cap with gray-white pores and a
white to gray stem covered with gray-
black scales are key identification
marks of this species, which is
treated in a broad sense here:
distinguishing between it and
its near relatives is difficult, and
Leccinum scabrum is often used as
a collective name for all brown-
capped *Leccinum* species (see also
L. variicolor, inset). The flesh is soft in the
bun-shaped cap, fibrous in the club-shaped
stem; unlike that of some relatives, it hardly
stains. Although edible, it is not choice and,
once gathered, does not keep well.
• **OCCURRENCE** Mycorrhizal with birch,
often on damp ground. Widespread in eastern
North America.

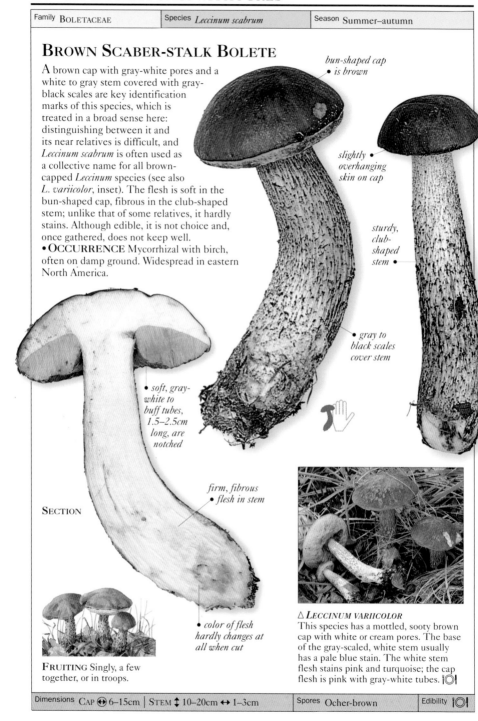

*bun-shaped cap
• is brown*

*slightly •
overhanging
skin on cap*

*sturdy,
club-
shaped
stem •*

*• gray to
black scales
cover stem*

*• soft, gray-
white to
buff tubes,
1.5–2.5cm
long, are
notched*

*firm, fibrous
• flesh in stem*

SECTION

*• color of flesh
hardly changes at
all when cut*

FRUITING Singly, a few
together, or in troops.

△ *LECCINUM VARIICOLOR*
This species has a mottled, sooty brown
cap with white or cream pores. The base
of the gray-scaled, white stem usually
has a pale blue stain. The white stem
flesh stains pink and turquoise; the cap
flesh is pink with gray-white tubes. |○|

Dimensions CAP ⊕ 6–15cm	STEM ↕ 10–20cm ↔ 1–3cm	Spores Ocher-brown	Edibility |○|

Family BOLETACEAE	Species *Leccinum versipelle*	Season Summer–autumn

ORANGE SCABER-STALK BOLETE

A very handsome mushroom, this species, also known as *L. testaceoscabrum*, has a bun-shaped, orange cap contrasting with its tall, black-scaled, white stem; the cap skin overhangs the cap margin and has a finely felted surface. The pores vary from pale gray to ocher-gray, while the notched tubes, 1–3cm long, are dirty white. Staining gray-black, the firm, off-white flesh is reasonably tasty but lacks the quality of some of the *Boletus* species.

• **OCCURRENCE** Mycorrhizal with birch in damp woods. Widespread and common in northern temperate zones; north-eastern North America.

tubes are notched and dirty white to buff

gray-black staining on off-white flesh

SECTION

bun-shaped mature cap

cap skin overhangs cap margin

pores may be pale gray to ocher-gray

black scales cover tall stem

very dark stem of immature specimen

bright orange cap surface is finely felted

FRUITING Singly or a few fruitbodies together.

Dimensions CAP ⊕ 8–15cm	STEM ↕ 10–18cm ↔ 1.5–4cm	Spores Ocher-brown	Edibility ¡◎!

| Family BOLETACEAE | Species *Leccinum quercinum* | Season Summer–autumn |

EURO SCABER-STALK

This bolete belongs to a group of red-capped *Leccinum* species and is distinguished in the group by its mycorrhizal partner and by the reddish brown scales on the stem. Its bun-shaped cap is orange-brown, the pores are off-white to gray or olive-yellow, and its firm white flesh stains almost black. It makes a good edible.

• OCCURRENCE
Mycorrhizal with oak trees in forests. Widespread and common in some regions of northern temperate zones.

• SIMILAR SPECIES
L. aurantiacum has a more orange cap and is associated with aspen and poplar trees. *L. insigne* is common under aspens in the Rockies and has flesh that stains lilac-gray.

pale gray tubes, 2–3cm long, are notched •

SECTION

• cap is bun-shaped

• cap skin is dark chestnut-brown and overhangs margin

almost • black stains on firm white flesh

• reddish brown scales cover stem surface

• almost cylindrical stem widens at base

FRUITING Typically a few fruitbodies together.

| Dimensions CAP ⊕ 8–15cm | STEM ↕ 10–15cm ↔ 1.5–3cm | Spores Ocher-brown | Edibility 🍽 |

| Family BOLETACEAE | Species *Suillus luteus* | Season Late summer–autumn |

SLIPPERY JACK BOLETE

Short-stemmed and slimy, this species has a convex, purple-brown cap, whose skin is easily peeled. It has adnate to slightly decurrent tubes, and fine, lemon-yellow pores. The stem ring has a dark purple underside. Below it, the stem is white, aging purple; above, it is pale yellow with darker dots. Some people are allergic to this species.

• OCCURRENCE Mycorrhizal with pine trees. Widespread and common in eastern North America under two- and three-needled pine.

short tubes, 0.8–1.2cm long, are pale yellow •

purple-• brown cap

off-white • or pale yellow flesh does not stain

SECTION

• ring is off-white above, purple below

fine, • pale lemon-yellow pores

FRUITING Typically in troops under two-needled pine trees.

| Dimensions CAP ⊕ 5–10cm | STEM ↕ 5–10cm ↔ 1.5–3cm | Spores Ocher-brown | Edibility 🍽 |

| Family BOLETACEAE | Species *Suillus grevillei* | Season Autumn |

LARCH BOLETE

This vividly colored bolete has a convex, bright yellow to yellowish orange cap, which is very slimy, and lemon-yellow pores that bruise cinnamon-brown. The white and yellow ring near the top of the yellow-brown stem is also slimy. It is edible, without a distinctive flavor, and, when young, has firm yellow flesh that does not stain; the slimy cap skin is best peeled off when gathering for eating.

• **OCCURRENCE**
Mycorrhizal with larch trees in woods, stands, and gardens; may be found some distance from the host tree. Widespread and common in northern temperate zones.

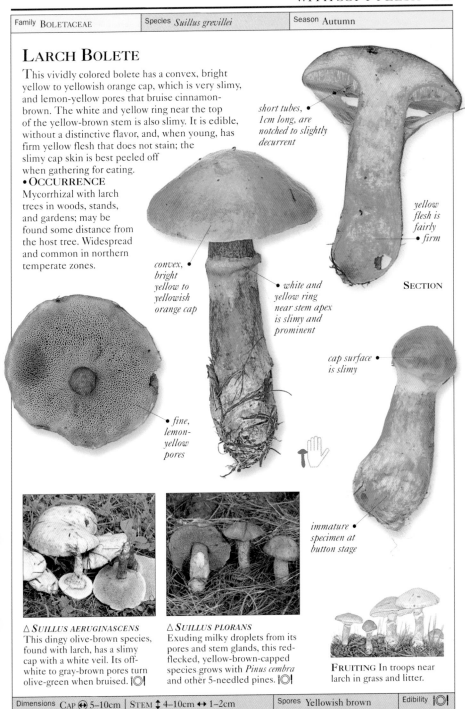

short tubes, • *1cm long, are notched to slightly decurrent*

yellow flesh is fairly • firm

SECTION

convex, • bright yellow to yellowish orange cap

• white and yellow ring near stem apex is slimy and prominent

cap surface • is slimy

• fine, lemon-yellow pores

immature • specimen at button stage

△ *SUILLUS AERUGINASCENS*
This dingy olive-brown species, found with larch, has a slimy cap with a white veil. Its off-white to gray-brown pores turn olive-green when bruised. ¶◎|

△ *SUILLUS PLORANS*
Exuding milky droplets from its pores and stem glands, this red-flecked, yellow-brown-capped species grows with *Pinus cembra* and other 5-needled pines. ¶◎|

FRUITING In troops near larch in grass and litter.

| Dimensions CAP ⊕ 5–10cm | STEM ↕ 4–10cm ↔ 1–2cm | Spores Yellowish brown | Edibility ¶◎| |

Family BOLETACEAE	Species *Suillus bovinus*	Season Late summer–autumn

EURO COW BOLETE

This usually small, orange-rusty brown bolete, with its convex to flat cap and short, ringless stem, is notable for its compound pores: the olive-green pore layer has an outer layer of coarse, angular pores and an inner layer of fine pores. The stem is often barely visible until the fruitbody is picked. The Euro Cow Bolete is edible, with soft, pink-flushed to brownish cream flesh, but it lacks flavor.

• **OCCURRENCE** Mycorrhizal with two-needled pine trees. Often found with *Suillus variegatus* (p.201) and *Gomphidius roseus* (p.38). Widespread and common in Europe and parts of Asia including Japan; absent in North America.

1cm

PORE SURFACE

cap greasy • when wet

adnate-decurrent • tubes are 0.3–1cm long and yellow to olive-yellow

orange-rusty • brown cap

compound pores are • more or less olive-green

FRUITING In troops, often with moss or on sandy soil.

Dimensions CAP ⊕ 3–7cm	STEM ↕ 3–6cm ↔ 0.5–1cm	Spores Brownish olive	Edibility ⭤

Family BOLETACEAE	Species *Suillus granulatus*	Season Late summer–autumn

DOTTED-STALK BOLETE

This species has a ringless stem with distinctive yellow dots and a pointed base. The cap is rusty brown to yellow-orange. In young fruitbodies, the fine, rounded pores exude milky droplets, as do the stem glands. The white to pale yellow flesh is firm with a mild, nutty flavor.

• **OCCURRENCE** Mycorrhizal with two-needled pine, on alkaline soil. Widespread in northern temperate zones.

• **SIMILAR SPECIES** A similar form occurs under 5-needled white pine and may be a different species. *S. placidus* and *S. americanus* occur under eastern white pine; *S. sibiricus* under western white pine.

adnate, pale yellow or pale brown tubes, 0.3–1cm long •

cap surface becomes greasy and slimy in wet • weather

SECTION

pale yellow stem with yellow to red glands

dry, • shiny cap is convex to flat

fine, rounded • yellow pores

FRUITING In troops or a few together near pines.

Dimensions CAP ⊕ 4–10cm	STEM ↕ 4–8cm ↔ 1–1.5cm	Spores Pale brown	Edibility ⭤

Family BOLETACEAE	Species *Suillus variegatus*	Season Summer–autumn

VARIEGATED BOLETE

Tall-stemmed and fleshy, the Variegated Bolete rarely exhibits the sliminess that is characteristic of the genus *Suillus*. Its convex, orange-brown cap has a felty to finely scaly surface. The small pores are brown to olive-brown and, like the pale yellow flesh, stain blue when pressed. The stem is brown with olive-green or pale red tints. Although edible, it has a metallic smell and unpleasant taste.

• **OCCURRENCE** Mycorrhizal with two-needled pine trees, often found with heathers and other acid-loving plants, on sandy soil. Widespread and common in Europe and nearby parts of Asia.

• **SIMILAR SPECIES** *S. tomentosus* is the equivalent species in western North America.

notched to slightly decurrent, short brown tubes, 0.8–1.2cm long

SECTION

blue staining on cut pale yellow flesh

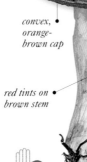

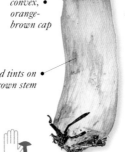

convex, orange-brown cap

cap surface is almost dry with small, grainlike scales

red tints on brown stem

pores to 1mm across

pores are olive-brown, staining blue if pressed

FRUITING Appears a few together or in troops.

Dimensions CAP ⊕ 7–13cm | STEM ↕ 6–10cm ↔ 1.5–2cm	Spores Brownish olive	Edibility

Family BOLETACEAE	Species *Suillus spraguei*	Season Summer–autumn

PAINTED BOLETE

With its dry, scaly red cap, partial white veil, and large yellow pores, this species is very easily recognized. The cap is convex, and the red-flecked, yellow stem may be somewhat club-shaped. The partial veil, which covers the immature pores at first, leaves a cobweblike ring on the upper part of the stem. The tubes are adnate to slightly decurrent. The yellow flesh, which becomes pink tinged on exposure to air, has a firm texture and a mild taste.

• **OCCURRENCE** Mycorrhizal with eastern white pine (*Pinus strobus*) in woods and parks. Widespread and common in eastern North America, wherever eastern white pine grows.

dry, convex cap is red with pale background

scales cover surface of cap

yellow stem is flecked with red

FRUITING Appears in scattered fruitbodies or in large groups under eastern white pine trees.

Dimensions CAP ⊕ 3–12cm | STEM ↕ 4–12cm ↔ 1–2.5cm	Spores Olive-brown	Edibility

WITH TOUGH FLESH

T HE MUSHROOMS in this subsection are known as polypores; they have pores on the cap underside and tough flesh. The polypores featured here also have a more or less distinct stem (for polypores with a bracketlike fruitbody and no stem, see pp.211–233).

Unlike the boletes (pp.184–201), the tube layer of polypores is not easy to separate from the flesh.

Family POLYPORACEAE	Species *Albatrellus ovinus*	Season Summer–autumn

SHEEP POLYPORE

From above, this creamy to pale gray-brown polypore looks like an agaric (see p.28) or a hedgehog mushroom (p.238), but it has minute pores on the underside. It stains lemon or greenish yellow, particularly on the pores. The skin of the convex cap often cracks with age. It has a sturdy stem and very firm, mild to slightly bitter white flesh.

• **OCCURRENCE** Under conifers, mycorrhizal with spruce on moss-covered soil. Widespread throughout northern temperate zones; locally common.

• **SIMILAR SPECIES** *Albatrellus confluens* is more orange and does not stain yellow; it tastes bitter. *A. subrubescens* stains orange.

cap margin is often wavy

angular pores, 2–4 per mm on underside

short, sturdy, cream to gray stem

convex cap is creamy to pale gray brown

FRUITING Appears in troops and groups under established stands of spruce trees.

Dimensions CAP ⊕ 7–18cm | STEM ↕ 3–7cm ↔ 1–3cm	Spores White	Edibility |◎|

Family POLYPORACEAE	Species *Polyporus umbellatus*	Season Summer–early autumn

UMBRELLA POLYPORE

This large, fleshy polypore has a single, multi-branched stem that supports many centrally stemmed, small, circular, pale gray to gray caps. The underside has angular pores, 1–3 per mm, which are white to pale yellow. A choice edible, it has firm, mild-tasting, white to cream flesh. Unlike most polypores, this species has a large black pseudosclerotium with an interior marbled black and white by a mixture of hyphae and earth.

• **OCCURRENCE** On the ground in open deciduous woods. Scattered in northern temperate zones.

• **SIMILAR SPECIES** The individual brackets of *Grifola frondosa* (p.216) do not have central stems.

overlapping, pale gray to gray caps

each cap has a small central stem

clustered fruitbody up to 50cm high

FRUITING On the ground, springing from pseudosclerotium; appears in large clusters.

Dimensions CAP ⊕ 1–4cm | STEM ↕ 5–7.5cm ↔ 2–3cm	Spores White	Edibility |◎|

Family POLYPORACEAE	Species *Polyporus squamosus*	Season Late spring–summer

DRYAD'S SADDLE POLYPORE

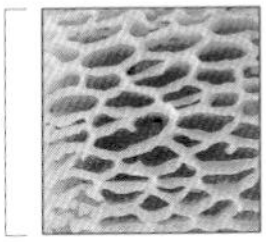

A circular to fan-shaped bracket, covered with brown scales, a black stem positioned to one side, and a decurrent off-white to ocher tube layer, 0.5–1cm thick, make this mushroom unmistakable. Early in the season, it seems to explode out of half-dead trees or stumps; it becomes very large, but is soon devoured by a multitude of insects, leaving only a dried-up carcass, which is broken down by other fungi. The white flesh is soft and smells and tastes of watermelon rind. It can be eaten when very young.

• **OCCURRENCE** Parasitic or saprotrophic on deciduous trees in woods, on street trees, and in parks. Widespread and common in northern temperate zones.

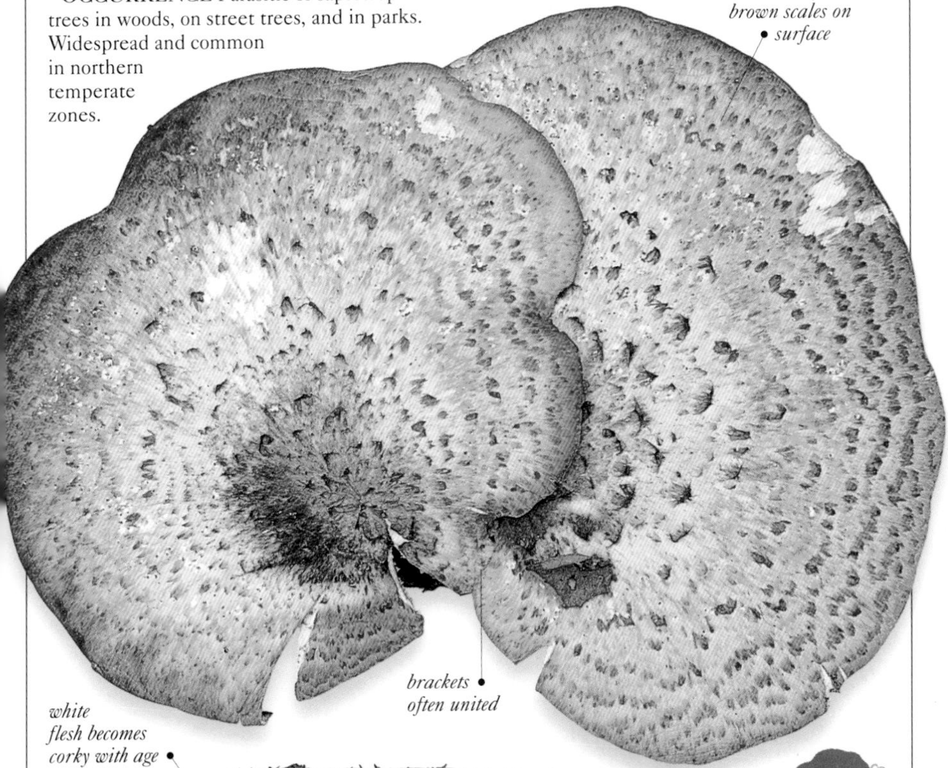

1cm

PORE SURFACE

concentric, flattened brown scales on • surface

white flesh becomes corky with age •

brackets • often united

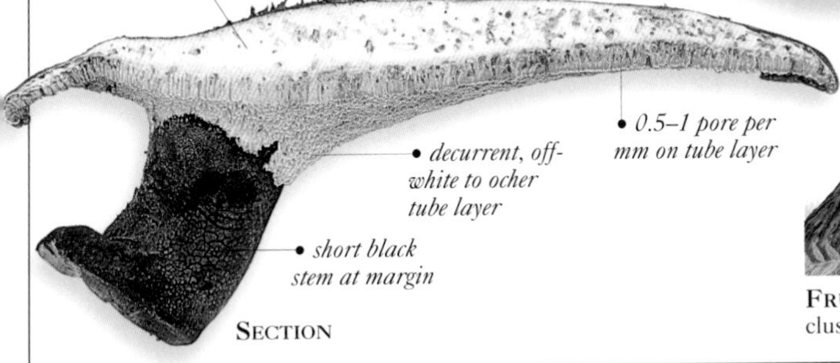

• decurrent, off-white to ocher tube layer

• 0.5–1 pore per mm on tube layer

• short black stem at margin

SECTION

FRUITING Appears in clusters or singly.

Dimensions BRACKET ⊕ 10–60cm × 10–30cm ⊕ to 5cm	Spores White	Edibility

Family POLYPORACEAE	Species *Polyporus tuberaster*	Season Late spring–autumn

TUBEROUS POLYPORE

This species has a flat cap with a distinct central depression and raised brown scales on a paler background. Its central brown stem may root to large underground storage organs; small forms without such organs can also be found. The flesh is edible but tough. The white tubes are up to 5mm long.

• **OCCURRENCE** In deciduous woods, often on calcareous soil; causes white-rot wood decay. Widespread but local in northern temperate zones; western North American in the aspen zone.

raised brown scales on cap surface

hairy cap margin

stem positioned centrally beneath cap

radial pattern of elongated pores

stem is brown and may root to underground storage organs

FRUITING Singly, often from underground storage organs.

up to 2 pores per mm

| Dimensions CAP ⊕ 5–20cm | STEM ↕ to 8cm ↔ 1.5cm | Spores White | Edibility |

Family POLYPORACEAE	Species *Polyporus badius*	Season Late spring–autumn

LIVER-BROWN POLYPORE

This species has a smooth and shiny funnel-shaped cap, which is pale gray-brown when young, then rich dark chestnut with a bright orange-brown margin; in wet weather it is greasy. The short, gray-black stem is attached off-center or at the margin. There are 4–8 pores per mm, and the decurrent tube layer is 0.5–2mm thick. The white flesh is too tough to be edible.

• **OCCURRENCE** In damp woods, on deciduous trees causing white rot. Widespread, local to common in northern temperate zones.

• **SIMILAR SPECIES** *Polyporus melanopus* is rarer and has a felty cap surface. *P. squamosus* (p.203).

1cm

PORE SURFACE

wavy cap margin

smooth, shiny cap surface, dark chestnut with age

tiny, creamy white pores age yellowish brown

short, brown to black stem is off-center

decurrent tube layer is white to cream

FRUITING Singly or a few fruitbodies together.

| Dimensions CAP ⊕ 5–20cm | STEM ↕ 2–4cm ↔ 0.5–2cm | Spores White | Edibility |

| Family POLYPORACEAE | Species *Polyporus varius* | Season Late spring–autumn |

BLACK-FOOTED POLYPORE

The wavy-margined cap of this species is a uniform golden yellow to cinnamon-brown and smooth. The off-center stem becomes black with age, in contrast to the lighter cap, and the decurrent, white to pale cream tube layer is less than 1mm thick. The inedible, white to pale wood-brown flesh is tough with a faint mushroomy smell. Tiny forms with a central stem may be found.

margin is wavy and often lobed

white pores, 4–6 per mm, age ocher-brown

stem slowly turns black from base

• OCCURRENCE On a range of deciduous trees in woods and parks, causing a white rot. Widespread and common in northern temperate zones.

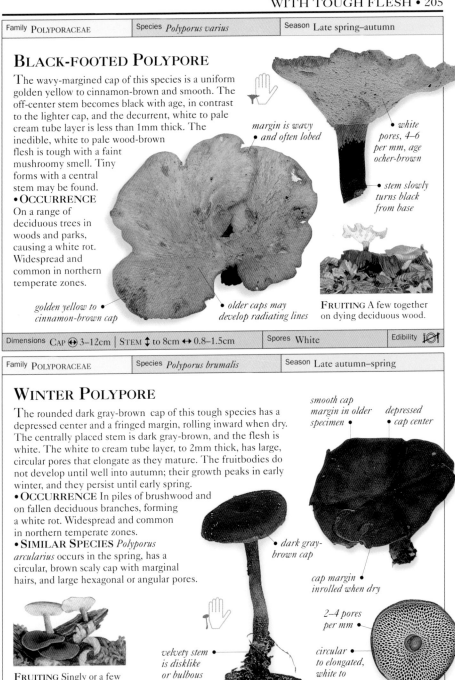

golden yellow to cinnamon-brown cap

older caps may develop radiating lines

FRUITING A few together on dying deciduous wood.

| Dimensions CAP ⊕ 3–12cm \| STEM ↕ to 8cm ↔ 0.8–1.5cm | Spores White | Edibility |

| Family POLYPORACEAE | Species *Polyporus brumalis* | Season Late autumn–spring |

WINTER POLYPORE

The rounded dark gray-brown cap of this tough species has a depressed center and a fringed margin, rolling inward when dry. The centrally placed stem is dark gray-brown, and the flesh is white. The white to cream tube layer, to 2mm thick, has large, circular pores that elongate as they mature. The fruitbodies do not develop until well into autumn; their growth peaks in early winter, and they persist until early spring.

smooth cap margin in older specimen

depressed cap center

• OCCURRENCE In piles of brushwood and on fallen deciduous branches, forming a white rot. Widespread and common in northern temperate zones.

• SIMILAR SPECIES *Polyporus arcularius* occurs in the spring, has a circular, brown scaly cap with marginal hairs, and large hexagonal or angular pores.

dark gray-brown cap

cap margin inrolled when dry

2–4 pores per mm

FRUITING Singly or a few fruitbodies together.

velvety stem is disklike or bulbous at base

circular to elongated, white to cream pores

| Dimensions CAP ⊕ 3–8cm \| STEM ↕ 2–6cm ↔ to 5mm | Spores White | Edibility |

Family HYMENOCHAETACEAE	Species *Coltricia perennis*	Season Summer–winter

FUNNEL POLYPORE

This annual polypore is very unusual in that it grows in the soil rather than on dead wood. The cap is more or less funnel-shaped with fairly tough, rusty brown flesh. Its shiny upper surface has concentric zones in the golden brown shades typical of many Hymenochaetaceae. The tubes, 2mm long, are decurrent on the short, felty stem.
• OCCURRENCE On the ground, mostly on sandy soil in conifer woods, rarely among deciduous trees. Widespread and rather common in northern temperate zones.
• SIMILAR SPECIES Several tooth-fungi (pp.234–39) are similar above but have spiny undersides.

SECTION

• *thin, rusty brown flesh*

• *underside has grayish brown pores*

• *2–4 pores per mm*

thin, wavy margin of funnel-shaped cap

• *concentric zones in shades of brown, ocher, yellow, and pale gray*

FRUITING Appears in small groups of fruitbodies.

Dimensions CAP ⊕ 2–10cm │ STEM ↕ 2–6cm ↔ 3–8mm	Spores Golden brown	Edibility 🖐🍴

Family GANODERMATACEAE	Species *Ganoderma lucidum*	Season All year

VARNISHED POLYPORE

This annual species has an oyster-shaped, shiny red and purple-black bracketlike cap with concentric ridges, a paler margin, and a lacquered brown stem to one side. The tube layer is brown with off-white pores, 3–4 per mm. The tough flesh, although off-white at first, also turns brown. Known as *Ling Chih* or *reishi*, it is a popular herbal tea.
• OCCURRENCE On the stumps or logs of deciduous trees. Widespread but local in northern temperate zones.
• SIMILAR SPECIES There are several closely related species, including *Ganoderma tsugae*, *G. oregonense*, and *G. curtissii*, some of which grow on conifers.

concentric ridges on surface •

shiny, lacquered surface of oyster-shaped cap •

margin of cap is slightly • *paler*

bracketlike cap is shades of purple and red •

distinct • *lacquered stem*

FRUITING Singly or in groups of fruitbodies around the stumps of deciduous trees.

Dimensions CAP ⊕ 10–30cm ⊕ to 3cm │ STEM ↕ 5–20cm ↔ 1–3cm	Spores Brown	Edibility 🖐🍴

HONEYCOMB-, BRAIN-, OR SADDLELIKE CAP

Most of the species in this section are thought to have evolved from cup fungi (see p.264). Their "cup" is heavily folded and is raised on a stem. The spore-producing surface, or hymenium, is smooth and sited on the folds. The choice morels, with a honeycomb-like structure, are found here.

saddlelike cap

brain-like cap

Family HELVELLACEAE	Species *Helvella crispa*	Season Summer–autumn

COMMON WHITE SADDLE

This species is easily identified by its furrowed, hollow, and chambered stem, its saddle-shaped cap, and its pale creamy white coloring. It varies in size but is typically large. With its thin flesh, it is not recommended and should be eaten only after being carefully dried until crisp or after boiling in water.

• **OCCURRENCE** In deciduous or coniferous woods on calcareous soil, often along paths and roads. It, and several other *Helvella* species, is frequently found alongside species of *Peziza* (pp.266–67) and *Inocybe* (pp.98–102). Widespread and common in most northern temperate regions.

cap underside is tan or pale buff •

SECTION

• *convoluted, saddle-shaped cap is cream colored*

hollow stem

chambers in stem

smooth, spore-producing surface •

stem is white with longitudinal grooves

• *base is slightly rooting*

△ **STEREOPSIS HUMPHREYI**
This North American species has a saddle-shaped, dull white cap and a white stem. It is thought to be related to coral fungi (pp.248–51) and appears in large troops.

FRUITING In troops of fruitbodies or singly.

Dimensions CAP ⊕ 2–6cm	STEM ↕ 3–12cm ↔ 0.5–2.5cm	Spores White	Edibility

Family HELVELLACEAE	Species *Helvella lacunosa*	Season Summer–autumn

COMMON GRAY SADDLE

Perhaps the most common *Helvella* species, this fungus is extremely variable in size, shape, and color. It can be any shade of gray, and its cap is either saddle-shaped or convoluted and lobed. The stem has distinct grooves on the outside and is chambered within. The flesh is thin and gray to dirty white; like *Helvella crispa* (p.207), it is edible after thorough drying or boiling but is not recommended.
• **OCCURRENCE** In forests and more open areas on calcareous soil and gravel. Widespread in temperate and alpine zones of both the northern and southern hemispheres.

upper, spore-producing surface

SECTION

gray to near black lobes are paler beneath

deep longitudinal grooves in stem

chambers inside stem

stem is any shade of gray

FRUITING In troops or singly on disturbed soil.

Dimensions CAP ⊕ 1–5cm | STEM ↕ 2–8cm ↔ 0.5–1.5cm	Spores White	Edibility

Family HELVELLACEAE	Species *Gyromitra esculenta*	Season Spring

CONIFER FALSE MOREL

A brainlike, dark brown cap with a chambered interior characterizes this easily identified species. The short white stem is almost hollow, with white flesh. Despite being poisonous, in parts of Europe it is eaten after careful drying or repeated boiling in fresh water.
• **OCCURRENCE** Near conifers on sandy soil or on wood chips. Widespread in northern temperate zones.
• **SIMILAR SPECIES** *Gyromitra gigas*, *G. brunnea*, *G. caroliniana*, and *G. korfii* are often larger and more vivid orange-brown; common in parts of North America.

△ *GYROMITRA INFULA* Appearing in autumn, this species has a lobed brown cap and a chambered, lavender to white stem. ☠

short white stem with slightly grooved surface

brainlike cap surface

cap interior is chambered

white flesh in hollow stem

SECTION

FRUITING In troops, often on disturbed soil near pine.

Dimensions CAP ⊕ 5–15cm | STEM ↕ 1–5cm ↔ 2–4cm	Spores White	Edibility ☠

| Family MORCHELLACEAE | Species *Verpa conica* | Season Spring |

BELL MOREL

The smooth, hoodlike cap of this species is attached only at the very top of the stem. It is ovoid, becoming bell-shaped with age, and dark brown, paler within. The cylindrical stem is off-white with a mealy surface. Although edible, the flesh is thin; many fruitbodies are needed to make gathering this species worthwhile, and they are so rare in some areas that picking it is discouraged, but see SIMILAR SPECIES.

• **OCCURRENCE** On the ground, in rich soil, in mixed deciduous woods. Widespread in northern temperate zones, locally fairly common; rare in cold regions.

• **SIMILAR SPECIES** Also edible, *Verpa bohemica* has a wrinkled cap and 2-spored asci – those of *V. conica* are 8-spored. It can occur en masse.

FRUITING In troops among leaf litter, usually in undergrowth.

narrow point of attachment of cap to stem •

• almost smooth cap surface

• mealy surface on cylindrical stem

hollow center •

SECTION

| Dimensions CAP ⊕ 2–3cm ↕ 2–4cm | STEM ↕ 3–10cm ↔ 0.5–1.5cm | Spores Cream | Edibility |

| Family MORCHELLACEAE | Species *Morchella esculenta* | Season Spring |

COMMON MOREL

This distinctive species has a ridged, honeycomb-like cap, ranging from ovoid to round or conical and fading to pale brown from dark brown as the spores mature on its surface. The white to cream stem is wider at the base and has a mealy surface. The off-white to pale brown flesh tastes and smells pleasant. Varying greatly in size and shape, *Morchella esculenta* is divided into several species by some mycologists.

• **OCCURRENCE** Under dead elms, old apple trees, poplars, tulip poplars, and conifers. Almost worldwide but less common in very cold or warm to hot regions.

• **SIMILAR SPECIES** *Gyromitra esculenta* (p.208) has a brainlike cap and is poisonous.

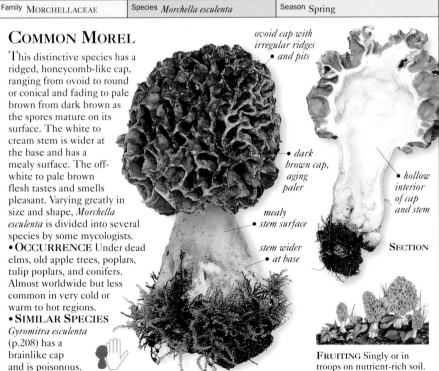

ovoid cap with irregular ridges • and pits

• dark brown cap, aging paler

• hollow interior of cap and stem

mealy • stem surface

stem wider • at base

SECTION

FRUITING Singly or in troops on nutrient-rich soil.

| Dimensions CAP ⊕ 2–10cm ↕ 5–12cm | STEM ↕ 3–15cm ↔ 1–6cm | Spores Ochre-brown | Edibility |

Family MORCHELLACEAE	Species *Morchella elata*	Season Spring

BLACK MOREL

This morel has a conical cap with distinct black ridges and brown to smoky-gray pits. The stem is white with a rough, mealy or granular surface and a hollow center. A popular edible with a crunchy texture and nutty flavor, the Black Morel can cause stomach upsets in some people.

• **OCCURRENCE** On the ground, in parks and open woods. Another form can appear in mountainous areas in summer. Widespread in northern temperate zones.

• **SIMILAR SPECIES** *Morchella esculenta* (p.209) is yellow and has pale ribs along the length of its cap. *Gyromitra* species (p.208), which are poisonous, lack the pitted cap and have chambered, rather than hollow, stems.

pits on cap are brown to smoky-gray •

cap is conical and tapers at top •

brown to black cap with longitudinal ridges •

white stem • with granular surface

FRUITING In large numbers under trees; especially in burned areas.

Dimensions CAP ⊕ 5–10cm ↕ 2.5–5cm │ STEM ↕ 5–10cm ↔ 2.5–5cm	Spores White to cream	Edibility ⦿

Family MORCHELLACEAE	Species *Morchella semilibera*	Season Spring

HALF-FREE MOREL

The conical, dark gray-brown cap of this small morel is free at the rim, with honeycomb-like ridges and pits. It has a slender, hollow, white to cream stem with a mealy surface. It is edible but the cream flesh is too thin to make it choice.

• **OCCURRENCE** Dense woodland on rich soil, along paths in damp places. Widespread and common; in eastern North America and the Pacific Northwest.

• **SIMILAR SPECIES** *Verpa* species (p.209) have small hood-like caps that are attached only to the very top of the stem.

• ridges and pits on cap surface

rim of cap is free of stem •

• cap is conical and taller than it is wide

stem has • hollow center

SECTION

stem is cylindrical • and white to cream

stem is not • very fleshy

slender stem has mealy surface •

• cap is dark gray-brown

FRUITING Often in troops hidden in dense vegetation.

Dimensions CAP ⊕ 1–2.5cm ↕ 1–4cm │ STEM ↕ 3–10cm ↔ 1–2cm	Spores Cream	Edibility ⦿

BRACKET- OR SKINLIKE

This section features fungi that have shelflike fruitbodies, which grow from trunks or branches, as well as species that grow flat (resupinate) against a woody substrate, forming a skinlike crust. The spore-producing surface (hymenium) may consist of tubes, with pores on the surface, or may be smooth to wrinkled.

• *bracketlike*

• *skinlike*

WITH PORES

THE SPECIES in this subsection are known as polypores. Their spores are produced in tubes sited on their undersides and are dispersed through pores that can be rounded to elongated or mazelike in shape. The fruitbodies can be produced annually or continue to grow as long as the substrate lasts.

Family POLYPORACEAE	Species *Tyromyces stipticus*	Season Mainly autumn

BITTER POLYPORE

A very bitter taste is one of the best indicators of this species that produces semicircular to kidney-shaped, off-white annual brackets. Distinctly triangular in cross-section, they have a rough, warty surface and soft white flesh. In humid weather the pores exude an off-white liquid that dries to cream-white. The tube layer is 0.5–1cm thick; there are 4–6 pores per mm.
• **OCCURRENCE** Causes a brown rot on stumps or trunks of conifers; thus it is sometimes placed in the genus *Oligoporus*. Widespread and common in northern temperate zones, especially in the boreal regions.

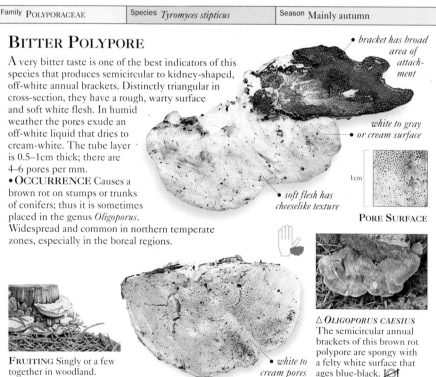

• *bracket has broad area of attachment*

white to gray or cream surface •

1cm

• *soft flesh has cheeselike texture*

PORE SURFACE

FRUITING Singly or a few together in woodland.

• *white to cream pores*

△ *OLIGOPORUS CAESIUS* The semicircular annual brackets of this brown rot polypore are spongy with a felty white surface that ages blue-black.

Dimensions BRACKET ⊕ 5–12cm × 3–7cm ⊕ to 2.5cm	Spores White	Edibility

Family POLYPORACEAE	Species *Piptoporus betulinus*	Season All year

BIRCH POLYPORE

This semicircular annual bracket fungus has a skinlike, brownish gray surface. It is stemless or has a rudimentary stemlike attachment. The soft but firm white flesh smells pleasant but is inedible. It was once used for sharpening razors and as a polishing agent in the watchmaking industry. The brackets are often attacked by flask fungi *Hypocrea pulvinata* when on the tree or by the orange *Hypomyces aurantius*, once the tree or polypore has fallen.

• **OCCURRENCE** In damp woods, often alongside *Fomes fomentarius* (p.219). It is parasitic on older birch trees, causing brown rot. The trees eventually die, but the polypore can continue fruiting on them for some time. Widespread and common in northern temperate zones.

bracket often swollen near attachment point •

brownish • gray surface may crack to reveal white flesh

SECTION

white tube • layer is up to 1cm thick

• white flesh is soft but tough

smooth, • rounded margin

• white pore surface with 3–4 pores per mm

FRUITING A few together on rotten birch trunks.

Dimensions BRACKET ⊕ 5–30cm × 5–20cm ⬍ 2–6cm	Spores White	Edibility

Family POLYPORACEAE	Species *Hapalopilus rutilans*	Season All year

PURPLE-DYE POLYPORE

All parts of this fan-shaped annual bracket fungus are reddish cinnamon in color – the surface, the flesh, and the tube layer, which is up to 1cm thick. It has a remarkable reaction with an alkaline solution, turning brilliant purple, a characteristic that is exploited for dyeing wool. The relatively soft-textured flesh is inedible.
• **OCCURRENCE** On dead deciduous trees, where it produces white rot, in woods. Widespread and common to local in northern temperate zones.
• **SIMILAR SPECIES** *Pycnoporus cinnabarinus* (p.225) is tougher and a brighter cinnabar-red.

broad area of • attachment to substrate

• bracket surface is downy when young

reddish cinnamon • tube layer

SECTION

FRUITING Singly, in groups, fused, or in tiers, on dead wood.

2–4 pores per mm •

1cm

PORE SURFACE

Dimensions BRACKET ⊕ 2–12cm × 2–8cm ⊕ 1–4cm	Spores White	Edibility

Family FISTULINACEAE	Species *Fistulina hepatica*	Season Late summer–autumn

BEEFSTEAK POLYPORE

This species produces a tonguelike annual bracket with red tubes 1–1.5cm long and 2–3 pale red pores per mm. The tubes are easily separated, unusual for a polypore. The bracket is pink- to orange-red then purple-brown and may have a short stem. The flesh looks like beef or liver. It exudes a blood-red liquid; it smells pleasant and has the texture and flavor of beef tongue seasoned with lemon juice.
• **OCCURRENCE** Grows on mature living oaks; causes brown heart rot. Widespread but local in northern temperate zones.

SECTION

tongue-shaped bracket •

• upper surface is sticky or moist

flesh • with veins and blood-red juice

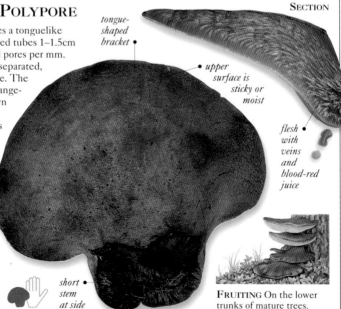

short • stem at side

FRUITING On the lower trunks of mature trees.

Dimensions BRACKET ⊕ 10–25cm × 10–20cm ⊕ 2–6cm	Spores White	Edibility

Family POLYPORACEAE	Species *Meripilus giganteus*	Season Autumn

BLACK-STAINING POLYPORE

This massive species produces several densely layered annual brackets from a single short stem; a composite fruitbody can be up to 1m across. Each fan-shaped bracket has a smooth surface with concentric, golden brown zones and a wavy margin. The pleasant smelling white flesh is soft and fibrous; it is edible when young – turning gray to black when cooked – but has a poor flavor. The off-white tube layer is up to 1cm thick.

• **OCCURRENCE** In woods and parks, causing a white rot on dying deciduous trees. Widespread and fairly common in eastern North America.

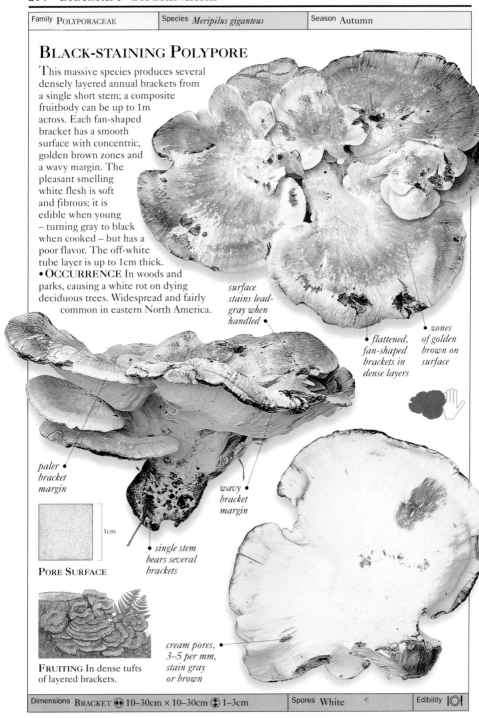

surface stains lead-gray when handled •

• *flattened, fan-shaped brackets in dense layers*

• *zones of golden brown on surface*

paler • bracket margin

wavy • bracket margin

1cm

PORE SURFACE

• *single stem bears several brackets*

FRUITING In dense tufts of layered brackets.

cream pores, 3–5 per mm, stain gray or brown •

Dimensions BRACKET ⊕ 10–30cm × 10–30cm ⊕ 1–3cm	Spores White	Edibility

Family POLYPORACEAE	Species *Laetiporus sulphureus*	Season Early summer–late autumn

CHICKEN POLYPORE

This splendid, annual bracket fungus has an almost luminous quality with its large, quick-growing, yellow or yellow-orange fruitbodies. The thick, fleshy brackets are fan-shaped or irregularly semicircular with an uneven, suedelike surface. The flesh is pale yellow with a crumbly texture, especially when old, and smells of fresh lemon. A choice edible, it requires thorough cooking; some people are allergic to it.

• **OCCURRENCE** On deciduous trees in some regions, conifers in others; mostly attacks the heartwood, causing a brown rot. Widespread and common in eastern North America.

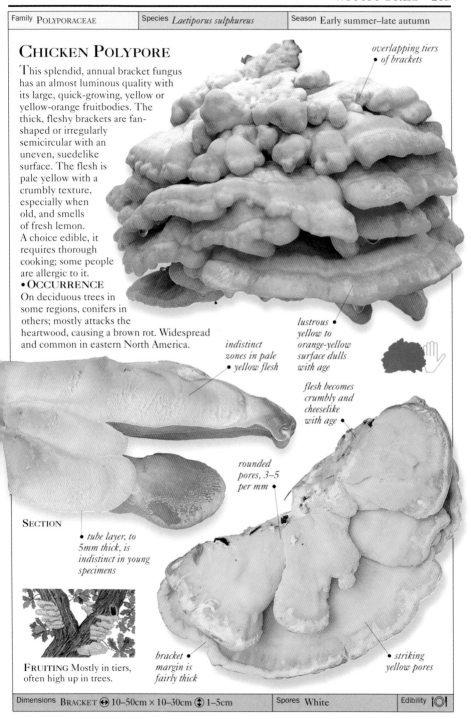

overlapping tiers of brackets

lustrous yellow to orange-yellow surface dulls with age

flesh becomes crumbly and cheeselike with age

indistinct zones in pale yellow flesh

rounded pores, 3–5 per mm

SECTION

tube layer, to 5mm thick, is indistinct in young specimens

bracket margin is fairly thick

striking yellow pores

FRUITING Mostly in tiers, often high up in trees.

Dimensions BRACKET ⊕ 10–50cm × 10–30cm ⊕ 1–5cm	Spores White	Edibility

Family POLYPORACEAE	Species *Grifola frondosa*	Season Summer–autumn

HEN-OF-THE-WOODS POLYPORE

This species has an annual fruitbody with tongue-shaped brackets branching off a central stem. Leathery with a wavy margin, the upper surface is gray, aging to brown. The decurrent tube layer is up to 5mm thick and off-white. The white flesh smells unpleasant when it ages. It is a choice edible, avidly collected in fall in eastern parks and woods.
• OCCURRENCE At the base of oak trees; produces a white rot. Widespread and common in eastern North America.
• SIMILAR SPECIES *Meripilus giganteus* (p.214).

small, tongue-shaped bracket

gray upper surface ages to brown

wrinkled and streaky upper surface

composite fruitbody, to 50cm wide

FRUITING Clusters of brackets branch off from a thick, central stem near the base of trees.

Dimensions BRACKET ⊕ 2–6cm × to 7cm ‡ 0.2–1cm	Spores White	Edibility

Family GANODERMATACEAE	Species *Ganoderma pfeifferi*	Season All year

EURO VARNISHED POLYPORE

The upper surface of this hoof-shaped perennial bracket has concentric, orange-brown ridges covered by a thick, copper-colored lacquer that melts when exposed to a flame. The brown tube layer, to 10cm thick, is protected by a thick, waxy yellow substance in winter. The woody brown flesh has a pleasant smell.
• OCCURRENCE At the base of living beech trees, rarely other hosts, where it forms white rot. Widespread but local in central and southern Europe.

hoof-shaped bracket is orange-brown

5–6 pores per mm

waxy yellow covering on pores in winter

thick lacquer on upper surface

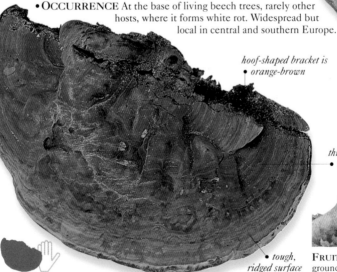

tough, ridged surface

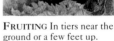

FRUITING In tiers near the ground or a few feet up.

Dimensions BRACKET ⊕ 20–50cm × to 25cm ‡ to 15cm	Spores Brown	Edibility

Family GANODERMATACEAE	Species *Ganoderma applanatum*	Season All year

ARTIST'S POLYPORE

The upper surface of this semicircular perennial bracket is uneven, with concentric ridges and a thin margin. Beginning off-white, it becomes pale ocher-brown and is often covered with a brown spore deposit. The upper surface is easily broken; the pale buff underside can be scratched with a sharp point to produce a brown "artwork," hence the common name. The tube layer is brown and 0.5–4cm deep. The thin, dark brown flesh, often with pockets of white tissue, has a bitter taste and a "mushroomy" smell.

• **OCCURRENCE** On stumps and trunks of trees in parks and woods. Widespread and common in northern temperate zones.

• **SIMILAR SPECIES** Other species of *Ganoderma* have a shiny, lacquered upper surface.

bracket has grown around strand of ivy

pale buff pores, 4–6 per mm

uneven, tough bracket surface

thin layer of lacquer just visible •

SECTION

thick brown spore deposit covers upper surface

FRUITING Singly or in groups, mostly on dead trees.

flesh is dark brown, typically with pockets of white tissue •

brown tubes

Dimensions BRACKET ⊕ 10–60cm × to 30cm ⊕ 2–8cm	Spores Brown	Edibility

Family HYMENOCHAETACEAE	Species *Phellinus igniarius*	Season All year

GRAY FIRE POLYPORE

Gray to almost black in color, this perennial bracket is hoof-shaped and extremely woody, with thick margins. The bracket may remain on living host trees for many years. The hard flesh and tubes are rusty brown; new tubes, 1–5mm long, grow annually on the previous year's tubes. Tiny hairs, called setae, characteristic of the family, are concealed in the hymenium. Experts disagree on the exact identity of this species; a range of forms is covered here.

• **OCCURRENCE**
Parasitic on a number of deciduous trees, commonly birch, willow, and apple, causing white rot. Widespread and fairly common in northern temperate zones.

moss and lichen grow on the upper surface of older specimens •

some cracking • often occurs on gray to almost black surface

• concentric ridges appear with age

broad area of • attachment

1cm

PORE SURFACE

• gray to gray-brown pores

5–6 pores • per mm

FRUITING Singly or a few together on living trees.

| Dimensions BRACKET ⊕ 10–40cm × 10–20cm ⊕ to 20cm | Spores White | Edibility |

| Family POLYPORACEAE | Species *Fomes fomentarius* | Season All year |

TINDER POLYPORE

This polypore has a hoof-shaped, woody perennial bracket with zones varying from dark brown in older areas to pale brown at the growing margin, which is downy or felty. A new brown tube layer grows annually. Each year's tube layer is 5mm thick. The pore surface is gray to gray-brown. Existing in several forms, depending on the host, this species has been used as tinder and to make hats and other clothing.
• **OCCURRENCE** Parasitic on deciduous trees, especially beech and birch, and forms white rot. It fruits on fallen wood. Widespread and often common in northern temperate zones.
• **SIMILAR SPECIES** *Fomitopsis pinicola* (inset, right).

△ *FOMITOPSIS PINICOLA*
This gray perennial species has bright yellow and red zones near its margin. The bracket surface feels lacquered and melts under a flame. The pores are pale yellow, and the hard flesh is white to yellow with a characteristic acidic smell. ✙✕

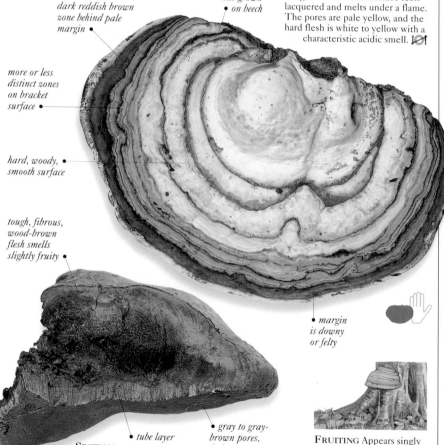

this specimen has grown on beech

dark reddish brown zone behind pale margin

more or less distinct zones on bracket surface

hard, woody, smooth surface

tough, fibrous, wood-brown flesh smells slightly fruity

margin is downy or felty

SECTION

tube layer

gray to gray-brown pores, 2–3 per mm

FRUITING Appears singly or in rows of brackets.

| Dimensions BRACKET ↔ 5–30cm × to 25cm ↕ 5–30cm | Spores White | Edibility ✙✕ |

Family POLYPORACEAE	Species *Phaeolus schweinitzii*	Season Summer–winter

PINE DYE POLYPORE

Impressive when actively growing, this annual
bracket mushroom arises from a very short, more or
less central brown stalk, and has a brilliant sulfur-
yellow margin surrounding concentric zones of rusty
brown. As the bracket ages, it turns dirty brown then
slowly rots away. The sulfur-yellow tube layer is up to
1cm thick with pores, 1–4mm in diameter, that are
greenish yellow when young, turning dark brown
when touched. The inedible, fibrous, yellow to
brown flesh contains a pigment used in dye.
• **OCCURRENCE** Around living or dead conifers
and Douglas fir, especially pine, causing brown
rot. Widespread and common in northern
temperate zones; cosmopolitan.

*sulfur-
yellow
young
specimen*

*uneven surface
with color
zones •*

*bracket •
surface is
very felty
or hairy*

1cm

PORE SURFACE

*• old specimen
is dark brown
all over*

FRUITING Mostly solitary
from underground roots.

Dimensions BRACKET ⊕ 15–30cm × 10–25cm ⊕ 1–4cm	Spores White	Edibility

Family HYMENOCHAETACEAE	Species *Inonotus hispidus*	Season Summer–autumn

SHAGGY POLYPORE

The thick-fleshed, fan-shaped annual bracket of this species is distinguished by its shaggy surface. Flame-red when young, it gradually turns brown from the inner part of the fruitbody outward; the pore surface is white to pale brown, becoming darker with age, and often appears shiny. There are 2–3 pores per mm. The pale brown tube layer is 1–3cm deep. Scattered, short, thick hairs (setae) are enclosed in the spore-bearing tissue (hymenium).
• **OCCURRENCE** Parasitic on deciduous trees such as ash, pear, apple, and walnut, causing white rot. Widespread and common to rare in northern temperate zones.
• **SIMILAR SPECIES** *Inonotus cuticularis* has smaller brackets and occurs on beech and oak. *I. rheades* is also smaller and occurs on aspen.

flame-red • bracket ages to brown

white to pale • brown pore surface becomes darker with age

bracket surface is very shaggy •

FRUITING Appears singly or in fused groups on living deciduous trees, stumps, and logs.

Dimensions BRACKET ⊕ 15–40cm × 10–20cm ⬧ to 10cm	Spores Yellow	Edibility

Family HYMENOCHAETACEAE	Species *Inonotus radiatus*	Season All year

ALDER BRACKET POLYPORE

SECTION

This polypore forms semicircular, wavy-margined annual brackets. The upper surface is bright yellow to orange-red when young, becoming zoned in shades of rusty brown. When young and growing, the pore surface often has yellow drops on it; with age, it reflects the light and appears shiny and silvery. The tubes are 1cm long, and the hymenium encloses tiny, short, curved hairs (setae).
• **OCCURRENCE** Parasitic, mostly on standing alder trunks or on birch trees. On fallen tree trunks it may develop just the tube layer over the bark (resupinate). Widespread and common in northern temperate zones.
• **SIMILAR SPECIES**
Inonotus nodulosus has less distinct brackets and occurs on beech.

tough flesh is • zoned with shades of rusty brown

tube layer may be decurrent, • running down the substrate

semicircular brackets have • wavy margins

top surface • is orange when young

2–4 • pores per mm

pore surface looks • shiny silvery gray from some angles

FRUITING Tiers and rows on dead wood.

Dimensions BRACKET ⊕ 3–8cm × 1–3cm ⬧ to 3cm	Spores Pale yellow-brown	Edibility

Family POLYPORACEAE	Species *Heterobasidion annosum*	Season All year

CONIFER-BASE POLYPORE

The perennial bracket of this species is irregular with a very uneven surface and a corklike texture. The crust darkens with age; the margin is white, often with an orange band just behind it. The white to cream tube layer is up to 1cm thick or more, and the inedible flesh is pale yellow. Occasionally, this species grows against the substrate, without brackets (resupinate).

• **OCCURRENCE** Causes a white rot on conifer stumps, rarely on deciduous trees. In densely planted conifer stands, it can spread underground to infect healthy trees. Widespread in northern temperate zones.

white to • cream pores, 2–4 per mm

growing margin is • white

1cm

PORE SURFACE

light brown • crust darkens with age

SECTION

• corklike, pale yellow flesh

FRUITING In groups of brackets or singly.

Dimensions BRACKET ⊕ 5–25cm × 3–15cm ⑂ 1–3cm	Spores White	Edibility 🚫

Family POLYPORACEAE	Species *Gloeophyllum odoratum*	Season All year

ANISE-SCENTED POLYPORE

This species develops perennial brackets, which are cushion-shaped and slightly felted. The margin is golden yellow to orange; older parts are almost black. There are 1–2 golden yellow pores per mm and the tube layer is up to 1cm thick. The corklike flesh is rust-brown. Although not edible, it smells pleasantly of fennel and oranges.

• **OCCURRENCE** On conifers, usually spruce; causes brown rot. Widespread in northern temperate zones.

• **SIMILAR SPECIES** Widespread and common, *Gloeophyllum abietinum* and *G. sepiarium* have gill-like pores and typically occur on sun-baked conifers.

dark • brown to black inner area

golden yellow • to orange margin

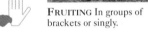

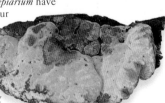

1cm

PORE SURFACE

golden • yellow young specimen

FRUITING Mostly singly or in groups on tree stumps.

Dimensions BRACKET ⊕ 5–20cm × 5–20cm ⑂ 2–5cm	Spores White	Edibility 🚫

Family POLYPORACEAE	Species *Trametes gibbosa*	Season All year

EURO BEECH POLYPORE

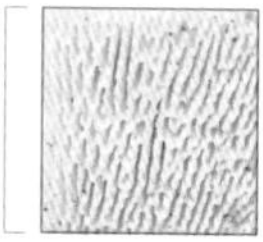

Annual or perennial, the large brackets of this species are semicircular with the inner part of the upper surface usually stained green by algae. Concentric color zones occur near the smooth margin. Young specimens are chalk-white with a downy or minutely hairy surface, becoming smooth with age. The white flesh is tough and inedible; the tube layer, to 4mm thick, has elongated cream pores.

• **OCCURRENCE** In woods; typically forms white rot on beech. Widespread and rather common in northern temperate zones.

• **SIMILAR SPECIES** *Trametes hirsuta* (p.224) is thinner and hairier with less elongated, grayer pores.

1cm

PORE SURFACE

green algal growth on bracket surface

• characteristic hump where bracket joins substrate

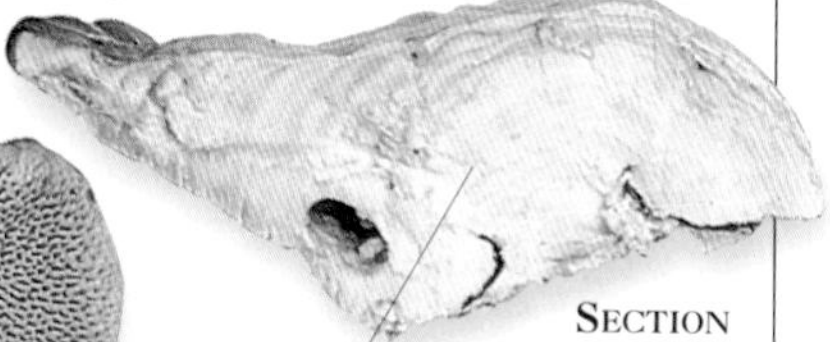

SECTION

thick, corky • white flesh

• cream pores are elongated

• mazelike pore surface with 1–2 pores per mm

FRUITING Singly or in tiers on deciduous stumps.

| Dimensions BRACKET ⊕ 10–30cm × 5–20cm ⬦ 1–4cm | Spores White | Edibility |

Family POLYPORACEAE	Species *Trametes hirsuta*	Season All year

HAIRY POLYPORE

This species produces annual brackets with straight surface hairs, which are stiff and upright on the inner areas. The surface has concentric ridges and off-white to yellow-brown zones, which become darker with age. The pores are angular, and the white tube layer is 1–4mm thick. The white flesh is tough.
• **OCCURRENCE** Appears in woodland sites that have been exposed to sun through wood cutting or storm damage. It produces white rot on a range of deciduous trees. Widespread and fairly common in northern temperate zones.
• **SIMILAR SPECIES** *Trametes pubescens*, a more northerly species, has yellower pores. *Cerrena unicolor*, also occurring in more northerly areas, has more irregular pores and a black line above the tube layer.

off-white pores, 2–4 per mm, become pale gray

short hairs lie flat at smooth margin

off-white to yellow-brown zones

FRUITING In rows and tiers on fallen deciduous trunks.

Dimensions BRACKET ⊕ 5–12cm × 3–8cm ⊕ 0.3–1cm	Spores White	Edibility

Family POLYPORACEAE	Species *Trametes versicolor*	Season All year

TURKEY-TAIL POLYPORE

Thin, layered brackets with alternating zones of either gray or brown shades characterize this familiar fungus. The fruitbody is annual but may develop further in spring. Narrowly attached to the substrate, the brackets are widely fan-shaped. The tube layer, to 3mm thick, is white, drying to pale yellow, and there are 3–4 pores per mm. The tough flesh is white. The smaller specimen shown here is a typical form, zoned gray and dark blue-gray.
• **OCCURRENCE** On deciduous trees, in woods, parks, and gardens; forms white rot. Widespread and very common throughout northern temperate zones.
• **SIMILAR SPECIES** *Trametes ochracea*, a more northerly species, is slightly thicker and browner, with larger pores.

1cm

PORE SURFACE

narrow attachment area

wavy, irregular margin

overlapping, tiered brackets

silky surface with dense zones of gray and brown

FRUITING In dense rows and tiers on tops or sides of stumps.

Dimensions BRACKET ⊕ 2–7cm × 1–5cm ⊕ 1–5mm	Spores White	Edibility

Family POLYPORACEAE	Species *Bjerkandera adusta*	Season All year

SMOKY POLYPORE

Abundant in suitable habitats, this species produces a thin annual bracket with concentric zones of gray-brown, a wavy felted surface, and a lobed margin. The tube layer, which is up to 2mm thick, has distinctive, tiny, ash-gray pores; in cross-section, a thin, dark layer is visible between the off-white flesh and the tube layer. It smells strongly "mushroomy."
• **OCCURRENCE** Parasitic or saprotrophic on deciduous trees, particularly beech, in woods; forms white rot. Widespread and common in northern temperate zones.
• **SIMILAR SPECIES** *Bjerkandera fumosa*, often on willow or ash, is rarer. It is larger and has paler pores.

PORE SURFACE

• *old specimen has dark margin; white when young*

• *felty surface has zones of gray-brown*

• *rounded pores, 4–6 per mm*

• *light gray-brown pores age ash-gray*

FRUITING Grows in rows or tiers of fruitbodies.

Dimensions BRACKET ⊕ 3–7cm × 1–5cm ‡ to 8mm	Spores White-cream	Edibility

Family POLYPORACEAE	Species *Pycnoporus cinnabarinus*	Season All year

CINNABAR POLYPORE

The uniform bright cinnabar-red coloring of this species makes it easy to identify. The annual bracket is semicircular to fan-shaped, with fine, silky hairs on the upper surface. It becomes paler as it ages and almost smooth, with a thin, sharp margin. The tube layer is 4–6mm thick. The flesh becomes corky when dried.
• **OCCURRENCE** On dead deciduous trees in warm, sunny, exposed areas; forms a white rot. Widespread and common to rare in northern temperate zones.
• **SIMILAR SPECIES** *Pycnoporus sanguineus* is thinner and is found in similar sites but in warmer climates.

PORE SURFACE

more or less smooth surface is slightly wrinkled • *when mature*

• *fine, rounded to elongated pores, 2–3 per mm*

bracket shape may be almost circular •

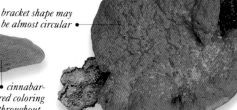

• *cinnabar-red coloring throughout bracket*

FRUITING Appears singly or a few together.

Dimensions BRACKET ⊕ 3–10cm × 2–6cm ‡ 0.5–2cm	Spores White	Edibility

Family POLYPORACEAE	Species *Trichaptum abietinum*	Season All year

PURPLE-TOOTH POLYPORE

pale gray surface is felty •

Tending to be abundant where it occurs, this widely fan-shaped annual bracket fungus has concentric grooves on the felty, pale gray surface, which is often tinged green by algae; the purple margin is typically wavy and lobed. When young, the tube layer, to 5mm thick, is purple, becoming reddish brown. The angular pores often split with age. It has tough, pale brown or purple flesh.

• green algal growth on bracket

• concentric grooves

pores tend to split
• *with age*

• *wavy, lobed bracket margin*

• **OCCURRENCE** On conifers, mostly spruce; it causes white rot. Widespread and common in northern temperate zones.
• **SIMILAR SPECIES** *Trichaptum biforme* has wider, less resupinate brackets, and grows on deciduous trees. Other *Trichaptum* species found on conifers, such as *T. fusco-violaceum* on pine, are distinguished by teeth or gills on the underside.

• *3–6 angular pores per mm*

FRUITING In rows and tiers, often fused in groups.

Dimensions BRACKET ⊕ 2–4cm × 2cm ⊛ 2–3mm	Spores White	Edibility

Family POLYPORACEAE	Species *Daedalea quercina*	Season All year

THICK-MAZE POLYPORE

This species produces a thick, semicircular perennial bracket with a smooth but uneven surface that is creamy yellow or dull ocher-brown to pale gray. Slightly flexible when fresh, it dries wood-hard. The inedible, pale wood-brown flesh smells faintly "mushroomy." Young pores near the growing margin are rounded but develop into a maze of thick plates radiating from the attachment point; the tube layer is 1–3cm thick, the separating walls 1.5–2mm thick.

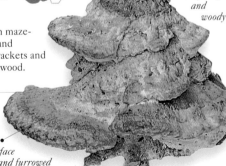

• *mazelike pores with woody walls*

• *very tough and woody*

• **OCCURRENCE** Parasitic or saprotrophic on oak trees in woods and parks; forms brown rot. Widespread in northern temperate zones; common in eastern North America.
• **SIMILAR SPECIES** Other polypores with maze-like pores, including *Daedaleopsis confragosa* and *Lenzites betulina* (both p.227), have thinner brackets and do not occur on oak heartwood.

FRUITING Singly or in tiers; may be in shelved groups.

bracket is • creamy yellow to pale gray

smooth to • downy surface is uneven and furrowed

Dimensions BRACKET ⊕ 10–30cm × 5–20cm ⊛ 3–7cm	Spores White	Edibility

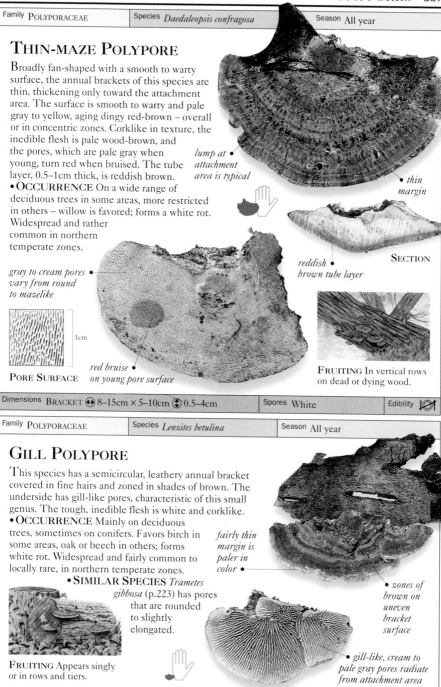

Family POLYPORACEAE	Species *Daedaleopsis confragosa*	Season All year

THIN-MAZE POLYPORE

Broadly fan-shaped with a smooth to warty
surface, the annual brackets of this species are
thin, thickening only toward the attachment
area. The surface is smooth to warty and pale
gray to yellow, aging dingy red-brown – overall
or in concentric zones. Corklike in texture, the
inedible flesh is pale wood-brown, and
the pores, which are pale gray when
young, turn red when bruised. The tube
layer, 0.5–1cm thick, is reddish brown.
• OCCURRENCE On a wide range of
deciduous trees in some areas, more restricted
in others – willow is favored; forms a white rot.
Widespread and rather
common in northern
temperate zones.

lump at
attachment
area is typical

• thin
margin

gray to cream pores •
vary from round
to mazelike

reddish •
brown tube layer

SECTION

1cm

PORE SURFACE

red bruise •
on young pore surface

FRUITING In vertical rows
on dead or dying wood.

Dimensions BRACKET ⊕ 8–15cm × 5–10cm ⊕ 0.5–4cm	Spores White	Edibility

Family POLYPORACEAE	Species *Lenzites betulina*	Season All year

GILL POLYPORE

This species has a semicircular, leathery annual bracket
covered in fine hairs and zoned in shades of brown. The
underside has gill-like pores, characteristic of this small
genus. The tough, inedible flesh is white and corklike.
• OCCURRENCE Mainly on deciduous
trees, sometimes on conifers. Favors birch in
some areas, oak or beech in others; forms
white rot. Widespread and fairly common to
locally rare, in northern temperate zones.
• SIMILAR SPECIES *Trametes*
gibbosa (p.223) has pores
that are rounded
to slightly
elongated.

fairly thin
margin is
paler in
color •

• zones of
brown on
uneven
bracket
surface

• gill-like, cream to
pale gray pores radiate
from attachment area

FRUITING Appears singly
or in rows and tiers.

Dimensions BRACKET ⊕ 3–10cm × 1–5cm ⊕ 1–2cm	Spores White	Edibility

WRINKLED OR SMOOTH UNDERNEATH

NOT ALL BRACKETLIKE mushrooms produce fruitbodies with a tube layer and pores on their underside (pp.211–27); some have the spore-producing cells (basidia) sited on a wrinkled, veined, warty, spiny, or completely smooth surface. This type of bracket is featured in this subsection. The other species featured here have tubes and pores but occasionally bear fruitbodies that grow flat against the substrate surface (resupinate). These species have a layer of flesh supporting the spore-producing tissue.

Family CORTICIACEAE	Species *Phlebia tremellosa*	Season Autumn–early winter

TREMBLING PHLEBIA

Exceptional among *Phlebia* species, which are usually resupinate, this mushroom has well-developed, protruding annual brackets, although part of the spore-producing layer runs down the bark. The upper side is velvety and almost white, while the underside is yellow to orange and covered with dense ridges and veins. The structure is soft and gelatinous.

• **OCCURRENCE** On the stumps of deciduous trees, such as birch and beech; very rarely on conifers. Widespread and common in northern temperate zones.

• **SIMILAR SPECIES** The closely related *P. radiata* is common on similar substrates, but is bright orange and thinner; it is fully resupinate, without brackets. The underside has radiating veins and wrinkles.

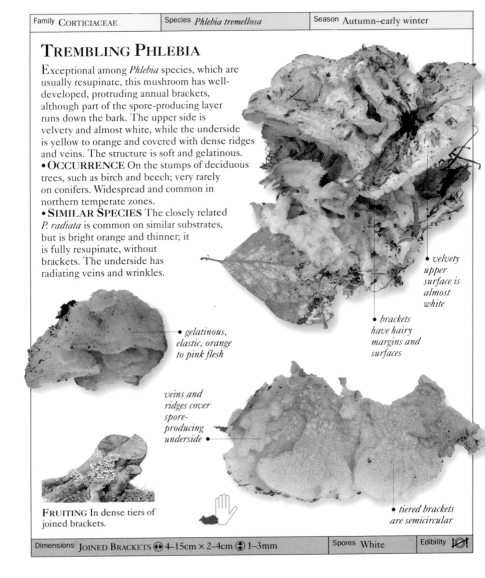

velvety upper surface is almost white

brackets have hairy margins and surfaces

gelatinous, elastic, orange to pink flesh

veins and ridges cover spore-producing underside

tiered brackets are semicircular

FRUITING In dense tiers of joined brackets.

Dimensions JOINED BRACKETS ⊕ 4–15cm × 2–4cm ⊕ 1–3mm	Spores White	Edibility

Family THELEPHORACEAE	Species *Thelephora terrestris*	Season All year

COMMON THELOPHORA

Similar in appearance to some lichens, the fringed, fan-shaped fruitbodies of this fungus are well camouflaged by their earthlike colors. The upper surface is uneven and fibrous; the spore-producing underside is warty and slightly paler in color. The inedible flesh is thin and brown.

underside is paler in color than upper side

• **OCCURRENCE** Mycorrhizal with trees in woods and waste ground, on acidic soil or decayed stumps; often found along paths and trails. Also found in plant nurseries with conifer seedlings. Widespread and common in northern temperate zones.

warty, spore-producing underside

often fruits at soil level

layers of fan-shaped brackets

uneven, felty upper surface

• **SIMILAR SPECIES**
Thelephora caryophyllea is deeply funnel-shaped and has a less felty surface. An uncommon resupinate form of *T. terrestris* is similar to species of *Tomentella*.

white to pale brown margin is fringed

distinctly fibrous structure of fruitbody

FRUITING Appears in layered, joined brackets.

Dimensions JOINED BRACKETS ⊕ 4–10cm × 1–6cm ⊕ 2–3mm	Spores Brown	Edibility

Family CONIOPHORACEAE	Species *Serpula lacrymans*	Season All year

DRY-ROT MUSHROOM

This mushroom is well known for the brown rot it causes, which severely weakens construction lumber inside houses. The semicircular, veined, resupinate or bracket-forming fruitbody is in shades of brown and exudes acidic white droplets from the growing margin. It stains red-brown when touched and is rubbery in texture. The fungus also produces a copious white weft of mycelium.

brackets growing from wooden windowsill

acidic white droplets exuded at growing margin

concentric zones in shades of brown

• **OCCURRENCE** Thrives inside poorly ventilated buildings where alkaline substances, such as mortar, neutralize its acidic droplets, which would otherwise make its growing environment too acid. Widespread and common in buildings; in the wild, on the east and west coasts of North America and in the Himalayan foothills of India.

spreading fruitbody is mostly resupinate

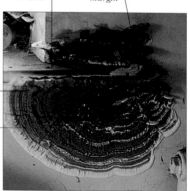

FRUITING Fully resupinate or with brackets on wood and walls in houses.

Dimensions FRUITBODY ⊕ to 50cm × to 10cm ⊕ 0.5–2cm	Spores Yellow to olive-brown	Edibility

Family AURICULARIACEAE	Species *Auricularia mesenterica*	Season All year

BRACKET JELLY

At first glance, this annual bracket could be mistaken for species of *Trametes* (pp.223–24) or *Stereum* (p.232 and below), but it is distinguished by, among other features, its gelatinous flesh. The zonation on the top surface is due to fine velvety hairs. The spore-producing underside of the bracket is wrinkled and veined. Although edible, it is not worth eating.

• OCCURRENCE Found on deciduous wood; where there is dead elm, it can be abundant with other elmwood species. Absent in all but the southernmost part of the United States, but it is reported from Mexico south to Argentina.

rubbery, jelly-like flesh

velvety upper side zoned in brown and gray-brown

wrinkled and veined spore-producing surface

green coloring due to algae

FRUITING In tiers on trunks and stumps.

Dimensions BRACKET ⊕ 4–15cm × 1–5cm ⊕ 2–5mm	Spores White	Edibility ⓉⓄ❙

Family CORTICIACEAE	Species *Stereum hirsutum*	Season All year

HAIRY STEREUM

This species produces a long-lived, fan-shaped, bright yellow to tan bracket with a smooth spore-bearing surface that often runs down the substrate. The upper surface is hairy, with indistinct concentric zones; it is paler at the margin. The similarly colored flesh is thin but tough and does not stain. The spores are amyloid.

• OCCURRENCE On deciduous trees, especially oak, birch, and beech; often on bark or on the cut surfaces of stored wood. Widespread in northern temperate zones; common in eastern North America.

• SIMILAR SPECIES *Stereum gausapatum* and *S. rugosum* (p.232) are more resupinate and stain red. *S. ochraceo-flavum* is smaller with duller undersides.

brackets can be densely layered

smooth, spore-producing underside

concentric zones in shades of yellow to tan

FRUITING Appears in abundant linked brackets.

wavy, lobed margin

hairy upper surface

△ *STEREUM SUBTOMENTOSUM*
This species has wide, less resupinate brackets with more distinct zones. Its flesh stains yellow. ⓉⓄ❙

Dimensions BRACKET ⊕ 2–6cm × to 3cm ⊕ 1–2mm	Spores White	Edibility ⓉⓄ❙

Family CORTICIACEAE	Species *Chondrostereum purpureum*	Season All year

PURPLE SILVER-LEAF STEREUM

This fungus is easy to identify because of its habit of producing a multitude of wavy-margined brackets, which are purple when young. The upper surfaces are white-downy; the undersides are smooth and purple-brown. When dry, they tend to be hornlike in texture. The flesh is waxy and somewhat gelatinous. Unlike *Stereum* species, the spores do not develop a blue coloring with iodine reagents.

• OCCURRENCE Parasitic or saprotrophic on many deciduous trees; causes silver-leaf disease on cherry and plum trees, eventually producing white rot in the wood. Widespread in northern temperate zones; common in most regions.

• fused and tiered brackets

• tough, leathery flesh is somewhat gelatinous

smooth spore-producing surface is purple-brown

felty or downy upper surface often looks almost white

• undulating bracket margin

FRUITING In tiers and rows of linked brackets.

Dimensions LINKED BRACKETS ⊕ 2–5cm × to 4cm ‡ 1–2.5mm	Spores White	Edibility

Family HYMENOCHAETACEAE	Species *Hymenochaete rubiginosa*	Season All year

RIGID LEATHER BRACKET

This well-camouflaged, rigid, perennial bracket fungus with wavy margins occurs in abundant tiers. The top surface is marked with concentric brown zones, increasing in number and becoming very dark with age; the cocoa-brown underside seems smooth, but examination with a powerful hand lens reveals a covering of tiny rigid hairs (setae). The flesh is very tough, thin, and cocoa-brown.

• OCCURRENCE Grows on the stumps or fallen branches of oak. Widespread and common in eastern North America.

• zones increase with age

• margins wavy and sometimes lobed

• minute, stiff hairs cover underside

upper surface brown, becoming very dark with age •

cocoa-brown • underside

• underside appears smooth

• dark brown zones on upper surface

FRUITING In crowded tiers of brackets.

Dimensions BRACKET ⊕ 1–6cm × 1–4cm ‡ 1mm	Spores White-cream	Edibility

SKINLIKE; GROWING FLAT OR CRUSTLIKE

I N THIS SUBSECTION are some of the many fungi that produce fully resupinate, skinlike fruitbodies on the underside of fallen wood. They range from white to pink or deep blue. The spore-producing surface (hymenium) of these species can be smooth, warty, spiny, or veined. (See also pp.228–31.)

Family CORTICIACEAE	Species *Stereum rugosum*	Season All year

RED-STAIN STEREUM

This abundant woodland fungus, which may grow for several seasons, forms a thick, flat, rather featureless, pale gray skin on bark; brackets rarely occur. Scraping the surface of the fungus soon produces blood-red marks. The spores are amyloid.
• **OCCURRENCE** On deciduous trees, often standing dead trunks; frequently found on hazel, birch, and alder. Widespread and common in Europe; probably also in a wider area in northern temperate zones.
• **SIMILAR SPECIES** *Stereum sanguinolentum* also stains red when damaged, but it is found on bark of conifers and has distinct brackets.

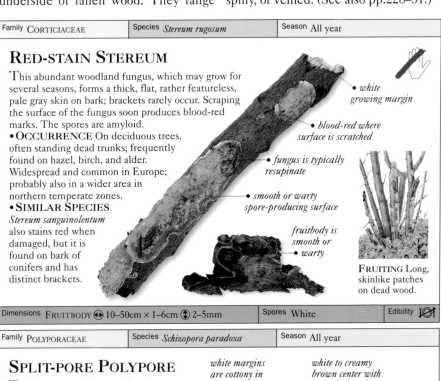

white growing margin

blood-red where surface is scratched

fungus is typically resupinate

smooth or warty spore-producing surface

fruitbody is smooth or warty

FRUITING Long, skinlike patches on dead wood.

Dimensions FRUITBODY ⊕ 10–50cm × 1–6cm ⊕ 2–5mm	Spores White	Edibility

Family POLYPORACEAE	Species *Schizopora paradoxa*	Season All year

SPLIT-PORE POLYPORE

This fungus usually grows flat, but may produce tiny brackets when on vertical surfaces. It is fairly tough and white to creamy brown with cottony white margins and teeth up to 4mm long in the center. The tube layer is 1–4mm thick and has 1–3 pores per mm; when examined under a hand lens, the pores often resemble flattened teeth.
• **OCCURRENCE** Mainly on deciduous trees, particularly beech, in woods; causes white rot. Widespread and common in northern temperate zones; cosmopolitan.

white margins are cottony in texture

white to creamy brown center with toothed surface

fruitbody usually resupinate

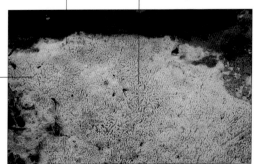

FRUITING Appears in skinlike, spreading patches on the underside of fallen branches.

Dimensions FRUITBODY ↕ 5–50cm × 2–10cm ⊕ 3–7mm	Spores White	Edibility

| Family CONIOPHORACEAE | Species *Coniophora puteana* | Season All year, mainly autumn |

WET-ROT MUSHROOM

The spreading fruitbodies of this wet-rot fungus are soft textured and grow flattened against the substrate, never forming brackets. Maturing spores make the centers yellow to olive-brown, whereas the margins are white and fringed. Typically, the fruitbody surface becomes wrinkly and warty with age. Unlike most resupinate species, which are firmly fixed to the substrate, Wet-rot Mushroom fruitbodies can be lifted gently off.
• **OCCURRENCE** On wet wood indoors, causing wet brown rot, and on all types of wood outdoors. Widespread in the wild and in buildings, in northern temperate zones.
• **SIMILAR SPECIES** *Serpula lacrymans* (p.229) exudes droplets and may form brackets.

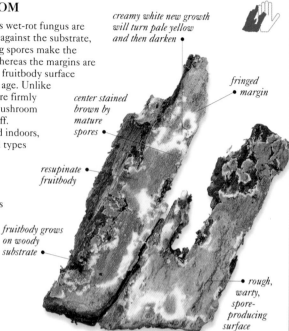

creamy white new growth will turn pale yellow and then darken

fringed margin

center stained brown by mature spores

resupinate fruitbody

fruitbody grows on woody substrate

rough, warty, spore-producing surface

FRUITING Resupinate fruitbodies over substrate.

| Dimensions FRUITBODY ↔ 5–100cm × 2–20cm ↕ 0.5–1mm | Spores Yellow-brown | Edibility |

| Family POLYPORACEAE | Species *Oligoporus rennyi* | Season Autumn |

POWDER-PUFF POLYPORE

This spreading polypore is most easily recognized by its two growth stages, which occur almost simultaneously, next to each other. The resupinate, crustlike sexual stage is white at the edge, creamy white in the center, with 2–3 pores per mm. The pores become torn with age and release white spores. The asexual stage is puffball-like at first, shredding open at maturity to expose a great mass of powdery, olive-brown spores.
• **OCCURRENCE** Small patches on stumps and fallen branches of conifers; produces a brown rot in the wood. Widespread and rare to common, but usually overlooked, in northern temperate zones.

puffball-like asexual stage

crustlike sexual stage

cream-white with pores in center

fuzzy white periphery

FRUITING Grows in small patches, sometimes many together, along wood.

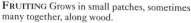

| Dimensions PATCHES ↔ to 7.5cm | "PUFFBALL" ↕ ↔ 2–4cm | Spores Olive-brown/white | Edibility |

FUNGI WITH SPINES

The fungi in this section are not closely related, but they all have their spore-producing cells (basidia) on a toothed or spiny surface. The spines are found under the cap, on the underside of a bracket, or hanging from the branches of coral-like fruitbodies. Some resupinate species (not featured) have spines all over their surface.

• *spines on cap underside*

Family AURISCALPIACEAE	Species *Auriscalpium vulgare*	Season All year

PINECONE TOOTH

Among the most distinctive of fungi, this mushroom has a characteristic kidney-shaped cap, which has a furry or hairy surface with the stem attached to one side. The cap is brown with a paler margin, and its underside is hung with long, gray spines. The stem is a darker brown than the cap and has a felty covering. It is attached to the substrate by a felted pale brown mycelium. The brown coloring makes this species difficult to spot, despite the fact that it is common. It has tough, inedible flesh.
• **OCCURRENCE** On decaying pine and, to a lesser degree, spruce cones in needle litter, in mature conifer woods or stands. Widespread in pine, spruce, and Douglas fir forests of northern temperate zones.

• *dark brown stem attached at cap margin*

pale cap • *margin*

felty brown covering • *on stem*

fine hairs on cap surface •

• *kidney-shaped brown cap*

stem attached to • *cone by felted, pale brown mycelium*

attachment • *point for stem*

• *fruitbody springs from buried or half-buried pine cone*

• *pale gray to gray-brown spines on cap underside*

FRUITING Appears singly or in pairs of fruitbodies.

Dimensions CAP ⊕ 0.5–2cm | STEM ↕ 3–10cm ↔ 2–3mm	Spores White	Edibility

Family TREMELLACEAE	Species *Pseudohydnum gelatinosum*	Season Autumn–winter

TOOTHED JELLY

Varying in color from almost white to dark gray-brown, this bracketlike jelly mushroom has a more or less semicircular cap, with a slightly rough or downy surface, and a short, fat stem, often attached at the side. The underside is covered with pale spines. Although edible, it is not worthwhile.

• **OCCURRENCE** On rotting conifers; rarely on well-rotted deciduous stumps or fallen branches. Widespread in northern temperate zones. Also occurs in warmer regions throughout North America.

gray-white to dark brown cap surface is downy or rough

flesh is gelatinous and semitranslucent

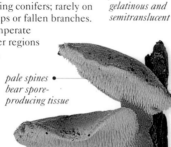

pale spines bear spore-producing tissue

bracketlike fruitbody

short stem at side of cap

1cm

spines are arranged vertically

SPINES

FRUITING Typically appears in groups of a few together.

Dimensions CAP ⊕ 1–8cm | STEM ↕ 0.5–3cm ↔ 0.5–1.5cm	Spores White	Edibility

Family THELEPHORACEAE	Species *Bankera fuligineoalba*	Season Autumn

BLUSHING FRAGRANT TOOTH

Misshapen caps are common in this species because it tends to lift part of the substrate as it emerges. It has a pale brown cap, which becomes red tinged with age; the spore-bearing spines beneath are dense and gray to white. The stem is white to gray toward the top, brown at the base. The relatively soft, unzoned flesh is fragrant and turns pale pink with age.

• **OCCURRENCE** Mycorrhizal with pine. Widespread in northern temperate zones.

• **SIMILAR SPECIES** *Bankera violascens* has a clean, regularly shaped cap with lilac tints; it grows with spruce. *Sarcodon* species have colored spores.

cap incorporates debris from substrate

white to gray zone at stem top

cap develops central depression with age

brown lower stem

SECTION

gray to white spines, to 5mm long

stem central or positioned near margin

FRUITING Singly or in small clusters on dry, sandy soil.

Dimensions CAP ⊕ 5–10cm | STEM ↕ 2–6cm ↔ 1–3cm	Spores White	Edibility

Family THELEPHORACEAE	Species *Phellodon niger*	Season Late summer–autumn

BLACK TOOTH

Fruitbodies of this species are often fused together. The cap is flat or has a slightly depressed center and is pale gray to purplish black; in young specimens the margin is a distinct pale blue. The spines are blue-gray at first, turning gray. The leathery black flesh smells of curry.

• **OCCURRENCE** Mycorrhizal with conifers in woods or stands, sometimes among deciduous trees, on calcareous soil. Widespread but local in northern temperate zones.

• **SIMILAR SPECIES** *Phellodon melaleucus* smells similar but is thinner, paler, and less felty. It is found on poor, acidic soil in woods.

faint zones on cap surface, which is covered in dense felt

blue-gray spines, to 3mm long, darken with age

spines are decurrent

densely felty, dark brown stem

fused fruitbodies

FRUITING Singly or in dense clusters among moss.

Dimensions CAP ⊕ 3–10cm	STEM ↕ 2–5cm ↔ 0.5–2cm	Spores White	Edibility 🚫

Family THELEPHORACEAE	Species *Phellodon tomentosus*	Season Late summer–autumn

FUNNEL TOOTH

This tooth fungus has a centrally depressed cap with the surface marked in zones of shades of brown, vertical spines on the underside, and a fibrous dark brown stem. The growing margin on the cap is thin and white, and caps are often fused together. The inedible, tough flesh is thin and brown. Dried fruitbodies smell of curry or fenugreek.

• **OCCURRENCE** Mycorrhizal with conifers or, rarely, deciduous trees in woods, on sandy soil. Widespread but local in northern temperate zones.

• **SIMILAR SPECIES** A range of tooth fungi look fairly similar, including some species of *Hydnellum* (see p.237), which have brown spores. *Phellodon confluens* has a more felty surface, has fewer zones, and is paler in color with more irregularly shaped caps.

spines, to 3mm long, are arranged vertically

fibrous, dark brown stem

stem slightly twisted and uneven

thin, sharp cap margin

cap flesh is thin but tough

cap has depressed center and clear zones

FRUITING In groups among mosses and lichens.

Dimensions CAP ⊕ 2–6cm	STEM ↕ 2–5cm ↔ 4–7mm	Spores White	Edibility 🚫

| Family THELEPHORACEAE | Species *Hydnellum peckii* | Season Autumn |

BLOODY TOOTH

The cap of this fleshy species is flat to depressed with a knobby surface and a spiny underside. It is velvety white at first, darkened by blood-red droplets exuded as the fruitbody grows. Later it becomes brown with wine-red tinges. The tapering stem is a similar color. The corky brown flesh has an extremely unpleasant taste.
• **OCCURRENCE** Mycorrhizal with pine and spruce in woods and stands, including sand dunes planted with pine. Widespread but local in northern temperate zones.
• **SIMILAR SPECIES** *Hydnellum ferrugineum* has a mild taste. Other species do not develop the red droplets.

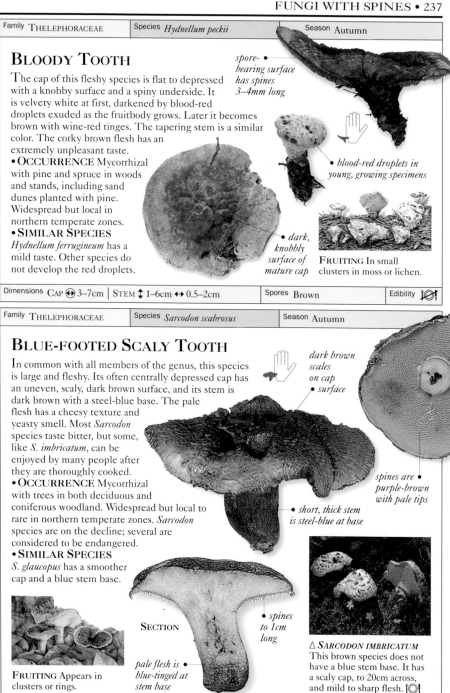

spore-bearing surface has spines 3–4mm long

• *blood-red droplets in young, growing specimens*

• *dark, knobbly surface of mature cap*

FRUITING In small clusters in moss or lichen.

| Dimensions CAP ⊕ 3–7cm \| STEM ↕ 1–6cm ↔ 0.5–2cm | Spores Brown | Edibility |

| Family THELEPHORACEAE | Species *Sarcodon scabrosus* | Season Autumn |

BLUE-FOOTED SCALY TOOTH

In common with all members of the genus, this species is large and fleshy. Its often centrally depressed cap has an uneven, scaly, dark brown surface, and its stem is dark brown with a steel-blue base. The pale flesh has a cheesy texture and yeasty smell. Most *Sarcodon* species taste bitter, but some, like *S. imbricatum*, can be enjoyed by many people after they are thoroughly cooked.
• **OCCURRENCE** Mycorrhizal with trees in both deciduous and coniferous woodland. Widespread but local to rare in northern temperate zones. *Sarcodon* species are on the decline; several are considered to be endangered.
• **SIMILAR SPECIES** *S. glaucopus* has a smoother cap and a blue stem base.

FRUITING Appears in clusters or rings.

dark brown scales on cap • surface

spines are • purple-brown with pale tips

• *short, thick stem is steel-blue at base*

SECTION

• *spines to 1cm long*

pale flesh is • blue-tinged at stem base

△ *SARCODON IMBRICATUM*
This brown species does not have a blue stem base. It has a scaly cap, to 20cm across, and mild to sharp flesh.

| Dimensions CAP ⊕ 4–14cm \| STEM ↕ 3–8cm ↔ 1–3.5cm | Spores Brown | Edibility |

Family HYDNACEAE	Species *Hydnum repandum*	Season Autumn

COMMON HEDGEHOG TOOTH

This very fleshy fungus has a massive, slightly off-center stem and a large, convex or centrally depressed cap, which is often irregular in shape. It has a smooth or slightly felty upper surface and fragile spines on the underside. Pale cream to ocher in color, the whole fruitbody stains orange with age and when bruised. This is a choice edible; older specimens should be cooked thoroughly, as the flesh can become bitter with age.

• **OCCURRENCE** Mycorrhizal with both deciduous trees and conifers in woods. Widespread in northern temperate zones, including cold regions.

• **SIMILAR SPECIES** *Hydnum albidum* has a white cap, smaller spores, and occurs on alkaline soil. Closely related *H. rufescens* is smaller and orange.

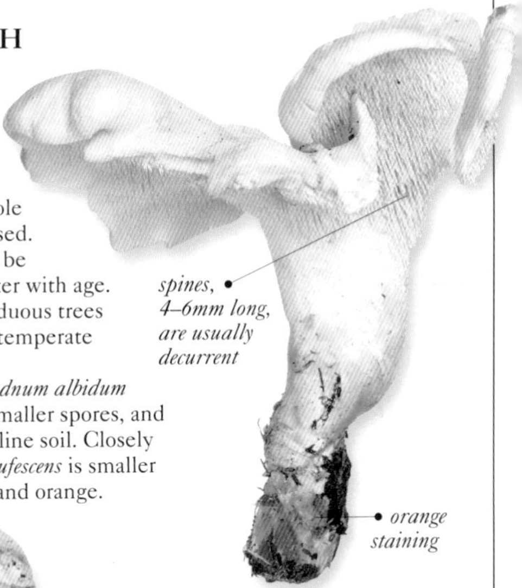

spines, 4–6mm long, are usually decurrent

orange staining

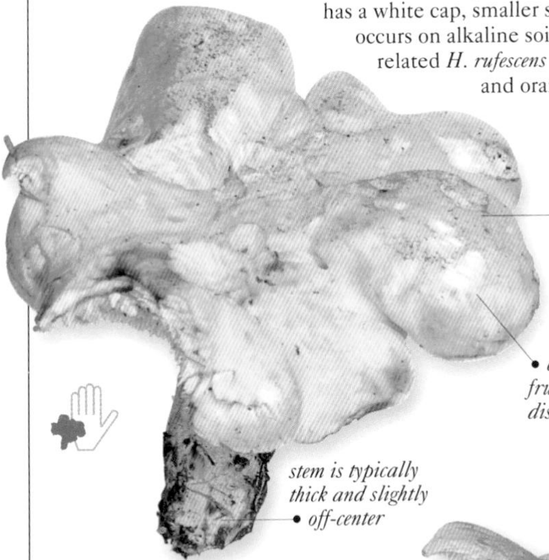

fruitbody is pale cream to ocher

closely clustered fruitbodies result in distorted caps

1cm

CAP UNDERSIDE

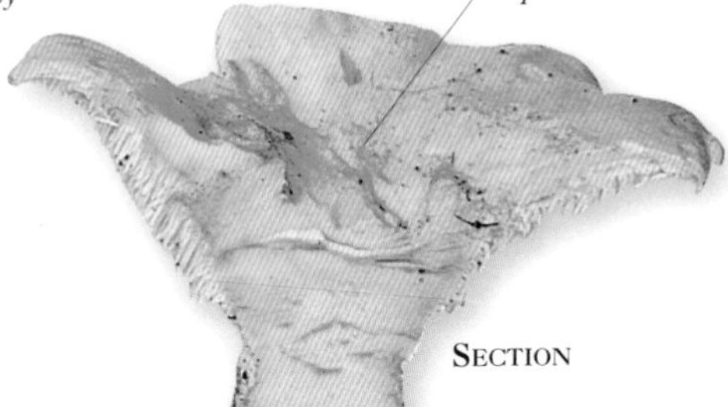

stem is typically thick and slightly off-center

depressed cap center

SECTION

firm, white to cream or buff flesh

△ *HYDNUM UMBILICATUM*
This is a choice edible that resembles the Common Hedgehog Tooth, but is smaller, thinner, typically orange, and has a hole or cavity in the center of the cap. Widespread in North America. |◯|

FRUITING Appears in troops and clusters.

| Dimensions CAP ⊕ 5–15cm \| STEM ↕ 3–7cm ↔ 1–3cm | Spores White | Edibility |◯| |

Family HERICIACEAE	Species *Hericium coralloides*	Season Late summer–late autumn

CORAL TOOTH

multibranched, coral-like fruitbody •

When it is spotted growing along a fallen trunk or similar substrate, this fungus is a breathtaking sight, with its off-white to dirty yellow fruitbody consisting of numerous brittle, coral-like branches, the lower surfaces of which are densely covered with long, pendent spines. The off-white or cream flesh has the texture of fresh crabmeat and greatly resembles it in appearance and taste when shredded and cooked.

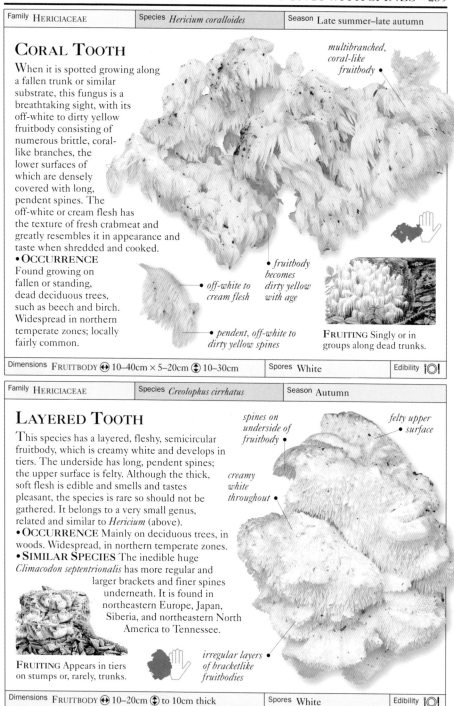

• OCCURRENCE
Found growing on fallen or standing, dead deciduous trees, such as beech and birch. Widespread in northern temperate zones; locally fairly common.

• off-white to cream flesh

• fruitbody becomes dirty yellow with age

• pendent, off-white to dirty yellow spines

FRUITING Singly or in groups along dead trunks.

Dimensions FRUITBODY ⊕ 10–40cm × 5–20cm ⬍ 10–30cm	Spores White	Edibility

Family HERICIACEAE	Species *Creolophus cirrhatus*	Season Autumn

LAYERED TOOTH

spines on underside of fruitbody •

felty upper • surface

This species has a layered, fleshy, semicircular fruitbody, which is creamy white and develops in tiers. The underside has long, pendent spines; the upper surface is felty. Although the thick, soft flesh is edible and smells and tastes pleasant, the species is rare so should not be gathered. It belongs to a very small genus, related and similar to *Hericium* (above).

creamy white throughout •

• OCCURRENCE Mainly on deciduous trees, in woods. Widespread, in northern temperate zones.
• SIMILAR SPECIES The inedible huge *Climacodon septentrionalis* has more regular and larger brackets and finer spines underneath. It is found in northeastern Europe, Japan, Siberia, and northeastern North America to Tennessee.

irregular layers • of bracketlike fruitbodies

FRUITING Appears in tiers on stumps or, rarely, trunks.

Dimensions FRUITBODY ⊕ 10–20cm ⬍ to 10cm thick	Spores White	Edibility

CLUB-SHAPED FUNGI

The species in this section have more or less club-shaped fruitbodies. In most of those featured, the fruitbody is fertile over its entire surface, or the base may be sterile. In the flask-fungi (see p.244), the spore-producing surface (hymenium) is in tiny, flask-shaped fruitbodies embedded in a fleshy, club-shaped structure (stroma).

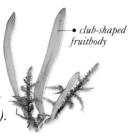
• club-shaped fruitbody

SMOOTH OR HAIRY

S PECIES FEATURED HERE have club-shaped fruitbodies with a smooth or hairy surface. (For species with a pimply or dusty surface, see p.244.) They vary from the very slender *Typhula* species to the much thicker *Clavariadelphus pistillaris* (p.241). Some, such as *Leotia lubrica* (p.243), have well-defined fertile heads, but in most, the fertile part merges with the stem.

Family CLAVARIACEAE	Species *Clavulinopsis helvola*	Season Autumn

YELLOW SPINDLE CORAL

Just one of several unbranched, club-shaped yellow species in this genus, Yellow Spindle Coral can be correctly identified only by examining the spores under a microscope: they have prominent warts on them, unlike the smooth spores of other members. The pale yellow flesh is rather brittle and odorless.
• **OCCURRENCE** In moss-rich meadows, mature lawns, and some wooded areas. Widespread in temperate regions of southeast Asia; common in Europe and northeastern North America.
• **SIMILAR SPECIES** *Clavulinopsis fusiformis* has large clubs and tends to grow in dense clusters. *C. laeticolor* is odorless and yellow to orange-yellow. *C. luteoalba* is apricot-orange and has a musty smell. *Clavaria angillacea* is dull yellow-brown and grows on heathland.

tip may be darker in • color

more or less flattened fruitbody •

FRUITING Appears singly or a few together in small groups.

smooth, • spore-producing surface

△ *CLAVARIA VERMICULARIS*
This species produces tufts of unbranched, club-shaped white fruitbodies. The tip of the club often dries yellow or tan. Fragile with brittle flesh, the fruitbody is hollow and may flatten as it ages.

• club-shaped fruitbody with lengthwise groove

Dimensions CLUB ↕ 3–7cm ↔ 2–4mm	Spores White	Edibility

| Family CLAVARIACEAE | Species *Clavariadelphus pistillaris* | Season Autumn |

GIANT CLUB CORAL

An impressive size for a club-fungus, this species is lemon flushed when young but becomes dull tan with age as the spores mature on the fruitbody surface. When bruised it stains reddish brown. Firm at first, becoming soft and spongy with age, the white flesh smells fairly pleasant but has a bitter taste.
• **OCCURRENCE** Found in woodland, often with beech. Widespread in northern temperate regions; local but can be common where habitats are suitable.
• **SIMILAR SPECIES** *Clavariadelphus ligula* and *C. sachalinensis* are smaller and less distinctly club-shaped; both occur with conifers. *C. truncatus* has a flat top and a sweet taste; it occurs in coniferous woods on rich soil.

large fruitbody is distinctly club-shaped •

much of surface is covered with spore-bearing hymenium

fruitbody is lemon flushed when young, aging dull tan •

FRUITING Appears in troops on soil among leaf litter in calcareous woodland.

| Dimensions CLUB ↕ 10–20cm ↔ 2–6cm | Spores White to pale yellow | Edibility |

| Family CLAVARIACEAE | Species *Macrotyphula fistulosa* | Season Late autumn |

PIPE CLUB CORAL

Unmistakable when found, the Pipe Club has a slender, club-shaped, yellow to tawny-brown fruitbody; it looks similar to a leaf stalk so is easily overlooked. A fairly stunted and twisted form is less easy to identify and is sometimes considered an independent species, *Macrotyphula contorta*.
• **OCCURRENCE** On buried deciduous wood in damp leaf litter, especially among beech trees. Widespread in northern temperate regions and subarctic areas; across northern North America.
• **SIMILAR SPECIES** The closely related *M. juncea* has much thinner fruitbodies. It is common in damp woods and grows on leaf litter.

• spores produced all over surface except on stem

• pointed tip of fruitbody

club varies considerably • in thickness

club darkens • from yellow to tawny brown with age

stem and • spore-bearing area merge subtly

club looks like leaf stalk •

• club tapers toward base

FRUITING Appears singly on decaying sticks.

| Dimensions CLUB ↕ 5–20cm ↔ 2–8mm | Spores White | Edibility |

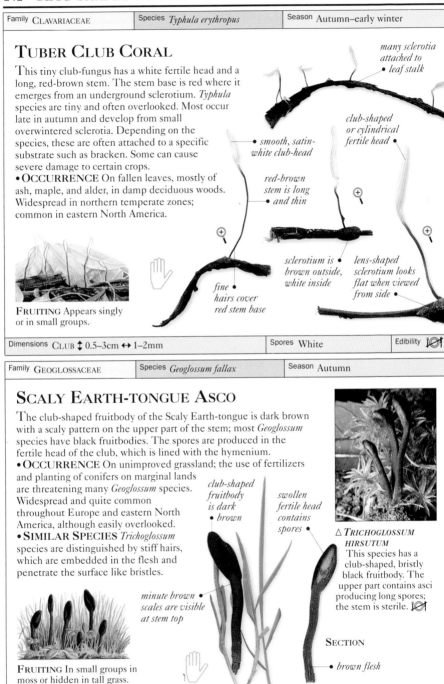

| Family CLAVARIACEAE | Species *Typhula erythropus* | Season Autumn–early winter |

TUBER CLUB CORAL

This tiny club-fungus has a white fertile head and a long, red-brown stem. The stem base is red where it emerges from an underground sclerotium. *Typhula* species are tiny and often overlooked. Most occur late in autumn and develop from small overwintered sclerotia. Depending on the species, these are often attached to a specific substrate such as bracken. Some can cause severe damage to certain crops.
• **OCCURRENCE** On fallen leaves, mostly of ash, maple, and alder, in damp deciduous woods. Widespread in northern temperate zones; common in eastern North America.

many sclerotia attached to • leaf stalk

club-shaped or cylindrical fertile head •

• smooth, satin-white club-head

red-brown stem is long • and thin

sclerotium is • brown outside, white inside

lens-shaped sclerotium looks flat when viewed from side •

fine • hairs cover red stem base

FRUITING Appears singly or in small groups.

| Dimensions CLUB ↕ 0.5–3cm ↔ 1–2mm | Spores White | Edibility |

| Family GEOGLOSSACEAE | Species *Geoglossum fallax* | Season Autumn |

SCALY EARTH-TONGUE ASCO

The club-shaped fruitbody of the Scaly Earth-tongue is dark brown with a scaly pattern on the upper part of the stem; most *Geoglossum* species have black fruitbodies. The spores are produced in the fertile head of the club, which is lined with the hymenium.
• **OCCURRENCE** On unimproved grassland; the use of fertilizers and planting of conifers on marginal lands are threatening many *Geoglossum* species. Widespread and quite common throughout Europe and eastern North America, although easily overlooked.
• **SIMILAR SPECIES** *Trichoglossum* species are distinguished by stiff hairs, which are embedded in the flesh and penetrate the surface like bristles.

club-shaped fruitbody is dark • brown

swollen fertile head contains spores •

△ *TRICHOGLOSSUM HIRSUTUM*
This species has a club-shaped, bristly black fruitbody. The upper part contains asci producing long spores; the stem is sterile.

minute brown • scales are visible at stem top

SECTION

• brown flesh

FRUITING In small groups in moss or hidden in tall grass.

| Dimensions CLUB ↕ 3–7cm ↔ 3–7mm | Spores Dark brown | Edibility |

| Family LEOTIACEAE | Species *Leotia lubrica* | Season Autumn |

JELLY BABIES ASCO

This distinctive species produces a small, pestle-shaped fruitbody with a rubbery texture and gelatinous flesh. The well-defined, convex, lobed head is greenish yellow with a clear, recurved margin and contains the spore-producing tissue. The orange-yellow stem is covered with minute green scales or dots and is often hollow. *Leotia lubrica* can develop a blackish green hue as a result of a fungal infection, but even healthy specimens often turn olive-green when they are fully mature.

• OCCURRENCE Found growing in damp woods among leaf litter and moss. Widespread and common in most northern temperate zones; cosmopolitan.

well-defined fertile head with indistinct lobes •

gelatinous flesh • is sterile in stem

• rubbery stem is orange-yellow

SECTION

convex head • contains spore-producing tissue

minute green • scales or dots cover stem

fruitbodies appear in • clusters

FRUITING Appears in clusters, often in large troops.

| Dimensions CLUB ↕ 2–5cm ↔ 0.3–1cm | Spores White | Edibility |

| Family GEOGLOSSACEAE | Species *Mitrula paludosa* | Season Early summer–autumn |

BOG BEACON ASCO

With its glistening orange head and cylindrical white stem, this attractive, club-shaped mushroom is very aptly named. It has a smooth surface and watery, soft, yellow flesh. The club head contains the spore-bearing hymenium; the stem is sterile.

• OCCURRENCE In unpolluted, stagnant water with leaf litter. Prefers northern areas and higher altitudes in northern temperate zones.

• SIMILAR SPECIES *Bryoglossum rehmii* is found in drier areas and placed in the Leotiaceae family (above, pp.269, 271–73). *Heyderia* species are smaller and mostly occur on needle litter. *Spathularia flavida*, also found on needle litter, has a very flat, somewhat lobed, head.

yellow head • contains spore-producing tissue

shape of head may • vary

• base of stem is darker than top

cylindrical stem • is dingy white

grows in moss or on leaves or twigs •

• fruitbody is club-shaped

FRUITING In small or large troops of fruitbodies.

| Dimensions CLUB ↕ 2–5cm ↔ 0.2–1cm | Spores White | Edibility |

WITH PIMPLES OR A DUSTY SURFACE

THE FUNGI in this subsection are mainly characterized by their pimply surface. The pimples are caused by flask-shaped fruitbodies embedded in the fleshy tissue (stroma). They are visible when the club is cut in half lengthwise. One species featured here, *Paecilomyces farinosus* (below), produces masses of loose, asexual spores on its surface, making it look dusty.

Family CLAVICIPITACEAE	Species *Cordyceps militaris*	Season Summer–autumn

ORANGE CATERPILLAR ASCO

This parasitic flask-fungus emerges from its host as a club-shaped, orange-red composite fruitbody, called a stroma. The spore-producing asci are contained in flasks seen as spikes breaking through the surface on the upper region of the club, which is slightly swollen. The spores themselves are long and cylindrical and break into segments. The stem is smooth and paler in color.
• **OCCURRENCE** Mycelia invade and kill the larvae and pupae of moths, either in woods or grassland. Widespread in northern temperate zones. Other *Cordyceps* species parasitize insects, spiders, or *Elaphomyces* truffles (p.259). The majority are tropical.
• **SIMILAR SPECIES** *C. bifusispora*, which is also parasitic on moths, is more yellow and has spores with club-shaped end cells.

• *swollen fertile head of club*

• *flasks appear as spikes or pimples on upper part of club*

host may be deeply • *buried*

• *lower part of club has no flasks and is smooth*

• *disfigured moth larva is host*

FRUITING Appear singly or in small groups.

Dimensions CLUB ↕ 2–5cm ↔ 3–8mm		Spores White	Edibility

Family CLAVIVIPITACEAE	Species *Paecilomyces farinosus*	Season Summer–autumn

COTTON CATERPILLAR ASCO

Thought to be the asexual stage of *Cordyceps militaris*, this fungus attacks the larvae and pupae of moths and, after consuming the host, produces erect, club-shaped structures. These may be orange or yellow, but their color is obscured by fluffy white masses of asexual spores (conidia), which are easily detached.
• **OCCURRENCE** Always grows on buried or partially buried larvae and pupae of moths, both in open grassy areas and in woodland. Widespread and common in northern temperate zones.

fungus is branched • *or unbranched*

surface with • *white conidia*

orange, yellow, or brown base •

FRUITING Appears singly or in small groups from the larvae and pupae of moths.

Dimensions CLUB ↕ 2–5cm ↔ 2–5mm		Spores White	Edibility

| Family CLAVICIPITACEAE | Species *Cordyceps ophioglossoides* | Season Autumn–early winter |

TRUFFLE CATERPILLAR ASCO

Parasitic on *Elaphomyces* truffles (p.259), this flask-fungus is attached to the underground fruitbody of the host by yellow threads that merge to form the stem above ground level. The head of the club, the stroma, is olive-brown to black; its surface is roughened by tiny flasks embedded in the yellow-brown flesh and containing spore-producing asci.

• OCCURRENCE
Parasitic on *Elaphomyces muricatus* or *E. granulatus* in conifer and deciduous woods. Widespread and locally common in northern temperate zones.

• SIMILAR SPECIES
Cordyceps capitata and *C. longisegmentatis*, both with rounded heads, can also occur on the same host as *C. ophioglossoides*.

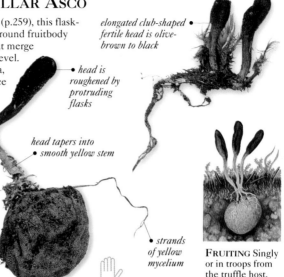

elongated club-shaped fertile head is olive-brown to black

head is roughened by protruding flasks

head tapers into smooth yellow stem

strands of yellow mycelium

FRUITING Singly or in troops from the truffle host, which is buried.

| Dimensions CLUB ↕ 5–13cm including root ↔ 0.5–1cm | Spores White | Edibility |

| Family XYLARIACEAE | Species *Xylaria polymorpha* | Season Summer–winter |

DEAD-MAN'S FINGERS ASCO

This well-known flask-fungus has club-shaped composite fruitbodies, or stromata with thick white flesh. Each has a short, cylindrical stem and a rounded tip. Just below the surface and embedded in the flesh are flask-shaped organs that contain the spore-producing asci. The asci eject the long, mature spores by force through a tiny opening in the top of the flask, the ostiole.

• OCCURRENCE Often found at soil level attached to rotten wood such as tree stumps, especially of beech and elm trees but also birch and linden. Widespread and rather common in northern temperate zones, its range extending to the subtropics.

• SIMILAR SPECIES The more slender *Xylaria longipes*, which also has shorter spores, is largely confined to dead deciduous wood in northern temperate zones.

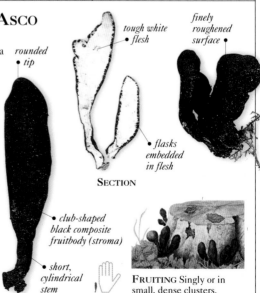

tough white flesh

finely roughened surface

rounded tip

flasks embedded in flesh

SECTION

club-shaped black composite fruitbody (stroma)

short, cylindrical stem

FRUITING Singly or in small, dense clusters.

| Dimensions CLUB ↕ 3–10cm ↔ 1–4cm | Spores Black | Edibility |

PHALLUS-SHAPED

T HIS SMALL SUBSECTION comprises fungi with phallic fruitbodies, the Stinkhorns, which belong to the genera *Phallus* and *Mutinus*. They bear spores in a sticky, slimy substance, known as the gleba. In *Phallus* the gleba sits on a caplike structure; in *Mutinus* it is part of the top of the stem. When young, the fruitbodies are egg-shaped and are surrounded by a skinlike structure called the peridium. It has a gelatinous, watery inner layer that protects the maturing gleba.

When mature, all fungi in this group have a penetrating putrid smell. This attracts flies, which aid spore dispersal.

Family PHALLACEAE	Species *Mutinus caninus*	Season Summer–autumn

DOG STINKHORN

The long-stemmed, off-white to dirty orange fruitbody of this species emerges from an egg-shaped structure with a leathery, off-white skin. The orange stem tip merges with the stem. It is covered with a foul-smelling slimy, olive-green spore mass, which attracts insects for dispersal.
• **OCCURRENCE** On thick leaf litter or needle litter, often around rotten stumps, in conifer and deciduous woods. Fairly common in Europe; worldwide distribution unclear.
• **SIMILAR SPECIES** *Mutinus elgans*, from North America but also spreading in Europe, has red stem coloring. It prefers gardens and parks. *Phallus impudicus* (p.247) and its relatives have distinct caps at the stem tip.

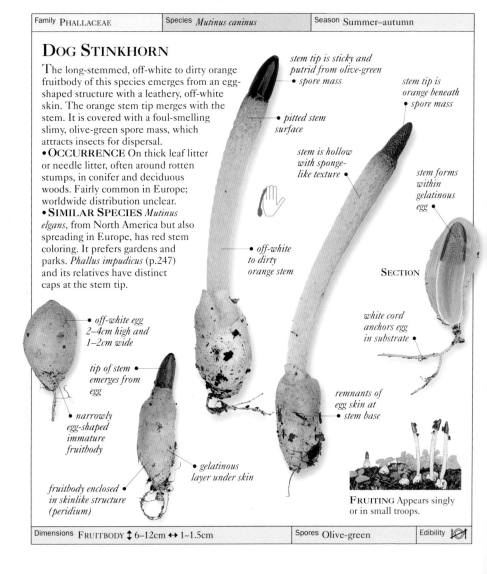

stem tip is sticky and putrid from olive-green • spore mass

stem tip is orange beneath • spore mass

pitted stem surface

stem is hollow with sponge-like texture •

stem forms within gelatinous egg •

SECTION

• off-white to dirty orange stem

white cord anchors egg in substrate •

• off-white egg 2–4cm high and 1–2cm wide

tip of stem • emerges from egg

• narrowly egg-shaped immature fruitbody

remnants of egg skin at • stem base

• gelatinous layer under skin

fruitbody enclosed • in skinlike structure (peridium)

FRUITING Appears singly or in small troops.

Dimensions FRUITBODY ↕ 6–12cm ↔ 1–1.5cm	Spores Olive-green	Edibility

| Family PHALLACEAE | Species *Phallus impudicus* | Season Summer–autumn |

SHAMELESS STINKHORN

This species is often smelled before it is seen; members of the Phallaceae family are famous for their foul-smelling fruitbodies, which attract insects to disperse the spores. Mature specimens are easy to recognize by their phallic shape, formed by the white stem and the slimy, olive-green cap. Young fruitbodies are enclosed in an egglike structure with a thin, leathery skin that breaks open as the stem emerges. The section that becomes the stem is edible and can be extracted from the egg.

• **OCCURRENCE** In acidic conifer or deciduous woods and in sand dunes. Widespread and common in areas of northern temperate zones.

• **SIMILAR SPECIES** *Phallus ravenellii* is the common eastern North America species, differing by minor characteristics. *P. duplicatus* (inset, below).

thimble-shaped cap

beneath slime, cap is honeycomb-like and white

spores are contained within olive-green slime covering cap

stem just about to emerge from egg

SECTION

thick white cord anchors egg to substrate

spongy white stem has a cellular structure and is hollow

intact egg 4–7cm high and 3–5cm wide

egg skin around base is thin and leathery

FRUITING Appears singly or in small troops on acidic soil.

△ *PHALLUS DUPLICATUS*
This species has a distinctive, delicate, netted white skirt of tissue that flares out from beneath the base of the slime-covered, dark green cap. |◎|

| Dimensions FRUITBODY ↕ 15–20cm ↔ 1.5–3cm | Spores Olive-brown | Edibility |◎| |

ANTLER- TO CORAL-LIKE FUNGI

These species are an elaboration of the club-shaped mushrooms on pp.240–45. Some have only a few branches; others are more complex. In most cases, the branches are entirely covered with spore-bearing tissue, but those of Sparassis crispa *(p.252) are fertile on one side only, and* Xylaria hypoxylon *is a flask-fungus (see p.244).*

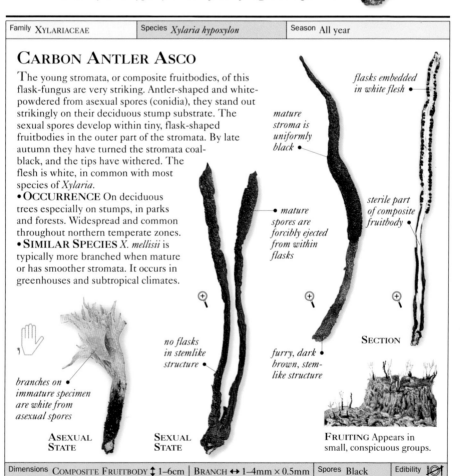

coral-like fruit-body

Family XYLARIACEAE	Species *Xylaria hypoxylon*	Season All year

CARBON ANTLER ASCO

The young stromata, or composite fruitbodies, of this flask-fungus are very striking. Antler-shaped and white-powdered from asexual spores (conidia), they stand out strikingly on their deciduous stump substrate. The sexual spores develop within tiny, flask-shaped fruitbodies in the outer part of the stromata. By late autumn they have turned the stromata coal-black, and the tips have withered. The flesh is white, in common with most species of *Xylaria*.

• OCCURRENCE On deciduous trees especially on stumps, in parks and forests. Widespread and common throughout northern temperate zones.

• SIMILAR SPECIES *X. mellisii* is typically more branched when mature or has smoother stromata. It occurs in greenhouses and subtropical climates.

flasks embedded in white flesh •

mature stroma is uniformly black •

• mature spores are forcibly ejected from within flasks

sterile part of composite fruitbody •

no flasks in stemlike structure •

furry, dark brown, stem-like structure

SECTION

branches on immature specimen are white from asexual spores

ASEXUAL STATE

SEXUAL STATE

FRUITING Appears in small, conspicuous groups.

Dimensions COMPOSITE FRUITBODY ↕ 1–6cm	BRANCH ↔ 1–4mm × 0.5mm	Spores Black	Edibility

Family CLAVARIACEAE	Species *Clavulinopsis corniculata*	Season Late autumn

MEADOW CORAL

One of the more common *Clavulinopsis* species, the Meadow Coral typically has many antlerlike branches, but the shape alters greatly with habitat. The fruitbody varies in color from sulfur-yellow to orange or tan; the base is white and has a feltlike surface, which turns green in contact with either dissolved or solid iron sulfate ($FeSO_4$). The duller, thin, rather fragile flesh has a yeasty smell.

• **OCCURRENCE** In unimproved, moss-rich meadows, in some coastal scrub with hawthorn, and in damp, ash-dominated woods. Widespread in temperate regions.

• **SIMILAR SPECIES** *Ramariopsis crocea* has more pointed tips, is more golden, and does not react with $FeSO_4$. It typically occurs in woods.

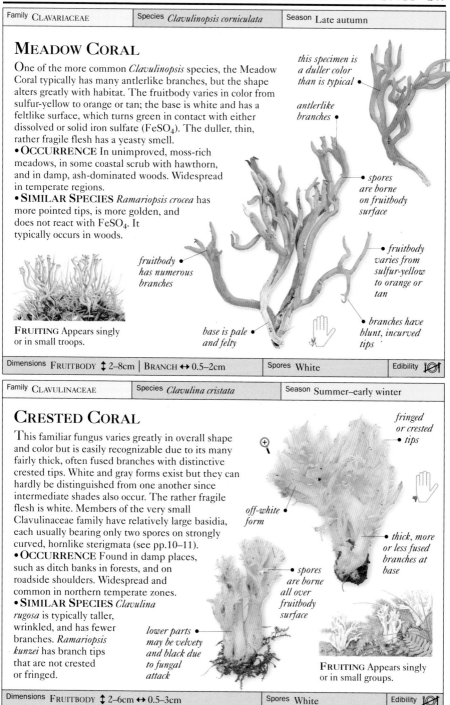

this specimen is a duller color than is typical •

antlerlike branches •

• spores are borne on fruitbody surface

• fruitbody varies from sulfur-yellow to orange or tan

fruitbody • has numerous branches

• branches have blunt, incurved tips

FRUITING Appears singly or in small troops.

base is pale • and felty

Dimensions FRUITBODY ↕ 2–8cm │ BRANCH ↔ 0.5–2cm	Spores White	Edibility

Family CLAVULINACEAE	Species *Clavulina cristata*	Season Summer–early winter

CRESTED CORAL

This familiar fungus varies greatly in overall shape and color but is easily recognizable due to its many fairly thick, often fused branches with distinctive crested tips. White and gray forms exist but they can hardly be distinguished from one another since intermediate shades also occur. The rather fragile flesh is white. Members of the very small Clavulinaceae family have relatively large basidia, each usually bearing only two spores on strongly curved, hornlike sterigmata (see pp.10–11).

• **OCCURRENCE** Found in damp places, such as ditch banks in forests, and on roadside shoulders. Widespread and common in northern temperate zones.

• **SIMILAR SPECIES** *Clavulina rugosa* is typically taller, wrinkled, and has fewer branches. *Ramariopsis kunzei* has branch tips that are not crested or fringed.

fringed or crested • tips

off-white • form

• thick, more or less fused branches at base

• spores are borne all over fruitbody surface

lower parts • may be velvety and black due to fungal attack

FRUITING Appears singly or in small groups.

Dimensions FRUITBODY ↕ 2–6cm ↔ 0.5–3cm	Spores White	Edibility

Family DACRYOMYCETACEAE	Species *Calocera viscosa*	Season Autumn–winter

ANTLER JELLY

The many-branched fruitbody of this jelly-fungus is bright orange with tough, rubbery flesh. Members of the Dacryomycetaceae family are distinguished under a microscope by their tuning-fork-shaped basidia (see pp.10–11); spores are borne over most of the fruitbody.

• OCCURRENCE Only on dead or decayed wood of conifers. Widespread and common in northern temperate zones.

• SIMILAR SPECIES *Calocera cornea* has small, unbranched clubs and grows on deciduous twigs. *C. furcata* is forked and grows on pine wood. Paler *C. pallido-spathulata* is flattened and irregular; it can be locally common. *Gymnosporangium clavariiforme*, found on juniper, is less erect and without branches at the tips. Club-fungi (pp.240–47) grow mostly on the ground and are more fragile.

flesh is rubbery and same color as surface •

branches are bright • orange

• forking branches of antlerlike fruitbody

decayed conifer substrate •

• fruitbody is strongly attached to substrate

FRUITING Appears singly or in small, clustered groups.

Dimensions FRUITBODY ↕ 3–10cm ↔ 0.5–4cm	Spores Yellow	Edibility

---

Family RAMARIACEAE	Species *Ramaria abietina*	Season Autumn

GREENING CORAL

The verdigris coloring that stains the whole fruitbody of this fungus as it ages makes it easy to identify among the small, less fleshy *Ramaria* species. It is densely branched and dull brown to olive-brown when it first emerges, slowly turning green. The flesh is dull pale brown and fairly firm.

• OCCURRENCE On thick needle beds under conifers, especially spruce. Widespread throughout conifer forests of northwestern North America.

• SIMILAR SPECIES Larger *R. apiculata* is green on the branch tips only. *R. eumorpha*, *R. flaccida*, and *R. myceliosa*, among others, are similar but do not stain green.

densely branched • upper fruitbody

verdigris • staining appears with age

• detached spores collect in branch angles

• short, felted, pale stem

FRUITING Almost always found in fairy rings.

Dimensions FRUITBODY ↕ 3–8cm ↔ 1.5–4cm	Spores Ocher	Edibility

Family RAMARIACEAE	Species *Ramaria botrytis*	Season Autumn

PINK-TIPPED CORAL

Dense, white to pale brown branches with purple tips help to identify this fungus, which is typically very fleshy. The lower part of the stem is very thick and stubby. The white flesh is firm with a pleasant, fruity smell, but eating it cannot be recommended because of identification problems (see SIMILAR SPECIES).
• **OCCURRENCE** On the ground under conifers, especially fir and spruce. Widespread in northern temperate and warm-temperate zones.
• **SIMILAR SPECIES** *Ramaria formosa* is a more colorful orange-pink without contrasting tips and is poisonous. There are 20 other similar species.

distinct purple tips on dense • branches

△ *RAMARIA SANGUINEA*
Rarer than *R. botrytis*, this species has thick yellow branches, the lower surfaces of which develop red spots with age or if bruised. 🖐

• numerous crowded branches with 5–7 forks

• white to pale brown fruitbody

• thick, stubby lower stem

FRUITING Appears singly or in fairy rings or lines.

Dimensions FRUITBODY ↕ ↔ 7–15cm	Spores Ocher	Edibility 🖐

Family RAMARIACEAE	Species *Ramaria stricta*	Season Later summer–winter

BITTER CORAL

This many-branched fungus is typically erect and taller than it is wide, but size and shape vary greatly. Its branches are pale orange-yellow, aging to ocher-brown, with pale yellow tips. The fairly firm, bitter-tasting flesh stains wine-red and has a spicy smell. Young fruitbodies can be citrus-yellow all over.
• **OCCURRENCE** Usually on half-buried deciduous wood, often beech, but also on sawdust. Widespread and common in northern temperate zones.
• **SIMILAR SPECIES** *Ramaria gracilis* is paler with a distinct anise smell. It occurs mostly with conifer litter.

older specimens can be • fairly dark red-brown

branches have pale • yellow tips

detached spores collect in the • branch angles

• erect fruitbody

firm, comparatively thin base

white mycelial cords attach fruitbody to substrate •

FRUITING Singly or in lines on rotten branches.

Dimensions FRUITBODY ↕ 4–12cm ↔ 3–8cm	Spores Ocher	Edibility 🖐

Family SPARASSIDACEAE	Species *Sparassis crispa*	Season Late summer–autumn

CAULIFLOWER MUSHROOM

A multitude of lobes forming an impressive fleshy, cream to pale yellow-brown fruitbody are characteristic of this species, which is borne on a short, thick, rootlike stem. The lobes are branched, flattened or ribbon-like, and fairly firm; like all members of this small family, the spore-producing layer is on one side only. Although difficult to clean, its pleasant taste and large size make it a very popular edible.

• **OCCURRENCE** Mostly on pine, in stands and native woods; causes brown rot. Widespread in northern temperate zones; common in western North America.

• **SIMILAR SPECIES** *Sparassis brevipes* is paler and tougher. It grows mostly on oak, beech, or fir. In eastern North America *S. herbstii* (*S. spathulata*) occurs on deciduous trees.

SECTION

• *densely packed, branched lobes*

strongly folded, cauliflower-shaped • fruitbody

spore-producing layer on one side • of lobes only

fruitbodies may • weigh up to 30lb; 2–20lb is typical

FRUITING Mostly singly on dead or dying conifer stumps.

Dimensions FRUITBODY ↕ ↔ 10–40cm	Spores White to pale yellow	Edibility 🍴

ROUNDED FUNGI

The fungi in this section are varied, but all produce rounded fruitbodies. With the exception of the Aborted Entoloma (below), those that occur above ground are puffballs, earthballs, and some flask-fungi (see p.244). Rounded fungi below ground are the truffles (pp.258–59), some of which are famous for their flavor.

• *rounded fruitbody*

ABOVE GROUND

THE FUNGI in this subsection are characterized by their stemless, rounded fruitbodies. (For rounded fruitbodies with stems see pp.260–63.) Some of the species are Basidiomycetes (see pp.10–11). They produce their spores within the fruitbody. The spores are released when its skin breaks down with age or when a pore develops on its top at maturity. Other species that are featured here are flask-fungi (see p.244). These have tiny, flask-shaped fruitbodies embedded in compound structures known as stromata.

Family ENTOLOMATACEAE	Species *Entoloma abortivum*	Season Autumn

ABORTED ENTOLOMA

A choice edible, the Aborted Entoloma normally produces rounded, lumpy white fruitbodies. These are thought to be the result of parasitizing the Honey Mushroom, *Armillaria mellea* (p.80). Cap and stem fruitbodies are occasionally produced, with caps to 10cm across and stems to 10cm high and 1.5cm wide. They are gray with decurrent pink gills. The white flesh smells of cucumber or fresh bread; in aborted forms it is pink-veined.

• **OCCURRENCE** On deciduous trees in open woodland. Widespread and common in eastern North America.

• **SIMILAR SPECIES** No other fungus produces aborted forms like this, but the cap and stem fruitbody are similar to other *Entoloma* species. However, they typically occur on the ground and lack decurrent gills. Many are poisonous, so it is unwise to eat isolated unaborted forms of *Entoloma abortivum*.

cap is convex and gray to gray-brown •

decurrent, off-white gills age to grayish white or pink •

stem is not always central under cap •

firm white aborted form is irregularly rounded •

pale yellow patches may be visible •

FRUITING Clusters of rounded forms with scattered cap and stem fruitbodies.

Dimensions ABORTED FORM ↕ 2.5–5cm ↔ 2.5–10cm	Spores Pink to salmon-pink	Edibility

Family LYCOPERDACEAE	Species *Calvatia gigantea*	Season Summer–autumn

GIANT PUFFBALL

This is one of the best-known edible fungi. Its huge, ball-shaped, white or cream fruitbodies regularly weigh above 9lb, and record finds are over 44lb. Most of the interior of the fruitbody consists of a huge number of spores; the lower, sterile part is much reduced. Its flesh is firm in texture and white when young.

• **OCCURRENCE** Saprotrophic; in disturbed sites with nutrient-rich soil, in fields, woodland edges, and parks. Widespread and locally common in northern temperate zones. Other giant puffball species are common in western North America.

huge, ball-shaped, white or cream fruitbody

SECTION

• *flesh is edible when white and firm*

leathery, smooth outer skin rots away to allow spores to escape

FRUITING Mostly appears in small fairy rings.

spore-producing tissue becomes yellow then olive-brown with age

Dimensions FRUITBODY ↕ ↔ 20–50cm	Spores Olive-brown	Edibility

Family LYCOPERDACEAE	Species *Bovista plumbea*	Season Summer–autumn

COMMON TUMBLING PUFFBALL

The white outer skin of this rounded fungus peels
off at maturity, like the shell of a boiled egg, revealing
a gray inner layer. Inside the ball is pale yellow tissue,
which produces a huge number of spores. At maturity,
the fruitbody of this and other *Bovista* species often
becomes detached and rolls about, increasing spore
dispersal, which occurs from a pore in the top.
This *Bovista* is not of great culinary interest.
• **OCCURRENCE** Saprotrophic; it is confined to
grassland, especially dry grassland, and it tolerates
fairly high fertilizer levels in the soil. Cosmopolitan
except for humid lowland tropics.
• **SIMILAR SPECIES** The inner covering layer
of *B. pila* is dark brown to bronze.

*golfball-
like in size
and shape*

*distinct pore in
top allows spores
to escape* •

SECTION

*pale yellow spore-
• producing tissue*

*two-layered
• skin (peridium)*

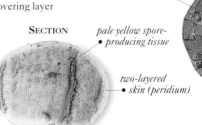

*• outer skin
peels to reveal
papery gray
inner layer*

FRUITING Mostly appears
in groups or a few together.

• base is also fertile

Dimensions FRUITBODY ↕ ↔ 1–3cm	Spores Olive- to sepia-brown	Edibility

Family LYCOPERDACEAE	Species *Vascellum pratense*	Season Summer–autumn

MEADOW PUFFBALL

The key identification characteristic of this spiny, white
to pale brown species can be difficult to see: it is a kind of
membrane separating the fertile, globe-shaped top part from
the short, sterile stem part. The fruitbody usually has a rather
flattened top with a large opening, through which the spores
escape; the sterile part often persists until the next spring.
Firm, fresh specimens can be eaten but taste bland.
• **OCCURRENCE** Saprotrophic; it is found growing on soil
and organic matter in grassy areas such as lawns, parks, golf
courses, and pastures. Virtually
cosmopolitan, but absent in
lowland tropics.

*fertile tissue
is minutely
chambered* •

SECTION

*very thin, skin-
like tissue
separating sterile
and fertile parts*

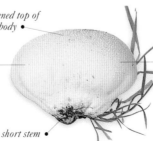

*flattened top of
fruitbody* •

*white •
fruitbody
becomes pale
yellow then
pale brown*

*• mealy surface
covered in fine
spines*

FRUITING Mostly appears
in small groups.

short stem •

Dimensions FRUITBODY ↕ 1.5–3.5cm ↔ 2–4.5cm	Spores Gray-olive to olive-brown	Edibility

Family SCLERODERMATACEAE	Species *Scleroderma citrinum*	Season Summer–autumn

COMMON EARTHBALL

This hard, potato-like fungus, which is a familiar sight in damp woodland, has pale yellow skin covered with scales. It has a tough, pale yellow outer skin, which is 2–5mm thick, and its distinctive spore-filled, black interior is somewhat marbled. Inedible and poisonous, it can develop a strong metallic smell.

• **OCCURRENCE** Mycorrhizal with deciduous trees, mostly in damp woodland; it can be found with *Boletus parasiticus* (p.194). Widespread and common in areas of northern temperate zones.

• **SIMILAR SPECIES** Edible *Lycoperdon* species (pp.260–61) and *Tuber* species (pp.258–59) differ in overall shape, color, smell, and spore shape.

firm black spore-bearing tissue is powdery when mature

SECTION • *tough skin is 2–5mm thick*

• *surface skin rots away, exposing spores for dispersal*

fruitbody • resembles a potato

brown scales • on thick, pale yellow skin

FRUITING Often appears in clusters among moss.

Dimensions FRUITBODY ⊕ 4–10cm	Spores Purplish black	Edibility ☠

Family RUSSULACEAE	Species *Zelleromyces cinnabarinus*	Season Summer–autumn

RED GASTROID LACTARIUS

Looking like a misshapen puffball, this species has the microscopic characteristics of a member of the *Lactarius* genus (pp.43–55) and, like *Lactarius* species, produces white "milk" when cut. The milk tastes mild and does not change color as it dries. The spores are produced in chambers in the cinnamon-buff flesh. They are released as the fungus decays or are spread by animals, which eat the rounded fruitbodies.

• **OCCURRENCE** Mycorrhizal with pine trees in areas of open woodland. Widespread and common in eastern North America, but easily overlooked in its habitat.

surface is smooth and • dull

irregularly rounded to ovoid • fruitbody

thin skin is • cinnabar-red to cinnamon-brown

chambered, • spore-bearing tissue is cinnamon-buff

FRUITING Scattered or several fruitbodies under pines, either on the soil surface or just beneath.

Dimensions FRUITBODY ⊕ 3–5cm	Spores Pale cinnamon-buff	Edibility

Family XYLARIACEAE	Species *Daldinia concentrica*	Season All year

CRAMP BALLS ASCO

The rounded, rusty brown composite fruitbodies, or stromata, of this flask-fungus are large and have flesh that is zoned in dark and light bands. When the spores are mature, they are forcibly ejected from asci inside the spore-producing chambers, or flasks, just beneath the surface. The long-lasting stromata eventually turn black and become crumbly in texture.
• OCCURRENCE Mostly on still-standing, dead, or dying trunks of ash trees; also birch and other deciduous trees in parks and forests, especially following fire damage. Widespread in northern temperate zones; most of North America and in the United Kingdom.
• SIMILAR SPECIES *Hypoxylon* species (below) have unzoned flesh.

rounded, stemless composite fruitbody has rough surface •

surface is rusty brown when • *young*

• *minute, spore-producing flasks are found just beneath surface*

flesh is silver-gray • *and black in concentric zones*

SECTION

FRUITING Appears singly or in large or small groups.

Dimensions COMPOSITE FRUITBODY ⊕ 2–10cm	Spores Black	Edibility

Family XYLARIACEAE	Species *Hypoxylon fragiforme*	Season All year

BEECH CUSHION ASCO

The fruitbodies (stromata) of this flask-fungus are stemless and range from pink through brick-red, becoming black when overmature. They have a hard, rough, warty surface, just beneath which are the spore-producing, flask-shaped chambers. The flesh is black and hard.
• OCCURRENCE On bark of freshly fallen beech trees in forests. Widespread and common wherever beech occurs in northern temperate zones.
• SIMILAR SPECIES *Hypoxylon howeianum* occurs on other deciduous trees. *H. rubiginosum* is flat, spreading, and reddish brown. *H. fuscum* is purplish brown.

hemispherical composite fruitbody • *(stroma)*

deposited spores darken surrounding • *bark*

overmature black • *composite fruitbodies*

FRUITING Appears in spreading troops on bark.

Dimensions COMPOSITE FRUITBODY ⊕ 0.5–3cm	Spores Black	Edibility

BELOW GROUND

T HE MUSHROOMS featured here are among many that have tuberlike fruitbodies, produced below ground. The spore-bearing asci are enclosed in the fruitbodies. The *Tuber* species, "truffles," have fairly solid interiors and are related to *Peziza* (pp.266–67). Species of *Elaphomyces*, which are not true truffles, have a powdery interior when they reach maturity.

Family TUBERACEAE	Species *Tuber aestivum*	Season Summer

EURO SUMMER TRUFFLE

The least expensive of the true edible truffles, *Tuber aestivum* has a more or less round fruitbody with a rough surface covered in pyramidal black warts. Within the fungus, the solid flesh is gray-brown with white veins. Like its relatives, this truffle has a distinct aroma, reminiscent of seaweed, and a faint nutty taste. Flies are attracted to *Tuber* fruitbodies, helping collectors to pinpoint truffle sites.
• OCCURRENCE Found among roots of beech, birch, and oak trees. Widespread in southern and central Europe and southern Scandinavia.

white veins run through solid, gray-brown flesh

SECTION

fruitbody surface is covered with pyramidal black warts

FRUITING Grows singly or in groups among tree roots.

Dimensions FRUITBODY ⊕ 2–5cm	Spores Yellow-brown	Edibility ⭐

Family TUBERACEAE	Species *Tuber melanosporum*	Season Late autumn–early spring

PERIGORD TRUFFLE

The rough, coal-black surface of the irregularly shaped Perigord Truffle consists of many tiny, polygonal warts. The solid flesh is made brown by the spores and turns black with age; it has white veins and a distinctive smell and taste. Perigord Truffles are collected from the wild by skilled pickers using specially trained dogs or pigs, but inoculated seedlings of host trees are now commercially available.
• OCCURRENCE Under species of Mediterranean oaks and other host trees on alkaline, red Mediterranean soils. It is a warmth-loving species, confined to southern Europe where the annual yield is about 330 tons. Other edible *Tuber* species are found in North America.
• SIMILAR SPECIES *Tuber brumale* is found farther north. *T. macrosporum* has an almost smooth surface. SECTION

rough rind is made up of hundreds of polygonal warts

coal-black surface on irregularly shaped fruitbody

solid brown flesh with white veins

FRUITING Grows singly, buried among tree roots.

Dimensions FRUITBODY ⊕ 2–7cm	Spores Dark brown	Edibility ⭐

Family TUBERACEAE	Species *Tuber magnatum*	Season Autumn–winter

EURO WHITE TRUFFLE

The fruitbody of this choice edible is irregularly round in shape, pale ocher to cream, and has a smooth surface. Its cream-colored flesh has a spicy odor and flavor. The spores can be seen as darker cream-brown areas in the flesh. Attempts are being made to cultivate the species on a large scale by inoculating suitable host roots; if this is successful the prevalent high prices may drop.
• **OCCURRENCE** Buried in alkaline soil among the roots of oak, but also found among poplar and willow. Found in the Piemonte region of northwestern Italy and in France.
• **SIMILAR SPECIES** *Tuber gibbosum*, found in North America, also has pale flesh and is edible.

△ *TUBER CANALICULATUM*
This is a rounded to egg-shaped, warty, reddish brown truffle. Its flesh is tan with white streaks. At maturity, the fruitbodies push up above ground or are uprooted by animals. It is a choice edible of North America. {O}

cream flesh is marbled with white veins •

• *fruitbody looks somewhat like a potato*

SECTION

FRUITING Grows singly, or in groups among tree roots.

Dimensions FRUITBODY ⊕ 2–8cm	Spores Brown	Edibility {O}

Family ELAPHOMYCETACEAE	Species *Elaphomyces granulatus*	Season All year

COMMON FALSE TRUFFLE

This truffle has a thick-fleshed, scaly, warty, uniformly yellow-brown surface. Within the fruitbody, the spores are produced in a powdery mass that disperses when the skin breaks down at maturity.
• **OCCURRENCE** Mycorrhizal with a wide range of conifers and deciduous trees in woods and parks. *Cordyceps ophioglossoides* (p.245) parasitizes it and can be used to locate it. Widespread and common in Europe; also found in North America and Japan.
• **SIMILAR SPECIES**
E. muricatus has a marbled outer layer, just beneath the warty, yellow-brown rind.

powdery black interior at maturity •

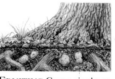

SECTION

SECTION

• *fertile tissue is pale brown when immature*

scaly, warty surface is golden brown

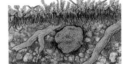

FRUITING In large or small groups underground.

Dimensions FRUITBODY ⊕ 1.5–4.5cm	Spores Blackish brown	Edibility {O}

PEAR- TO PESTLE-SHAPED FUNGI

This section features puffballs and earthballs that typically have a short, stemlike base supporting the rounded, fertile top (see also pp.253–57). At maturity, the spores are released either through a pore in the top or as the outer skin breaks down. Drops of rain or other disturbance of the fruitbody helps to disperse the spores.

• *pestle-shaped fruitbody*

Family LYCOPERDACEAE	Species *Lycoperdon pyriforme*	Season Autumn–winter

STUMP PUFFBALL

This is one of the more easily identified *Lycoperdon* species: identification marks include its elongated pear shape, its smooth surface at maturity, white cords at the base, and its occurrence on woody substrates – others in the genus grow on the ground. Young fruitbodies have a warty to spiny skin. They are edible, but not choice, when their flesh is firm and white.

• **OCCURRENCE** Saprotrophic; on rotten deciduous wood and, more rarely, conifers in woods, open parks, and gardens. Almost cosmopolitan; absent in extreme climatic zones.

• **SIMILAR SPECIES** Found in open, wooded areas, *L. lividum* is also smooth, but is grayer and has warty spores (those of *L. pyriforme* are almost smooth).

young specimens have firm white flesh •

SECTION

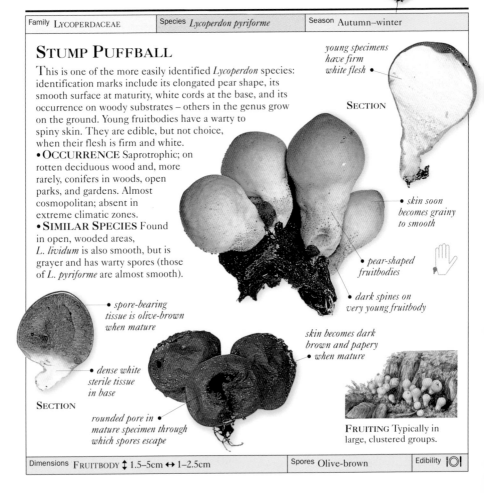

• *skin soon becomes grainy to smooth*

• *pear-shaped fruitbodies*

• *dark spines on very young fruitbody*

skin becomes dark brown and papery • when mature

• *spore-bearing tissue is olive-brown when mature*

• *dense white sterile tissue in base*

SECTION

rounded pore in • mature specimen through which spores escape

FRUITING Typically in large, clustered groups.

Dimensions FRUITBODY ↕ 1.5–5cm ↔ 1–2.5cm	Spores Olive-brown	Edibility 🍴

| Family LYCOPERDACEAE | Species *Lycoperdon echinatum* | Season Autumn |

HEDGEHOG PUFFBALL

Long brown spines on the surface of the globe-shaped, tapering fruitbody give the Hedgehog Puffball its name. The spines fall off at maturity, leaving a distinctive net pattern on the dark brown surface. The spore-bearing tissue is white and firm when young, becoming brown at maturity when the lilac-tinted, chocolate-brown spores escape through a pore on the top; the sterile basal flesh also darkens with age.
• **OCCURRENCE**
Saprotrophic; on alkaline soil in beech woods. Sometimes found beside the rarer, pink-tinged *Lycoperdon mammiforme*. In warmer parts of Europe and nearby parts of Asia.
• **SIMILAR SPECIES**
L. americanum is similar in appearance and occurs in North America.

groups of 3 or 4 long spines meet at tips •

pore in top of mature • fruitbody

• net pattern left where spines have fallen off

• globe-shaped fruitbody tapers at base

white • mycelial cords attach fruitbody to litter

FRUITING A few together, often on ditch banks.

| Dimensions FRUITBODY ↕ 3–7cm ↔ 1–3cm | Spores Chocolate-brown | Edibility |

| Family LYCOPERDACEAE | Species *Lycoperdon perlatum* | Season Autumn |

COMMON PUFFBALL

pore •

spore mass brown and powdery when mature •

Rounded, typically with a distinct stem, this white to yellowish brown species is covered with short spines, each surrounded by smaller, grainlike scales. A projection on the top marks where the pore, through which the spores escape, will form. At maturity, the spines fall off, leaving a regular pattern on the skin. The firm white flesh is edible when young, becoming darker and unpalatable with age.
• **OCCURRENCE** Saprotrophic; on soil, mainly in woods but also in grassland. Widespread; common in northern temperate zones.
• **SIMILAR SPECIES**
Lycoperdon nigrescens has longer, darker spines in groups, like those of the much longer-spined *L. echinatum* (above). The surface of both has a similar pattern when the spines fall off.

• conelike spines are lost with age

SECTION

• projection where pore will form

spore-producing • tissue ages darker

SECTION

• grainlike spines around conical spines

sterile stem • tissue is spongy

FRUITING In dense groups or occasionally singly.

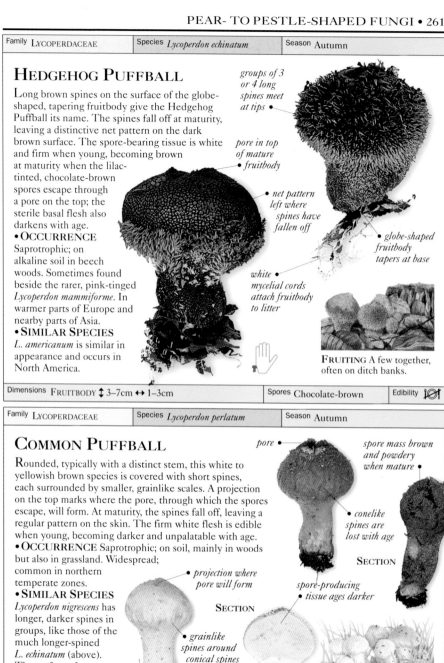

| Dimensions FRUITBODY ↕ 4–7cm ↔ 2–4cm | Spores Pale yellow to olive-brown | Edibility |

Family LYCOPERDACEAE	Species *Calvatia excipuliformis*	Season Autumn

PESTLE-SHAPED PUFFBALL

This buff-brown fungus typically has a tall stem with a rounded upper fertile part; short-stemmed specimens also occur. When mature, the outer skin breaks open and the brown spores within are dispersed by wind and rain. When young and firm, the fruitbodies are edible but fairly tasteless. The stem part becomes very tough as it matures and may even persist into the following season.

• **OCCURRENCE** Saprotrophic; on soil or turf in woods or open areas. Widespread and common in most parts of northern temperate zones, extending to subarctic and subtropical zones.

• **SIMILAR SPECIES** *C. elata* is widespread and common in North America. *Lycoperdon molle* resembles a short-stemmed specimen.

• *fine-pointed scales on surface of upper part when young*

• *pale buff-brown immature fruitbody*

outer skin breaks at maturity, revealing rich brown spore mass •

fairly long stem • *develops furrows on surface when mature*

fairly firm, white, spore-producing tissue in young specimen •

SECTION

• *stem does not produce spores*

• *appears among moss or leaf litter*

stem flesh • *is spongy in texture*

SECTION

FRUITING Mostly in small groups of fruitbodies.

Dimensions FRUITBODY ↕ 5–20cm ↔ 5–10cm	Spores Olive-brown to brown	Edibility

| Family LYCOPERDACEAE | Species *Calvatia utriformis* | Season Summer–autumn |

MOSAIC PUFFBALL

This large species has pear-shaped fruitbodies with coarse scales, which are lost at maturity. The top skin rots away to reveal the powdery brown spore mass. The lower, sterile part is white, aging to brown. Edible when young but not tasty.
• **OCCURRENCE** Saprotrophic; found growing in open, often coastal, areas. Widespread in northern temperate zones.
• **SIMILAR SPECIES** *C. cyathiformis* has a lilac-tinted spore mass; common in eastern North America.

spore mass visible through hole in top •

coarse, mealy, white scales •

pear-shaped fruitbody with flat top •

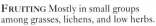

FRUITING Mostly in small groups among grasses, lichens, and low herbs.

| Dimensions FRUITBODY ↕ 5–10cm ↔ 5–15cm | Spores Chocolate-brown | Edibility |

| Family SCLERODERMATACEAE | Species *Scleroderma verrucosum* | Season Autumn |

SCALY EARTHBALL

This fairly large species is pale yellow to brown and covered with irregular brown scales. It has a stemlike projection and thin skin, to 1mm thick. The spore-bearing tissue is white and smells metallic, soon turning dark purple-brown as it matures. The spores are dispersed by wind as the outer skin of the fruitbody distintegrates.
• **OCCURRENCE** Mycorrhizal with deciduous trees such as oak and beech, growing in wooded areas and open parks. Widespread and common in both northern and southern temperate zones.

brown scales on rounded fruitbody •

partly buried stem under main fruitbody •

white mycelial cords •

FRUITING Mostly a few together or singly, often on bare soil.

| Dimensions FRUITBODY ↕ 5–10cm ↔ 2–5cm | Spores Purple-black | Edibility |

| Family CALOSTOMATACEAE | Species *Calostoma cinnabarina* | Season Late summer–autumn |

PUFFBALL-IN-ASPIC

This species has a gelatinous outer layer and a red inner layer, breaking up to enclose the stem in a thick jelly, dotted with red pieces. The exposed, ovoid top is coated in a red powder that wears away to reveal a pale yellow ball with a cross-shaped opening for spore release.
• **OCCURRENCE** Found growing on the ground in open woods. Widespread and common in eastern North America.
• **SIMILAR SPECIES** *Calostoma lutescens* is yellow and extremely small. *C. ravenelii* is straw-yellow and not gelatinous.

red powder covers immature spore ball •

stem sheathed in jelly filled with red pieces •

red mouth for spore release •

FRUITING Appears in small groups on the ground in open wooded areas.

| Dimensions FRUITBODY ↕ 2–5cm ↔ 1–2cm | Spores White to cream | Edibility |

CUP- TO DISK-SHAPED

Although they all produce cup- or disk-shaped fruitbodies, the mushrooms in this section belong to two separate groups. The first group has more or less circular fruitbodies that are shallowly cupped or flat (pp.264–73); the second group has deeply cupped, nestlike fruitbodies containing tiny, lentil-shaped structures (p.274).

• *cup-shaped fruitbody*

WITHOUT "EGGS"

THIS SUBSECTION features fungi that produce cup- or disk-shaped fruitbodies with a smooth, spore-bearing surface (hymenium) on the inner side of the cup or on the top of the disk. When mature, the spores are discharged violently (see p.16–17).

The morels (pp.209–10) evolved from simple cup-fungi, but have distinct stems and are more elaborate in shape.

Family SARCOSCYPHACEAE	Species *Sarcoscypha austriaca*	Season Late autumn–early summer

CURLY-HAIRED ELF CUP

This fungus has tiny, corkscrewlike white hairs on the outside of the long-lasting, cup-shaped fruitbody, making it appear pale in contrast to the interior, which is bright scarlet. The cup margin is also fairly pale and may be finely toothed. The pale stem is often hidden in the substrate, and the pale red flesh is fairly firm but brittle. There is also a pure white form.
• **OCCURRENCE** Grows on wood substrates in deciduous areas. Widespread throughout Europe and probably in other parts of northern temperate zones.
• **SIMILAR SPECIES** *Sarcoscypha coccinea* has straight hairs on the outside of the cup. Other species of *Sarcoscypha* have more localized distributions and differ in spore characteristics and germination.

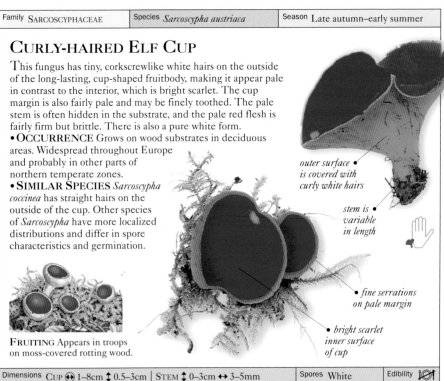

outer surface •
is covered with curly white hairs

stem is •
variable in length

• *fine serrations on pale margin*

• *bright scarlet inner surface of cup*

FRUITING Appears in troops on moss-covered rotting wood.

Dimensions CUP ⊕ 1–8cm ↕ 0.5–3cm | STEM ↕ 0–3cm ↔ 3–5mm	Spores White	Edibility

Family OTIDEACEAE	Species *Tarzetta cupularis*	Season Summer–autumn

DENTATE ELF CUP

The wine goblet-shaped fruitbody of the Dentate Elf Cup has small, triangular teeth at the cup margin and a short stem. Unlike other cup fungi that expand with age, its shape remains the same as the fruitbody matures. The outer surface of the fruitbody has a granular texture and is pale buff; inside the cup, the spore-producing layer (hymenium) is grayish cream.

• **OCCURRENCE** Found growing on nutrient-rich, calcareous or clay soil in parks and conifer forests. Widespread and fairly common in northern temperate zones.

• **SIMILAR SPECIES** Other members of this small genus occur in the same habitat. Size is the major distinguishing feature: *Tarzetta caninus* has the largest cup, reaching 5cm in diameter. Otherwise it is very difficult to differentiate between the species, although stem development and microscopic features can help.

fine teeth at cup margin •

spore-producing inner surface of cup is grayish cream SECTION

fruitbody is shaped like a wine goblet •

• *light buff-colored exterior*

short stem •

FRUITING Appears in small groups, mostly on bare soil.

Dimensions CUP ⊕ 0.5–1.5cm ↕ 0.5–2.5cm | STEM ↕ 0.3–1cm ↔ 2–4mm	Spores White	Edibility

Family MORCHELLACEAE	Species *Disciotis venosa*	Season Spring–early summer

CUPLIKE MOREL

Initially cup-shaped, the rich, dark brown fruitbody of the Cuplike Morel flattens and may become convex as it ages. Its surface is distinctly ribbed and furrowed, particularly in larger specimens; the underside is off-white with a scurfy covering. The reduced stem is thick and off-white; the pale flesh is brittle and thick. Although eaten in parts of Europe, this species is hard to identify in North America; little is known about the edibility of its look-alikes.

• **OCCURRENCE** In parks and woods, often alongside *Morchella semilibera* (p.210). In deciduous woods in eastern North America; under conifers in the West. Widespread in most regions except arctic-alpine and tropical zones; worldwide distribution unclear.

flesh smells of • *chlorine*

inner surface of cup is brown to dark brown •

flesh is pale with thick but brittle texture •

ribs and • *furrows on surface of this mature specimen*

FRUITING Appears singly or in groups on the ground, always growing on nutrient-rich soil.

Dimensions CUP ⊕ 4–10cm| STEM ↕ ↔ 2mm	Spores Cream	Edibility

Family PEZIZACEAE	Species *Peziza vesiculosa*	Season All year

BLADDER CUP

This fungus has a tightly rolled, curved margin and a distinctive bladder shape with blisterlike pustules developing in cups. The outer surface is pale buff and granular; the inner spore-bearing surface (hymenium) is pale yellow-brown. The opening through which the spores are released is small and, unlike most other *Peziza* species, it barely expands with age.

• OCCURRENCE In parks, gardens, and around farm buildings on nutrient-rich substrate such as composted manure, mulch in flower beds, and rotting straw. It is often found near other cup-fungi and ink caps (*Coprinus* species, pp.174–76). Widespread and common in northern temperate zones.

mealy, granular covering on outer surface •

pale yellow-brown inner surface

incurved • cup margin

small opening for • spore escape

FRUITING Appears in dense clusters or singly.

• brittle flesh is comparatively thick

Dimensions CUP ⊕ 3–10cm ↕ 1–4cm	Spores White	Edibility

Family PEZIZACEAE	Species *Peziza badia*	Season Summer–autumn

OLIVE-BROWN CUP

A liver-brown fruitbody that becomes darker olive-brown inside as it matures is characteristic of this species, although it is positively distinguishable from other brown *Peziza* species only with the use of a microscope. This reveals, among other things, an incomplete net ornament on the spores. The fruitbody is stemless with a granular, reddish brown outer surface and thin, reddish brown flesh.

• OCCURRENCE On sandy soil by paths in conifer stands, or banks of ditches in boggy areas close to birch trees. Widespread and common in northern temperate zones.

• SIMILAR SPECIES Paler brown species, such as *P. micropus*, *P. repanda*, and *P. varia*, can be found on rotten trunks.

• inner surface is liver-brown, becoming darker with olive tinges

cup • expands with age

irregular cup margin •

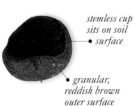

stemless cup sits on soil • surface

• granular, reddish brown outer surface

FRUITING Grows in troops and small clusters.

Dimensions CUP ⊕ 1.5–7cm ↕ 0.5–3cm	Spores White	Edibility

Family PEZIZACEAE	Species *Peziza succosa*	Season Summer–autumn

YELLOW-MILK CUP

Cup-shaped and yellow- to gray-brown, the
Yellow-milk Cup is distinguished from most other
Peziza species by its reaction when cut open: the
thin, yellow-brown flesh exudes a milky yellow
juice that gradually turns bright yellow. With age,
the cup expands and becomes irregular in shape.
• **OCCURRENCE** Along roadsides in deciduous
areas; often found with *Helvella* and *Inocybe* species.
Widespread and common in Europe;
also occurs in eastern and central North America.
• **SIMILAR SPECIES** Other *Peziza* species that
have yellow juice include *P. michelii*, with its lilac
tinges, and *P. succosella*, which has a greenish yellow
flesh reaction and smaller spores.

• *more or less
even margin*

• *fairly pale
specimen*

• *cup expands
with age*

*gray-brown spore-
producing
surface* •

*outer surface
is almost
smooth* •

*flesh stains •
yellow when
cut or broken*

FRUITING Singly or in
troops on clay-rich soil.

Dimensions CUP ⊕ 0.5–5cm ↕ 0.5–2cm	Spores White	Edibility

Family OTIDEACEAE	Species *Geopora arenicola*	Season Summer–autumn

SANDY EARTH CUP

This species produces a fairly large, cup-shaped brown
fruitbody with a hairy outer surface. The smooth interior
may contain the tiny flask-fungus parasite *Melanospora
brevirostris*. The spores of this mushroom are large
compared to those of its similar relatives.
• **OCCURRENCE** Buried in gravel or sand by roads
or in gravel pits, it is easily overlooked in its hidden
habitat. Widespread and common in Europe. Also found
in northeastern United States and in California.
• **SIMILAR SPECIES** All species of *Geopora* are sunk in the soil,
some producing only a tiny opening, others splitting in a starlike
pattern when very mature. *Humaria hemisphaerica* develops on the
soil surface. There is also a range of other similar species, but it is
very difficult to distinguish many species in this genus.

• *cup splits
open so that
spores can be
released*

• *cup margin
splits into
lobes with age*

*thin, brittle
brown flesh* •

*fruitbody is
buried in mossy,
sandy soil* •

*smooth •
interior is
creamy brown*

*brown
outer surface
is hairy*

FRUITING In troops breaking
through the soil surface.

Dimensions CUP ⊕ 0.5–2cm ↕ 1–2cm	Spores White	Edibility

Family OTIDEACEAE	Species *Aleuria aurantia*	Season Summer–autumn

ORANGE-PEEL CUP

With its vivid orange coloring and downy outer surface, the Orange-peel Cup is one of the most attractive cup-fungi. The cup margin is inrolled when young, becoming wavy. The cup flattens with age. The thin, brittle, white to pale flesh is edible but must be cooked because it is toxic when raw.

• **OCCURRENCE** Found on gravelly soil in disturbed sites, such as on dirt roads and on new lawns. Some *Scutellinia* species (see below) can also be found in similar sites. Widespread and common in European northern temperate zones.

• **SIMILAR SPECIES** Found on similar sites, *Melastiza chateri* is smaller, reddish orange, and has very short, pale brown hairs at the cup margin. Other *Aleuria* species have smaller cups and are rarer; a microscope is required to identify them correctly.

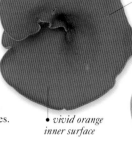

cup becomes wavy and flattened with age

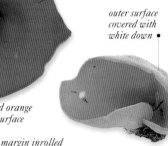

outer surface covered with white down

vivid orange inner surface

margin inrolled when young

stemlike base is visible on some specimens

FRUITING Appears in large groups and clusters.

Dimensions CUP ⊕ 2–10cm ↕ 0.2–3cm	Spores White	Edibility

Family OTIDEACEAE	Species *Scutellinia scutellata*	Season Late spring–winter

COMMON EYELASH CUP

This highly distinctive cup-fungus has conspicuous long black "eyelashes" at the margin of the disk-shaped, vivid orange-red cup; the outer surface is pale orange-brown. The presence of carotene causes the orange-red coloring on this and other orange-colored fungi. There are many similar species in this complex genus; under a microscope, spore shape and ornamentation offer the best clues for positive identification.

• **OCCURRENCE** On wet, mossy wood near ponds, occasionally on organic soil. Widespread and common in northern temperate zones.

inner surface is bright orange-red

when fully mature, dark brown hairs point outward

dark brown hairs project inward when young

grows on wet and rotten wood

FRUITING Typically appears in dense swarms on wood.

Dimensions CUP ⊕ 0.5–1cm ↕ 2mm	Spores White	Edibility

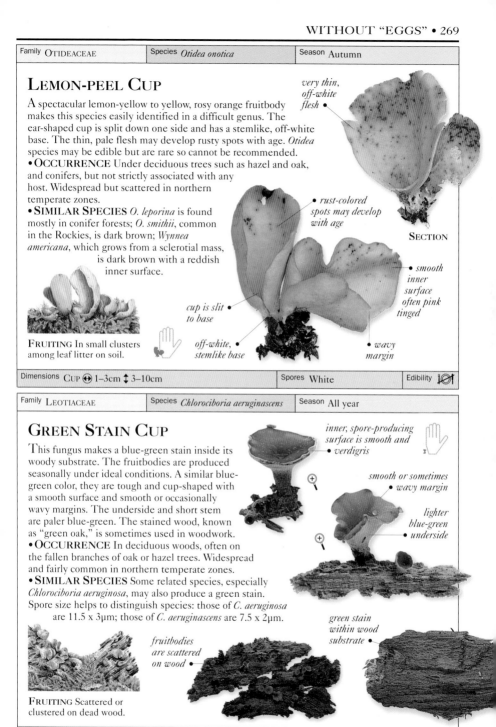

| Family OTIDEACEAE | Species *Otidea onotica* | Season Autumn |

LEMON-PEEL CUP

A spectacular lemon-yellow to yellow, rosy orange fruitbody makes this species easily identified in a difficult genus. The ear-shaped cup is split down one side and has a stemlike, off-white base. The thin, pale flesh may develop rusty spots with age. *Otidea* species may be edible but are rare so cannot be recommended.

• **OCCURRENCE** Under deciduous trees such as hazel and oak, and conifers, but not strictly associated with any host. Widespread but scattered in northern temperate zones.

• **SIMILAR SPECIES** *O. leporina* is found mostly in conifer forests; *O. smithii*, common in the Rockies, is dark brown; *Wynnea americana*, which grows from a sclerotial mass, is dark brown with a reddish inner surface.

very thin, off-white flesh •

• rust-colored spots may develop with age

SECTION

• smooth inner surface often pink tinged

FRUITING In small clusters among leaf litter on soil.

cup is slit to base •

off-white, • stemlike base

• wavy margin

| Dimensions CUP ⊕ 1–3cm ↕ 3–10cm | Spores White | Edibility |

| Family LEOTIACEAE | Species *Chlorociboria aeruginascens* | Season All year |

GREEN STAIN CUP

This fungus makes a blue-green stain inside its woody substrate. The fruitbodies are produced seasonally under ideal conditions. A similar blue-green color, they are tough and cup-shaped with a smooth surface and smooth or occasionally wavy margins. The underside and short stem are paler blue-green. The stained wood, known as "green oak," is sometimes used in woodwork.

• **OCCURRENCE** In deciduous woods, often on the fallen branches of oak or hazel trees. Widespread and fairly common in northern temperate zones.

• **SIMILAR SPECIES** Some related species, especially *Chlorociboria aeruginosa*, may also produce a green stain. Spore size helps to distinguish species: those of *C. aeruginosa* are 11.5 x 3µm; those of *C. aeruginascens* are 7.5 x 2µm.

inner, spore-producing surface is smooth and • verdigris

smooth or sometimes • wavy margin

lighter blue-green • underside

green stain within wood substrate •

fruitbodies are scattered on wood •

FRUITING Scattered or clustered on dead wood.

| Dimensions CUP ⊕ 0.2–1cm | STEM ↕ 1–5mm ↔ 1–3mm | Spores White | Edibility |

| Family SCLEROTINIACEAE | Species *Dumontinia tuberosa* | Season Spring |

TUBER CUP

This species has a chestnut-brown fruitbody that grows up out of a black underground organ, called a sclerotium. Cup-shaped, with a smooth margin, it has smooth surfaces, both inside the cup and out. The stem is long and black. This species has perhaps the largest fruitbodies in the Sclerotiniaceae.

• **OCCURRENCE** Sclerotia are formed inside the rhizomes of anemone species in Europe; reported on the ground in North America. Widespread; local to very common.

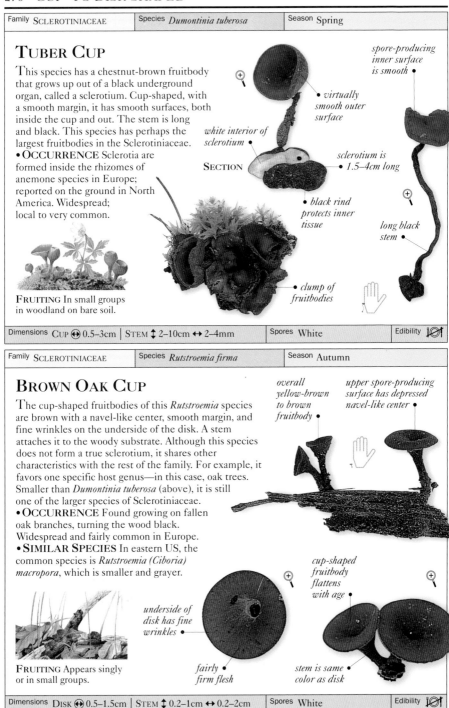

spore-producing inner surface is smooth •

• virtually smooth outer surface

white interior of sclerotium •

SECTION

sclerotium is • 1.5–4cm long

• black rind protects inner tissue

long black stem •

• clump of fruitbodies

FRUITING In small groups in woodland on bare soil.

| Dimensions CUP ⊕ 0.5–3cm | STEM ↕ 2–10cm ↔ 2–4mm | Spores White | Edibility |

| Family SCLEROTINIACEAE | Species *Rutstroemia firma* | Season Autumn |

BROWN OAK CUP

The cup-shaped fruitbodies of this *Rutstroemia* species are brown with a navel-like center, smooth margin, and fine wrinkles on the underside of the disk. A stem attaches it to the woody substrate. Although this species does not form a true sclerotium, it shares other characteristics with the rest of the family. For example, it favors one specific host genus—in this case, oak trees. Smaller than *Dumontinia tuberosa* (above), it is still one of the larger species of Sclerotiniaceae.

• **OCCURRENCE** Found growing on fallen oak branches, turning the wood black. Widespread and fairly common in Europe.

• **SIMILAR SPECIES** In eastern US, the common species is *Rutstroemia (Ciboria) macropora*, which is smaller and grayer.

overall yellow-brown to brown fruitbody •

upper spore-producing surface has depressed navel-like center •

underside of disk has fine wrinkles •

cup-shaped fruitbody flattens with age •

FRUITING Appears singly or in small groups.

fairly firm flesh

stem is same color as disk •

| Dimensions DISK ⊕ 0.5–1.5cm | STEM ↕ 0.2–1cm ↔ 0.2–2cm | Spores White | Edibility |

Family LEOTIACEAE	Species *Neobulgaria pura*	Season Late autumn

BEECH JELLY-DROP CUP

The fruitbodies of this fungus are pale pink, gelatinous, and translucent with a flat spore-producing surface and finely toothed margins. Tapering strongly to the base, they are cone-shaped in cross-section. Newly emerged specimens are very firm and rubbery. Exposure to the weather eventually makes them collapse and become much thinner, but they will persist from autumn into winter.

• **OCCURRENCE** On relatively fresh bark of fallen beech trunks and branches, often next to *Hypoxylon fragiforme* (p.257). Northern temperate zones; in most areas where beech occurs.

• **SIMILAR SPECIES** *Bulgaria inquinans* (below) is similar in habit and habitat but is harder and darker brown to black.

flesh is rubbery

cone-shaped fruitbody

disk-shaped surface

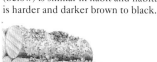

FRUITING In dense clusters on beech bark.

pale pink fruitbody is translucent

top surface is flat and produces spores

Dimensions DISK ⊕ 0.5–3cm ↕ 1cm	Spores White	Edibility

Family LEOTIACEAE	Species *Bulgaria inquinans*	Season Autumn–winter

BLACK JELLY-DROP CUPS

The disk-shaped mature fruitbodies of this licorice-like fungus are black, sometimes appearing blue. Unusual for the Leotiaceae, the spores here are very conspicuous and jet black; the nearby bark may be black with ejected spores, and touching the fruitbody produces black smudges on the fingers. Of the eight spores formed within each ascus (see pp.10–11), only the top four develop the dark coloring. The staining property of the spores has been used for dyeing wool.

• **OCCURRENCE** On the bark of recently fallen trunks of beech or oak trees; mostly on the upper surface. Widespread and common where host trees occur in northern temperate zones.

• **SIMILAR SPECIES** *Exidia glandulosa* (p.283), a true jelly mushroom, is even more jellylike and can revive after drying out.

SECTION

black spores collect on upper surface

firm but rubbery fruitbody

disk-shaped fruitbody

young specimens are scurfy and brown outside

FRUITING Appears in swarms on beech or oak bark.

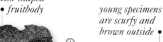

Dimensions DISC ⊕ 0.5–4cm ↕ 0.5–2cm	Spores Jet black	Edibility

Family LEOTIACEAE	Species *Ascocoryne cylichnium*	Season Autumn–winter

PURPLE JELLY-DROP CUP

This species produces a disk-shaped, gelatinous, reddish purple fruitbody with a smooth, shiny, spore-producing surface and an often irregularly lobed margin. It has a short stem, which makes the fruitbody appear to be cone-shaped when viewed from the side.
• **OCCURRENCE** Found growing on the bark and exposed wood of deciduous trees. Widespread and fairly common in northern temperate zones.
• **SIMILAR SPECIES** *Ascocoryne sarcoides* (below) has narrower disks and shorter spores. Several other smaller species occur in the northern hemisphere. The best way to distinguish between them is by microscopic examination of such features as the spores.

fruitbody is gelatinous

short stem attached to substrate

smooth lower surface

smooth, spore-producing upper surface

reddish purple coloring

specimen growing on bare wood

FRUITING In swarms on tree stumps and branches.

fruitbody is disk-shaped

Dimensions DISC ⊕ 0.5–2cm ↕ 2–4mm │ STEM ↕ to 5mm ↔ to 2mm	Spores White	Edibility

Family LEOTIACEAE	Species *Ascocoryne sarcoides*	Season Autumn–winter

BRAIN JELLY-DROP CUP

The disk-shaped, gelatinous, reddish purple fruitbody of this species may have a rudimentary stem. Along with the disk-shaped fruitbodies, brainlike asexual growths appear. They are paler and grayer.
• **OCCURRENCE** Mostly on bare deciduous stumps or trunks. Widespread and common in parts of northern temperate zones, and probably elsewhere.
• **SIMILAR SPECIES** *Ascocoryne cylichnium* (above) is best distinguished by microscopic examination. Its spores are larger and normally more than 3-septate at maturity. *A. turficola* is much rarer and more colorful and grows on sphagnum moss. *Ascotremella faginea* (p.283) has larger, brainlike fruitbodies.

brainlike, pale red-purple asexual state

disk-shaped fruitbody is gelatinous inside

fruitbodies grow on bare wood

FRUITING In clusters or singly, often with the asexual and fertile state appearing together.

Dimensions DISC ⊕ 0.2–1cm ↕ 1–4mm	Spores White	Edibility

Family LEOTIACEAE	Species *Bisporella citrina*	Season Autumn–early winter

LEMON CUP

The clustered habit and vivid yellow color of this tiny species enable it to be seen from a distance. The disks have a smooth, flat or slightly concave upper surface and a paler lower surface. White disks may occur. There is no true stem.
• **OCCURRENCE** Found growing on fallen deciduous wood, often beech, oak, and hazel; mostly grows on wood that lacks its bark. Widespread and very common throughout northern temperate zones.
• **SIMILAR SPECIES** Some species of *Bisporella* have fruitbodies that occur near or on top of their blackish, powdery asexual form, called *Bispora*. There are a number of other closely related yellow cup-fungi. Some may have a stem or may differ only in microscopic features.

rusty spots may appear on disk surface

looks like a nail-head in side view

smooth, spore-producing upper surface

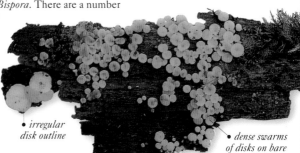

FRUITING Appears in conspicuous swarms on wood.

irregular disk outline

dense swarms of disks on bare wood

Dimensions DISC ⊕ 1–3mm ↕ less than 1mm	Spores White	Edibility

Family CORTICIACEAE	Species *Aleurodiscus amorphus*	Season All year

ORANGE DISCUS MUSHROOM

fruitbody is tough and leathery

pale orange or pinkish orange spore-producing surface

Although it looks like a cup-fungus, this skin-fungus is tougher and more leathery than many cup-fungi. The disk is pinkish orange with a mealy surface and a fringed white margin. It is firmly attached to the substrate at a point beneath its center. A gelatinous, transparent or white blob indicates that it has been parasitized by a species of *Tremella* such as *T. simplex*.
• **OCCURRENCE** On bark-clad fir or, more rarely, spruce. Widespread and fairly common across northern North America and Europe.
• **SIMILAR SPECIES** The cup-fungus *Lachnellula subtilissima* is hairier, brighter orange, and has a more distinct stem.

sterile, fringed, incurved white margin

gelatinous blob indicates parasite

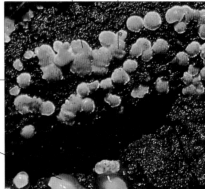

FRUITING Appears in massed, attached fruitings during damp periods.

Dimensions CUP ⊕ 1–8mm ↕ 2–3mm	Spores White	Edibility

CUP-SHAPED CONTAINING "EGGS"

T HE FUNGI here have unique fruitbodies consisting of a "cup," inside of which are tiny structures called peridioles. These contain the spore-producing hymenium. Initally, a protective skin covers the top of the "cup." It disappears at maturity and the peridioles are dispersed by raindrops.

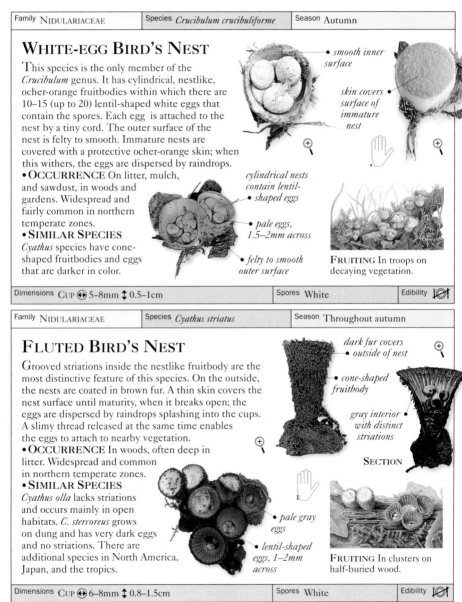

Family NIDULARIACEAE	Species *Crucibulum crucibuliforme*	Season Autumn

WHITE-EGG BIRD'S NEST

This species is the only member of the *Crucibulum* genus. It has cylindrical, nestlike, ocher-orange fruitbodies within which there are 10–15 (up to 20) lentil-shaped white eggs that contain the spores. Each egg is attached to the nest by a tiny cord. The outer surface of the nest is felty to smooth. Immature nests are covered with a protective ocher-orange skin; when this withers, the eggs are dispersed by raindrops.

• **OCCURRENCE** On litter, mulch, and sawdust, in woods and gardens. Widespread and fairly common in northern temperate zones.

• **SIMILAR SPECIES** *Cyathus* species have cone-shaped fruitbodies and eggs that are darker in color.

smooth inner surface

skin covers surface of immature nest

cylindrical nests contain lentil-shaped eggs

pale eggs, 1.5–2mm across

felty to smooth outer surface

FRUITING In troops on decaying vegetation.

Dimensions CUP ⊕ 5–8mm ↕ 0.5–1cm	Spores White	Edibility 🌂

Family NIDULARIACEAE	Species *Cyathus striatus*	Season Throughout autumn

FLUTED BIRD'S NEST

Grooved striations inside the nestlike fruitbody are the most distinctive feature of this species. On the outside, the nests are coated in brown fur. A thin skin covers the nest surface until maturity, when it breaks open; the eggs are dispersed by raindrops splashing into the cups. A slimy thread released at the same time enables the eggs to attach to nearby vegetation.

• **OCCURRENCE** In woods, often deep in litter. Widespread and common in northern temperate zones.

• **SIMILAR SPECIES** *Cyathus olla* lacks striations and occurs mainly in open habitats. *C. stercoreus* grows on dung and has very dark eggs and no striations. There are additional species in North America, Japan, and the tropics.

dark fur covers outside of nest

cone-shaped fruitbody

gray interior with distinct striations

SECTION

pale gray eggs

lentil-shaped eggs, 1–2mm across

FRUITING In clusters on half-buried wood.

Dimensions CUP ⊕ 6–8mm ↕ 0.8–1.5cm	Spores White	Edibility 🌂

TRUMPET-SHAPED FUNGI

The fungi featured in this section have trumpet-shaped, hollow fruitbodies with the spore-producing hymenium lining the more or less smooth outer surface. Most of the species here belong to the Cantharellaceae family (see also pp.28 and 30). The fruitbodies have fairly tough flesh and may persist for several weeks.

• *trumpet-shaped fruitbody*

Family CANTHARELLACEAE	Species *Craterellus cornucopioides*	Season Summer–autumn

BLACK TRUMPET

dark brown marbling on inner surface •

The fruitbody of this dark brown chanterelle is hollow and trumpet-shaped, tapering toward the base. The outer side has a paler gray spore-bearing layer. The thin gray flesh is mild and pleasant tasting with an aromatic smell. Its dark coloring makes it difficult to spot at first, but where found it typically occurs en masse.

hollow, • trumpet-shaped fruitbody

• **OCCURRENCE** Mycorrhizal with deciduous trees in woods, on fairly rich, often calcareous soil; more rarely with conifers. Widespread in northern temperate zones; abundant in some areas, but almost absent in others.
• **SIMILAR SPECIES** *Craterellus fallax*, a North American species, is more fragrant.

• wavy, irregular margin

SECTION

• off-white bloom on fertile outer fruitbody surface

• gray-brown base

FRUITING Appears in troops and small clusters.

Dimensions FRUITBODY ⊕ 3–10cm ↕ 5–12cm | BASE ↔ 0.5–2cm	Spores White	Edibility

Family CANTHARELLACEAE	Species *Cantharellus lutescens*	Season Early autumn–early winter

GOLDEN CHANTERELLE

yellow-orange stem •   • yellow-brown cap

This chanterelle has a somewhat funnel-shaped, yellow-brown fruitbody. It has a hollow, yellow-orange base, and rather thin, pale yellow flesh with a fruity smell. The pale spore-producing layer on the outer surface is almost smooth, resembling those of *Craterellus* species (above).
• **OCCURRENCE** Mycorrhizal with deciduous trees and conifers in damp, moss-rich woods. Widespread but rather local in temperate and warm-temperate regions, including North America, Europe, and Asia.
• **SIMILAR SPECIES** *C. tubaeformis* var. *lutescens* has distinct, veinlike gills on the outer surface.

FRUITING Appears in troops among mosses in damp forests.

Dimensions FRUITBODY ⊕ 2–7cm ↕ 3–7cm | BASE ↔ 3–8mm	Spores Pale cream	Edibility

Family CANTHARELLACEAE	Species *Cantharellus lateritius*	Season Summer–autumn

SMOOTH CHANTERELLE

Trumpet-shaped with a pendent, wavy margin, this orange-yellow species is closely related to *Cantharellus cibarius* (p.28), and differs from it mainly in having a smooth to faintly or partly veined outer surface. It is generally denser and stouter but just as fragrant, with the same taste. It was formerly known as *Craterellus cantharellus*, because it looks like *C. cornucopioides* (p.275) but with chanterelle colors.

poorly formed, gill-like folds sometimes occur •

cap margin is pendent • and wavy

trumpet-shaped, orange-yellow • fruitbody

smooth or • nearly smooth undersurface

• OCCURRENCE
Under oaks. Widespread and very common in eastern North America.

• SIMILAR SPECIES *C. cibarius* (p.28), has well-formed, forked, gill-like folds on its outer surface. *C. odoratus* appears in dense, flowerlike clusters.

FRUITING Appears singly or in large numbers on the ground under oak trees in open woods and parks.

Dimensions FRUITBODY ⊕ ↕ 2.5–10cm	BASE ↔ 0.5–2.5cm	Spores Pale yellow-orange	Edibility

Family GOMPHACEAE	Species *Gomphus floccosus*	Season Summer–autumn

SCALY VASE CHANTERELLE

This large, trumpet-shaped species is brightly colored, making it easy to spot in open woods. It has a variably scaly, red-orange to orange-yellow cap. The flesh has the same strong coloring.

large, trumpet-to vase-shaped fruitbody •

cap surface is red-orange to orange-yellow

The decurrent veined spore-producing surface is creamy white to ocher. This mushroom and its related look-alikes should not be eaten because they contain an indigestible acid.

scales on cap surface are red-orange •

creamy white to ocher spore-producing surface •

• OCCURRENCE On the ground under conifers and in mixed wooded areas. Widespread and common throughout North America.

tapering, • stemlike base

• SIMILAR SPECIES *Gomphus bonarii* is bright red with a milk-white spore-producing surface. *G. kauffmanii* is larger, more coarsely scaly, and yellowish tan.

FRUITING Singly or in large groups of fruitbodies on the ground under conifers and in mixed woods.

Dimensions FRUITBODY ⊕ 5–15cm ↕ 5–10cm	BASE ↔ 1.5cm	Spores Ocher-yellow	Edibility

STAR-SHAPED & CAGELIKE FUNGI

These fungi are called gasteroids because their spore-tissue (gleba) is enclosed, stomachlike, in the fruitbody. The earth stars (p.278–80) have fruitbodies that split into a star with an inner spore-ball. The two Clathrus *species (below and p.280) are related to stinkhorns (pp.246–47).*

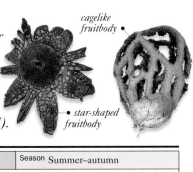

cagelike fruitbody

star-shaped fruitbody

Family CLATHRACEAE	Species *Clathrus archeri*	Season Summer–autumn

ARMED STINKHORN

This species produces spores in a foul-smelling slime to attract insects for dispersal. Its very characteristic fruitbody, with four to eight vivid red arms, emerges from a buff to pale pink base, or egg. The spore mass is on the inside of the arms. All Clathraceae have remarkable shapes; almost all are red tinged or white to off-white.
• **OCCURRENCE** Among woodland litter, or on sawdust or wood chips; in woods, parks, and flower beds. Inadvertently introduced from Australia or New Zealand, and now well established in Europe.
• **SIMILAR SPECIES** *Pseudocolus fusiformis*, found in North America, has only three or four joined arms. *Aseroë* species, for example *A. coccinea* from Japan, have stemlike bases.

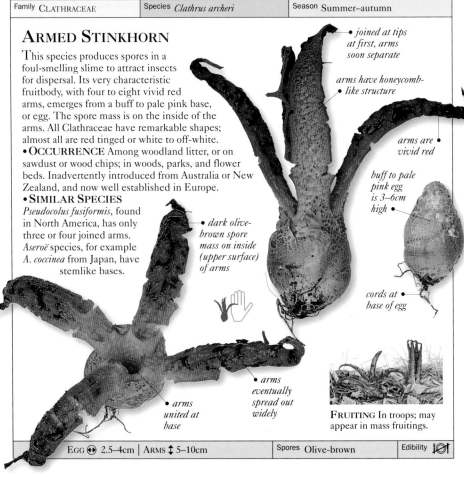

joined at tips at first, arms soon separate

arms have honeycomb-like structure

arms are vivid red

buff to pale pink egg is 3–6cm high

dark olive-brown spore mass on inside (upper surface) of arms

cords at base of egg

arms united at base

arms eventually spread out widely

FRUITING In troops; may appear in mass fruitings.

EGG ⊕ 2.5–4cm | ARMS ↕ 5–10cm	Spores Olive-brown	Edibility

Family SCLERODERMATACEAE	Species *Astraeus hygrometricus*	Season All year

BAROMETER EARTH STAR

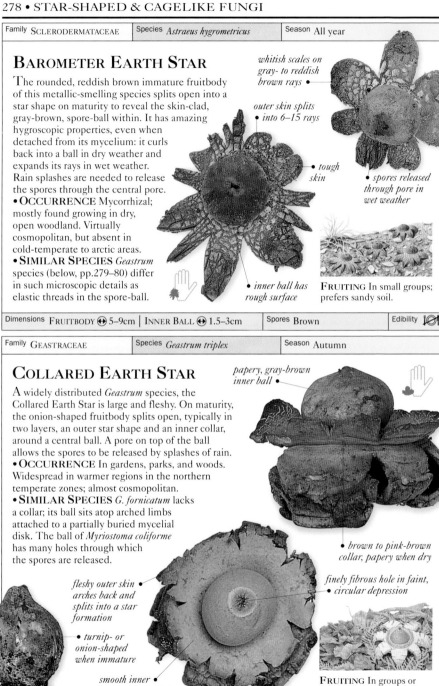

The rounded, reddish brown immature fruitbody of this metallic-smelling species splits open into a star shape on maturity to reveal the skin-clad, gray-brown, spore-ball within. It has amazing hygroscopic properties, even when detached from its mycelium: it curls back into a ball in dry weather and expands its rays in wet weather. Rain splashes are needed to release the spores through the central pore.
• **OCCURRENCE** Mycorrhizal; mostly found growing in dry, open woodland. Virtually cosmopolitan, but absent in cold-temperate to arctic areas.
• **SIMILAR SPECIES** *Geastrum* species (below, pp.279–80) differ in such microscopic details as elastic threads in the spore-ball.

whitish scales on gray- to reddish brown rays •

outer skin splits • into 6–15 rays

• tough skin

• spores released through pore in wet weather

• inner ball has rough surface

FRUITING In small groups; prefers sandy soil.

Dimensions FRUITBODY ⊕ 5–9cm | INNER BALL ⊕ 1.5–3cm	Spores Brown	Edibility

Family GEASTRACEAE	Species *Geastrum triplex*	Season Autumn

COLLARED EARTH STAR

A widely distributed *Geastrum* species, the Collared Earth Star is large and fleshy. On maturity, the onion-shaped fruitbody splits open, typically in two layers, an outer star shape and an inner collar, around a central ball. A pore on top of the ball allows the spores to be released by splashes of rain.
• **OCCURRENCE** In gardens, parks, and woods. Widespread in warmer regions in the northern temperate zones; almost cosmopolitan.
• **SIMILAR SPECIES** *G. fornicatum* lacks a collar; its ball sits atop arched limbs attached to a partially buried mycelial disk. The ball of *Myriostoma coliforme* has many holes through which the spores are released.

papery, gray-brown inner ball •

• brown to pink-brown collar; papery when dry

fleshy outer skin • arches back and splits into a star formation

finely fibrous hole in faint, • circular depression

• turnip- or onion-shaped when immature

smooth inner • surface of fruitbody

FRUITING In groups or fairy rings on rich soil.

Dimensions FRUITBODY ⊕ 4–12cm | INNER BALL ⊕ 2–4cm	Spores Chocolate-brown	Edibility

Family GEASTRACEAE	Species *Geastrum fimbriatum*	Season Autumn

SESSILE EARTH STAR

The globe-shaped, yellow-brown or pale brown fruitbody of the Sessile Earth Star opens on maturity, its outer skin splitting into a star shape. Inside is a pale gray to gray-buff ball, which contains the spores. Raindrops splashing on the ball make it contract, releasing the spores through a hole on the top, which is edged with fine hairs (fimbriate).
• **OCCURRENCE** Mostly on litter on calcareous soil, under trees. Widespread in northern temperate zones; common throughout eastern North America.
• **SIMILAR SPECIES** *Geastrum triplex* (p.278) is often found on similar sites; its outer skin splits into a star, and a collar surrounds the inner ball. *G. rufescens* is pink hued and develops a stalk on the inner ball when dry.

inner ball is pale gray to gray-buff

fimbriate mouth on top of ball

5–9 rays in fully expanded outer skin

papery ball releases spores when compressed by raindrops

outer skin is yellow-brown or pale brown

FRUITING Appears in small groups or fairy rings.

Dimensions FRUITBODY ⊕ 3–6cm | INNER BALL ⊕ 1–2.5cm	Spores Chocolate-brown	Edibility

Family GEASTRACEAE	Species *Geastrum schmidelii*	Season Autumn

DWARF EARTH STAR

This earth star is identified by its habitat and size. The inner spore-ball, which is exposed when the fruitbody splits open, has a beaklike, furrowed, and striated mouth. The immature brown fruitbody is nearly spherical and is usually encrusted with sand and debris; the fleshy skin splits open to form five to eight rays, which become papery when mature. The inner ball is gray-brown.
• **OCCURRENCE** On sand in fields and dunes or in open parts of coniferous forests on sandy soil. Widespread in Europe and neighboring parts of Asia; reported in southeastern and midwestern North America.
• **SIMILAR SPECIES** *Geastrum elegans* has a stemless inner ball. *G. pectinatum*, which grows with conifers, is larger; its inner ball has a grainy skin and a more distinct stem.

beaklike, dark brown "mouth" has distinct furrows and striations

ball containing spores is mealy when young, smooth in older specimens

lobes are fleshy when young, papery when mature

when dry, ball is lifted 1–2mm high by stem

lobes arch back to reveal inner ball

lobes arch right back under fruitbody

FRUITING In rings or groups of a few fruitbodies together.

expanding fruitbody forms 5–8 lobes

Dimensions FRUITBODY ⊕ 1.5–3.5cm | INNER BALL ⊕ 0.5–1.5cm	Spores Chocolate-brown	Edibility

Family GEASTRACEAE	Species *Geastrum striatum*	Season Autumn

STRIATED EARTH STAR

Like other earth stars, the outer skin of this species splits open to reveal a spore-ball. In the Striated Earth Star, the finely grainy, grayish white ball has a short stem, inserted into a collarlike rim. The immature fruitbody is near-spherical to onion-shaped and is strongly encrusted with soil and the debris of its habitat. After opening, the fleshy, gray-brown rays soon become papery in texture.

• OCCURRENCE On fertile soil, often under conifers in gardens and parks; also in mixed forest. Widespread in Europe; world distribution unclear.

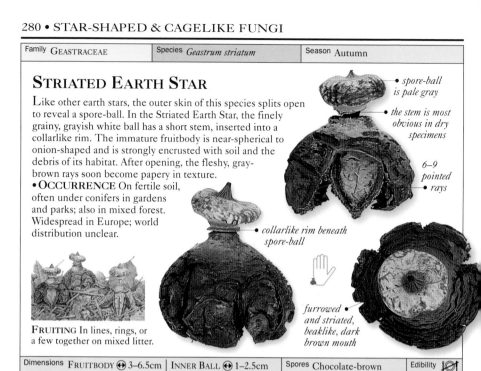

spore-ball is pale gray

the stem is most obvious in dry specimens

6–9 pointed rays

collarlike rim beneath spore-ball

furrowed and striated, beaklike, dark brown mouth

FRUITING In lines, rings, or a few together on mixed litter.

Dimensions FRUITBODY ⊕ 3–6.5cm	INNER BALL ⊕ 1–2.5cm	Spores Chocolate-brown	Edibility

Family CLATHRACEAE	Species *Clathrus ruber*	Season All year

CAGED STINKHORN

When mature, this mushroom turns a brilliant red and develops a spherical, cagelike structure. It emerges from a white or buff egg. Inside, the cage bars are smeared with an olive-brown spore mass, the foul smell of which attracts insects for spore dispersal.

• OCCURRENCE On leaf and wood litter, in parks and gardens; prefers warmth. Widespread but scattered; mostly in Mediterranean areas.

• SIMILAR SPECIES There are about 17 *Clathrus* species. They are mainly tropical. Some are bright red, others are white.

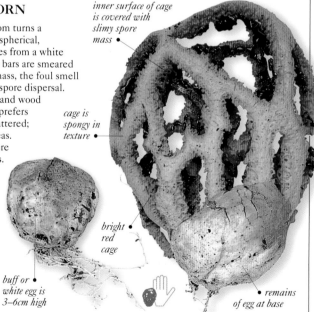

inner surface of cage is covered with slimy spore mass

cage is spongy in texture

bright red cage

buff or white egg is 3–6cm high

remains of egg at base

FRUITING Appears in small groups or troops.

Dimensions FRUITBODY ⊕ to 9cm ↕ to 12cm	Spores Olive-brown	Edibility

EAR- OR BRAINLIKE, GELATINOUS FUNGI

*M*ost of the fungi featured in this section have *gelatinous flesh. They desiccate in dry weather but rehydrate when wet and then continue to shed spores. Their shape varies from brainlike, with the spore-bearing tissue (hymenium) all over, to pendent and earlike, with the hymenium lining the inside and facing downward.*

brainlike
• fruitbody

earlike •
fruitbody

Family AURICULARIACEAE	Species *Auricularia auricula-judae*	Season All year

WOOD EAR JELLY

The fruitbody of this species is distinctively ear-shaped. It is gelatinous and smooth when fresh, but becomes hard and folded as it matures and dries out. The outer surface is tan-brown and covered in downy hairs, while the inner, spore-producing surface is more gray in color, veined, and wrinkled. Considered a bland edible in the West, this fungus and related species are valued as both a food and a medicine in China.
• **OCCURRENCE** On deciduous trees, often elder, in damp woods. Widespread in warmer parts of northern temperate zones.
• **SIMILAR SPECIES** *Auricularia polytricha* is the same color or darker, and its upper surface is very velvety. It is found mainly in the tropics.

closely attached to
• bark substrate

downy hairs on
• upper surface

spore-producing •
surface is veined
and wrinkled and
faces downward

tan to brown fruitbody •
is distinctly ear-shaped

• folds develop
as fruitbody ages
and dries out

• flesh dries
hard and horny

FRUITING Singly or in crowded tiers and rows.

Dimensions FRUITBODY ↔ 4–12cm ⬙ to 2mm	Spores White	Edibility

| Family TREMELLACEAE | Species *Tremella mesenterica* | Season Mostly late autumn–winter |

YELLOW BRAIN JELLY

The striking, almost transparent yellow coloring of the Yellow Brain Jelly makes it very easy to see. Prolonged rainfall can turn it white, but occasionally it may also produce true albino forms. In dry weather the fruitbody shrivels up, but it will rehydrate when moist conditions return. Although the flavor is very bland, this species can be eaten or used in soups.

• OCCURRENCE Parasitic on Corticiaceae species; growing on deciduous branches, often in piles of brushwood. Widespread and common in northern temperate zones.

fruitbody consists of soft, flabby lobes •

• spores are produced all over surface

• prolonged wet weather causes color loss

dried • flesh is brittle

• fruitbody dries to dark orange

FRUITING Mainly in small groups of lobed fruitbodies.

| Dimensions JOINED FRUITBODIES ↔ 1–6cm ⊕ 0.5–4cm | Spores White | Edibility |

| Family TREMELLACEAE | Species *Tremella foliacea* | Season Autumn–winter |

BROWN LEAFY JELLY

A strongly folded, gelatinous brown fruitbody, attached directly to bark with no stem, make this species easy to identify. The spores, produced on microscopic club-shaped basidia (p.11), cover the surface of the fruitbody.

• OCCURRENCE Parasitic on species of *Stereum* and Corticiaceae on deciduous trees, but also on pine, in parks and woods. Widespread in northern temperate zones.

• SIMILAR SPECIES *Ascotremella faginea* (p.283) and a folded form of *Neobulgaria pura* (p.271); they are distinguished by more rounded, brainlike lobes and spores in the asci (p.11).

flesh is brown and very gelatinous •

fruitbody • is strongly folded

fresh specimens • are glossy brown

dried-up • fruitbody is shrunken and black

• water can reconstitute dried-up specimens

FRUITING Appears singly or a few together.

| Dimensions FRUITBODY ↔ 4–12cm ↕ 3–7cm | Spores White | Edibility |

Family TREMELLACEAE	Species *Exidia glandulosa*	Season Late autumn–winter

BLACK BRAIN JELLY

Looking like blobs of tar, this jelly-fungus is comparatively firm and less gelatinous to touch than *Tremella mesenterica* (p.282). The brainlike surface consists of numerous folds that become deeper and more wrinkled with age. As with most other jelly-fungi, wet weather causes shriveled, dried-up specimens to rehydrate.

• OCCURRENCE On bare to bark-clad wood of deciduous trees. Widespread and common in northern temperate zones.

• SIMILAR SPECIES *E. truncata* is also common and is found mainly on oak trees. Its fruitbody is more button-shaped with a fine velvety outer surface and a pimpled fertile surface. *E. recisa* is yellow-brown.

black surface with numerous brainlike folds

mature specimen has even more marked folds and wrinkles

spores produced all over exposed surface

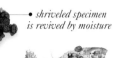

shriveled specimen is revived by moisture

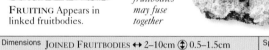

spreading fruitbodies may fuse together

FRUITING Appears in linked fruitbodies.

Dimensions JOINED FRUITBODIES ↔ 2–10cm ⊕ 0.5–1.5cm	Spores White	Edibility 🚫

Family LEOTIACEAE	Species *Ascotremella faginea*	Season Summer–autumn

RAISIN JELLY CUP

spores produced all over surface of fruitbody

dingy purple fruitbodies

This dingy purple fungus is most often seen in large, shiny, jellylike groups, up to 10cm across. The fruitbody consists of a mass of gelatinous, irregularly shaped blobs, the whole effect being almost brainlike. It is attached to the substrate by a short, stemlike point. It looks like a jelly-fungus, but microscopic characteristics, such as spores produced in cylindrical asci (pp.10–11), identify it as a cup-fungus.

• OCCURRENCE Typically on dead beech, but also on other deciduous trees. Widespread and locally common in northeastern North America and most of Europe.

fruitbody has jellylike texture

brainlike, irregular fruitbody

FRUITING Mostly singly or a few together on branches and trunks of dead deciduous trees.

Dimensions FRUITBODY ↕ 1–2cm ↔ 2–4cm	Spores White	Edibility 🚫

SPORE CHART

SPORES occur in many colors, shapes, surface textures, and sizes, and offer important clues to precise identification of a species. Spore color is included with each species main entry; size and shape are given in the table below. Spores vary from 2 to 500 microns (µm); average sizes are given here. A microscope is necessary to determine size and shape (see p.17). In the table below, ⊕ means diameter.

SPECIES	SIZE (µm)	SHAPE
Agaricus arvensis	7 × 5	broadly ellipsoid
Agaricus augustus	8.5 × 5	ellipsoid
Agaricus bernardii	6.5 × 5.5	broadly ellipsoid
Agaricus bisporus	6 × 5	broadly ellipsoid
Agaricus bitorquis	6 × 4.5	broadly ellipsoid
Agaricus californicus	5.5 × 4.5	ellipsoid
Agaricus campestris	8 × 4.5	ellipsoid
Agaricus hondensis	5 × 3.5	ellipsoid
Agaricus porphyrizon	5 × 3.5	ellipsoid
Agaricus praeclaresquamosus	5.5 × 3.5	broadly ellipsoid
Agaricus sylvaticus	5.5 × 3.5	broadly ellipsoid
Agaricus sylvicola	7 × 4.5	ellipsoid
Agaricus xanthoderma	6 × 4	ellipsoid
Agrocybe cylindracea	10 × 5.5	ellipsoid with a pore
Agrocybe pediades	12 × 8	ellipsoid with a pore
Agrocybe praecox	9 × 5.5	ellipsoid with a pore
Albatrellus ovinus	4 × 3.5	near spherical, amyloid
Aleuria aurantia	17.5 × 9	ellipsoid, reticulate, 2 drops inside
Aleurodiscus amorphus	28 × 23	near spherical, spiny
Amanita caesarea	10 × 7	broadly ellipsoid
Amanita citrina	9 × 8	near spherical, amyloid
Amanita crocea	10 ⊕	near spherical
Amanita fulva	11 ⊕	near spherical
Amanita gemmata	10 × 7.5	broadly ellipsoid
Amanita muscaria and *A. m.* var. *formosa*	9 × 6.5	ellipsoid
Amanita pantherina	11 × 7.5	broadly ellipsoid
Amanita phalloides	8.5 × 7	near spherical to broadly ellipsoid, amyloid
Amanita porphyria	9 ⊕	near spherical, amyloid
Amanita rubescens	8.5 × 6.5	broadly ellipsoid, amyloid
Amanita smithiana	12 × 7.5	ellipsoid, amyloid
Amanita spissa	9.5 × 7.5	near spherical, amyloid
Amanita vaginata	11 ⊕	near spherical
Amanita virosa	7.5 ⊕	near spherical, amyloid
Armillaria cepistipes	8.5 × 5.5	broadly ellipsoid
Armillaria mellea	8.5 × 5.5	broadly ellipsoid
Armillaria tabescens	8 × 6	broadly ellipsoid
Ascocoryne cylichnium	24 × 5	narrow ellipsoid, 5–7 septate
Ascocoryne sarcoides	14 × 4	narrow ellipsoid
Ascotremella faginea	8 × 4	ellipsoide, faintly striate
Asterophora parasitica	5.5 × 3.5	broadly ellipsoid
Astraeus hygrometricus	9 ⊕	spherical, spiny
Auricularia auricula-judae	14 × 5.5	sausage-shaped
Auricularia mesenterica	16.5 × 6	broadly sausage-shaped
Auriscalpium vulgare	5 × 4	oval, minutely spiny
Baeospora myosura	3.5 × 1.5	ellipsoid
Bankera fuligineoalba	5 × 3	oval, spiny
Bispora citrina	12 × 4	ellipsoid, 0–1 septate
Bjerkandera adusta	5 × 3	ellipsoid

SPECIES	SIZE (µm)	SHAPE
Boletus aereus	15.5 × 5.5	spindle-shaped
Boletus appendiculatus	14.5 × 4.5	spindle-shaped
Boletus badius	14 × 5	spindle-shaped
Boletus barrowsii	14 × 4.5	spindle-shaped
Boletus bicolor	10 × 4.5	near spindle-shaped
Boletus calopus	14 × 5.5	spindle-shaped
Boletus edulis	15.5 × 5.5	spindle-shaped
Boletus legaliae	13 × 6	spindle-shaped
Boletus luridiformis	15 × 5	spindle-shaped
Boletus luridus	13 × 6	near spindle-shaped
Boletus pascuus	13 × 5	spindle-shaped
Boletus parasiticus	15 × 5	spindle-shaped
Boletus pinophilus	17 × 5	spindle-shaped
Boletus porosporus	13 × 5	spindle-shaped, some have a pore and appear truncate
Boletus pulcherrimus	14.5 × 6	spindle-shaped
Boletus pulverulentus	13 × 5	spindle-shaped
Boletus reticulatus	15 × 5	spindle-shaped
Boletus rubellus	12.5 × 5	spindle-shaped
Boletus satanas	13 × 6	near spindle-shaped
Boletus subtomentosus	12.5 × 5	spindle-shaped
Bovista plumbea	5.5 × 5	near spherical with a long pedicel, warty
Bulgaria inquinans	12.5 × 6.5	kidney-shaped; in asci top 4 spores are brown, lower 4 (slightly smaller) are hyaline
Calocera viscosa	11.5 × 4	curved with rounded ends
Calocybe carnea	5.5 × 3	egg-shaped
Calocybe gambosa	5.5 × 3.5	egg-shaped
Calocybe ionides	6 × 3	egg-shaped
Calostoma cinnabarina	17 × 8	ellipsoid, pitted
Calvatia excipuliformis	5 ⊕	spherical, warty
Calvatia gigantea	4.5 ⊕	spherical, warty
Calvatia utriformis	4.5 ⊕	spherical, nearly smooth
Cantharellus cibarius	8.5 × 5	ellipsoid
Cantharellus cinnabarinus	9 × 5	ellipsoid
Cantharellus lateritius	10 × 5.5	ellipsoid
Cantharellus lutescens	10.5 × 7	broadly ellipsoid
Cantharellus subalbidus	8 × 5	ellipsoid
Cantharellus tubaeformis	10 × 8	ellipsoid
Chalciporus piperatus	9.5 × 4.5	oblong
Chlorociboria aeruginascens	7.5 × 2	spindle-shaped
Chlorophyllum molybdites	11 × 7.5	egg-shaped to ellipsoid with a pore
Chondrostereum purpureum	7.5 × 3	ellipsoid
Chroogomphus rutilus	19 × 6.5	spindle-shaped
Clathrus archeri	6.5 × 3	narrowly cylindrical
Clathrus ruber	5 × 2.5	ellipsoid to cylindrical
Clavaria vermicularis	7 × 4.5	oval
Clavariadelphus pistillaris	13.5 × 8	broadly ellipsoid
Clavulina cristata	9 × 7.5	broadly ellipsoid

SPECIES	SIZE (µm)	SHAPE
Clavulinopsis corniculata	6 ⊕	spherical
Clavulinopsis helvola	6.5 × 5	spherical to broadly ellipsoid, long warts, irregular outline
Clitocybe clavipes	8 × 4.5	ellipsoid
Clitocybe dealbata	5 × 3	tear-shaped
Clitocybe geotropa	8 × 6	tear-shaped
Clitocybe gibba	7 × 4.5	tear-shaped
Clitocybe metachroa	7 × 4.5	ellipsoid
Clitocybe nebularis	7.5 × 4	ellipsoid
Clitocybe odora	7 × 4.5	ellipsoid
Clitopilus prunulus	10.5 × 5	egg-shaped to ellipsoid, ribbed lengthwise
Collybia butyracea	7 × 3.5	oblong-ellipsoid
Collybia confluens	8 × 3.5	egg-shaped
Collybia dryophila	5.5 × 2.5	egg-shaped to ellipsoid
Collybia erythropus	7 × 3.5	ellipsoid
Collybia fusipes	5 × 3.5	broadly egg-shaped
Collybia maculata	5 × 4.5	near spherical
Collybia peronata	7.5 × 3.5	ellipsoid
Coltricia perennis	7 × 4.5	ellipsoid
Coniophora puteana	13 × 7	ellipsoid
Conocybe arrhenii	8 × 4.5	ellipsoid with a pore
Conocybe lactea	12.5 × 8	ellipsoid with a pore
Coprinus atramentarius	9 × 6	ellipsoid with a pore
Coprinus comatus	12 × 8	ellipsoid with a pore
Coprinus disseminatus	8.5 × 4.5	ellipsoid with a pore
Coprinus micaceus	8.5 × 6 × 4.5	flattened ellipsoid with a truncated pore
Coprinus niveus	15 × 10.5 × 8	flattened ellipsoid, slightly hexagonal, with a pore
Coprinus picaceus	16 × 11.5 × 9.5	flattened ellipsoid with a pore
Coprinus plicatilis	12 × 9 × 5	flat, heart-shaped with a pore
Cordyceps militaris	4.5 × 1.5	very long, cylindrical, breaking into part spores
Cordyceps ophioglossoides	4 × 2	very long, cylindrical, breaking into part spores
Cortinarius alboviolaceus	8.5 × 5.5	ellipsoid, rugose
Cortinarius anserinus	10 × 6.5	lemon-shaped, rugose
Cortinarius armillatus	10.5 × 6.5	almond-shaped, rugose
Cortinarius bolaris	6.5 × 4	near spherical, rugose
Cortinarius caerulescens	10 × 5.5	ellipsoid, rugose
Cortinarius calochrous	10 × 6	ellipsoid, rugose
Cortinarius cinnamomeus	7.5 × 4.5	almond-shaped, rugose
Cortinarius elegantissimus	14 × 8.5	lemon-shaped, rugose
Cortinarius mucosus	12.5 × 6.5	narrow lemon-shaped, rugose
Cortinarius orellanus	10.5 × 6	ellipsoid, rugose
Cortinarius paleaceus	8.5 × 5.5	ellipsoid, rugose
Cortinarius pholideus	7.5 × 5.5	near spherical, rugose
Cortinarius rubellus	10 × 7.5	near spherical to broadly ellipsoid, rugose
Cortinarius rufoolivaceus	13 × 7.5	almond- to lemon-shaped, rugose
Cortinarius semisanguineus	7 × 4.5	ellipsoid to lemon-shaped, rugose
Cortinarius sodagnitus	11 × 6	ellipsoid to almond-shaped, rugose
Cortinarius splendens	9.5 × 5.5	almond-shaped, rugose
Cortinarius torvus	9.5 × 6	broadly ellipsoid to egg-shaped, rugose
Cortinarius triumphans	12 × 6.5	almond-shaped, rugose

SPECIES	SIZE (µm)	SHAPE
Cortinarius violaceus	12.5 × 8	near spherical to almond-shaped, rugose
Craterellus cornucopioides	13 × 8	broadly ellipsoid
Creolophus cirrhatus	4 × 3	near spherical, amyloid, hyphae not amyloid
Crepidotus mollis	9 × 6	egg-shaped
Crepidotus variabilis	6.5 × 3	oblong-ellipsoid, warty
Crinipellis stipitaria	7.5 × 5	broadly ellipsoid
Crucibulum crucibuliforme	8 × 4.5	oblong-ellipsoid
Cyathus striatus	17 × 10	oblong-ellipsoid
Cystoderma amianthinum	6 × 3	egg-shaped, amyloid
Cystoderma carcharias	5 × 4	near spherical, amyloid
Cystoderma terrei	4.5 × 2.5	ellipsoid
Daedalea quercina	6.5 × 3	ellipsoid
Daedaleopsis confragosa	7.5 × 2.5	cylindrical, curved
Daldinia concentrica	14.5 × 7	ellipsoid to spindle-shaped, flattened on one side
Disciotis venosa	22 × 13.5	broadly ellipsoid
Dumontinia tuberosa	15 × 7.5	ellipsoid
Elaphomyces granulatus	30 ⊕	spherical, spiny
Entoloma aborticum	9 × 5	ellipsoid, angular
Entoloma cetratum	12 × 8	prism-shaped, nodular
Entoloma clypeatum	10 × 9.5	prism-shaped
Entoloma conferendum	10 × 9	cruciform, angular
Entoloma incanum	12.5 × 8.5	angular
Entoloma nitidum	8 × 7	angular
Entoloma porphyrophaeum	11 × 7.5	angular
Entoloma rhodopolium	8.5 × 7.5	prism-shaped
Entoloma sericeum	9 × 8	angular
Entoloma serrulatum	10.5 × 7.5	angular
Entoloma sinuatum	10 × 9	angular
Exidia glandulosa	13 × 4	sausage-shaped
Fistulina hepatica	5.5 × 4	near spherical
Flammulina velutipes	8.5 × 4	ellipsoid to cylindrical
Fomes fomentarius	17 × 6	cylindrical
Fomitopsis pinicola	7.5 × 4	slender ellipsoid
Galerina calyptrata	11 × 6	broadly spindle-shaped, warty, loosening outer wall
Galerina mutabilis	7.5 × 5	ellipsoid with a pore
Galerina unicolor	12 × 6	almond-shaped, rugose, loosening outer wall
Ganoderma applanatum	7.5 × 5	ellipsoid, truncated, warty
Ganoderma lucidum	10 × 7	ellipsoid, truncated, warty
Ganoderma pfeifferi	10 × 7.5	ellipsoid, truncated, warty
Geastrum fimbriatum	3.5 ⊕	spherical, warty
Geastrum schmidelii	5.2 ⊕	spherical, warty
Geastrum striatum	4.5 ⊕	spherical, warty
Geastrum triplex	4 ⊕	spherical, blunt spiny
Geoglossum fallax	75 × 6	near cylindrical, 0–7 septate
Geopora arenicola	25 × 15	ellipsoid, 1–2 drops inside
Gloeophyllum odoratum	8.5 × 4	cylindrical
Gomphidius glutinosus	19 × 5.5	near spindle-shaped
Gomphidius roseus	19 × 5.5	near spindle-shaped
Gomphus floccosus	13 × 7.5	ellipsoid, rugose
Grifola frondosa	5.5 × 4	broadly ellipsoid to near spherical
Gymnopilus penetrans	7.5 × 4.5	ellipsoid, rugose
Gymnopilus spectabilis	9 × 5.5	ellipsoid, rugose
Gyromitra esculenta	20 × 10	ellipsoid
Gyromitra infula	22 × 8.5	narrowly ellipsoid
Gyroporus castaneus	9.5 × 5.5	ellipsoid
Gyroporus cyanescens	10 × 5	ellipsoid

Species	Size (μm)	Shape
Hapalopilus rutilans	5 × 2.5	ellipsoid
Hebeloma crustuliniforme	11 × 6	almond-shaped, rugose
Hebeloma mesophaeum	9 × 5.5	ellipsoid, finely rugose
Hebeloma radicosum	9 × 5.5	almond-shaped, rugose
Helvella crispa	20 × 12	ellipsoid
Helvella lacunosa	19 × 12	ellipsoid
Hericium coralloides	4 × 3	oval, amyloid
Heterobasidion annosum	4.5 × 3.5	broadly ellipsoid to near spherical, warty
Hydnellum peckii	5.5 × 4	oval, warty
Hydnum repandum	7 × 6	oval
Hydnum umbilicatum	8.5 × 7	near spherical
Hygrocybe calyptraeformis	7.5 × 5	broadly ellipsoid
Hygrocybe chlorophana	8.5 × 5	ovoid to ellipsoid
Hygrocybe coccinea	9 × 5	ellipsoid to almond-shaped
Hygrocybe conica (4-spored)	9.5 × 6	ellipsoid or almond- to bean-
(2-spored)	10.5 × 7	shaped
Hygrocybe miniata	7.5 × 5.5	often pear-shaped
Hygrocybe pratensis	6 × 4.5	near spherical to ellipsoid or tear-shaped
Hygrocybe psittacina	8.5 × 5.5	oblong-ellipsoid
Hygrocybe punicea	9.5 × 5	oblong-ellipsoid
Hygrocybe virginea	8 × 5	narrowly ellipsoid
Hygrophoropsis aurantiaca	6.5 × 4	oblong-ellipsoid
Hygrophorus eburneus	8.5 × 4.5	ellipsoid
Hygrophorus hypothejus	8 × 4.5	ellipsoid
Hymenochaete rubiginosa	5.5 × 3	oblong-ellipsoid
Hypholoma capnoides	8 × 4.5	ellipsoid with a pore
Hypholoma fasciculare	7 × 4.5	ellipsoid with a pore
Hypholoma sublateritium	7 × 4	ellipsoid with a pore
Hypomyces hyalinus	19 × 5.5	spindle-shaped, 2-celled, warty
Hypomyces lactifluorum	40 × 4.5	spindle-shaped, 2-celled, warty
Hypoxylon fragiforme	13 × 6	ellipsoid to spindle-shaped, flattened
Inocybe asterospora	10.5 × 8.5	star-shaped, nodular
Inocybe erubescens	12 × 6	ellipsoid to bean-shaped
Inocybe geophylla	9.5 × 5.5	ellipsoid
Inocybe godeyi	10.5 × 6.5	almond-shaped
Inocybe griseolilacina	9 × 5.5	almond-shaped
Inocybe haemacta	9 × 5.5	ellipsoid to almond-shaped
Inocybe lacera	14 × 5.5	cylindrical
Inocybe rimosa	12 × 6	ellipsoid to bean-shaped
Inonotus hispidus	8.5 × 7	broadly ellipsoid
Inonotus radiatus	6 × 4.5	broadly ellipsoid
Laccaria amethystina	9.5 ⊕	spherical or near spherical, spiny
Laccaria laccata	9 × 8	spherical or near spherical, spiny
Lactarius blennius	7.5 × 6	near spherical, warty, veined, amyloid
Lactarius camphoratus	8 × 7	near spherical, spiny-rugose, veined, amyloid
Lactarius controversus	7 × 5	near spherical, rugose, veined, amyloid
Lactarius deliciosus	8.5 × 7	near spherical, warty, veined, amyloid
Lactarius deterrimus	9 × 7	near spherical, warty, veined, amyloid
Lactarius fuliginosus	9 ⊕	spherical, reticulate, crested, amyloid

Species	Size (μm)	Shape
Lactarius glyciosmus	8.5 × 7.5	near spherical, rugose, veined, amyloid
Lactarius helvus	8 × 6	near spherical, reticulate, veined, amyloid
Lactarius hepaticus	8 × 6.5	near spherical, reticulate, veined, amyloid
Lactarius hygrophoroides	8.5 × 7	near spherical, warty, veined, amyloid
Lactarius mitissimus	9 × 7	near spherical, rugose, amyloid
Lactarius necator	7 × 6	near spherical, veined, amyloid
Lactarius pallidus	8 × 6.5	near spherical, rugose, veined, amyloid
Lactarius piperatus	8.5 × 6.5	near spherical, warty, with connecting lines, amyloid
Lactarius pyrogalus	7 × 5.5	near spherical, reticulate, veined, amyloid
Lactarius quietus	8.5 × 7.5	near spherical, rugose, veined, amyloid
Lactarius rufus	9 × 6.5	broadly ellipsoid, reticulate, veined, amyloid
Lactarius sanguifluus	8.5 × 7	near spherical, warty, veined
Lactarius subdulcis	7.5 × 6	near spherical, reticulate, veined, amyloid
Lactarius theijogalus	8.5 × 6.5	near spherical, rugose, veined, amyloid
Lactarius torminosus	8.5 × 7	near spherical, rugose, veined, amyloid
Lactarius trivialis	9.5 × 8	near spherical, rugose, veined, amyloid
Lactarius vellereus	10.5 × 8.5	near spherical, warty, with connecting veins, amyloid
Lactarius volemus	8.5 ⊕	spherical, reticulate, veined, amyloid
Laetiporus sulphureus	6 × 4	broadly ellipsoid
Leccinum crocipodium	15 × 6	near spindle-shaped
Leccinum quercinum	13.5 × 4.5	near spindle-shaped
Leccinum scabrum	17 × 5.5	near spindle-shaped
Leccinum variicolor	14.5 × 5	near spindle-shaped
Leccinum versipelle	14.5 × 4.5	near spindle-shaped
Lentinellus cochleatus	4.5 × 4	near spherical, spiny
Lentinellus ursinus	4 × 2.5	egg-shaped, spiny, amyloid
Lentinus tigrinus	7.5 × 3.5	cylindrical
Lenzites betulina	5.5 × 2.5	more or less ellipsoid
Leotia lubrica	23 × 6	near cylindrical, somewhat curved, 4–5 septate
Lepiota aspera	8 × 3	ellipsoid
Lepiota brunneoincarnata	8 × 4.5	ellipsoid
Lepiota castanea	11 × 4	projectile-shaped
Lepiota clypeolaria	14 × 6	spindle-shaped
Lepiota cristata	7 × 3.5	projectile-shaped
Lepiota ignivolvata	12 × 6	broadly spindle-shaped
Lepiota oreadiformis	12.5 × 5	spindle-shaped
Lepista flaccida	3-4.5 ⊕	near spherical, fine spiny
Lepista irina	8 × 4.5	ellipsoid, rugose
Lepista nuda	7.5 × 4.5	ellipsoid, rugose
Lepista personata	7.5 × 5	ellipsoid, rugose
Leucoagaricus leucothites	8.5 × 5.5	broadly egg- to almond-shaped
Leucocoprinus badhamii	6.5 × 4.5	ellipsoid to spindle-shaped
Leucocoprinus luteus	8.5 × 6	almond-shaped with a pore

Species	Size (μm)	Shape	Species	Size (μm)	Shape
Leucopaxillus giganteus	7 × 4	tear-shaped	*Paxillus corrugatus*	3 × 1.75	ellipsoid
Limacella guttata	5.5 × 4.5	near spherical	*Paxillus involutus*	9 × 5.5	ellipsoid
Lycoperdon echinatum	4.5 ⊕	spherical, warty	*Peziza badia*	18.5 × 8.5	ellipsoid, 2 drops inside
Lycoperdon perlatum	3.5 ⊕	spherical, warty	*Peziza succosa*	20.5 × 11	ellipsoid, 2 drops inside, warty
Lycoperdon pyriforme	4 ⊕	spherical, nearly smooth			
Lyophyllum connatum	6 × 3.5	ellipsoid	*Peziza vesiculosa*	22 × 12	ellipsoid without drops
Lyophyllum decastes	5.5 ⊕	spherical	*Phaeolepiota aurea*	12 × 5	narrowly ellipsoid
Lyophyllum palustre	7 × 4	ellipsoid	*Phaeolus schweinitzii*	7 × 4	ellipsoid
Macrocystidia cucumis	9 × 4.5	ellipsoid	*Phallus duplicatus*	4 × 2	ellipsoid
Macrolepiota procera	15 × 10	ellipsoid with a pore	*Phallus impudicus*	5 × 2.5	ellipsoid
Macrolepiota rhacodes	10 × 6.5	ellipsoid with a pore	*Phellinus igniarius*	6 × 5	near spherical
Macrotyphula fistulosa	13 × 6.5	ellipsoid	*Phellodon niger*	4 × 3	oval, spiny
Marasmiellus ramealis	9 × 3	spindle-shaped to ellipsoid	*Phellodon tomentosus*	4 × 3	oval or spherical, spiny
Marasmius alliaceus	9.5 × 7	broadly ellipsoid	*Phlebia tremellosa*	4 × 1	sausage-shaped
Marasmius androsaceus	8 × 4.5	ellipsoid to tear-shaped	*Pholiota alnicola*	9.5 × 5	ellipsoid with a pore
Marasmius oreades	9 × 5.5	broadly ellipsoid	*Pholiota aurivellus*	9 × 5.5	ellipsoid with a pore
Marasmius rotula	8 × 4	ellipsoid or tear-shaped	*Pholiota gummosa*	7.5 × 4	ellipsoid with a pore
Megacollybia platyphylla	7.5 × 6.5	near spherical	*Pholiota highlandensis*	7 × 4.5	ellipsoid with a pore
Melanoleuca cognata	9.5 × 6	ellipsoid, fine spiny, amyloid	*Pholiota lenta*	6.5 × 3.5	ellipsoid with a pore
Melanoleuca polioleuca	8 × 5.5	ellipsoid, fine spiny, amyloid	*Pholiota squarrosa*	7 × 4	ellipsoid with a pore
Meripilus giganteus	6 × 5	broadly ellipsoid to near spherical	*Phylloporus rhodoxanthus*	12.5 × 4.5	ellipsoid to spindle-shaped
			Piptoporus betulinus	6 × 2	sausage-shaped
Micromphale foetidum	9 × 4	ellipsoid	*Pleurocybella porrigens*	7 × 5	near spherical to broadly ellipsoid
Mitrula paludosa	12.5 × 3	club-shaped to cylindrical			
Morchella elata	25 × 14	ellipsoid	*Pleurotus cornucopiae*	10 × 4.5	elongated ellipsoid
Morchella esculenta	20 × 12.5	ellipsoid	*Pleurotus eryngii*	11 × 5	elongated ellipsoid
Morchella semilibera	26 × 16	ellipsoid	*Pleurotus ostreatus*	9.5 × 3.5	elongated ellipsoid
Mutinus caninus	5.5 × 2.5	ellipsoid	*Pluteus aurantiorugosus*	6 × 4	broadly ellipsoid
Mycena acicula	11 × 3.5	near spindle-shaped to near cylindrical	*Pluteus cervinus*	7.5 × 5.5	broadly ellipsoid
			Pluteus chrysophaeus	7 × 6	near spherical
Mycena adonis	8.5 × 5	ellipsoid to oblong	*Pluteus umbrosus*	6.5 × 5	broadly ellipsoid
Mycena arcangeliana	9 × 5.5	ellipsoid	*Polyporus badius*	7.5 × 3.5	cylindrical
Mycena crocata	8.5 × 5	broadly ellipsoid	*Polyporus brumalis*	5.5 × 2.5	cylindrical
Mycena epipterygia	10 × 5	ellispoid	*Polyporus squamosus*	13 × 5	cylindrical
Mycena filopes	10 × 6	ellipsoid	*Polyporus tuberaster*	13 × 5	cylindrical
Mycena flavoalba	7.5 × 3.5	ellipsoid to near cylindrical	*Polyporus umbellatus*	9 × 3	cylindrical
Mycena galericulata	10 × 7.5	egg-shaped to oblong	*Polyporus varius*	8.5 × 3	cylindrical
Mycena galopus	12 × 6	ellipsoid to near cylindrical	*Porphyrellus porphyrosporus*	14 × 6	near spindle-shaped
Mycena haematopus	8.5 × 6	ellipsoid	*Postia caesia*	5 × 1.5	sausage-shaped, amyloid
Mycena inclinata	10 × 6.5	egg-shaped to ellipsoid	*Postia stiptica*	4.5 × 2	ellipsoid to cylindrical
Mycena leptocephala	10 × 5	ellipsoid to near cylindrical	*Psathyrella candolleana*	8 × 4.5	ellipsoid with a pore
Mycena olivaceomarginata	10 × 5.5	ellipsoid	*Psathyrella conopilus*	15.5 × 7.5	ellipsoid with a pore
Mycena pelianthina	6.5 × 3.5	ellipsoid	*Psathyrella multipedata*	7.5 × 4	ellipsoid with a pore
Mycena polygramma	9.5 × 6.5	ellipsoid	*Psathyrella piluliformis*	6 × 3.5	ellipsoid with a pore
Mycena pura	7 × 3.5	ellipsoid	*Psathyrella velutina*	9.5 × 6	lemon-shaped with a big pore, warty
Neobulgaria pura	9 × 4	ellipsoid, striped lengthways			
Oligoporus rennyi	4 × 2.5	oblong	*Pseudoclitocybe cyathiformis*	9 × 5.5	ellipsoid, amyloid
Omphalina umbellifera	8.5 × 6	near spherical to egg-shaped	*Pseudohydnum gelatinosum*	6.5 × 5.5	near spherical to broadly ellipsoid
Omphalotus olearius	5.5 × 5	near spherical	*Psilocybe cubensis*	14 × 9	ellipsoid with a pore
Otidea onotica	13 × 7	ellipsoid, 2 drops inside	*Psilocybe cyanescens*	11.5 × 7 × 6	ellipsoid to almond-shaped with a pore
Oudemansiella mucida	16 × 14	near spherical to spherical, thick-walled			
			Psilocybe semilanceata	13 × 8	ovoid to ellipsoid with a pore
Oudemansiella radicata	13.5 × 10	broadly ellipsoid	*Psilocybe squamosa*	14 × 8	ellipsoid with a pore
Paecilomyces farinosus	2.5 × 1.5	ellipsoid	*Pycnoporus cinnabarinus*	5 × 2.5	ellipsoid
Panaeolina foenisecii	13.5 × 8	lemon-shaped with a pore, warty	*Ramaria abietina*	8 × 4	ellipsoid, short spiny
			Ramaria botrytis	15 × 5.5	narrowly ellipsoid, striped
Panaeolus papilionaceus	16 × 9	lemon-shaped with a pore	*Ramaria sanguinea*	10 × 4.5	narrowly ellipsoid, warty
Panaeolus semiovatus	18 × 10	broadly ellipsoid with a pore	*Ramaria stricta*	9 × 4.5	ellipsoid, warty
Panellus serotinus	5 × 1.5	sausage-shaped	*Rickenella fibula*	4.5 × 2.5	narrowly ellipsoid
Panellus stypticus	4.5 × 2	egg-shaped	*Rickenella setipes*	5 × 3	ellipsoid
Paxillus atrotomentosus	5 × 4	broadly ellipsoid	*Rozites caperata*	12.5 × 8	almond-shaped, rugose

Species	Size (µm)	Shape
Russula aeruginea	8 × 6	near spherical, warty, veined, amyloid
Russula atropurpurea	8 × 6.5	near spherical, warty, partially reticulate, amyloid
Russula claroflava	8.5 × 7	near spherical, warty, veined, amyloid
Russula cyanoxantha	8.5 × 7	near spherical, warty, veined, amyloid
Russula delica	9.5 × 7.5	near spherical, rugose, amyloid
Russula emetica	9.5 × 8	near spherical, warty, veined, amyloid
Russula fellea	8.5 × 6.5	near spherical, veined, amyloid
Russula foetens	8.5 × 8	near spherical, warty, amyloid
Russula fragilis	8.5 × 7	near spherical, reticulate, warty, amyloid
Russula integra	10.5 × 8.5	near spherical, spiny, amyloid
Russula mairei	7.5 × 6	near spherical, reticulate, warty, amyloid
Russula nigricans	7 × 6.5	near spherical, reticulate, amyloid
Russula ochroleuca	9 × 7.5	near spherical, partly reticulate, warty, amyloid
Russula paludosa	9.5 × 8	near spherical, warty, some connecting veins, amyloid
Russula puellaris	8 × 6	near spherical, warty-spiny, amyloid
Russula rosea	8.5 × 7.5	near spherical, reticulate, warty, amyloid
Russula sanguinaria	8.5 × 7.5	near spherical, spiny, some connecting veins, amyloid
Russula sardonia	8 × 6.5	near spherical, warty-crested, veined, amyloid
Russula turci	8 × 7	near spherical, warty-crested, veined, amyloid
Russula vesca	7 × 5.5	near spherical, warty, amyloid
Russula vinosa	10 × 8	near spherical, spiny, amyloid
Russula virescens	8 × 6.5	near spherical, reticulate, warty, amyloid
Russula xerampelina	9 × 8	near spherical, warty, amyloid
Rutstroemia firma	17 × 5.5	narrow ellipsoid, 3–5 septate
Sarcodon imbricatum	7.5 × 5	near spherical, warty
Sarcodon scabrosus	7.5 × 6	spherical with coarse warts
Sarcoscypha austriaca	28 × 13	narrowly ellipsoid
Schizophyllum commune	5 × 2	cylindrical or curved
Schizopora paradoxa	5.5 × 3.5	oval
Scleroderma citrinum	11.5 ⊕	spherical, spiny, partially reticulate
Scleroderma verrucosum	10 ⊕	spherical, spiny
Scutellinia scutellata	19 × 12	ellipsoid, warty
Sepedonium chrysospermum	20 ⊕	spherical, warty
Serpula lacrymans	12 × 7	ellipsoid
Sparassis crispa	7 × 4.5	ellipsoid
Spinellus fusiger	40 × 20	lemon-shaped, variable
Stereopsis humphreyi	7.5 × 4.5	ellipsoid to egg-shaped
Stereum hirsutum	6 × 2.5	ellipsoid to cylindrical, amyloid
Stereum rugosum	7.5 × 4	ellipsoid to cylindrical, amyloid
Stereum subtomentosum	6 × 2.5	ellipsoid to cylindrical, amyloid

Species	Size (µm)	Shape
Strobilomyces strobilaceus	11 × 10	near spherical, reticulate
Strobilurus esculentus	5 × 2	ellipsoid
Stropharia aurantiaca	14 × 7	ellipsoid with a pore
Stropharia coronilla	8.5 × 4.5	ellipsoid with a pore
Stropharia cyanea	8.5 × 4.5	ellipsoid with a pore
Stropharia rugoso-annulata	11.5 × 8	ellipsoid with a pore
Stropharia semiglobata	18 × 9	ellipsoid with a pore
Suillus aeruginascens	11.5 × 5	near spindle-shaped
Suillus bovinus	9 × 3.5	near spindle-shaped
Suillus granulatus	9 × 3	near spindle-shaped
Suillus grevillei	9.5 × 3.5	near spindle-shaped
Suillus luteus	8.5 × 3.5	oblong to spindle-shaped
Suillus plorans	9 × 4.5	ellipsoid
Suillus spraguei	10 × 4	ellipsoid
Suillus variegatus	9 × 3.5	near spindle-shaped
Syzygites megalocarpus	25	globose
Tarzetta cupularis	20 × 13	narrowly ellipsoid, 2 drops inside
Thelephora terrestris	9 × 7	oval to ellipsoid, warty-spiny
Trametes gibbosa	5 × 2.5	cylindrical to curved
Trametes hirsuta	6 × 2	cylindrical
Trametes versicolor	6.5 × 2	cylindrical
Tremella foliacea	9.5 × 8	oval
Tremella mesenterica	12.5 × 8.5	oval
Trichaptum abietinum	7.5 × 2.5	cylindrical
Trichoglossum hirsutum	125 × 7	near cylindrical, pointed ends, 15 septate
Tricholoma atrosquamosum	6.5 × 4	ellipsoid
Tricholoma auratum	5.5 × 3.5	ellipsoid
Tricholoma caligatum	7 × 5	ellipsoid
Tricholoma flavovirens	7 × 4.5	ellipsoid
Tricholoma fulvum	6.5 × 4.5	broadly ellipsoid
Tricholoma lascivum	7 × 4	ellipsoid to near spindle-shaped
Tricholoma magnivelare	6 × 5	ellipsoid to near spherical
Tricholoma pardinum	10 × 6.5	broadly ellipsoid
Tricholoma portentosum	6.5 × 4.5	ellipsoid
Tricholoma saponaceum	6 × 4	ellipsoid
Tricholoma scalpturatum	5 × 3	ellipsoid
Tricholoma sciodes	7 × 6	broadly ellipsoid
Tricholoma sejunctum	5.5 × 4	ellipsoid
Tricholoma sulphureum	10 × 6	ellipsoid to almond-shaped
Tricholoma terreum	6.5 × 4.5	ellipsoid
Tricholoma ustale	7 × 5	ellipsoid
Tricholomopsis rutilans	6.5 × 5	broadly ellipsoid to near spherical
Tuber aestivum	30 × 24	egg-shaped, reticulate, spiny
Tuber canaliculatum	60 × 50	ellipsoid to near spherical, reticulate
Tuber magnatum	40 × 35	egg-shaped, reticulate
Tuber melanosporum	35 × 25	ellipsoid, curved spiny
Tylopilus felleus	13 × 4.5	near spindle-shaped
Typhula erythropus	6 × 3	ellipsoid
Vascellum pratense	3.5 ⊕	spherical, warty
Verpa conica	22 × 13	ellipsoid
Volvariella bombycina	9 × 6	ellipsoid
Volvariella gloiocephala	15 × 9	egg-shaped to ellipsoid
Xylaria hypoxylon	12.5 × 5.5	spindle-shaped, flattened
Xylaria polymorpha	25 × 7	spindle-shaped, flattened
Zelleromyces cinnabarinus	15 x 12	ellipsoid, reticulate, amyloid

GLOSSARY

Many of the terms described here are illustrated in the introduction (pp.6–23). Words in **bold** type are defined elsewhere in the glossary.

- **ADNATE GILLS**
Gills that are broadly attached to the stem.
- **ADNEXED GILLS**
Gills with a narrow attachment to the stem.
- **AGARIC**
Fungus with a cap and stem **fruitbody** with **gills** under the cap.
- **AMYLOID**
Refers to a reaction with an iodine reagent resulting in a blue stain.
- **ASCUS (pl. ASCI)**
The saclike organ in which ascomycetes (see p.11) produce sexual **spores**.
- **BASIDIUM (pl. BASIDIA)**
The club-shaped organ on which basidiomycetes (see p.11) form sexual **spores**.
- **BOLETE**
A bolete produces a fleshy cap and stem **fruitbody** with **pores** and soft **tubes** under the cap.
- **BOREAL**
Refers to northern conifer region.
- **CORTINA**
A weblike **veil**, found in the genus *Cortinarius*.
- **CYSTIDIUM (pl. CYSTIDIA)**
Special sterile cells that can be found in various places on **fruitbodies** of basidiomycetes (see p.8). Cystidia on the **gill** sides and the stem can be important in identifying species of *Conocybe* and *Inocybe*.
- **DECURRENT GILLS**
Gills that run down the stem.
- **DELIQUESCENT GILLS**
Gills that dissolve as they mature, releasing an inky liquid full of black **spores**. They are peculiar to the genus *Coprinus*.
- **FIBRILLOSE**
With threadlike fibers.
- **FIMBRIATE**
With prominent projecting hairs on the cap margin.
- **FLASK FUNGUS**
Fungus with tiny, flask-shaped **fruitbodies**, sometimes enclosed within a protective **stroma**.
- **FREE GILLS**
Gills with no stem attachment.

- **FRUITBODY**
A structure that supports the cells required for sexual reproduction in fungi.
- **GILLS**
The bladelike, **spore**-bearing structures found under the caps of **agarics**.
- **GLEBA**
The fertile tissue occuring in the group of fungi that includes puffballs, stinkhorns, earth stars, earth balls, and bird's nest fungi.
- **HYALINE**
Colorless.
- **HYGROPHANOUS**
Usually refers to the caps of **agarics** drying from the center and becoming paler in zones until they are completely dry. When damp, the dark color reappears from the margin inward. Such fungi are typically **striate** at the cap margin.
- **HYPHA (pl. HYPHAE)**
The threadlike structures that make up a fungus, including its **fruitbodies**.
- **KOH**
Potassium hydroxide. This aids identification by producing stains on the flesh of certain fungi.
- **MYCORRHIZAL**
A relationship between plants and fungi that benefits both partners.
- **NOTCHED GILLS**
Gills that are indented just before reaching the stem.
- **OSTIOLE**
The opening or neck of the **spore**-producing organ in **flask fungi**.
- **PARTIAL VEIL**
Thin, skin- or threadlike tissue that protects the **gills** or **pores** of the immature **fruitbody**. It splits as the fruitbody matures, often leaving traces at the cap margin or as a ring around the stem.
- **PEDICEL**
A cylindrical or tapering appendage on the **spores** of some fungi, such as *Bovista plumbea*.
- **PORES**
The opening of the **tubes** through which the **spores** are released in fungi such as **boletes**.
- **RESUPINATE**
Refers to a **fruitbody** that grows completely flat against the **substrate** without producing a cap or free margin.

- **RETICULATE**
With a net pattern.
- **RHIZOIDS**
Tightly spun **hyphae**.
- **RUGOSE**
With a rough surface.
- **SCLEROTIUM (pl. SCLEROTIA)**
A storage organ with a dense pale interior and a black protective rind produced by some fungi. It contains nutrients that will enable the fungus to grow when conditions are favorable.
- **SEPTATE**
Refers to **hyphae** or **spores** with transverse partitions or walls.
- **SETA (pl. SETAE)**
Thick-walled hairs (on caps, **gills**, stems, or in the flesh).
- **SINUATE GILLS**
Curved **gills**.
- **SPORES**
Microscopic cells produced by fungi for reproduction.
- **STRIATE**
Refers to lines on the cap caused by underlying **gills**.
- **STROMA (pl. STROMATA)**
A protective tissue, formed by **flask fungi** for example; it normally contains the tiny **fruitbodies**.
- **SUBSTRATE**
The medium, such as soil or bark, in which a fungus grows.
- **TUBES**
Tubular structures under the caps of fungi such as **boletes**, where the fertile, **spore**-producing tissue is found. Tubes are visible as **pores** on the undersurface.
- **UMBO**
A raised boss in the center of a cap.
- **UNIVERSAL VEIL**
Thin skin- or weblike tissue covering the whole of the immature **fruitbody**. It splits as the fruitbody grows, sometimes leaving a **volva** at the stem base or loose scales on the cap.
- **VEIL**
Thin skin- or weblike tissue that may protect entire **fruitbodies** (universal veil) or just the **gills** or **pores** (partial veil).
- **VISCID**
Slimy-sticky.
- **VOLVA**
A saclike remnant of the **universal veil** at a stem base.

INDEX

C

D

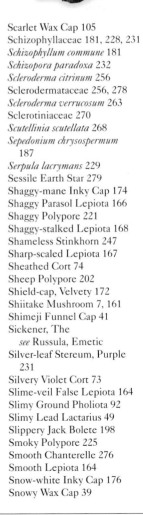

ACKNOWLEDGMENTS

GARY LINCOFF thanks all those amateur mushroom hunting clubs in the United States and Canada that, over the years, have so generously shared with him what they know about their local mushrooms. He also wishes to thank all those mycologists in North America whose passion for taxonomy over the past quarter century has sparked a renaissance in our understanding of fungal relationships.

DK would like to thank Phoebe Todd-Naylor for her constant attention.

THOMAS LÆSSØE would like to thank Colin Walton and Jo Weeks for their work on this book, as well as all those involved in *The Mushroom Book* who did much of the groundwork for this project, including Paul Copsey, Neil Fletcher, Sharon Moore, Joyce Pitt, Bella Pringle, and Jo Weightman.

PICTURE CREDITS
All photographs are by Neil Fletcher with the exception of those listed below. Dorling Kindersley would like to thank the following illustrators and photographers for permission to reproduce their artwork and photographs.

Illustrations by Pauline Bayne, Evelyn Binns, Caroline Church, Angela Hargreaves, Christine Hart-Davies, Sarah Kensington, Vanessa Luff, David More, Leighton Moses, Sue Oldfield, Liz Pepperell, Valerie Price, Sallie Reason, Elizabeth Rice, Michelle Ross, Helen Senior, Gill Tomblin, Barbara Walker, Debra Woodward.

Photographs by A-Z Botanical Collection Ltd 97tr (J M Staples), 20cl, 38tr, 187bc, 210tr, 219tr (Bjorn Svensson); Harley Barnhart 42cr, 81br, 84tr, 159crb, 237br; Kit Skates Barnhart 28crb, 35br, 43br, 81tr, 146br, 148br, 159bc, 170br, 186br, 191cr, 202cr, 207clb, 208cr; Biofotos 229br (Heather Angel), 32br, 110br, 138tr, 180tr, 272br (Gordon Dickson); Morten Christensen 187br, 275br; Bruce Coleman Collection 216tr (Adrian Davies); Dr. Ewald Gerhardt 36crb, 97br, 192tr, 199bc; Jacob Heilmann-Clausen 163br; Emily Johnson 89tr, 147bl, 178br, 244br, 253br, 263br, 276tr; Peter Katsaros 114crb, 136crb; Thomas Læssøe 11br, 16c, 42tr, 60cra, 62cla, 63br, 72br, 96tr, 110tr, 110c, 128tr, 131br, 132cra, 141br, 150tr, 164br, 167br, 179br, 206br, 221tr, 232br, 242crb, 263tr, 265br, 283br; N W Legon 46bl, 230br; Natural History Photographic Agency 16cr (Stephen Dalton), 19c (Martin Garwood), 179cl, 184br (Yves Lanceau), 21tr (David Woodfall); Natural Image 68bl, 240crb, 263cr (John Roberts), 17c (courtesy of Olympus Microscopes), Alan R. Outen 68tr; Jens H. Petersen 11tr, 11cra, 11cr, 16cl, 17bl, 17bcl, 17bcr, 17br, 18br, 19bc, 124bc, 251tr; Planet Earth Pictures 18c (Wayne Harris); Erik Rald 169crb, 191br; Samuel Ristich 233br, 273br; William Roody 30tr, 42br, 52tr, 54br, 166br, 182br, 190bc, 202br, 238bl, 247br, 256br, 259tr, 276br; Royal Botanic Gardens Kew 8tc; A. Sloth 11crb; Ulrik Søchting 6br, 20cra; Paul Stamets 84tr; Walter Sturgeon 201br; Jan Vesterholt 21cl, 46bc, 70br, 73tr, 74br, 76crb, 80tr, 102br, 116tr, 124crb, 130br, 143br, 153bl, 161tr, 177br, 189cla, 190bl, 191tr, 192cr, 196br, 199bl, 211br, 241tr.

(a=above; b=below; c=center; l=left; r=right; t=top)

Mushroom silhouettes by Colin Walton

Jacket design by Nathalie Godwin

579.6 LAE

Laessoe, Thomas.

Mushrooms

LOWER MERION LIBRARY SYSTEM

30043000403091

9/98

GLADWYNE FREE LIBRARY
GLADWYNE, PA 19035